THE JOHN GOULD FLETCHER SERIES

Lucas Carpenter, General Editor
Volume III

John Gould Fletcher

ARKANSAS

John Gould Fletcher

Introduction by Harry S. Ashmore

The University of Arkansas Press
Fayetteville London 1989

Manufactured in the United States of America

99 98 97 96 95 5 4 3 2 1

First paperback printing 1995

Designed by Chiquita Babb

∞ The paper used in this publication meets the minimum requirements of the American National Standard for Permanence of Paper for Printed Library Materials Z39.48-1984.

LIBRARY OF CONGRESS CATALOGING-IN-PUBLICATION DATA

Fletcher, John Gould, 1886-1950.
Arkansas.

(The John Gould Fletcher series; v. 3)
Reprint. Originally published: Chapel Hill:
University of North Carolina Press, 1947.
Includes index.
1. Arkansas—History. 2. Folklore—Arkansas.
I. Carpenter, Lucas. II. Title. III. Series:
Fletcher, John Gould, 1886-1950. Works. 1988; V. 3.
PS3511.L457 1988 VOL. 3 [F411] 976.7 88-17188
ISBN 1-55728-040-1 (alk. paper)
ISBN 1-55728-379-6 (paper)

CONTENTS

GENERAL EDITOR'S PREFACE

John Gould Fletcher was well qualified to write a history of Arkansas. As the only son of a prominent Little Rock family, he grew up steeped in the traditions of his native state. Even during his years as a cosmopolitan expatriate in England, he was conscious of his heritage, and despite his early reputation as a leading innovator in the vanguard of the modernist movement, he remained a profoundly Southern writer. Upon his return to Arkansas for good in 1933, after twenty-four years of self-imposed exile abroad, he devoted much of his time to such concerns as founding the Arkansas Folklore Society and writing a panoramic verse history of the state that appeared as the centerpiece of the *Arkansas Gazette* statehood centennial issue on June 15, 1936. This strikingly original poem was the first evidence of a unique mode of historical vision that, eleven years later, would result in the poetic prose of *Arkansas*. First published by the University of North Carolina Press in 1947, *Arkansas* is not a formal historical narrative, as historian Harry S. Ashmore points out in his introduction to this reissue of Fletcher's book, but rather an "interpretation of the unique development of one of the most misunderstood states in the union by one uniquely qualified to make it." More than anything else, *Arkansas* is history viewed from the perspective of a poet, and it remains valuable for its imaginative treatment of historical materials and its beauty and power of expression.

Lucas Carpenter
Oxford College of Emory University

INTRODUCTION

If there existed in Arkansas an FFA equivalent to the FFV (First Families of Virginia) the Fletchers undoubtedly would be near the top of the roster. Henry Lewis Fletcher was among the earliest white settlers, coming over from Tennessee in 1825 to stake out a homestead in the hill country west of Benton. Six years later, while Arkansas was still a territory, he sired the first John Gould, one of six sons recalled by his namesake as "fine, upstanding, resolute pieces of American timber."

These early Fletchers were upland farmers who owned few slaves, but when the Civil War came all joined the Confederate Army. And if their plain life style contrasted with that of the plantation aristocracy, John Gould Fletcher broke the mold when he returned from service at the age of thirty-four. Moving to Little Rock, he survived Reconstruction to become a successful merchant, cotton factor, and banker, and by 1889 he had acquired the state's grandest mansion—the stately edifice built in 1840 by Albert Pike as a dwelling fit for a Mexican War captain, celebrated duelist, Whig newspaper editor, Confederate brigadier general, contributor to leading literary journals, and national leader of the Masonic Order.

There John Gould Fletcher, Jr., grew up, surrounded by loving relatives and faithful black servants, safely removed from the ruder contemporaries who lived beyond the ornate iron fence that set apart an entire city block in downtown Little Rock:

> It was from this house, with its ten lofty rooms, its wide hall with great folding doors, its six white columns, its green wooden-shuttered windows, its broad lawn dotted with oaks two hundred years old, vast locust and magnolia trees, that I learned what it was to have been a southerner of the aristocratic sort in the days before the Civil War. The flavor of the old South hung around that house and hangs around it still . . . The influence of the house, in its magnifi-

cence and decay, the qualities of mind and heart that I inherited from my parents, and my own education all urged me later on to become a poet.*

The aesthetic propulsion was primarily that of his mother, who came of the pioneer German stock that also contributed to the FFA. She was an accomplished musician and an admirer of the German classicists, whom she read in the original. John Gould, Sr., was not a bookish man, but his presence, if not his tutelage, left a deep imprint upon the sensitive youth who recalled "the six-foot, robustly built, solid figure in the broadcloth coat, the wide-brimmed soft black hat, with the massive hands and feet and features, the candid open blue eyes, the great flowing beard of gray, who had so overawed my boyhood." In 1901, when he was fifteen, his father stood as the Bourbon establishment's champion in a race for governor against the flamboyant populist, Jeff Davis. The elder Fletcher lost, and the younger came away from the campaign with a life-long loathing for "the sham and corruption that went on in the name of democracy . . ."

What was considered a proper education for the children of a family of such standing was not available in Arkansas at the turn of the century. His older sister was dispatched to Vassar and John Gould was destined for Harvard, but his preparation at a local private academy, and for the last three years at Little Rock's new public high school, did not equip him to cope with the entrance examination. So he spent his sixteenth year among the most proper of New Englanders at Philips Academy, and then settled in at Cambridge, Massachusetts. In retrospect he saw himself as "a shy, sensitive, possibly spoilt only son . . . I already stood at an immense 'aesthetic distance' from my own past."

At Harvard, where he spent four unhappy years and departed without bothering to qualify for a degree, that distance grew. He could not be said, then or later, to have suffered from an inferiority complex. When he began to achieve recognition as an Imagist poet, standing as he said "arm-in-arm" with the Boston Brahmin, Amy Lowell, he wrote, "Her family, I knew, was one of wealth and social importance. So, too, was mine, in my own community." But wealth and status, interlocked as they usually were in America, had become

*John Gould Fletcher, *Life is My Song,* (New York: Farrar & Rinehart, 1937). Unless otherwise credited, the quotations in the preface are from this autobiography. The author's older sister, Adolphine Fletcher Terry, maintained the Pike mansion essentially unchanged throughout her long life, and left it to the city as a public monument. It now serves as a Center for the Decorative Arts.

anathema to him, and he fled to Europe in an unsuccessful quest for aesthetic fulfillment.

". . . I regarded myself, and continued to regard myself until my return in 1914, as a complete rebel against the intellectual, moral, and spiritual standards of the United States," he wrote in 1937, adding, "I know now that it was my heritage, no less than my own will, that dictated my expatriation." On that wartime visit he commemorated his boyhood home with a poem, "Ghosts of an Old House," and began to formulate the regionalist concepts that in time would dominate his thought and writing.

Back in England, he was inspired by a reading of Henry Adams's *Education* to begin sketching out a plan for treating his own upbringing in a fictional narrative, but he put it aside in favor of the experimental poetry that in time would bring him a Pulitzer Prize. In the postwar years he acquired an English wife and stepdaughter, and this, along with the standing he enjoyed in London intellectual circles, subordinated the tug of his Arkansas heritage. He did not come again to Little Rock until Christmas, 1926.

The second visit to the Old House was protracted, and it served as the occasion for a lecture tour that took him to Nashville, and a meeting with the young poets grouped around Vanderbilt University who called themselves Fugitives. They, like Fletcher, were devotees of "a purposeful and purified romanticism," and they shared his growing conviction that salvation lay in somehow restoring the classic traditions of pre-Civil War America. And they were, as he was to become, unreconstructed Southerners, convinced that, despite the blight of slavery, the ancient virtues had survived only in the Old South.

He stayed in touch with the Fugitives after his return to England, contributing poetry to their journal, and in 1929 he was one of twelve prominent authors and academicians invited to join in issuing a defiant manifesto, *I'll Take My Stand.* Now calling themselves Agrarians, the contributors declared holy war on the apostles of progress and their works—industrialization, urbanization, materialism, mass culture, centralized government—all of which they saw embodied in the emerging New South.

In 1931 Alan Tate, the Agrarians' prime mover, asked Fletcher to represent the group in a symposium at the University of Virginia. He came back from London to confront a distinguished panel of critics including Lewis Mumford, Stuart Chase, and Howard Odum. "I sustained my position of a lone hand battling against the tide of modernity for four days," he wrote, "and managed at least to keep most of my ground and cause one or two to revise their extremely urban-centered views."

In his early days in London Fletcher had considered himself a Fabian socialist, but his ingrained pessimism had long since overcome any utopian leanings. The Agrarians appealed to what he called "my rebellious Americanism, my individualistic anarchism." His contribution to *I'll Take My Stand,* an essay on "Education—Past and Present," affirmed "my faith in my own country—the genuine rural America of the beloved community . . ." At a time when Marxism was making converts among the literary avant garde, the Agrarians considered titling their manifesto "Tracts Against Communism" before they settled on the provocative excerpt from the Confederate anthem.

England was now blighted for Fletcher by a failing marriage, and he found he could not abide clamorous New York, where his eminence as a poet brought him offers of editorial employment he needed to supplement the modest income from a trust left by his father. As recurring bouts of depression abraded his naturally thorny temperament he became estranged from most of his artistic companions, and began increasingly to think of himself as an exiled Arkansan. In March, 1933, he came home to stay.

The transmogrification of the passionate seeker after Truth and Beauty was not an easy one, and in many ways it was never completed. If, in England, Fletcher considered himself an expatriate from Arkansas, in Arkansas he found himself expatriated from the world of fine art, belles lettres, and classical music he considered his natural habitat.

On the previous visit he had resisted the impulse to put down new roots in his native soil: ". . . I would rapidly have grown as insignificant as anyone there—and I could find no painters, no musicians, and only one possible writer of any importance in the entire length and breadth of my state." But now he was buoyed by optimism that the shattering impact of the depression and the subsequent ferment of the New Deal might open the way for a renascence of early American values. This, he thought, could be achieved "only by a development of regional culture on an enormous scale, as a deliberate antidote to the pseudo culture, equally compounded of sophistication and commercialization, of such a city as New York . . . I saw no reason why Arkansas should not achieve a genuine culture of its own, as significant in the pattern of American living as the culture of New England or New York had been."

As for his own role, "it was primarily as a cultural agent that I had come back, and as a cultural agent that I chose to remain." And this time he discovered a kindred spirit in the Arkansas backwoods: Charlie May Simon, who had spent her own expatriate years in the Paris art colony, and had now launched a distinguished career as the author of children's books. A refugee from the depression, she had returned to her native hills to homestead in the Ouachita National Forest, bringing with her the reluctant New York artist who was then her husband. The dissolution of her marriage, and of Fletcher's, made possible a union that was to be fondly memorialized by both.

"At forty-nine, but now feeling twenty years younger, I knew at last that the gods had relented and given me their greatest gift—a mate," he wrote in the volume he dedicated to her "in homage and adoration." And in the tender memoir she published after his death in 1950, she attested that their deep devotion never flagged despite the stormy passages brought on by the recurring sieges of mental illness that led him to end his own life.*

Although he doggedly pursued his mission as an apostle of high culture, lecturing throughout the state, organizing a folklore festival, raising funds to support a variety of artistic endeavors, and making himself available to aspiring students, he could not have succeeded without his gentle bride's insights and soothing interventions. "He was all fire, and like fire he could give a glow of warmth," she wrote, "but he could also flare up and burn."

Unless his illness forbad, Fletcher put in the forenoon at his writing desk in the charming, book-lined stone cottage he and his new wife christened Johnswood when it was built to their specifications on a wooded tract overlooking the Arkansas River west of Little Rock. He

*Charlie May Simon, *Johnswood,* (New York: E. P. Dutton & Company, Inc., 1953).

continued to write poetry, and also kept up a voluminous correspondence, which included often caustic exchanges with those Arkansans who challenged the views he expressed in his role as the state's most eminent literary figure.

The regionalism he had espoused in *I'll Take My Stand* was accentuated by his exposure to the rural Arkansans he had known only by reputation during his sheltered youth. He shared with his homesteading wife a special affection for upland Arkansas—"those long, wooded ridges, those dense forests and those lonely mountain settlements with their unspoilt people." *Johnswood* contains an unforgettable vignette of the aging poet, clad in his habitual dark city suit topped off with a broad-brimmed boulevardier's fedora, sitting on a log in the remote Ozarks listening to the sounding of Old Belle as she led a pack of hounds on a nocturnal fox hunt.

Although he shared his fellow Arkansans' often exaggerated resentment of the outsiders who inveighed against the South's repression of its black citizens, he recognized the palpable injustices of the segregated society and openly expressed his contempt for many of its practices. Charlie May Simon summed up his attitude by quoting a letter to Lawrence A. Davis, then president of the state's Negro college, A.M.&N. at Pine Bluff:

> I cannot see . . . any reason why the idea of "States' Rights" should be used as a smoke-screen to keep race-prejudice, discrimination and absence of elementary human rights firmly in place. Nor can I see any reason why responsible Negro leaders should not frankly recognize the fact that the South intends, if it can, to maintain the idea of "States' Rights" against Washington, or any other outside agency. In short, if some progress toward tolerance, mutual understanding, or elementary justice between your people and mine is going to be achieved, it will have to come from within the South, from Negro-white cooperation and better understanding.

This blend of enlightened humanism and stubborn parochialism represented about as advanced a view on race relations as was to be found in the South at the end of World War II. Harry Truman's Civil Rights Commission, the Dixiecrat rebellion, and the Supreme Court's abrogation of the states' rights doctrine were still in the future in the summer of 1946 when Fletcher and his wife repaired to the endowed retreat for creative artists maintained at the MacDowell Colony in

New Hampshire. He finished writing *Arkansas* there, but the historical grounding that provides the context of his ultimate appraisal of his native state goes back at least to 1914, when on his first return to the Old House he discovered Thomas Nuttall's remarkable *Journal of Travels in the Arkansas Territory During the Year 1819,* by far the most perceptive firsthand account of the earliest white settlers and their surroundings.

Commissioned by the *Arkansas Gazette* to write an epic poem for its June 15, 1936, statehood centennial issue, Fletcher necessarily drew upon his imagination to elaborate on the scarce original sources on Arkansas' colonial and territorial past. He had completed four books of narrative verse, beginning with the arrival of the DeSoto expedition in 1541, when he came to the post-Civil War period. Recalling the anger aroused in his parents by their memories of Reconstruction, he responded to a stirring of his own inherited outrage:

> I decided to make this book of my poems more detailed, more realistic, and to draw the clear lesson, apparent in all American history for the past seventy years, that all gangs of politicians in power—whether Democrat or Republican, it matters not—can, under democracy, not only despoil the people but go on corrupting and despoiling them forever, while mouthing the shibboleths of democracy meanwhile, unless the people themselves, through the threat of revolution, take the issue into their own hands. This was the opinion of Thomas Jefferson, and it is also mine; but it was difficult to embody all this in poetry.

It was even more difficult to sell it to J. N. Heiskell, the editor and president of the *Gazette,* and the poet "had to be satisfied with a far briefer, more generalized and less accurately pointed account." He attributed this to concern that the original version might offend descendants of the carpetbag aristocracy, but this seems unlikely in the case of Heiskell, whose father had been a Confederate colonel and one of the Redeemers who restored native white rule. It seems more likely that the editor simply saw no point in re-igniting revolutionary fervor against the Yankee occupation so long after the fact; in any case he held out until, as Fletcher put it, "he succeeded at last in curbing my unreconstructed southernism."

Ten years later, when he set about writing *Arkansas,* his Confederate fervor had obviously moderated. His treatment of the broad issues of the Civil War does not differ significantly from that of most contemporary historians, but he does part company with many of those who have dealt with Arkansas' special role in the great conflict. His focus is narrow, and his sympathy is with the leaders who went so far as to propose secession from the Confederacy when the troops defending the state's northern border were shifted across the Mississippi to meet Grant's invasion of Tennessee: "It was the people of the state who had to make this war, abandoned and betrayed and alone." Abraham Lincoln and the Yankee invader, General Frederick Steele, came off far better in *Arkansas* than did Jefferson Davis and General Theophilus Hunter Holmes, Confederate commander in the Trans-Mississippi.

Fletcher was hardly a convert to the view of the revisionists who had begun to discount the horrors of Reconstruction as embroidered by the Dunning school,* but here too he passes over the larger issues—including most notably the profound, and in many ways still unresolved social questions raised by emancipation. His concentration is on such events as the Brooks-Baxter "War," a comic opera confrontation between contending carpetbag factions, and on the personalities of the major participants.

The book drew generally favorable reviews when it was published by the University of North Carolina Press in 1947, and sold 3,837 copies before it was declared out of print in 1961—a considerable sale for a work of this character. It is not, of course, a formal history, but rather an interpretation of the unique development of one of the most misunderstood states in the union by one uniquely qualified to make it. Although scholarly critics inevitably found fault with some of its omissions and interpretations, all greeted it as a welcome, extraordinarily insightful addition to the sparse literature on the last frontier of the Old South.

Arkansas was still current in 1948 when I first encountered it, and I found it an invaluable introduction to what was to be my own home country after I joined the *Arkansas Gazette.* My background was in the

*In the 1890s followers of Prof. William A. Dunning of Columbia University reversed the harsh view non-Southern historians had generally taken of the defeated Confederates' response to Reconstruction, and the Dunning school left its imprint on the textbooks in general use during the first half of this century. "The intellectual heirs of Charles Sumner and Henry Adams gushed sentimentally about the decline of the great plantations and the trials of Southern womanhood," Frances Fitzgerald wrote in *America Revised.*

Carolinas, my experience of the Trans-Mississippi limited to World War II tours of duty at army posts in Louisiana and Texas. As the years passed and I had my own reactions to compare with his, I found little to fault in Fletcher's panoramic view of the state and its origins.

Three decades after that first reading, I was commissioned by the American Association of State and Local History to write an appraisal of the historic relationship between Arkansas and the nation,* and again turned to Fletcher's handiwork, this time measuring it against the considerable volume of pertinent material that had become available since its publication. I found that *Arkansas* still stands up as its author intended, a poet's imaginative treatment of "a history both tragic and comic—with its deep legendary roots going far back into the remote prehistoric past." It has earned a permanent place among the books that must be read by those who seek to understand the matrix in which new forces of economic and social change are reshaping Arkansas' traditional society.

Harry S. Ashmore
Santa Barbara, California

*Harry S. Ashmore, *Arkansas: A Bicentennial History,* (New York: W. W. Norton & Company, Inc., 1978).

ARKANSAS

To Wayman Hogue

true chronicler of the Arkansas Backwoods

NOTE TO THE READER

In March, 1881, both houses of the Arkansas legislature, by concurrent resolution, affirmed that "the true pronunciation of the name of the State, in the opinion of this body, is that received by the French from the native Indians, and committed to writing in the French word representing the sound, and that it should be pronounced in three syllables, with the final *s* silent, the *a* in each syllable with the Italian sound, and the accent on the first and the last syllables; being the pronunciation formerly universally and now still most commonly used; and that the pronunciation with the accent on the second syllable, with the sound of *a* as in man, and the sounding of the terminal *s*, is an innovation to be discouraged."

Before that date, the name of the state had been spoken in various ways, thus giving rise to a folk tale of considerable grossness, which need not here be recalled. But however Kansans may enunciate the name of a river which flows through their territory also; or however other midwesterners may think the name of Arkansas should be pronounced, to the natives it has always been sounded in only one way—as "Arkansaw." Therefore I have seen fit to designate the name of the natives of the state, throughout this narrative, as "the Arkansawyers."

One

A LOOK AROUND THE LAND

Where the Mississippi River cuts the southern border of Missouri lies the State of Arkansas. Except for an area roughly forty miles square between the Saint Francis and the Great River where Missouri bites a chunk off its northeast corner, the state stretches westward for over three hundred miles to the prairies of eastern Oklahoma. Most of those miles are in the Ozarks, the mountain region. From the north boundary, Arkansas runs southward for about two hundred and fifty miles to the northern edge of Louisiana. Here, thanks to another chunk of about the same size bitten off the southwest corner by Texas, and thanks, too, to the generally southwest trend of the Great River, the state is no more than a hundred and seventy miles across from east to west. Every foot of this is river-delta plain. Hence one may say that there are roughly two regions in Arkansas: the highlands, occupying the northwestern half, and the lowlands, occupying the southeastern half of the area. These two are distinct in types of population, in scenery, and in culture.

But to the native Arkansawyer, each of these two regions falls into at least two subdivisions. The lowland area, densely forested, when the first man entered it, with oak, elm, ash, sweetgum, hickory, and cypress, was broken, from the beginning, by a great prairie extending northward from the first settlement at Arkansas Post to the present city of Brinkley—a distance of at least seventy miles north and south and from fifteen to twenty miles east and west. This prairie, since the first road in Arkansas ran directly across it, afforded an early access to the interior; and except for a few smaller prairies along the western border, it is the chief treeless region in the state. It has its own peculiar history.

The upland region, too, is cut into irregular halves by two different types of mountain formation. North of the Arkansas River, which cuts diagonally through the center of the state, are the Ozarks proper, composed mainly of limestone rocks lying in flat strata, which have been worn down through ages on ages of rainfall into flat-topped plateaus. These are divided by steep winding hollows, through which the streams straggle irregularly like the branches of a vine. South of the river, in the Ouachitas, the rocks are more varied and uptilted in their strata; their ridges run more regularly east and west and the valleys are usually wider, with parallel east-west-running streams in them. Also, the southern mountain region and the northern are different in the appearance of their forests. The Ozarks, to the north and west, are clad for the most part in dense hardwoods: oak, hickory, ash, with occasional patches of dark cedar and the shortleaf pine. But south and west of Little Rock, a dense, unvaried shortleaf pine forest extends for miles, with patches of sweetgum, scrub oaks, and, by the bed of rock-bordered, leaf-hidden streams, the wild holly sometimes growing in dense groves.

Each of these two mountain areas is distinct from the other; and both, in turn, vary greatly from the flat monotony of the lowlands, covered originally with trackless forest, broken only by immense swamps of cypress and cane and vine. Through the midst of this lowland area runs the Grand Prairie region already mentioned, so named by the earliest settlers, now the great rice field of the state and an important factor in its history.

These distinctions between Ozark and Ouachita, between rice and cotton lowland, and fruit-growing or forested upland are important; for, possibly more than in any other Southern state, the native of this region is dependent, not on industry, but on nature for his material well-being. Of the small number of manufactures in the state, over half are directly connected with the forests and with lumbering. Up to a period which may be set roughly as about fifty years ago, a considerable proportion of the population lived largely on fish caught in the rivers and wild game shot in the forest; and to this day, the state is known as a paradise for sportsmen. Except for the counties bordering directly on the Mississippi and those along the Arkansas River southeast of Little Rock, the plantation system, so important elsewhere in the South, never took firm hold. The typical Arkansawyer was far more likely to be a frontier settler in coonskin cap, blanket cape, and buckskin trousers—or its modern equivalent of blue denim jumper, checkered shirt, blue overalls, and greasy black hat—than a planter in broadcloth coat, satin vest, and ruffled shirt, drinking his mint julep on a pillared verandah while his Negro slave waved palm-leaf fans in his direction.

One thing, however, the sections of Arkansas all have in common—the climate. For the last sixty years, since temperature records were first kept, these records have shown a remarkable uniformity. For the northwestern third of the state, to a line beginning about Corning and running thence southwest to about Searcy, thence due west to Fort Smith, the average annual temperature has been between 56 and 60 degrees. South of this, to a region which begins about at DeQueen or Nashville on the west and ends at the site of Arkansas Post on the east, runs a belt which averages between 60 and 62. Still farther south, for the lower third of the state, the average is between 62 and 66. The average winter temperature, for the state as a whole, is about 42, the spring 61, the summer nearly 80, the fall 61. These seasons, too, are uniformly divided, spring running usually from March to June, summer from June to October, fall from October to the end of December, winter from Christmas to March. Summer, however, as any native son or daughter can testify, is actually longer than the other seasons; it often starts in May, and does not end till the middle of November. Its first part is usually humid, with tremendous thunderstorms; its last part is usually intensely scorching and dry. Indeed, as an early traveller wisely observed, "Throughout this territory, there are no grasses nor other vegetables of consequence in agriculture (except the cane) which retain their verdure beyond the close of September." And I myself have seen, as early as the middle of July, pavements thick with those yellow leaves which usually drift down in heaps by August.

It is probably this climate—capricious in winter, when December rains drench the bottomlands and sudden, hard February freezes sweep from Nebraska and Kansas down across the Ozarks, and also in spring, when violent April winds of tornado intensity come up from Texas and Oklahoma, while in summer all is an overpowering blaze of humid torpor under an eternal scorching sun—that has made Arkansas a Southern state. Southern and yet Southwestern. With Texas we share the distinction of being the only Southern state that lies altogether west of the Mississippi. But where Texas is overwhelmingly a plains state, Arkansas is a mixed mountain and lowland state. Yet the Ozarks, though having six peaks of over two thousand feet, will never be a successful summer resort. Nothing is more strange as an experience than to attempt a motor trip among them at the close of June, when windless stillness holds rigid the endless rows of scalloped-leaved oaks and pointed-leaved hickories at the roadside, and a heat of tropic intensity broods over the densely thicketed hollow and beyond to where another rugged ridge, showing no sign of human habitation, cuts the sky. Then one understands why the true Arkansawyer, from June to September, moves slowly, if he moves at all.

The inhabitant of the Ozarks, though much has been written about him to prove his culture unique, is, in fact, extremely like any other Southern mountaineer. In the lowlands bordering on the Mississippi or on the lower Arkansas there are great cotton plantations, akin to those elsewhere in the South, staffed by armies of tenant sharecroppers—at first almost altogether Negro but now becoming increasingly white. But in the Ozarks it is only with difficulty that the forests are cleared and a few stony acres kept plowed to receive the seeds of cotton or of corn. There are far fewer people; and these are invariably white. The five hundred thousand Negroes of the state have, for the most part, never seen, let alone known, the quality of life of the mountain region.

This region is unique in yet another way. Circumstances made of the inhabitant of the Ozarks—and the inhabitant of the Ouachitas differed in no way from him except that he lived in still greater isolation—not alone a mountaineer, but still more, a frontiersman facing the semi-civilized Indian Territory. Up to about fifty years ago, well within the lifetime of persons now living, the Ozarker was self-contained and self-dependent. He ground his own corn. His women spun their own thread, made their own clothes. He distilled his own whisky. Crude furniture was made by whittling, and chairs were seated with twisted withes of willow or untanned oxhides. Houses were built by unskilled labor; and I have seen and spent hours in a four-room log cabin—with two massive stone chimneys—built by unskilled mountaineers as late as 1932. Bedspread coverlets there were elaborately made out of patchwork pieces, or woven; and many days in the year were spent in the woods near by, recruiting the scanty larder with squirrels, rabbits, deer, or possums. The life of the Ozarks was wild and primitive, but not without its savor. The proximity of the Indian Territory—it must be remembered that the Cherokee Strip was not opened to settlers before 1889—and the scarcity of all settlements served not only to preserve old mountaineer traditions brought from Tennessee or the Carolinas, but to intensify the frontier type. It is not too much to say that the Ozarker was, if not himself an outlaw, at least in sympathy with the outlaw breed. His favorite heroes had all a strong touch of Jesse James about them and were good men with a gun.

All this is different enough from the life of the lowlands, where, from the eighteen-thirties on, the plantation system, resting on its basis of Negro slavery, crept westward and northward from Alabama, Mississippi, Tennessee, Louisiana, to shape much of the State's political life previous to the Civil War and to resume its control after: for the plantation system held the predominant economic power up to the threshold of the twentieth century. One can see the plantation system still in full flower along any of the highways between Little Rock and Memphis. Here, in a land as flat as any table, are the endless rows of cotton, plowed in March, seeded in April. Here, bordering the "turn row," are lines of two-roomed cabins of unpainted lumber, sometimes whitewashed and sometimes not, looking intensely hot and shadeless and comfortless, as indeed they are. Here are the houses of the "riding bosses" and overseers, made of better lumber, neatly painted, with small flower gardens and shade trees. Here, occasionally, is the two-story house of an owner, usually on higher ground. Here is where cotton grows up to the front doors, and to the back doors as well—and here are rows of Negroes swinging their hoes in May, June, July, under the blazing sun: creeping with long sacks at their shoulders through the fields from September to past Thanksgiving, picking. Here is the corrugated iron gin house—ugly, yet useful. Here is the commissary store, with its advertisements of chill-remedy and of snuff—which are seen frequently, too, in the highlands—and the usual group of listless sharecroppers in their high boots, sitting on its porch. And here, finally, is the dense cypress swamp, with its lightly plumed arms, green in summer, brown in winter, blocking the flat horizon.

It is all very different from those lonely unpainted cabins with a "dog-run" between two rooms, resting on their rickety unmortared stone foundations, half-disengaged from the surrounding forest, which surprise the traveller at a sudden turning on a narrow solitary road in the Ozarks. There, not infrequently, the towheaded native children still run to the doors to stare at the uncommon spectacle of a passing car; and Negroes are unknown. In fact, in spite of the similarity of climate, the mountain region and the plantation region of this state might well belong to two different continents, to two different worlds.

Out of the interactions of highland upon lowland, of lowland upon highland; out of the significant historic fact that slavery existed here from the beginning of the state's existence as a territory, and that southwest lay Texas, and west the region designed for the Indians as early as Jefferson's day; out of all these has emerged a history both tragic and comic—with its deep, legendary roots going far back into the remote, prehistoric past.

Two

A SPANIARD COMES TO SEE THE LAND AND DOES NOT DEPART

On an April morning in 1538, Hernando de Soto, Spanish conquistador, newly appointed adelantado of Florida, set sail from San Lucar, Spain, with some six hundred men and two hundred horses, to explore the North American continent, of which Cabeza de Vaca, recently returned Indian captive, was telling golden tales. On May 30, 1539, after a delay of some months in Cuba, the expedition landed in the bay of Espiritu Santo (now generally believed to be Tampa Bay), and began at once to look for Indian guides. By a strange stroke of luck, they found Juan Ortiz, a refugee castaway from an earlier expedition, now living as an Indian, who could act as both guide and interpreter.

Of the ensuing adventures of De Soto's expedition as it struggled through forest and swamp, with its pack horses, its foot-soldiers, its cavalry, its bloodhounds, its herd of swine, its Indian captives, we who are here interested in De Soto only as the discoverer of Arkansas will have little to say. Two years later, in May, 1541, this same expedition—its horses reduced to around a hundred, its fighting strength diminished by at least two hundred dead, its survivors wearing raccoon and wildcat furs under their rusty armor—beating desperately northwestward up through the Chickasaw country from their most terrible defeat at Mauvilla, in the Mobile region, suddenly stumbled upon the Mississippi.

As they stood on the bank of the Great River (facing Arkansas, although they did not know it), De Soto and his men had lost all their baggage, including two hundred pounds of mussel pearls found in Georgia, as well as their supply of wafers and wine for celebrating mass. The two priests of the expedition wore rude cassocks of deerskin. And all the men were reduced to such a state that an eyewitness could write: "I saw a gentleman, called Don Antonio de Osorio, . . . with a jacket made of skins of the martens of that country, all broken at the sides. His flesh showed through. He had no hat; was barefoot and without breeches; a buckler at his shoulder, girt with a sword without a sheath; and thus he marched in all the frost and cold. He endured his toil without laments, such as many others made, for there was no one to help him, although he had in Spain two thousand ducats of income through the church. And the day I saw him, he had not eaten a mouthful; and if he wished to sup, he had to dig the earth with his nails to get something to eat."

It is worthy of note, and a measure of the kind of man their leader was, that the Great River—a mile wide here, and, as these grim, unshaven creatures remarked among themselves, far broader than the Danube—did not daunt them. They prepared to cross it. It took the best part of a month. Having encamped at the spot selected on the twenty-first of May, 1541, for the crossing, on the eighteenth of June they crossed in boats built by themselves.

The effort that crossing must have cost them is hard to imagine. Pines were felled, were daubed with pitch, and were fashioned into four large "piraguas"—probably akin to the flat-bottomed barges of the present-day Mississippi. A bellows, made perhaps of deer-leather or bearskin, was set up, and precious iron halberds and broken sword blades and stirrups were melted down into bolts to fasten the crude timbers together. All this went on to the accompaniment of incessant attacks from the opposite shore.

Every afternoon from around two o'clock until sunset, two hundred canoes filled with naked and painted savages—the first Arkansawyers—swarmed within bowshot and sent over clouds of arrows. These Indians had heard beforehand that the white strangers were in the country, and they were prepared to oppose all further exploring. Finally, the attacks stopped for some reason, and the Spaniards got over, taking with them apparently the remnant of the huge herd of swine with which they had started out in Florida two years before, and which still formed their main food supply. As they slowly crossed the river, they dragged up great catfish and the shovel-nosed gar from the turbid water.

The exact spot of that crossing has never been clearly determined, but modern geographers are sure that it could not have been at the lower Chickasaw Bluff, where Memphis now stands, although Memphis has always been eager to claim that distinction. The finding of some authentic Spanish halberds, much waterworn, in a creek bed in the present Phillips County in Arkansas had led most students of the subject to suppose that the crossing must have been near Sunflower Landing, south of Helena—especially as the three authentic accounts of the expedition agree that a large Indian town named Casqui or Icasqui lay northward up the river, three days' march through swampy country from the point of disembarkment. The present city of Helena in Phillips County, it is believed, occupies the site of a prehistoric Indian town; and the country southward is exceedingly swampy. So somewhere near Sunflower Landing may have been the spot where the historic crossing actually took place.

At all events, they crossed into Arkansas—only to find the first Indian village, Aquixo, deserted. Three days of struggling through swamps brought them to Casqui (the Indian village already mentioned as probably occupying the site of the present town of Helena); and they entered it on St. John's Day, June 24, 1541. The land hereabouts lay somewhat higher and freer of swamps. And the town, behind its stockade, was well built, was surrounded with fields of pecan trees and persimmons; while the chief's house, standing upon a small mound, was decorated in front with two skulls of buffalo. There was probably corn, too, left in the storehouses; and here, for nearly the last time, fortune turned in De Soto's favor.

The chief of Casqui, having no doubt long been aware that the hairy white strangers who bestrode strange beasts were now in his country, thought it best to dissemble and to maintain a friendly attitude. He sent out from the town an embassy, bearing presents of "skins, shawls, and fish," and welcomed De Soto to his territory. But, with true Indian cunning, he decided to test the Spaniards. He affected to believe what De Soto himself had proclaimed to be the truth, that the Spaniards were in reality divine creatures, children of the sun. And so he ordered some lame and blind people to be brought before De Soto and bade the bearded stranger to heal them.

This put the Spaniard into a quandary, from which he extricated himself by means of a long discourse, no doubt roughly translated to the chief by Juan Ortiz, the Spanish castaway. After much talk about God, Jesus Christ, the Blessed Virgin, and the Trinity, De Soto ordered a cross to be made and set up on the mound beside the chief's house—the first cross on Arkansas soil—and he bade the Indians adore it rather than himself. He told the chief that if the Indians knelt and kissed the foot of the cross, a sign from heaven would be given, as showing that their requests had received favorable attention.

But this did not satisfy the chief; and very soon he began to look for an excuse to get rid of his hungry and ill-clad guests. He told them that he was at war with the chief of another prosperous town, named Pacaha, which lay two days' journey up the river. Whether this was actually true or was merely a ruse, De Soto did not discover. He marched on to Pacaha, where he found most of the inhabitants gone and their chief fled to an island in the river. The town turned out to be a rich one; its stockaded wall was equipped with towers, and a moat rich in fish, connected by a canal with the Great River, lay surrounding it. The Spaniards were about to enter when they saw a body of Indians hurrying up. These, strangely enough, were the chief of Casqui and his warriors. Rain, they said, had fallen on their fields the previous night; and so the medicine of the cross that De Soto had ordered set up was a true medicine. They promptly enlisted in the forces set to take Pacaha.

In this town were found many skins, some shell beads, and a little maize, which De Soto offered to the chief of Casqui in return for his assistance in subduing the place. Whereupon, loaded with all this loot, the chief immediately decamped, leaving De Soto again without an ally in a territory more populous than any the Spaniards had seen for over a year.

But De Soto was shrewd enough to perceive that he was now in a position to play both ends against the middle. Summoning the fugitive chief of Pacaha to his presence, he offered him an immediate alliance if he would attack the chief of Casqui. And on these terms the chief of Pacaha formally submitted and came to De Soto in the Spanish camp, which lay some distance from the town. Because of the heat and the perpetual dangers of a night ambush, De Soto had long since learned to insist on this point.

To the Spanish camp now came also the chief of Casqui, who realized what a mistake he had made in running away to cache his loot before he of Pacaha had been safely put out of the way. So he instantly returned to De Soto, along with fifty Indians in full war-paint, bringing with him "a clown to make merriment," in the hope of softening the hearts of these strange, bearded creatures who were continually getting the better of them.

De Soto thus gained two possible allies instead of one, and the expedition rested in the territories of these two chiefs—both vying with each other to win the favor of the Spaniards—for a full month, till the end of July. No doubt the weary explorers were grateful for being at last housed, fed, and clad.

Presently De Soto sent northward a scouting party of thirty horsemen and fifty foot soldiers to look for a place which the Indians called Chisca, where they said there was some sort of foundry producing copper and gold. After seven days' travel through uninhabited country, the Spaniards were forced to turn back, eating cornstalks and green persimmons en route. They had learned only that to the northward there were no more cornfields, but rather herds of "wild cattle" (undoubtedly buffalo) upon which the inhabitants, living in houses of skins which could be taken down, rolled up, and dragged away, alone subsisted. De Soto then asked the two chiefs to be directed to another populous country, and was told to go southwest, towards a place called Aquigate, or Quigate, which lay on another river—presumably the Arkansas. The chiefs of Pacaha and Casqui continued their friendship and supplied De Soto with canoes, bridge-builders, and porters to make the way to Quigate easier.

At Quigate, a populous town lying in the midst of fields of pumpkins, squash, and ripening corn, trouble arose. Whether it was caused by the Indians, who, to delude De Soto, had invented tales of fabulous wealth in far-away places, or whether it came from De Soto's own men, who were, for the first time in many months, reasonably well clad and fed and who all wanted to get back to Cuba as soon as possible, we do not know. At any rate, De Soto, having occupied half of the town of Quigate, promptly burned down the other half; to avoid, as he said, being attacked by the Indians.

It was now late August. De Soto and his men had been in the Arkansas country for two months; and it was imperative for him either to discover the gold he had vainly sought for more than two years or to quit the country. But he did not yet leave the region of Arkansas.

When he learned that there were other populous settlements farther down the river which emptied into the Mississippi, but that there was also some sort of trail which led north and west along the bank of the Arkansas itself, he decided to try the up-stream trail, on which lay, he was told, a settlement called Caligua, in hilly country. There, amid the hills of Caligua, he could perhaps find the gold which he could take back with him to Spain as proof of his success. And, apparently by sheer force of will, he succeeded in persuading his men to follow him off towards the Ozarks.

Caligua was reached about the first of September after a four days' march through terrific swamps. It lay in hilly country as the Indians had said. Salt, which the Spaniards now ate in great lumps, having had none for many months, was brought in from places where the Indians extracted it from the sands of various streams—another indication that they were close to the first mountain ridges. The fields were still rich in corn, beans, and pumpkins. After a brief pause, the expedition set out again—presumably still following the bank of the Arkansas northwestward—to another small place of scattered houses, called Tatilcoya. Here they heard that still farther up the river was a rich province called Cayas, where they could find good provisions, although it lay amid ridges in rough, rocky country.

Just where in Arkansas this region of Cayas was, is a matter of much dispute among present-day geographers. We nowhere read that the explorers had crossed the Arkansas, nor is the river anywhere given its name. But the time was September, when the river is usually much shrunken by drought; so fording it would not have been difficult. All three chroniclers—Luís Hernandez de Biedma, factor of the Crown, whose report is brief and impersonal, Rodrigo Ranjel, De Soto's own private secretary whose day-by-day diary was followed by Oviedo in his *La historia natural y general de las Indias,* and the mysterious Portuguese known as the "Gentleman of Elvas," whose book was first published in 1557 at Evora, are agreed that this "province" lay in a rough and mountainous region in a land of scattered dwellings rather than of compact, stockaded towns.

And the Gentleman of Elvas adds this precious detail: "The Governor [De Soto] tarried a month in the Province of Cayas. In this time the horses fattened and throve more than they had done at other places in a longer time, in consequence of the large quantity of maize there. The blade of it, I think, is the best fodder that grows. The beasts drank so copiously from the very warm and brackish lake, that they came in having their bellies swollen with the leaves, when they came back from their watering."

Now the only place in Arkansas where a "very warm and brackish lake" could ever have existed is at Hot Springs—and so we must suppose De Soto to have been there. And it is but natural that this meagre sentence, revealing only that a seepage basin of warm water (for there are no genuine lakes in the Ouachitas or the Ozarks), was actually visited, should have been embroidered upon later by the romantic Garcilaso de la Vega, whose imagination ran riot among legends, as well as by the later Arkansawyers themselves, and made into a vast myth which says that Indians came here annually in large numbers, like the invalids of today, to seek healing; that by lasting agreement they did not here make war on each other; that De Soto had a fine time combing the near-by mountains for gold. But the chronicles we follow say nothing of these things. They merely remark that here De Soto learned of another province "to the southward named Tulla, where the folk spoke another language that no Indian of Cayas understood and were very warlike"—and that De Soto determined to go thither, and promptly did, getting well banged about by the redskins for his pains.

The fact that a blade of an old Spanish halberd has been dug up recently at Caddo Gap, southwest of Hot Springs, has led modern students of De Soto's expedition to identify Tulla with the ancient Caddo country, whose Indians, as we know, spoke a language akin to the Pawnee, entirely different from any other in Arkansas, and were noticeably hostile to all the other tribes. There is no proof, however, that this halberd may not have been passed westward from hand to hand by tribes settled near Hot Springs. All that is clear from the chronicles is that De Soto remained in the mountain country around Hot Springs till the middle of October, when the corn by which he kept his horses and men alive was already diminishing and the starving time of winter was upon them. Then the expedition beat south and east again, descending to the plains at a spot called variously Autianque, Viranque, or Utiangue, where De Soto had heard that there was a large body of water. He supposed that it was an arm of the sea, but it turned out to be merely the bed of another river descending to the Mississippi. This place is generally thought to have been at present-day Calion, near Eldorado, on the lower Ouachita.

Here the forlorn expedition remained all winter, behind a stockade which De Soto ordered built, set well away from the rest of the Indian settlement in case of attack by fire; and here they eked out their lives on the corn, beans, pecans, and dried persimmons provided unwillingly by the Indians—a diet varied mainly by rabbits, which the savages had taught the Spaniards to catch in snares. Their numbers were much reduced—about three hundred and forty Spaniards and a pitiful lot of some forty unshod, scarecrow horses alone remaining. At this time, or perhaps earlier, their drove of hogs took to the woods—to provide respectable ancestry for the Arkansas razorback of later years.

During this last winter on Arkansas soil, the snow lay on the ground for an entire month; and Juan Ortiz, invaluable Florida Spaniard, sickened and died. As for the expedition itself, the men must at last have realized just how desperate their position was.

From November to March they stood watch behind their stockade, ready to beat off attacks; and their leader kept them on the alert by ordering a guard to sound the alarm frequently and cry out that he spied Indians. Meanwhile death, stinging with sluggish insistence at their wasted bodies, was reducing them, one by one, through its chosen medium of malaria.

On Monday, the sixth of March, 1542, the encampment was broken up, and the sorry lot of scarecrows pushed southward. . . .

Some leagues farther down the river, below the present Arkansas region, lay a country called Quigualtam, the chief of which was said to be the greatest in that country. De Soto, racked by malaria, was now on the point of taking to his bed for good. He determined, however, to make some further show of force, some attempt to bring about the rescue and assistance that still evaded him. Accordingly he sent off to the chief of Quigualtam a messenger with a pompous proclamation saying that inasmuch as he, De Soto, was the child of the sun and was obeyed in all the lands from which he came, he commanded the chief to value his friendship and to come to where he was; that he would be rejoiced to see him; and that in token of love and obedience the chief should bring with him "something that was in esteem among his countrymen."

The reply of the proud chief is worth preserving, since one of the three accounts gives it in the full splendor of its Indian rhetoric. He said, according to the Gentleman of Elvas: "As to what you say of being the son of the Sun, if you will cause Him to dry up the great river, I will believe you. As for the rest, it is not my custom to visit anyone. Rather, all of whom I have ever heard, have come to visit me, to serve and obey me, and to pay me tribute either of their own free will, or by force; so if you desire to see me, come where I am. If you come in peace, I will receive you with goodwill; if for war, I will await you in my town; but neither for you nor for anyone, will I stir forth one foot after the other." Since De Soto was now bedridden, this reply must have been particularly galling.

As the days passed, it became clear that the great Spaniard was dying; and when, after many months, the remnant of his expedition at last disembarked, from roughly-made boats, at a Mexican village—three hundred and eleven shaggy, half-naked men, red as any Indians—and fell on their knees before God in the tiny church, their leader, significantly, was not with them. He had remained behind, somewhere close to the Arkansas region he had discovered; his body concealed forever under the floods of the Great River he had been the first to cross.

And there, I think, he is to this day. Anyone who is at all familiar with Garland and Montgomery counties, which lie to the west of Hot Springs, or with Cleburne County, on the other side of the river, north of Searcy, can testify that the inhabitants of these regions frequently profess a belief in what they call the "Spanish diggins"—a cave somewhere in the hills, where a great treasure amassed by some mysterious Spanish expedition still lies hidden from men. A frequent variant of the tale is that an old priest, left behind by the Spaniards, had in his possession a map drawn on buffalo hide, showing the exact location of a valuable deposit of gold or silver, which he gave to an Indian, who in turn sold it to some whites, who are now looking for this spoil. Another version is that the cave has actually been seen by some recent wanderer in the hills, with the tools of the original Spanish digging-party still in position. I have heard, far in the northwest corner of the state, beyond the Boston Mountains and Fayetteville, that people there believe in the existence of the "Spanish diggins" somewhere in their neighborhood and hold that the treasure can yet be found.

Now this tale can derive ultimately only from a vague knowledge of De Soto, who, as we know, came across the Mississippi to look for gold, and who was led into the mountain region, where are many small limestone caves, to search for it in vain. There is no record, however, that De Soto's expedition took much time to look for, let alone find, anything of value in the whole of Arkansas. If they had, the chroniclers, we may be sure, would have well advertised the fact—as they did in the case of the pearls previously found in Georgia, and lost. Nor, so far as we know, did any other Spaniard ever come to Arkansas to explore it. But it is true that in the fifties of the last century, and for some time after the Civil War as well, silver was found in the Caddo Gap region, in Pike and Montgomery counties, in small quantities; and it was also long believed that the same metal lay in the Maumelle and Big Rock region, north and west of Little Rock. The present city of North Little Rock was in fact originally called "Argenta"—a name sufficiently symptomatic. As for the old mining tools to be found in some caves around Hot Springs and elsewhere, they are presumably the property of the prospectors that tramped over this region after the fifties—for after the discovery of gold in California in 1849, most of the southwestern states believed that they, too, would soon make similar discoveries. And the last "gold boom" in Arkansas occurred as late as 1880.

That all this activity, centering around the mineral resources of the Ouachitas and Ozarks, tends to fasten itself to the fame of a mysterious Spanish expedition is more than a romantic circumstance; it justifies the presence of this black-bearded and desperate conquistador among present-day Arkansawyers. He came here, to the territory that is now our state, long ago—sixty-six long years before the settlement at Jamestown, seventy-nine years before the Mayflower sighted Plymouth Rock. When he came, Henry VIII sat on the throne of England, Francis I on that of France; Michelangelo had just painted his "Last Judgment" on the Sistine wall, and Elizabeth of England was only eight years old. But he came to stay. We, Arkansawyers of a different race, are the heirs of his legendary legacy. Now and again, we too go off seeking forgotten gold—in the market place of some great Northern city, or in the blue-shadowed, deepwooded Ozark hollows. Whether we find it or not does not matter. There is always a map, drawn on deer or buffalo hide, left behind in somebody's hands, showing how, amid the densely wooded ridges, the narrow and trackless hollows, the lost path that leads to that remote burying spot can somehow be found.

Three centuries after De Soto rode through the Indian Country and summoned the chief of Quigualtam to appear before him, the following dialogue, classic to all genuine Arkansawyers, took place. A traveller, riding through the remote Ozarks, with nightfall fast coming on and his horse spent, approached the cabin of a squatter, who was sitting at his door on the upturned end of an old whisky barrel, sawing briefly and furiously away at an old fiddle. The traveller, still sitting on his horse, spoke first:

TRAVELLER: Hello, stranger!

SQUATTER: Hello, yourself.

TRAVELLER: Can you tell me where this road goes to?

SQUATTER: Hit's never gone anywhar since I've lived here; hit's always thar when I git up in the mornin'.

TRAVELLER: Well, how far is it to where it forks?

SQUATTER: Hit don't fork noways, but hit splits up like the devil.

TRAVELLER: Can I get to stay all night with you?

SQUATTER: You kin git to go to hell.

TRAVELLER: Have you got any spirits?

SQUATTER: Plenty of 'em. Sall saw one down by the old holler gum thar, the other night, and hit like to skeered her to death.

TRAVELLER: I don't mean that kind of spirits. I want some liquor. Have you got any liquor?

SQUATTER: Had some yestidy, but old Bose, he got in and lapped all of hit clean outen the pot.

TRAVELLER: You still don't understand me. I don't mean pot liquor. I'm wet and cold, and I want some whisky. Have you got any whisky?

SQUATTER: Oh, yes—I drunk the last of hit this mornin'.

TRAVELLER: Well, I'm hungry and I want something to eat. Have you got anything to eat?

SQUATTER: Hain't a damned thing in the house. Not a mouthful of meat, nor a dust of meal.

TRAVELLER: Well, can't you feed my horse?

SQUATTER: Hain't got nothin' to feed him on.

TRAVELLER: How far is it to the next house?

SQUATTER: Dunno, stranger; I hain't never measured hit, nor been thar.

TRAVELLER: Well, do you know who lives here?

SQUATTER: I do.

TRAVELLER: Then what might your name be?

SQUATTER: Hit mout be Dick and hit mout be Tom; but hit lacks a damn sight of either.

TRAVELLER: Since I'm not likely to get to any other house tonight, can't you let me sleep in yours? I'll tie my horse to that tree, and do without anything to eat or to drink.

SQUATTER: The house leaks. Thar's only one dry spot in hit, and me and Sall has to sleep on that. And that thar tree is the ole woman's persimmon. Yer cain't tie yore hoss to hit, caze she don't want the 'simmons shuck down. She 'lows to make beer out'n em.

TRAVELLER: Why don't you finish covering your house then, and stop the leaks?

SQUATTER: Hit's been a-rainin' all day.

TRAVELLER: Why don't you do it in the dry weather, then?

SQUATTER: Hit don't leak, then.

TRAVELLER: I am puzzled to see how you manage to make a living here. How do you do, anyhow?

SQUATTER: Purty well, thank ye; how do yew do yerself?

TRAVELLER: I mean, what do you do for a living?

SQUATTER: Keep a tavern, and sell whisky.

TRAVELLER: Well, I told you that I wanted some whisky.

SQUATTER: Stranger, I bought a bar'l more'n a week ago. Yew see, me and Sall went shares on hit. Arter a while, we had made only a bit betweenst us, and Sall, she didn't want to use her share fust, nor me mine. I had a spiggin in one end, and she in tother. So she takes a drink out'n my end, and pays me the bit for it; and then I took one out o'hern, and give her back the bit. We were gittin' along fust rate, till Dick, that damn skulking skunk, bourn a hole on the bottom to suck at, and the next time I went to fotch me a drink, I'll be danged but thar wurn't none thar.

TRAVELLER: Well, I'm sorry that your whisky's all gone; but, my friend, why don't you play the balance of that tune?

SQUATTER: Hit's got no balance to it.

TRAVELLER: I mean, you don't play the whole of it.

SQUATTER: Stranger, kin yew play the fiddul?

TRAVELLER: I can saw a little, sometimes.

SQUATTER: Wal, if I was a-goin' to kill a fiddler, I'd never shoot at yew; but if yew think yew kin play any more onto that thar tune, yew kin jist git down and try.

(The Traveller gets down, and plays through the tune. The Squatter starts dancing.)

SQUATTER: Stranger, take half a dozen cheers and sot down. Sall, stir yourself round like a six-mule team in a mudhole. Go down in the holler whar I killed that buck this mornin', cut off some of the best pieces, and fotch and cook hit for me and this gentleman. Till, drive old Bose out'n the bread tray, then climb up in the loft and git the rag that's got the sugar tied in it. Tom, raise up the board under the head of the bed, and git the old black jug I hid from Dick, and give us some whisky; I know thar's some left yit. Dick, take this gentleman's hoss around under the shed, and give him some fodder and cawn, all that he kin eat.

TILL: Dad, thar ain't knives enuf to sot the table with.

SQUATTER: Whar's Big Butch, Little Butch, Old Case, Cobhandle, Granny's Knife, and the one I handled yistidy? That's 'nuff to sot any man's table with, withouten yew've lost 'em. Damme, stranger, yew kin stay here jist as long as ye want to, and I'll give ye plenty to eat and drink. Will yew have coffee for yore supper?

TRAVELLER: Yes, sir.

SQUATTER: I'll be hanged if ye do; we ain't got nothin' that way here, but Grub Hyson, and I reckon hit's mightly good with long sweetenin'. Play away, stranger, yew kin sleep on the dry spot tonight.

TRAVELLER: (*after about two hours fiddling*): My friend, can't you tell me about the road I'm to travel tomorrow?

SQUATTER: Tomorrow! Stranger, yew won't git out'n these diggins for six weeks. But when hit gits so yew kin start, ye see that big sloo over thar? Wal, yew haf to git crost that fust, then yew take the big road up the bank, and in about a mile, yew'll come to a two-acre-and-a-half cawn-patch, the cawn's mightily in weeds, but yew needn't mind that, jist ride on. In about a mile and a half, or mebbe two miles, yew'll come to the damndest swamp yew ever seen. Hit's boggy enuf to mire a saddle blanket. Thur's a fust rate road about six feet under thar.

TRAVELLER: How am I to get at it?

SQUATTER: Yew cain't get at hit noways, till the weather stiffens down some. Wal, about a mile from thar, yew'll come to whar thur's two roads. Yew kin take the right-hand one, if yew want to; yew'll foller hit a mile or so, and yew'll find hit's just plum run out; then come back and try the left one; when yew git about two miles along on that, you may know ye air wrong; for thur ain't no road thar. Then yew'll think yerself mightly lucky if yew git back here, where yew kin play that tune, and stay jist as long as yew please."

If the reader will but compare this authentic folktale, written down, since its first telling by Sandy Faulkner, in many versions, of which I give here my own, with that haughty reply which the chief of Quigualtam made to De Soto (not to mention the attitude of benign skepticism displayed by that other chief—he of Casqui—towards the same Spanish gentleman) he will learn that the natives of Arkansas, though they may have changed their clothes and the color of their skins since 1540, have never lost their dominant traits when it comes to receiving "furriners."

Three

THE FRENCH MAKE A MAP AND LEAVE BEHIND SOME NAMES

Hernando de Soto was dead, and the meagre relics of his expedition—including, as it later proved, an Italian silver medal struck off by Sigismundo Pandolfo Malatesta of Rimini in honor of his consort, about 1460, some thirty years before Columbus set sail for his mysterious new world—had been left behind to moulder slowly in Arkansas soil. It was not until 1673, over a century after De Soto crossed the Great River, that another white man was permitted to glimpse what was going on in Arkansas.

The French had been in Canada since 1604, and the British, by 1673, had become masters of the Atlantic seaboard. A certain amount of trade in guns and ammunition exchanged for valuable furs had been opened with the tribes of the remote interior—by the British through the Iroquois and by the French through the Hurons. Down south, in Mexico, Spain controlled everything from the Isthmus to the upper Rio Grande. To the west and the southwest lay the Pacific and the long sea-route to China. It was known that the region around the Great Lakes, dotted with missionary outposts through the heroic efforts of a few French Jesuits and Recollet friars, was immensely rich in furs and in game; and the Indians had already told tales of a Great River, which ran through the land southward and westward of the Great Lakes to an unknown ocean. These tales had come to the ears of René Cavelier, Sieur de la Salle, a young Norman seminarian turned adventurer, who had settled in Canada by the spring of 1666 and who soon became convinced that this river the Indians talked about would afford a passage for his countrymen to the Vermillion Sea, as the Gulf of California was then called. Such a passage would soon put France ahead of Spain, which since the defeat of the Great Armada in 1588, had declined; and ahead of England, which had only begun to colonize after 1600.

In the winter of 1669–1670, La Salle went to find out for himself just what lay to the south and west of Lake Erie. What he did during this season and the following summer is altogether mysterious; but there seems small reason to doubt that he discovered the Ohio, went down it possibly as far as its confluence with the Wabash, and may have made also a journey down the Illinois as far as the Mississippi itself, though this last is exceedingly questionable. Even Louis Joliet, the good-tempered giant Canadian fur-trader, who was later to rob him of the honor of being the first explorer of the Great River, frankly admitted the validity of his rival's claim to being the discoverer of the Ohio and a portion of the Illinois. We know, however, that whatever La Salle did discover on this trip remained his own profound secret; which may have been the reason why Talon, then Intendant of Louis XIV in Canada, refused to give him the assignment of looking for the Great River, but passed it on to Joliet instead. Unfortunately for himself, La Salle, though one of the greatest explorers in all French history, was haughty, overbearing, and profoundly suspicious of all men. In his whole lifetime he had but one loyal friend, the Sicilian-born Henri de Tonti, who, because of an accident in his youth, was known to the Indians as "the man with the iron hand."

Louis Joliet had lived much among the Indians, had explored as far as Lake Superior, was young, hardy, and resourceful. He also stood well with the Jesuits, whom La Salle especially hated, but who were favored by Louis XIV. Indeed, it was a young Jesuit missionary priest, Jacques Marquette, extremely pious and the possessor of a good knowledge of Indian languages, who was selected to accompany Joliet on his famous voyage.

In two canoes, with only five boatmen and a small supply of smoked meat and dried corn, the two explorers set out from Michilimackinac, a missionary outpost where Lake Michigan empties into Lake Huron, on the seventeenth of May—a day duly noted down by the pious Marquette as the Feast of the Immaculate Conception. They skirted the northwestern shore of Lake Michigan to Green Bay, where they entered the Fox River. Up this they paddled to Lake Winnebago; and across the mile-and-a-half portage to the Wisconsin. Although the Indians at Green Bay had attempted to dissuade the two travellers from their enterprise, by telling all manner of tall tales concerning monsters and demons and great rapids in the river, these had not shaken either Joliet's stolid determination or Marquette's devotion to the idea that he must go on and spread the gospel to far-away peoples. On the seventh of June, a month after their departure, the Mississippi lay before them, beautiful in all the freshness of the summer green along its banks. Down the Great River they went for a full month, passing rock and rapid and river outlet, descending into the south steadily, till they came near the mouth of the Arkansas. For three hundred miles, since they had passed the mouth of the Ohio and the Illinois village there—where they had been well received—they had seen no more Indians; but now another cluster of wattled cabins suddenly appeared above the west bank and they boldly steered towards it.

The reception they received in Arkansas on that hot morning of mid-July was—to say the least—tumultuous. A number of canoes, filled with whooping Indians, took to the water above and below them. Other warriors waded into the shallows, armed for the attack—and a war-club, skillfully thrown, whistled past Marquette's ear. But the courageous priest, standing in the prow, still held aloft the feathered calumet given him by the Indians at the mouth of the Ohio. It finally had its effect. The older Indians quieted the young warriors, and the two canoes drew to the shore.

They stayed there for only one night, not without qualms. Their hostile reception, even though it was followed by the usual feast, had daunted them. None of the Indians here knew enough of the Illinois dialect to be able to answer Marquette's questions concerning the distance that still lay before them ere the sea could be reached. Farther down, they learned, lay another town, on the east bank directly opposite the mouth of the Arkansas; and there in the morning they repaired. The chief had already heard of their coming and had prepared a magnificent feast. One dish succeeded another in endless succession: a platter of sagamite, followed by broiled fish; a roasted dog, with the skin taken off; cornmeal porridge cooked with bear's grease; and so on. A young Indian was discovered in the village, who had a good knowledge of the Illinois language, and to him Marquette addressed himself. He told how he had come to spread a knowledge of Christianity, the one true religion, among them; and he requested information about the course of the river below. In reply the young Indian dissuaded his guests from proceeding farther. His people, he said, were the Oguapas—sometimes called the Akansea—the downstream people—and along the river were hostile tribes, armed with guns procured by barter from the white men. His people, he said, were in such fear of those others that they dared not even hunt the buffalo, but were forced to live solely on their corn, of which they raised three crops a year. As for where the great river emptied, he could not say; but he knew that it ran south continuously.

The feast at last drew to an end; and the guests staggered away to their lodges, their bellies distended, to digest all this food and information at their leisure. But the danger of a surprise attack such as they had already experienced at the village across the river now returned. They might have been seized in the darkness and put to death by some of the young hotheads if the head chief had not learned of the plot, scared the plotters away, and solemnly danced the dance of the calumet before their lodges to reassure them. Later on in the night, the two Frenchmen held counsel together. They decided to return. They had learned enough to judge that the Great River probably discharged itself, not into the Gulf of California, but into that of Mexico; and they were not sufficiently strong in numbers to go on through hostile territory. So the next day, the two canoes were pointed up stream, and the explorers started the long journey northward. It was not until the end of September that they came again to Green Bay.

Now La Salle, whose haughty pride must have rankled deep within him at the thought of how his enemies, the Jesuits, had nearly snatched away the prize from him, was still determined not to be beaten. Whether the newly discovered river—which Marquette had named, provisionally, Rivière de la Conception—entered into the Gulf of Mexico or not, he decided to traverse its entire length and to claim for France all the territory through which it passed.

It was on the thirteenth of March, 1682, almost ten years after Marquette and Joliet had explored the Great River, that La Salle entered the Arkansas region. On that day, floating in their canoes down the Great River, with spring already in the air, La Salle and his fifty-four followers in some six or eight canoes, now far below the mouth of the Ohio, found themselves wrapped in a thick fog. Neither bank was visible, but from the right (the Arkansas side) came the insistent booming of a drum and the shrill yelps of a scalp dance. La Salle immediately landed on a point of land on the west bank and within an hour ran up a rough stockade, which he prepared to defend. He then sent forward some of his party towards the invisible village, whence the sound of the war drums had come across the water. The chiefs proved to be unexpectedly friendly and entertained the Frenchmen and the Indians who were with them for three days, even offering them some of their own war captives for slaves. They were engaged in warring, not on the French, but on other Indians.

These people were the same that Marquette had seen ten years before. They called themselves most commonly the Oguapas, a name often shortened to Kappas, or Quapaws. Their country, rather than their tribe, was known as Akansea or Arcança—the land of the downstream folk—so Marquette had been in error in giving that name to the people rather than the land. They were remarkably fine-looking Indians, the men all practically stark naked, the women clad in skins, with their long hair clumped into a mass behind each ear when unmarried, braided into two plain pigtails after marriage. They wore silver pendants at the nose and in the ears; and were, by comparison with the Iroquois and other northern nations, open hearted, free, and gay. Father Zenobius, the missionary whom La Salle brought along, was delighted with them and dubbed them "*Les Beaux Hommes.*"

Here in the Arkansas country, on the fourteenth of March, a cross was erected, and La Salle formally took possession of the land for his royal master. (On his return journey he again visited the spot, to find that the friendly Indians had carefully surrounded the cross with a neat cane palisade.)

Two of the Indians now offered to guide him farther downstream; and on the seventeenth of March the expedition proceeded, passing two more villages of the same people and reaching the land of the Taensas on the twenty-second. On the ninth of April, after further adventures that need not detain us, they stood at the mouth of the Mississippi, at the opening on the Gulf; and, returning, came again by way of the Arkansas village on the eighteenth of May. . . .

With the misadventures of La Salle's tragic attempt four years later to found a colony at the mouth of the Mississippi, there is no need here to deal. In the end, with the ships of his colonizing expedition lost in the Gulf, and his men bewildered and starving on the Texas prairies, he chose a strange and fantastic course. He decided to march back northward, with his best men, and to keep on for a thousand miles until he found the Illinois—and Tonti, who was now living among them. But he fell ill on the way, and all his further efforts were halted while another summer waned to fall.

Meanwhile, La Salle's faithful lieutenant, Henri de Tonti, had not been idle. In the spring of 1686 he had organized an expedition to go down the river to look for his missing leader. On his way, he stopped in the Arkansas country, some fifteen miles or so inland, close by the junction of the White and Arkansas rivers with the Mississippi and near the place where an old trail, much used by the Indians, crossed the lower Arkansas, going southwest. Here he established a post, where he left six determined Frenchmen, with instructions to watch and wait. He then went south, failed to discover any trace of La Salle after searching the coast for some thirty leagues westward and eastward, and finally came back in the fall of 1686 to take four of the Frenchmen at the Arkansas Post back to the Illinois and to leave only two volunteers, Couture and De Launay, behind.

Henri de Tonti and La Salle—faithful follower and baffled master—were destined never to meet. Seventeen men had set out with La Salle on a last forlorn hope to beat northward after the New Year's Day of 1687; but only seven, with the aid of horses taken from the Indians, finally reached the fort that Tonti had built in the Arkansas country. They arrived on the twentieth of July. On their way they had witnessed scenes of horror and desperation—a wild buffalo hunt on the Texas prairies; a quarrel between Moranget, La Salle's nephew, and two others; the hunting down and killing of their own leader by his mutinous followers; the mutineers squabbling among themselves and killing each other; one party turning back to Texas, while the other went northward. They had sat, unwillingly, through tedious Indian ceremonial feasts and had endured dreary marches through an endless forest, plagued by flies, mosquitoes, and all the other insects of the lower Mississippi region. Now on the other side of the muddy Arkansas, they suddenly saw, as one Joutel tells us, a tall cross and a house built "in the French fashion": two Frenchmen, clad in buckskins, came out and fired their guns in the air as a salute; and the seven men, saved, wept and went almost mad with joy.

La Salle had died, a failure to the last. But his idea of colonizing at the mouth of the Mississippi was not allowed to perish. In January, 1699, Le Moyne d'Iberville landed at last with a small colony, which pushed up the Mississippi just in time to displace the British and to build a fort on Mobile Bay. There, about 1702, D'Iberville was joined by Henri de Tonti, who still, at the Illinois, had cherished his master's forgotten dreams. One hopes that Tonti died honored and happy, at the new flourishing colony of New Orleans, for he deserved it.

From the beginning of the century up to 1763, the close of the Seven Years' War, which was so disastrous for France, the interior of the American continent lay entirely in that country's hands; and her trading posts—Sault Sainte Marie, Michilimackinac, Fort Crèvecoeur, Kaskaskia, Sainte Geneviève, Arkansas Post, Saint Louis, New Orleans—grew and flourished. The *coureur de bois*—the Frenchman turned Indian—went everywhere, had his squaws in every Indian village and supplied the merchants of Paris with their most valuable furs. Though the Court at Versailles made edicts to suppress him, the spirit of France, so far as he was concerned, could not be suppressed. Had the blundering ministers, the corrupted favorites of Louis XIV and Louis XV, not interfered, France might soon have become far more wealthy and powerful on the American continent than England was. But of all that effort, all that adventure, nothing now really remains but a faint flavor of France at Quebec, at New Orleans, perhaps also at Sainte Geneviève, in Missouri; and a map well sown with French names.

There were thirteen French maps of the interior between 1670 and 1684, according to Parkman; and still more extraordinary ones came later, like the map published in Paris by Guillaume de Lisle in 1718, in which the course of practically every river emptying into the Gulf or the Mississippi is fairly accurately laid down under the name it bears today. Yet a goodly proportion of these same rivers had not, as yet, been completely explored, unless by the *coureurs de bois* and by their cousins the Indians.

In 1719, a year after the De Lisle map, Bernard de la Harpe pushed up the Red River from the tiny French outpost of Natchitoches and crossed the plains to a spot well along the upper course of the Arkansas. Two years later, urged by some strange Indian tales of an emerald rock in the stream, he came up the Arkansas itself, sighting the first small outcropping of greenish-brown schist and sandstone where the city of Little Rock later was built on the south bank of the river, and giving it the name that has persisted to this day. Arkansas Post, as the chief center of the fur trade through the territory during all this time, had remained more or less occupied. But that spot, though then protected in part by a high sandy bluff, which has long since gone into the river with every other vestige of settlement, was always subject to great floods. Long after the Spanish occupation, it was described, in 1770, as comprising a square, long-walled, stockaded fort, about one hundred and eighty feet across each face, with several half-ruinous buildings inside the stockade and a garrison of some thirty soldiers; while outside the fort area proper lay eight houses, whose occupants—since the area was too often flooded for farming to prosper—did not till the soil, but lived by hunting in the adjoining woods and prairies. And so Arkansas Post remained, to survive down to the Civil War.

A glance at any century-old map of Arkansas will show how thorough the French were in giving to places their names. Here are the rivers: Saint Francis, Fourche l'Anguille, Cache, Bayou d'Arc, Bayou Bartholomew, Maumelle, Fourche la Feve, Petit Jean, Saline, Two (for Deux) Prairie, Cosatot (for Casse-Tête). Here are the mountains: Ozark (an obvious abbreviation of Aux Arkansas), Masserne (for Montcerne). Petit Jean (more probably named after the hero of some folk tale than after the girl disguised as a French soldier of the later legend), Magazine, Dardanelle (though this last may be derived from the Cherokee rather than from any fancied resemblance to the Dardanelles). Here are the settlements: Ecore à Fabre—apparently Fabre's Bluff—the first name for the spot where now stands the town of Camden and mentioned as early as 1805; La Grange, New Gascony, Cadron (formerly Quadrant), Saint Charles, Saint Martin's, Desarc, possibly Lewisburg. This array of French names across the old map serves to convince us that French exploration, at least, was thorough.

Of the few families with French names that Thomas Nuttall found in Arkansas on his journey of exploration in 1819, none now remains, so far as I know. The Bougies, the Notrebes, and the Vaugines are long gone, though Lefevre, corrupted to Lefever, still exists. Concerning the fate of the last holder of the name of one of these families, I have heard an interesting, though a grisly, story. As it seems to me to symbolize, in its mingled tragedy and grotesque farce, much of the dubious mystery that accompanied the French attempt at colonization, I give it here.

After a fairly recent great flood, during which the Arkansas River vastly changed its course, cutting through its banks both below and above Little Rock, a skeleton was discovered washed out from a forgotten graveyard some miles below the capital city. The skeleton lay long unnoticed, till it was brought to a farmer's front yard near by, where it decked a tree for some months, the children playing with the bones. A very old woman of French descent, living in Little Rock, heard that the skull contained some teeth that were plainly artificial and concluded that it had belonged to her grandfather, a pioneer from Canada back in 1770, who had lived nearly up to the Civil War. She of course had never seen him but had heard about him from their parents in her childhood. She had the bones carefully collected and laid out in an inner room in her own home. There they were dusted and polished daily by a Negro servant, while she set about arranging for their reburial in Mount Holly, Little Rock's famous historic cemetery, which at first had been open to Catholic, Protestant, and Jew without distinction, but which had become, and now is, open exclusively to Protestant burials. Finally a Protestant clergyman was found who agreed to officiate at the reburial of the bones on the existing family plot; but by a mistake they were put into the ground at a spot somewhat over the boundary of the plot of another family. Meanwhile, an aged Negro man, tottering and feeble, appeared and solemnly declared that the bones in fact had been those of one of his long-dead wives, a woman who also had artificial teeth in her head in the same position as those in the skull. The family on whose plot the bones had been reburied promptly objected to their presence; they had no desire to allow any of their members to lie next door to a Negro, even if that Negro was only a skeleton. The unfortunate woman was forced to take the bones up again and rebury them, this time on the other side of the central monument, mossy with age, which the family had long ago set up. And there they remain to this day.

The influence of the French effort, which was carried on so long, though only sporadically, and through so many disasters and failures, has long since mingled and become assimilated with the Anglo-Saxon culture of Arkansas. It has become, in its essence, much like those old disputed bones—a thing of doubtful antiquity of paternity, a legend, a myth, a remote shadowy survival, although, as late as beyond the Civil War, cases based on French or Spanish land grants—usually to French families—still occurred in the Arkansas courts. Like the French celebration of Mardi Gras, still honored by masking on the streets of Little Rock during the days of my boyhood—and earlier celebrated by great parades and balls—the French influence has, to all intents and purposes, disappeared. But the symbol of France, seen dimly in the great figures of La Salle and Tonti, of La Harpe, in the records of Arkansas Post, or in the mythical, unrealized Alsatian colony of John Law, serves to haunt us still, as a shadow crossing the familiar sunlight.

Under the Spanish occupation (1763–1800) the first white child—at least of Anglo-Saxon descent—was born in Arkansas. This was John Patterson, who, born in 1790, lived up to 1886 and described himself as "uncultivated as a poke stalk, unlettered as a savage; birthplace caved in the river when I was young; father was shot from ambush while asleep at home." In his old age he frequently recited his own epitaph:

> "I was born in a Kingdom,
> Raised in an Empire;
> Attained manhood in a Territory;
> Am now a citizen of a State;
> And have never been one hundred
> miles from where I live."

This epitaph not only seems to be characteristic, but it also describes well the fate of the first French settlers in Arkansas.

Four

A TRAVELLER SEES ARKANSAS BECOME A TERRITORY

Thomas Nuttall was, by any standard, a remarkable man. Born into poverty in Yorkshire, England, in the year 1786, and apprenticed in boyhood to a printer, he soon developed such a love for the natural sciences that when he emigrated to Philadelphia in 1808 he was already beginning those researches into botany that later made him famous. In 1818 he published in two volumes the first comprehensive book on American botany, for which he is said to have set most of the type personally. It formed the basis for all later works on the subject.

At the end of the year which saw the production of his great botanical work, Nuttall, then thirty-two, was fired with the idea of visiting the Arkansas country, which offered him a practically virgin field. The region had been added to the territory of the United States by the Louisiana Purchase in 1803; and Jefferson, then president, urged on by his usual curiosity concerning all natural rarities, had, in the following year, dispatched William Dunbar and Dr. George Hunter, both natives of Natchez, Mississippi, up the Red and the Ouachita rivers to look for some hot springs, which—as reported by the Indians—lay in the mountains near the headwaters of the Ouachita. The journal of the Dunbar-Hunter trip is extant and has been published. But it reveals nothing of importance concerning the kind of man and woman who later were to come to Arkansas, for the region through which the travellers passed was practically uninhabited, though a rough, one-roomed log cabin stood at Hot Springs itself. In 1806 Lieutenant James B. Wilkinson, of the Zebulon Pike expedition, had also descended, in two canoes, the Arkansas River from the Great Plains to the Mississippi, but all that he had to record, apart from some topographical notes, concerned the unchanging forests, the great herds of buffalo, of deer, of other wild animals. Now Nuttall had the field to himself and was likely to make the most of it. His chief interest, apart from botany and geology, lay in the unexplored field of American Indian ethnology.

A man who could say of himself, "My chief converse had been in the wilderness with the spontaneous productions of nature; and the study of these objects and their contemplation has been to me a source of constant delight," is certainly not to be expected to give us any strong insight into the manners and customs of the first pioneer American settlers in Arkansas. Yet Nuttall gives us enough, by way of casual comment, to enable us to deduce what these settlers were like and how they lived. The year 1818 in itself was momentous. Cotton—and the Arkansas land was known to be favorable to cotton—had risen to the unprecedented price of thirty-four cents a pound. Missouri, in whose territory the Arkansas region lay, was clamoring for admission as a slave state, a move which agitated the aging Jefferson and set the North fairly ablaze, since it meant the abandonment of Mason and Dixon's line west of the Mississippi. In 1820, by means of a great compromise, Missouri was admitted as a slave state; and in the year earlier, as we shall see, the southern portion, south of the Saint Francis lowland, was separated from it and admitted as a new territory. A vast scramble for western lands was already in progress and was accompanied by a wildcat inflation of the national currency. The first uprising of the West in American history, which was to destroy eventually the Bank of the United States and to send Andrew Jackson to the White House, was already under way.

It was on the eve of such stirring events that Nuttall visited the region later to become "Arkansaw Territory" and the State of Arkansas. Still other and equally stirring events lay in the background. In the late fall of 1811, while the first steamboat, the "New Orleans," was making her maiden voyage from Pittsburgh to the Gulf, the mysterious New Madrid earthquakes had taken place—a series of events to this day insufficiently documented. These shakings, which went on for some time, were caused apparently by some slipping and shifting of rock in strata deep underground. They lowered the fertile regions on both sides of the river, in many places, from ten to twenty feet, changed the bed and shifted the current of the Great River itself, and created many new swamps and lakes—such as Reelfoot Lake in West Tennessee, or the Sunken Lands of the Saint Francis in Arkansas. As late as the time of his southward journey, according to Nuttall, small earthquakes still persisted in the New Madrid region, two or three tremors being sometimes felt in a single day. As a result, the region was rapidly becoming depopulated, its pioneer settlers moving south to more favorable locations along the banks of the White River and the Arkansas itself. The United States had encouraged this movement by granting to most of the dispossessed settlers certificates entitling them to a free equivalent of their present holdings, southward and westward as far as the Arkansas River.

Thus Arkansas, discovered by the tragic figure of the gold-seeking De Soto, first explored by the unsettled and unrooted persistence of the French, was at last becoming populous, thanks to a cotton boom and a great natural disaster. The rich lowlands of southeastern Missouri, settled far earlier, were losing both French and American residents; and around the Mississippi, as far as the Saint Francis, lay great swamps, newly formed and enlarged, which persist to this day. When Nuttall set out from Philadelphia to explore and to botanize, the crest of the first wave of Anglo-Saxons to reach the interior of the continent beyond the Mississippi was just coming into Arkansas; but at least two sections of the new territory were still entirely Indian. On the south bank of the Arkansas River, beginning at Arkansas Post itself and running due southwest to a point close to the confluence of the Ouachita and the Saline, then up this latter stream north to near the eastern boundary of the present city of Little Rock, and from thence down the line of the Arkansas again, lay the lands already allotted to the Quapaws by a treaty signed at Saint Louis in 1817. These were descendants of those Indians visited by Joliet and by Tonti. Further to the northwest, on the opposite bank, between Point Remove and Bellepointe, which was just becoming a new American army garrison under the name of Fort Smith, lay lands granted to the eastern Cherokees by the treaty of 1817. We shall have more to say of the Quapaws and the Cherokees later, as we follow Nuttall's travels.

Nuttall left Philadelphia on October 2, 1818, and reached Pittsburgh by way of a partly completed, very rough stagecoach road on October 16. There he found "the shores of the Monongahela lined with boats of all descriptions, steamboats, barges, keels, and arks, or flats." The Ohio was too low to descend above Wheeling. It was not until the twenty-first of October that he was able to get away from Pittsburgh. Accompanied by a young man who understood the handling of a boat, he started out in a skiff that had cost six dollars. The first of November found him below Marietta, Ohio; and the sixteenth of that month brought him to Cincinnati, "by far the most agreeable and flourishing of all the western towns." Leaving again on the seventeenth, he reached Louisville on the twenty-third of November, only to be detained till the seventh of December by his companion's abandoning him. He was faced with the impracticability of going on. A steamboat passage to Natchez from this point cost as much as fifty dollars; in the end, it seemed much cheaper to buy another small flatboat and go on.

At last, on the seventeenth of December, the Great River was reached, rolling through what Nuttall called "an occidental wilderness" which "appears here to retain its primal solitude." Settlement there was none on the site of the present-day Cairo; and the Mississippi there was bank-full with blocks of floating ice. Accordingly the three travellers (for here Nuttall was accompanied by an elderly gentleman and his son, bound for New Orleans), tied up to the bank for two days, inspected a canebrake growing on the top of the bank, with canes growing thirty feet high, and talked with some wandering Delaware and Shawnee Indians. Proceeding on the nineteenth, despite the floating ice, they soon grounded on Wolf Island—well named, for it cost them about fourteen dollars to get off with the assistance of passing boatmen who were thorough rascals. On the twenty-second they arrived at New Madrid, an insignificant and already dying "French hamlet," as Nuttall calls it, containing little more than twenty log houses and "stores miserably supplied." Here in these same "miserably supplied" stores, prices ruled as follows: eighteen cents a pound for lead, five dollars a bushel for salt, thirty-one and a quarter cents a pound for sugar, a dollar and twenty-five cents a gallon for whisky, twenty-five cents for a dozen apples, fifty cents a bushel for corn, thirty-seven and a half cents a pound for butter; eggs the same price per dozen, and beef and pork five and six dollars for a hundred pounds—which suggests that the man who wished to explore this remote frontier would better go equipped with a good gun and the knowledge of how to use it on the plentiful game of the region.

The settlement at New Madrid, however "miserable," was nearly the last till Arkansas Post was reached. Through tremendous flooded lands the travellers moved, passing innumerable floating, or half-floating, logs fixed to sandbars, which were called, in river speech, "snags" or "sawyers." On the sixth of January, 1819, near some widely scattered log houses at the mouth of the Saint Francis, they came upon a scene, then frequent but lost after the Civil War: a flock of screaming Carolina parrots were feeding on buttonwood seeds. The button willow still grows here, no doubt, as elsewhere along swampy rivers in Arkansas; but the parrots have long since disappeared before the guns of white hunters.

On the twelfth of January, they arrived at Mr. McLane's, "a house of entertainment," opposite the mouth of the "White River Cut-Off," that common bayou route for all travellers to the Arkansas River from the Mississippi. Here Nuttall parted from his companions, the elderly gentleman and his son, who went on. For five dollars, a new boatman was hired; and Nuttall notes in his journal, "The idea of so soon arriving on the ground which I more immediately intended to explore, did not fail to inspire me with hope and satisfaction"—a commentary which our modern generation, which covers the same ground by airplane or motor in a number of hours far less than it took Nuttall days, might take to heart.

It was not until the sixteenth of January, after the first boatman hired had turned out to be a drunken scoundrel, that Nuttall, with the aid of another boatman, reached the Arkansas, or, as he spells it, the "Arkansa"—muddy and turbid then as now, chocolate-red in the strong sunlight. The thermometer at noon stood at 67; birds were already singing; and flowers were already peeping out. But progress was slow, for the boat had to be pulled, foot by foot, up the river and against the current, by means of the cordelle, or towrope. It was the twenty-second of January before our traveller, by walking through the last stretch, found himself at the "Post, now town, of Arkansas." That he spelled the name of the river and also the name of the Indians without the final, silent *s*, and the name of the Post with it, is one of the minor mysteries of his engaging narrative.

The Post, lying about twenty miles up the river from the Mississippi, was found to be a settlement of some thirty or forty log houses, scattered for almost three miles around a sandy bluff, almost as "elevated as the Chickasaw Bluffs" at the site which later became Memphis. A straggling road of sorts led directly north across the Grand Prairie at the back of the settlement. Here were again merchants, of whom Nuttall had seen none since New Madrid. They were supplied here mostly from New Orleans: Messrs. Braham and Drope; Mr. Lewis—later found, according to the first issue of the first newspaper in Arkansas—in partnership with a certain Thomas. Above all, here was Frederick Notrebe (sometimes spelled Noteribe). This last personage, together with a certain Charles Bougie (or, as his name was usually spelled, Bogy), were the two most distinguished of the earliest settlers. The outlandishness of the country is sufficiently attested by the fact that, though both were Frenchmen, one had come from the South and the other from the far North. Bougie had entered Arkansas with the Federal troops who came to take possession of the Post after the Louisiana Purchase; he originally came from Canada by way of Kaskaskia, Illinois. Notrebe had taken part in the French Revolution, had been an army officer under the First Consul, and had left France in 1803, to come up the river from New Orleans about 1815. Bougie was now about seventy, and, like Notrebe, wore the garb then common: "A blanket capeau, buckskin leggins, and moccasins." Nuttall adds to this, that, from the scarcity of hats, most men and women wore a handkerchief tied over their heads. Whether this was true in the case of Bougie and Notrebe is not known.

The settlement itself consisted of one-storied log houses built after the French fashion, with unglazed windows, open hallways running through the center from front to back, and wide verandahs going all around. Its only communication with the outside world was by canoe or keelboat; no steamer was to arrive there until the "Comet" docked on April 1, 1820. Nuttall remained at Arkansas Post till the twenty-sixth of February, 1819, occupying his time in rambling over the country, botanizing at his leisure, hunting for wild fowl on the prairie, which was already in bloom, as were the redbud and the peach trees of the settlement, and reporting on the adjoining Indians. On the north bank, he learned, there were already several scattered settlements of whites all the way up to Cadron; but on the south bank, one Choctaw and four Quapaw villages stood, with their oblong huts made of bark and cane, with a hole in the center of the roof to let out the smoke from the hearthstone fire. Later on, he was destined to visit one of these villages and to remark on the foppishness of the dress of the young bucks: "covered with feathers, blazing calicoes, scarlet blankets, and silver pendants." A sober man of science, he was unable to appreciate the fact that human clothes were originally designed not for protection, but for adornment, to increase in his own eyes the dignity of that "forked radish" known as man. On a later visit Nuttall estimated that the Quapaws did not amount to more than two hundred warriors. Constant old campaigns with Chickasaws to the east and Osages to the west, as well as more recent addiction to the white man's firewater, had far reduced their numbers. They were strikingly handsome, dark-skinned rather than copper-colored, and markedly open and friendly with the whites. Their houses were always burnt down and destroyed, after a death took place, over the burial-spot of the body within; hence resulted low mounds, usually bare of grass, which Nuttall noted. At marriage, the husband presented his wife with a leg of deer; she responded with an ear of corn. The same division of labor took place in life: the males spent their time in hunting, usually with a bow fashioned out of the yellow-hued wood of the Osage orange, called *bois d'arc* by the French explorers, and still known as "burdock" in this part of the South; the wife hoed with bone hoes the patches of corn, squashes, and pumpkins. Before planting time, according to Nuttall, a dog was devoured alive by the women engaged in planting, as "an offering to the Indian Ceres"—or so at least he recorded. They had masks made out of deerhide and employed masked figures in their dances. This is practically all that is known about them, except that they had originally come, according to their tradition, from the Illinois country, and were of the Siouan stock. There they had divided into two parts, some going up the Missouri and becoming the Omahas, or up-stream people; others descending to the Arkansas and becoming the Oguapas, or Quapaws. Apparently they had come down to the river since De Soto's time; for there is nothing in the accounts of that expedition to indicate that they were actually then in Arkansas.

Meantime, still at Arkansas Post, and lacking any other means of transportation, Nuttall arranged to go up the river with a party of the native settlers, who proceeded, carousing on whisky, by easy stages, with numerous halts, to a small settlement just below the mouth of Plum Bayou.

There, on the ninth of March, Mr. Drope, one of the merchants established at the Post, took him aboard his "large and commodious trading boat of twenty-five tons burthen," which was now proceeding—with numerous halts—to supply the scattered settlements as far up-river as the garrison at Fort Smith. Thus Nuttall was enabled to visit the site of the future city of Pine Bluff, originally called "Mont Marie," in a region rich in aboriginal mounds and ancient Indian settlements, where a few half-breed families, boasting of their dubious descent from Tonti's original explorers, welcomed them. These settlers, he noted, lived in such close proximity to the Indians that they were "entirely hunters, or in fact Indians in their habits, and pay no attention to the cultivation of the soil." "In the evening," he says, "a ball or dance was struck up between them and the *engagés*"—these latter being Drope's boatmen. One would like, it must be confessed, to read some fuller account of that ball: to know what old French tunes were played, to hear how much corn whisky was drunk, to learn whether knives were drawn. Fancy dwells long on that far-off prospect, to bring back to mind the furiously sawing fiddler, with his forehead swathed in a red calico handkerchief, the shouted calls for the figures, the whirling brown homespun skirts, the blazing pine knots or tallow dips set against the naked walls, the pat of the deerleather moccasins on the puncheon floor. Not so very different, perhaps, from similar scenes witnessed in the Ozark region as recently as only yesterday.

On the sixteenth of March, Nuttall's thermometer dropped suddenly from 73 to 28 degrees, and the next morning "we had the disagreeable prospect of ice." Arkansas was already living up to its reputation as a land of uncertain springs. Here, in the latitude of Morocco, "we find the fig annually levelled to the ground by frosts," as Nuttall truly observes, and the peach, already naturalized from the East, as well as the native mulberry, no sooner bloomed than a frost came along to "despoil the possible fruit." "Not even the low palmetto is indigenous," he declares (though this last is a mistake, for I have seen the plant myself in low and swampy spots not far from Pine Bluff). "No olive," he continues, "nor any well-grounded prospect of its success; wines, for which Madeira has long been celebrated, appear also proscribed; no evergreens of any description, except the holly, appear throughout the dreary forests. The northwestern winds, sweeping over the arctic deserts of eternal winter, have extended the temperature of northern Europe over all the regions of the United States, nearly to the very limits of the tropic. The climate of Arkansas is not more ardent and less temperate than that of the south of France." Which—if we discount the effects produced by over a century of forest-cutting and of cultivation—remains largely true even today.

Four days later the travellers passed the point where the great military road from Saint Louis—running southwestward beyond the lead mines of lower Missouri, through the Saint Francis River country and so on past Hot Springs to Fulton and the "Lost Prairie" settlements at Red River—crossed the Arkansas: a road probably following, for the most part, the lines of prehistoric Indian trails and called even before Nuttall's day, "the southwest trail." Here, at a spot called "Mr. Hogan's, or the settlement of the Little Rock," the pine-clad hills began, hailed by Nuttall, who had been travelling for more than three months in deep-forested, flat alluvial lands, with much romantic joy. Some miles farther on, above the then unquarried bastion of Big Rock, in a temperature which had suddenly dropped to 22, "appeared again, on the left, very considerable round-top hills. One of them, called the Mamelle, in the distance, where first visible, appeared insulated and conic like a volcano. The cliffs bordering the river, broken into shelvings, were decorated with the red cedar and clusters of ferns." The transition to the Ozarks and the Ouachitas had come.

Here, east of "the Mamelle," now undignified under the more Puritanic name of "Pinnacle Mountain"—a favorite ground for picnics close to the site of present-day Little Rock—Nuttall observed the "pretended silver mine, about one mile below White Oak bayou or rivulet," where, between slate, schist, and sandstone, he saw veins of quartz containing the rock-crystals so often sold today to tourists around the Hot Springs area, as well as "round masses of imperfect crystals of a white and diaphanous talc, collected into radii, each plate forming the segment of a circle." And here, too, he exercised his—it must be admitted—mediocre skill as an artist, by making two sketches of Pinnacle Mountain, which show, remotely, how that land, so familiar to the present writer, looked in that day. Spring, after two false starts, was rapidly coming back again with a rising river, warning of the melting of snows on the northwest plains; and on the twenty-seventh of March, the travellers reached Cadron, which, along with Arkansas Post and Fort Smith, deserves mention here as the third of the earliest settlements in the Arkansas area.

The site of Cadron is still fairly accessible and can be reached—though it often is not, because of the badness of the road—a few miles from the highway west of Conway. I recall a midsummer afternoon passed there not long ago. On the north bank, at a point where the muddy, steady river changes its course from east-and-west to north-and-south, there are two outstretching capes of worn blue-gray slaty rock some fifteen or twenty feet high, enclosing a small space of high ground set well out of the reach of all floods. The site is at present covered densely with a thicket of cedars, not shown on Nuttall's sketch; and no one now lives on it. Here, in a solitude unknown to cities, one can sit on a waterworn ledge and dream of all that has gone by in this vicinity since the beginning: De Soto possibly, and La Harpe, Nuttall himself, and Governor Miller, as we shall soon see; the wild frontiersmen, whisky-guzzling, shooting, and cursing; the land-speculators and the silk-hatted gamblers; the coonskin-capped pioneers; the Chickasaws, the Cherokees, the Quapaws, and the Choctaws quitting their country; the desperate Confederates retreating before the Federals. For nearly a century, there has been no settlement at Cadron; once it was county seat of Pulaski and a bold contender for the site of the state capital, but it has now become a rarely visited park, with a board marking the supposed center of the state and a low cliff from which one can drop twigs into the muddy current below, to see them drift southward and eastward to the cottonwood-bordered horizon, where runs, back and forth, a small steam-ferry from Conway. There is peace now at Cadron; a peace such as Nuttall failed to find in its noisy tavern, crowded with frontiersmen.

At Point Remove Creek, which the modern traveller along Highway 64 crosses at the outset of the magnificent cottonplain west of Morrillton, Nuttall saw the lands which had been recommended to the Tennessee Cherokees as early as Jefferson's administration and which had been finally ceded to them by treaty in 1817. They began on the north bank of the creek and continued all the way to Fort Smith. Here, in what are now flourishing cotton bottoms, between northeast- and southwest-tending ridges, Nuttall was surprised to find the Indians living, on the whole, somewhat better than their neighbors the white men. Here were well tilled acres, established settlements representing a community of some two to three thousand souls, living in decently furnished houses and on farms "well-fenced and stocked with cattle." Some of the Indians, in fact, possessed property to the amount of many thousands of dollars; and, unlike the Quapaws, they were not being slowly worn away into extinction by the white man's whisky, nor by his improvements. Startling indeed was the contrast between these neat homes and the decayed, crumbling log huts of the Post or the rude shacks, doorless and windowless, which Nuttall had already seen at Cadron.

These Cherokees were indeed, and are still, remarkable people. Supposedly akin to the Iroquois, when first seen by the white men they occupied a highland region that ran south and west across present-day eastern Tennessee, from the Virginia border to west of Nashville and thence down across the Great Smoky Mountains into North and South Carolina, upper Alabama and Georgia. De Soto had probably visited them in 1540, on the way to his defeat at Mauvilla; and, in this region, mustering originally perhaps twenty thousand souls, they possessed no less than sixty-four towns, including their traditional capital of Echota in northern Georgia. Up to the time that gold was unfortunately discovered in Dahlonega near by, they held much of this vast territory and resisted all attempts at dispossession; but the main body of the tribe was finally removed by 1833–1835 to the Indian Territory as we shall see, the Arkansas Cherokees having already preceded them, having been forced out by white settlers. Even then, some escaped removal by taking refuge in the fastnesses of the Smokies, where they remain today.

At the time that Nuttall found them occupying the river banks above Point Remove, they had been there since 1818: and among them, from Tennessee, was soon to come George Guess—or Sequoyah, to give him his Indian name—product probably of a squaw and a white trader, who in his own way was to be one of the most remarkable people either white man or Indian has ever seen. Inventor of the only known alphabet achieved by an Indian for the correct transliteration of his own language, this "Cherokee Cadmus" left his tribesmen, before even most of the white men had letters, a literate people. The troubles that were later to disrupt the Cherokees utterly had not, when Nuttall saw them, yet made their appearance; they were eager to have missionaries come and live among them; most of the tribe had adapted themselves to the white men's way of living without losing any of their better Indian characteristics; they wore white men's clothes and were far more enterprising as farmers than many of the wild frontiersmen or decayed French half-breeds whom Nuttall had already seen. They were also about to experience the benefits of conversion to Christianity—the Reverend Cephas Washburn, a devoted Congregational missionary from Yale College, was coming to live among them in the following year, 1820.

From Point Remove, Nuttall moved on through this beautiful Cherokee country of ridge and valley, with many side excursions at Dardanelle and elsewhere, to examine the geology of the neighboring mountains, to admire the rich variety of the surrounding country, and to note the dogwoods now in full flower. He arrived at Fort Smith on the twenty-fourth of April and immediately became so attracted by the aspect of the nearby prairies with their innumerable grasses and flowers—coreopsis, larkspur, coneflowers—that he decided to remain all summer and to spend his time exploring the Osage country to westward. It was not until the sixteenth of October, after coming close to the gates of death through a violent attack of malaria, during the course of an excursion across the prairies to the Neosho (now Grand) River in August, that he returned again to Arkansas Post, to recuperate from his botanical efforts.

While he was away at Fort Smith, the new people in Arkansas had not been idle. The agitation to divide Missouri and to create out of the southern half of it a new territory, to be called "Arkansaw" (it is thus spelled several times in the original act of admittance) had led, during the previous year, to the circulation of a petition to Congress; and on January 30, while Nuttall was still at the Post, this petition duly made its appearance on the floor of Congress. It was promptly acted upon; and on March 2, President Monroe signed the act making "Arkansaw" a territory—the act to take effect on July 4, 1819.

The future state at that time, according to the census made a year later, had a population, exclusive of the Indians, of 14,255—most of them newly-arrived settlers. Two large sections of the area, as we have seen, had already been granted to the Indians by solemn treaty. Outside of this, there were enormous land grants, made mostly to French families during the latter days of the Spanish administration; which still had to be cleared up before settlement was possible; and litigation concerning them went on furiously till well beyond the forties. One grant of a million acres along the Arkansas had been made in 1797 to Elisha, William, and Gabriel Winter, Joseph Stilwell, and a certain William Russell—a name to recur ominously later on. Others, equally vast, had been made to Don Joseph Vallière, in the White River valley, in 1793; to Don Carlos de Villemont, Commandant at the Post, in 1795; and to Baron de Bastrop, probably the largest landowner of them all, the original settler at Camden in southwestern Arkansas, in 1799. The attitude of the United States to all these old Spanish titles was unknown; their sites were still largely uninhabited and in some cases unmarked and unsurveyed. Also to be legally settled was the vexed question of the New Madrid certificates recently issued by the government to refugees from the earthquake districts, allowing them to take up elsewhere the equivalent of their lost lands. What population there was, was scattered over a vast, densely forested area, with no roads. There was not a grist mill in the whole territory. Corn meal was still ground in wooden mortars. Flour sold for twelve dollars a barrel. Although President Monroe had appointed, as first governor, a full-fledged general from remote New Hampshire, who did not arrive till the day after Christmas of this eventful year 1819, it was left to the Secretary of the Territory, the young and ambitious Robert Crittenden, recently come from Kentucky, to summon the first legislature. And this body, made up of the three judges of the Superior Court and of Crittenden himself, met on July 28 for a period of seven days, established two circuit courts, and voted only that the laws of Missouri should be applicable to the new territory.

Before the mysterious new governor of Monroe's appointment could arrive, and before Nuttall, lying ill of his "bilious fever" at Fort Smith could return to the Post, civilization, in the shape of the printed word, had already reached Arkansas. William E. Woodruff, born at "Fire Place" on Long Island, on December 24, 1795, and early trained as a printer, had come down the Ohio River to Louisville, and from there—it is said—had walked overland to Franklin, Tennessee, south of Nashville; from there he had again started early in the year 1819, with a small hand press and types as his baggage, down the Cumberland and the Ohio to the Mississippi, and then down the Great River to the Arkansas. He was determined to become the first printer in the new-made territory, and he succeeded. By buying two log dugouts and by lashing them together, he contrived to bring his press and types safely to Arkansas Post that fall; and he gave to the world, on November 20, 1819, the first issue of the *Arkansas Gazette,* edited from a mean log cabin. Thus another man, and by no means an insignificant one, lived up to his own chosen motto: "It is the duty of every man to be useful, in whatsoever activity he may be placed in life."

Woodruff, remembered by one who saw him in 1832, as a short, thickset man, clean-shaven, with a fine forehead, thin dark-auburn hair, piercing dark eyes, and a reserved manner, was destined, through his energy, persistence, and determination to succeed, to remain a mighty force in the territory and the later state, down to the time when, full of many years of honors, he died in the year 1885.

General James Miller, the new governor by Monroe's appointment—shown in his fine later portrait by Samuel F. B. Morse as a handsome, kindly-looking gentleman—was destined to no such lucky fate. Born near Peterborough, New Hampshire, in the rocky Monadnock region, in the year of the Declaration of Independence, he had joined the American Army as major in 1808, became lieutenant colonel in 1810, and colonel of the Twenty-first Connecticut Volunteer Regiment at the outset of the War of 1812. At Lundy's Lane, July 25, 1814, having been ordered to take a British battery firing near by, he replied to his commanding officer, "I'll try, sir," and moved his men boldly forward. The charge was successful; and Congress had voted him a gold medal and made him a brigadier general for his exploit.

Whatever Miller's future might be, he at least set himself from the outset the task of impressing the native Arkansawyers. Since no steamboat had so far succeeded in penetrating up the Arkansas River, the government provided him with a keelboat for the long journey from Pittsburgh to the Post. This was fitted up with a large and well-furnished deck cabin, which Miller used as his office and living quarters during the first months of his stay. On both sides of the keelboat appeared the potent name "Arkansaw" in large gilt letters, while from a flagstaff above the cabin there floated a large banner bearing upon a scroll the magic phrase, "I'll try, sir!" Thus equipped, and ready, like Andrew Jackson, to capitalize to the utmost on his newly made military reputation, James Miller braved the wilderness.

He embarked at Pittsburgh in his keelboat in September; but unfortunately consumed three leisurely months in descending the Ohio and the Mississippi, and, as we have seen, did not arrive at the Post till the day after Christmas. Robert Crittenden was already on the ground and was not likely to yield precedence to the New Hampshire Yankee who happened to be governor. Young and handsome, with a tight-lipped mouth that bespoke contempt, and a chin that proclaimed determination, he had already witnessed, or heard, back in Kentucky, much concerning the intrigues whereby Kentucky had been almost detached from the Union to join Spain; and much concerning the high-handed methods whereby old settlers—such as Daniel Boone—

had already been dispossessed of their lands. He did not openly disapprove of such tactics, for he was determined to rise in the world and was not going to be overnice in the methods he used to achieve this object. An accomplished lawyer and debater, he meant to be the dominant man in Arkansas politics, let Miller say or do what he would. Most of the new settlers, having been bred to just such frontier conditions as he, were already on his side or could be bribed to come over to him. Or so he thought, as he prepared, even before Miller's advent or consent, to hold elections for a new legislature, to be summoned into session just after the new governor's arrival.

From the outset of his career in Arkansas, Miller proved a total failure as governor. It is said that he opposed the choice of Little Rock as the state capital and favored rather his own country seat chosen early in 1820, Crystal Hill, some twenty miles up the river and nearer Cadron and the geographic center of the state. Now Little Rock is a city, and Crystal Hill is merely a name on some maps. Miller's early actions, at all events, irritated those already in the field and thus killed him politically. For the whole of his term he was inactive, apparently at outs with the ruling Crittenden faction and their native support. When he retired in 1825, to be appointed collector of customs at the Port of Salem, he had already faded into obscurity, as far as Arkansas was concerned.

The selection of such a governor, and that governor's attempt to impress the natives with his importance, were symbolic acts. Arkansas was not actually the most remote frontier territory: but it was near it. Southwest lay Texas, nominally Spanish, but in reality a no-man's land. Its northeastern border still lacked the restraint of law. As in every frontier state later formed west of the Mississippi, the conduct of Arkansas, as Nuttall had already noted, was bold, reckless, lawless. To fit the natives to law-abiding civilization, it was indeed necessary to bring civilization to the wilderness and, as Miller's slogan said, to try. Miller could not find support; so his try had failed, from the outset. After all, he was a Yankee and a stickler for too much legality.

In November, 1819, on his way eastward and southward down the Arkansas, Nuttall, pausing from his observations of the autumn climate and of the dry land, sun-scorched and withered since September, filled now with the undulating haze of gray smoke uprising from narrow prairies and dense underwoods (burned at this season by both whites and Indians), recorded his disgust at the "dram-drinking, jockeying, and gambling" crowd already collecting at Cadron in the two-room log tavern recently set up there. As he notes, "a considerable concourse of travellers, and some emigrants began to make their appearance in this imaginary town." Farther down river, at Edmund Hogan's cabin and ferry, at a point southeast of "the Rock" itself, he heard talk of a plan already afoot to build another town. This western country, despite its malaria—which had nearly killed him—was filling up fast; and in the violence of the pioneer onrush, carrying numberless land speculators in its wake, there was good reason for Miller to have tested out his stubborn motto, "I'll try."

Three-fourths of the elements that later made the Arkansawyers what they were—and are—were already on the scene, or approaching it. There was Miller, the easygoing, open, well-bred country gentlemen, fundamentally honest, but too disposed to rest on precedent, and on acquired laurels. There was Woodruff, hard-working, serious, reserved, with a cautious eye to the main chance—since his livelihood depended upon it. There was Crittenden, flashy, unscrupulous, bold, determined to succeed by fair means or foul. And there were the "dram-drinking, jockeying, gambling" speculators, the rough-and-ready frontiersmen whom Nuttall had seen at Cadron. All these were types that later appeared in Arkansas history. Behind them, somewhat shadowy, lay the Indians: The Quapaws, already sinking in decline, and the more settled and peaceable Cherokees, who had quitted their eastern homes. Whoever won in the contest soon to develop, the Indians were bound to lose. Nuttall, no doubt, reflected with melancholy on these facts, as—soon after Miller's arrival at the Post—he prepared to quit Arkansas for good and all. He seems to have left, concluding that the new territory would never really be fit for human settlement—a conclusion shown to be remarkably wrong by the facts of later history.

Five

PISTOLS FOR TWO AND DUELS AT THE LAW

Arkansas, as we have seen, was already populated with men and women much like ourselves—that is, with white people whose parents had been born in some part of the United States. Up to 1930 this condition still prevailed—ninety-seven percent of the white population had both parents born in America. The Indian population, of which Nuttall tells us so much, was destined soon to disappear; the Negro population was to grow from a small handful of slaves to over twenty-five percent of the total. But the white men whom Nuttall described were prototypes of those who lived in Arkansas up to the Civil War and even later. They had come from Kentucky, from Tennessee, from Maryland, from the Carolinas, from Virginia—and, in a few cases, from New England. And they brought with them, or readily adopted, the code duello, the unwritten law of the Southern gentleman.

If a frontiersman insulted another frontiersman, the result was a fight, a mix-up, a brawl. Abraham Lincoln was in many such brawls in the New Salem of his young manhood; and he knew how to hold his own in them, wrestling, gouging, kicking, and pummelling. But if a Southern gentleman insulted another Southern gentleman, the result was a challenge to a duel, in which seconds were employed, duelling pistols were usually used, and the parties met in some secluded spot by arrangement, usually in the early morning. Many men famous in American history, most notably Andrew Jackson himself, lived and throve by the code duello during their early years. The distinctive mark of a gentleman, as distinguished from a mere commoner, was considered to be his ability to fight a duel; and those who opposed the practice were, as an old Arkansas authority said, "regarded as pseudo-moralists, and their sincerity and courage were alike doubted." Arkansas was a Southern state; and the duelling code was a part of its unwritten law, its prevailing folkways. And in Arkansas it stood out even more vividly than in other Southern states, since it was set there against the grim and dark background of frontier living.

One of the earliest duels of which we have any record was also one of the most foolish; and it arose from a cause more trivial than most. At a hotel in Arkansas Post, a wooden building with open hall and wide verandahs running around it, there lived in the winter of 1819 a man of about forty named William O. Allen. This man owned and commonly walked with a cane which had a small steel spear at its top. By pressing on a spring, the spear would jump out and could be held in position till the spring was again released. Also at the same hotel lived a young lawyer, aged twenty-two, named Robert C. Oden. This man showed a considerable interest in Allen's spear-topped cane. One day, when the two were at dinner together, Oden finished his meal before Allen; and as he went out of the dining room, he picked up Allen's cane and began practicing with it, releasing the spring and causing the spear to jump out. This he did for some time, up and down the hall. After a while Allen came out, and seeing Oden with the cane, he reached for it—but Oden retreated a few steps. Allen then walked up and asked for it. Oden, in a playful mood, according to the best account, "presented it towards him, and just as Allen was about to take it, jerked the cane back and again retreated."

A race commenced—Allen still advancing and reaching for the cane, and Oden alternately presenting it and jerking it back. It went on all around the porch and again into the hall; but Oden, "being young and active, easily eluded his pursuer." Allen at last became exasperated and sat down to write a challenge. The two men met on a sandbar on the south bank of the Arkansas River, away from the Post, and settled their difference with pistols, at ten paces. Allen's first ball struck Oden "on the suspender button of his pants, at the waist, under his right arm, and ranged around the body." As he was falling, he contrived to fire, and his bullet struck Allen in the forehead, cracking the skull. Allen was carried to the home of his second, to die in great agony a week later. Oden recovered.

A still earlier duel than this, happening before the territory was established, is noted by one authority. Frederick Notrebe, whom we have seen living at the Post during the time of Nuttall's visit there, was here the challenging party, and one Alexander Walker was the challenged. Both men were old friends; but a quarrel arose one day, and Walker made some remark about Notrebe which was taken as an insult. The usual meeting on the sandbar opposite the Post at sunrise the following morning was arranged. Notrebe was the first to arrive, and he brought with him not only his second and surgeon, but "a large crowd of his dependents, and nearly all of his negroes." When Walker arrived a few minutes later with his surgeon and second, all these supernumeraries were lined up on the bank in imposing array. Walker, as he stepped from the boat onto the sandbar exclaimed, "Well, Frederick, if I had known you were going to come with an army at your back, I would have come over during the night and thrown up some breastworks!"—at which several of Notrebe's friends laughed; while his second, stepping forward, asked if the duel need go on as arranged. Walker withdrew the remark to which Notrebe had taken exception; Notrebe withdrew his challenge; and promptly peace was made.

These two duels, one tragic, the other comic, have in them certain elements which recur in all these old tales of duelling. One reads over and over of the death of one of the parties; or else, the whole affair becomes so much comic stage-play. The fact that the duel was frequently practiced in Tennessee, Kentucky, and the Carolinas—not to mention the famous Hamilton-Burr duel, fought in New Jersey—suggests that the hot-blooded Americans of that day found this the easiest way of settling their private disputes. Duels were so common in New Orleans that the "duelling oaks" still stand in Audubon Park in that city—but duels were common elsewhere, too, all through the South. In Arkansas they seem to have arisen largely out of the violent political campaigns of the twenties and thirties; and though the newspapers, as early as 1833, published pieces directed against the practice, and though, no doubt, the ministers of the Gospel also denounced it, they went on, beyond the Civil War. Two political duels, both fought in the early days, are worth mentioning here. In one of them the meddlesome Oden reappears, though not as a leading actor.

In 1827 the Territory of Arkansas, as it had been for some years past, was sharply divided politically between the National Republicans and the Democrats, the former led by Robert Crittenden, the latter by Henry W. Conway. The real issue between them was, whether Jackson should succeed John Quincy Adams in the presidency; and feeling ran very high. The candidate of the Crittenden party for delegate to Congress was none other than Robert C. Oden, the survivor of the duel over the famous cane. Conway, however, won the election, thus succeeding himself for a third term; but during the contest, the criticism which Crittenden had brought to bear on him had been so great that as soon as the race was over, he immediately challenged Crittenden to a duel. The men met on October 29, 1827, on the east bank of the Mississippi, opposite the mouth of the White River. Crittenden is said to have been the first to arrive with his second, Ben Desha. Seeing that his adversary had not yet come, he put a blanket on the ground, lay down upon it, and drawing his overcoat over him, was fast asleep while the preliminaries were being discussed with Conway's second, Major Wharton Rector, of the United States Army. It was agreed upon by the seconds that the two men should stand with their right sides facing, and were not to stir from their places till the word "fire," when they should turn half-around and blaze away. This, it was thought later, gave Crittenden some advantage. At the first exchange, the bullet from Conway's pistol passed through the lapel of Crittenden's coat, causing the lint to fly from it. Desha, Crittenden's second, leaned forward and asked, "Mr. Crittenden, are you seriously hurt?"—to which the reply was, "No, but I fear I have killed Mr. Conway," and in the next instant Desha saw Conway fall to the ground, mortally wounded in the body. Crittenden survived to be, as we have seen, a powerful force in Arkansas politics, and to be nicknamed "Cardinal Wolsey" by his friends and opponents.

The other case was not, strictly speaking, a duel, but rather a murderous affray. It should be given here, however, as having marked the new-born State of Arkansas with a memory not to be effaced, and as being symptomatic of the temper which ruled many men at that time.

In December, 1837, during the session of the legislature—Arkansas now having been a state for over a year—the House of Representatives was discussing a bill which had just come from the Senate, called the wolf bill. This was ostensibly aimed at the extermination of all wolves; and it provided that when any citizen appeared before a justice of the peace in a particular district with the scalp of a wolf, he was to receive a certificate of the fact, which was to entitle him to a bounty. During the discussion of the bill, it had been pointed out by its opponents that hunters, under its provisions, could go into the adjoining districts of Texas or of Indian Territory, hunt wolves, and bring their pelts back into Arkansas, and thereby claim the bounty; also that the scalp of a wolf could be easily cut into small strips, could be sewed together with the scalp of a sheep, dyed and disguised; and that the individual claiming the bounty could then take this doctored scalp before a magistrate, and, holding it in his fingers, swear that it was the scalp of a wolf killed in that district. Criticism along these lines had gone on for hours.

Now the speaker of the House was one John Wilson, who had been appointed president of the recently established Real Estate Bank of Arkansas. This bank had enabled many squatters holding worthless lands to convert their holdings into bank stock—which could, though often at a heavy discount, be sold for ready money. The United States, be it remembered, was at that time moving into its second great financial crisis, the panic of 1837, which, caused in general by a period of wild over-speculation, was precipitated by the distribution of the surplus deposits in the United States Bank among the various state banks, by a vast over-inflation of paper currency in all local banks, and by the Specie Circular of 1836, applied by Jackson as a last desperate remedy, ordering that the United States Treasury should receive no further paper currency for its remaining public lands. The Real Estate Bank of Arkansas (its affairs were to plague the state up to the nineties), had been established in order to counteract the Specie Circular and to keep paper "shinplaster" money in circulation. The law establishing this bank had already been severely criticized as a piece of political jobbery, but it had passed. Now, in the person of John Wilson, both speaker of the house and president of the Bank, it was to become momentarily entangled with the opposition to the wolf bill.

In the midst of the debate, one J. J. Anthony, member of the House from Randolph County, offered an amendment to the effect that "the signature of the President of the Real Estate Bank should be attached to the certificate of the wolf scalp." At this suggestion that something in his own conduct had been dishonest, Wilson, as speaker of the House and also as president of the Bank, took offense, and asked Anthony if he meant to be personal. Anthony replied that he did not; that he could explain why he had offered this amendment; whereupon Wilson ordered him to sit down. Anthony refused to yield the floor, insisting on his right to offer an explanation. Wilson retorted, "Sit down, or I'll make you!"—and drawing a large knife from his breast, he advanced upon Anthony. Anthony stepped aside from his chair, retreated, and drew his own knife. A nearby legislator immediately caught up a chair and thrust it between the two men; but Wilson continued his advance. Anthony, now thoroughly panic-smitten, dropped his knife and snatched at the chair. Wilson threw up the chair with his left hand and, with the knife in his right, plunged at Anthony. The knife was driven full into Anthony's heart; he fell upon the floor and died in the presence of the entire legislative assembly. It is said that Wilson calmly pulled out the knife from Anthony's breast, looked on it, wiped it with his thumb and finger, and walked back to the speaker's desk. At this point a motion to adjourn was instantly made and voted unanimously.

Three days passed before any of the authorities took cognizance of what had happened. A relative, however, finally swore out a warrant against Wilson. Wilson came to the court in a carriage, it is said, with four horses, and followed by a number of his friends. The prosecuting attorney, by invoking one of the statutes, tried to prove that this was not a bailable offense; but Wilson was, nevertheless, admitted to bail. At the session appointed to try him, he duly appeared, with a clever lawyer in attendance who argued that feeling ran so high, in this particular county, that Wilson could not get a fair trial. The trial was therefore removed to an adjoining county, where Wilson, by lodging at the same house as his judge and paying for his dinners, as well as by hiring a mob to demonstrate in his favor outside the courtroom during the prosecuting attorney's address, managed to obtain an acquittal. He thereupon in open court asked the sheriff "to take the jury to a dram-shop, and he would pay for all that was drunk by them and everybody else." The whole proceeding ended with Wilson, his friends, and the jury parading through the streets till daylight, making a "shivaree" on drums, trumpets, and tin pans. The verdict stood, and the citizenry expended themselves in a wave of useless indignation.

The special breed of lawlessness produced by Arkansas in this period was undoubtedly of a far more intense kind and far more savagely vindictive in its violence than anything that had been seen in the states east of the Great River. Only Kentucky, "the dark and bloody ground," had anything at all like it: and in Kentucky formal duels—which were more respectable and gentlemanly—were probably far more common. In Arkansas most men soon learned not to wait for a formal challenge; most of them carried, in the bosom of their shirts or in a sheath on the right hip, a large knife of the sort which James Black, a blacksmith of the little southwestern town of Washington, had originally made for Reason (or Rezin) Bowie, a planter living near the Texas boundary; and which James Bowie, his younger brother, later carried on his body to the defense of the Alamo. These bowie knives became so common in the state that they were nicknamed "Arkansas toothpicks," and most fights were settled with them. They were later replaced throughout the Southwest with the Colt revolver, first patented in America in 1836, the year of Texas's independence and of Arkansas's admission as a state; these were manufactured commercially from 1838 onwards. By that time Arkansas had become—comparatively—more law-abiding and civilized, and knife brawls were less common.

The duelling, knifing, brawling period of Arkansas history, from 1820 to 1840, went on to the accompaniment of a series of "legal" manoeuvres also without precedent. Here in this trans-Mississippi frontier community, with the Indian Territory and the debatable ground of Texas as next-door neighbors, the lawyer rapidly became the arbiter of society; and the courts were soon choked with long-dragged-out lawsuits, endless legal battles over land claims. As regards robbery, murder, and violence the earliest settlers, harassed from the start by gangs of horse-thieves, bandits, land and river pirates, soon learned not to depend upon the courts but to take the law into their own hands and invoke Judge Lynch. Friedrich Gerstaecker's novel, *Die Regulatoren in Arkansas,* not unworthy of his master, Cooper, and still unfortunately inaccessible to those who cannot read German, reveals clearly the conditions faced by the frontiersmen. Land claims had still to be settled by law: in every county seat at every session of the court it was the lawyer, with his ruffled silk shirt, his tall beaver hat, his silver-topped cane, who appeared to dominate the scene; and at Little Rock particularly the big lawyers lived in state. They were the richest, the most honored men of the community. Many of them, despite their fine manners and their aptness at literary quotation, were undoubtedly corrupt, and arrogant in their corruption; but they gave to this frontier society the only tone it had.

The complicated story of the founding of Little Rock and of the establishment of the capital there is perhaps the best illustration that can be found of the growing power of the lawyer in this new territory. As early as 1812 the site of the future city of Little Rock was occupied by one William Lewis, a buffalo hunter, who built, it is said, some sort of rude shack on the spot and who took out a claim to the land at the nearest Federal land office (in Nashville, Tennessee), in 1814. This claim was sold in the fall of the same year, and passed into the hands of "the widow Martha White, Peter Franks, and others"—all of whose claims were finally bought up by one William Russell, of Saint Louis, Missouri, in 1819, the very year that Thomas Nuttall visited Arkansas.

The name of William Russell has already appeared in this story in connection with early land-grants under the Spaniards. He himself has a place upon the first and most important page of Arkansas's history as a state, not only as the greatest large-scale speculator in lands within its boundaries, but as the chosen agent, the prime mover appointed by fate, to induce a change of the capital site from the old Arkansas Post to new Little Rock. Russell was born in Virginia, about 1777, and he had come as a very young man to Saint Louis. Active and long used to the saddle, he had ridden all over the new territory. "The Little Rock" stood on lands covered by his claim.

To the modern traveller speeding along the motor highway from Memphis, who can see for himself that it is precisely at this point that the Arkansas River emerges from the highlands and that this point lies close to the geographical center of the state (as well as to the traveller of Nuttall's time, who saw that the old southwest trail from Saint Louis to the Red River settlements crossed the Arkansas River near here), it may seem strange that Little Rock was not immediately voted to be the capital, without any of Russell's solicitation. But though the site lay far enough above the river to protect it from all but the worst floods, and though it had on it good springs (one of them persisted down past the Civil War and is commemorated in the name of present-day Spring Street)—though all this is, or was, true, there were other opposing interests already in the field. These interests centered in the people who were thickly gathering at Cadron settlement, whom Nuttall had seen in November. Southeast of Cadron, it will be remembered, he had stopped for the night at Edmund Hogan's place. Hogan had already established a sort of ferry at the point where the military trail crossed the Arkansas—a point near the east limits of the present city of Little Rock—upon land already allotted to the Quapaw Indians. At Hogan's place, Nuttall heard of a plan to build another town on the yet uninhabited spot of "the Rock itself."

By the time the legislature met in February, 1820, Russell had taken care to buy out Hogan's claim, and thus became sole owner of all land at Little Rock and the leading competitor to the speculators already settling at Cadron. He also encouraged one Benjamin Murphy, another squatter, now represented as owning some share of the original Lewis claim, to build another rude shack of some sort on the site; then he rode east to the Post to work on the legislature itself. On Monday, February 7, 1820, the legislature duly convened; but there was a doubt raised by Governor Miller, which had to be settled in the law courts, as to whether this legislature was legally constituted, since Miller had not been present when it was called into being. Russell did not let this deter him. He was determined that the site at "the Little Rock" should be chosen as the future capital; and he soon won some leading legislators over to his side.

On February 22, one Joab Hardin, of Lawrence County, brought in a bill naming Cadron Settlement as the future capital. All that Russell could do, through his supporters in the legislature, was to have the name "Little Rock" substituted for that of Cadron in the text of the bill; but the House refused to consider the bill as amended. At the end of February the legislature adjourned without further action while its legality was being determined in the law courts. They decided to meet again in October to settle the question of the territorial capital. Meanwhile other events were shaping which made Little Rock the inevitable choice.

Moses Austin, a far-seeing pioneer from New England, was now living, at this very time, at Potosi, a lead-mining town in southeast Missouri. He had been there ever since 1797, had reared up sons and daughters to succeed him, and as early as 1814 had planned to colonize the remote Spanish province of Texas. The scheme had been discussed and had been entrusted to his son, Stephen Austin, to carry out. Stephen was now twenty-five and eager to do something noteworthy. The depression of 1818–1820 had already ruined his father's fortunes as a mine-owner in Potosi as well as his own prospects of success. In the Texas project lay now all the future hopes of the old pioneer's family.

Obstacles there were many, the chief one being that consent of the

Mexican authorities in Texas had first to be obtained. Meanwhile, it was also necessary that there should be a depot, a trading-post for needed supplies, somewhere near the area where the main colonizing effort was to take place. Young Stephen threw himself eagerly into this side of the enterprise, and in December, 1919, at the time of Governor Miller's arrival, the papers of both Arkansas and Missouri advertised a sale by auction of some fifty lots in a new town named Fulton, at Long Prairie on the Red River in southwestern Arkansas near the Texas border. The new town was described as being "handsomely situated on the northeast bank of main Red River, about two miles below the mouth of Little Red River, and near the center of the boundary of Arkansas Territory, on Red River. It is the principal landing, and place of deposit for the county of Hempstead, and also the point at which the most direct road, leading from Missouri Territory and many of the Eastern States, to the extensive and fertile province of Texas, will cross the river." What these advertisements did not state was that the land where lay the future town—still on the present-day map of Arkansas—belonged to James Bryan, Stephen Austin's own brother-in-law, and also that, associated with him in this enterprise, was one William O'Hara, cashier of a recently closed bank at Saint Louis, in which Moses Austin had been heavily interested and had lost a good part of his fortune.

The date of the auction of these lots at Fulton was set for April 29, 1820; but meanwhile events had moved very fast in Arkansas. The legislature, as we have seen, had almost made "the Little Rock" capital of the entire Arkansas Territory. This would hand the entire townsite into the hands of a rival of Austin, William Russell. Would it not be wise for Stephen Austin, since the road described in his advertisement would earlier cross the Arkansas at precisely this point of "the Little Rock," to look into that matter as well? If Fulton was to be laid out as a road-head from which future Texas colonization was to start, what about this other, more important site halfway along the same route? The question was no sooner asked than answered.

William O'Hara, cashier of the now closed bank at Saint Louis, had still in his possession, no doubt transferred to the bank long ago for cash, three of the still unused New Madrid land certificates issued to old French settlers by the United States government after the earthquake of 1811. On the basis of these certificates, Austin, Bryan, O'Hara, and Company acted at once. They decided to settle themselves upon the townsite at Little Rock before Russell could do so. The certificates would give them some kind of claim. To the group centering around Austin possession must have appeared to be nine points of the law. So they promptly planted a henchman, "Captain" Amos Wheeler, of Saint Louis, on the Little Rock townsite; and Wheeler, through connivance of the legislature, became thereby postmaster, storekeeper, and real-estate operator—as well as unquestioned tenant along with Murphy. "A small framed shanty, just by the Rock near the spring" now arose as the headquarters of the Austin Associates, as I shall henceforth call them. Streets were laid out by the simple method of chopping down a few trees; and Little Rock was duly, if illegitimately, born.

Russell, knowing well that his claim to the townsite was the earlier and the most valid one, but realizing that the legislature had in it factions hostile to his claim, was willing to bide his time. He contented himself with issuing a handbill warning the public against accepting at its face value "any sort or pretence to a title" which the Associates now claimed. Meanwhile, the Associates, disregarding the warning, set about laying out their new town. On July 3, of that year 1820, the Reverend Cephas Washburn, Congregational missionary from the Yale Divinity School to the Cherokees westward, and founder of the Dwight Mission, which stood near present-day Russellville till the Cherokees disappeared, halted for the night with his weary, "chillin' and feverin'," exhausted party of missionaries on the north bank of the river opposite to the Rock. He was promptly invited to preach a sermon on the following day by a committee composed of Stephen Austin himself, and Matthew Cunningham, the first physician to settle in the new town. And so, the next day, in that "small framed shanty, near the spring," in the midst of a scanty stock of medicines and much whisky, with barrels of flour, hogsheads of molasses, sacks of sugar and gunpowder lying about, the Reverend Cephas Washburn duly honored the day, in the presence of some dozen newly arrived settlers.

On October 2, the legislature met again at Arkansas Post; and now there was no longer a doubt as to what would be the outcome of the unfinished business of the capital. Disregarding momentarily the Austin Associates, Russell was determined to have his way. A few days after a block of lots in the townsite had been quietly and unostentatiously transferred, through a chosen intermediary, to Joseph Hardin, the brother of Joab, speaker of the House and once a leading supporter of the Cadron project, he saw reason to change his mind. So did Thomas Tindall and so did Radford Ellis, the two members from Pulaski County. They saved their faces, if not their consciences, before their constituents at Cadron and Governor Miller's own settlement at nearby Crystal Hill, by promoting a bill to make Cadron only the seat of Pulaski County and to erect a courthouse and a jail on that spot. And then, on October 25, 1820, the day the legislature finally adjourned, it was agreed not only that "the Little Rock" was to be the territorial capital, but that Amos Wheeler should erect a building there, on land provided by the Austin Associates, to be used as a place of assembly for the next legislature. This building, a two-roomed affair, with an open hall, or, as the Arkansawyers would say, a "dog-run" or "breeze-way" between the rooms, was hurriedly run up; and William E. Woodruff was able to announce in his newspaper in November, to the inhabitants of the Post, that he intended to pack up his presses once again and depart by the following New Year, as the official printer to the territory, for Little Rock.

Mrs. Matthew Cunningham, wife of the physician, in "a good two horse wagon, with new double harness," drawn by "a pair of handsome sorrel horses," was already on her way down from Missouri to the same point; and the Austin Associates, choosing to ignore William Russell and in undisputed possession of the future townsite, were triumphant. They went so far as to assert that their claim to the spot had been established as early as February, 1819, and that the mysterious shack of poles seen near the Rock by the earliest settlers, and presumably built by either Benjamin Murphy or William Lewis, had in fact been put up by no less a person than Moses Austin. They had, as Russell knew, no basis whatever for such a claim. Russell was content, however, to wait till the courts could decide on the validity of his title; for by now, as he realized, the Austin Associates had enlisted in their service a shrewd Yankee lawyer, the Massachusetts-born and bred Chester Ashley, who well deserved his later nickname of "Talleyrand" for his finesse in handling their interests at this juncture.

There is much that is striking and original about Chester Ashley. He was both cultivated and educated; a considerable cut above most pioneers. Born at Amherst (some authorities say Westfield), Massachusetts, in 1791, he was graduated from Williams College in 1813; and then, as a young lawyer, migrated west, moving first to Illinois and later on to Potosi, Missouri, where he came into contact with the

Austin Associates as early as 1819. A shrewd and unscrupulous lawyer was now required, if ever William Russell was to be beaten off; and Ashley was invincibly shrewd as regards his own interests. He came to Little Rock sometime by the fall of 1820. A little later, probably in November, for what many have been the first, and certainly proved to be the last time in his career, Moses Austin also passed through Little Rock on his way down to Texas. Ashley was already on the spot; and through Ashley, the claim of the Austin Associates increasingly acquired a higher status of legality. Ashley himself was destined to live on to 1848, and to be ranked as the wealthiest man in Arkansas, the most important lawyer of the early state. He returned, temporarily, to Missouri in the summer of 1821 to marry Mary Elliott, and to move with his new bride to Little Rock, where Mrs. Cunningham, later famed as the first woman resident of the town, was already established with her husband. In later years Ashley was to be William Woodruff's closest friend, destined to make a great fortune and to build himself a magnificent mansion, the forlorn shell of which still stood, in my own boyhood. It is said that he lived in such style there that he organized his own Negroes into a band, with which he entertained his guests by having it play on the lawn on moonlit nights.

The only portrait of Ashley that I have ever seen shows a portly, well-dressed old gentleman, with magnificent forehead surmounted by a shock of curly white hair, but with eyes too cunningly deep and too close-set for comfort; and a nose of vulpine shrewdness. Altogether the "Senator," as he became after 1844, was, one feels, a formidable man.

Ashley, though he exhausted every legal trick that he could muster in support of the Austin Associates' claim to the townsite, soon found that Russell was not disposed to let the battle go by default. On November 18, within a month after the legislature had rendered its decision, Russell issued an open declaration of war in the shape of a public letter to the *Gazette* which occupied six closely printed columns of that newspaper; and he followed this up promptly with a lawsuit for the forcible ousting of the Austin Associates. The suit, thanks to Ashley's persistence in inventing obstacles, dragged along; it was not until June, 1821, that the territorial supreme court, sitting, by supreme irony, at Cadron, brought in its verdict. All the New Madrid certificates on which the Austin Associates had chiefly based their claim for this land were ruled invalid for any lands south of the Arkansas River;

William Russell was, in fact and by law, sole owner of the townsite; and it must now, with all its new improvements, be restored to him by the associated interlopers.

There followed a scene which, remembered and described picturesquely and in part inaccurately very many years later by an eyewitness, is best given in that eyewitness's own words. Let me introduce, then, Thomas James, author of *Three Years Among the Indians and New Mexicans,* whose exceedingly rare book was written around 1847:

"I started from Saint Louis on the 10th day of May, A.D. 1821, and descended the Mississippi to the mouth of the Arkansas. . . . Ascending the Arkansas, the first settlement we reached was Arkansas Post. Dense and heavy woods of valuable timber lined both sides of the river . . . small fields of corn, squash, pumpkins, cultivated by the Indians, appeared in view on the low banks. Since entering the Arkansas, we had found the country quite level; after sailing and pushing about three hundred miles from the mouth, we now reached the first high land, near Little Rock, the capital of the territory, as established that spring. The archives had not yet been removed from Arkansas Post, the former capital. As we approached Little Rock we beheld a scene of true western life and character, that no other country could present. First, we saw a large wood and stone building in flames, and then about one hundred men, painted, masked, and disguised in almost every conceivable manner, engaged in removing the town. These men, with ropes and chains, would march off a frame house on wheels and logs, place it about three or four hundred yards from its former site, and then return and move off another in the same manner. They all seemed tolerably drunk, and . . . they were a merry company indeed. Thus they worked amid songs and shouts, until by nightfall they had completely changed the site of the town. Such buildings as they could not move, they burned down without a dissentient vote. . . . In one day and night, Mr. Russell's land was disencumbered of the town of Little Rock. Coolly and quietly, though not without much unnecessary noise, they took the town up and set it in a neighboring claim of the Quapaw tribe; while fire removed what was immovable in a more convenient way. The free and enlightened citizens of Little Rock made a change of landlords more rapidly than Bonaparte took Moscow."

Moses Austin, the old pioneer dreaming to the last of his dawning Texas enterprise, had sickened of pneumonia on the way home from the long ride down to San Antonio, and died at his Potosi residence on June 10, 1821. His son Stephen, having already conveyed all his claims to the Little Rock townsite by a deed made in favor of the shrewd Chester Ashley the previous winter, was now down in Louisiana, still planning to execute his father's unfulfilled and long-cherished Texas project; James Bryan, Moses' son-in-law, his Fulton townsite auction having proven a failure, was already a broken, ruined man; William O'Hara was destined to die, alone and unbefriended at the last, at Arkansas Post on July 21 of that year. Against Russell, the persistent and successful, stood no one but the crafty and shifty Ashley, now proprietor as well as lawyer. And though Russell had won his suit, he was not to obtain his town. Ashley had ordered the buildings moved off and set down among the Indians. And no doubt the townspeople painted their faces, put on feathers, and tricked themselves out in all the disguises they knew, in the spirit of a huge practical joke, to do this thing. They were not frontiersmen for nothing, those Arkansawyers.

A compromise had to be arranged. Russell, though the courts had just declared in his favor, had met at last his match. In November the two contenders, Russell and Ashley, met—no doubt by prearrangement—at the land office in Batesville; and Russell then and there deeded, for nothing, as it seems, exactly one half of his share in the original Lewis claim to Ashley. The buildings presented to the Quapaw Indians were no doubt dragged back; the great quarrel was over, only to be revived years later in an endless lawsuit between the heirs concerned. Little Rock was at last a city, with about a hundred permanent inhabitants; and on December 29, 1821, Editor Woodruff, in the first issue of his *Gazette* printed at the new capital, was able to comment:

"Until within the last few weeks, the title to the tract of land selected as the townsite has been in dispute; but happily for the place and the territory generally, the parties concerned became sensible of the propriety of settling their conflicting claims in an amicable manner. This circumstance places the prosperity of the town beyond doubt; and we feel satisfied from the high opinion which all who have seen the place and are acquainted with the country, express of its superior advantages, that in a few years we shall have one of the most flourishing and pleasant towns west of the Mississippi."

Woodruff was invincibly tactful in making this statement. A modern historian has stated that the story of the founding of Little Rock is a story without a moral. But the fact remains that, even had the Austin

Associates and Ashley not employed every device of legal trickery to possess themselves of the townsite, obtained already by the not-too-scrupulous Russell, Little Rock would still have become the chief city of Arkansas. The site was inevitable. From the time of the founding of Little Rock, the old Post rapidly declined. Little Rock was central to its territory; and the establishment of the capital there was no accident.

Six

THE INDIAN VANISHES ALONG THE TRAIL OF TEARS

Among the twelve million, eight hundred and sixty-six thousand people inhabiting the United States by the year 1830, the little more than thirty thousand persons who lived in the Territory of Arkansas stood out. Except for the even hardier souls who had followed Stephen Austin down into Texas (now attached to the troubled Republic of Mexico), and the two or three hundred "mountain men"—buffalo hunters, beaver trappers, and plainsmen extraordinary who had already got into the Rocky Mountains north of New Mexico to lead there a riotous existence—the Arkansawyers were America's foremost frontiersmen. With the Indian territory to the west of them already filling up with tribe after tribe driven west of the Mississippi, Arkansas had become an outpost, where every really good man had in him something of the frontiersman and knew how to use his knife and his gun.

Once across the Appalachians, and penetrating more deeply every year into the magnificent river valleys that ran down to the monotonous grandeur of the Mississippi, the Anglo-Saxons had produced a breed that Washington himself could not have foreseen. The men of this stamp wore the blanket cape, the buckskin leggings, the deer-leather moccasins, the knife in a sheath at the belt that made them look like Indians. They often had long hair falling to their shoulders and invariably carried rifles. Their women, clad in homespun butternut-stained linsey-woolsey or the even coarser osnaburg, were a match for the men. The smoking of corncob pipes—as well as prowess with the rifle—was not uncommon among them. Tobacco-chewing and spitting, as Mrs. Trollope soon saw, were very frequent. So was dram-drinking among both sexes, and strange outbursts of hysterical religious fervor. The women were much concerned over their "purity," or their reputation for such; the men were usually gamecocks in their youth, little scrupulous—since after all, they had descended from the eighteenth century—concerning their transient amours, but later on, as they became more established, were disposed to settle down. Both sexes ate omnivorously and coarsely. Manners, table or otherwise, were at a discount. Although the river steamboat, with its gamblers and shady characters, had already become the chief mode of transportation, these people were not industrial. They lived lives that might have been taken from the Middle Ages, and the popularity among them of romances by Scott, which Mark Twain later deplored, was, after all, natural. In many of their dozen heroes—half legendary, vast, and invincibly picturesque—men like Daniel Boone, Davy Crockett, Mike Fink, the King of Keelboatmen, or Kit Carson, we glimpse the true descendants of Robin Hood and Richard the Lion-Hearted: even of the Knights of the Round Table.

Andrew Jackson, who so much sums up their best characteristics as well as their worst, had dispossessed the last of the elder statesmen, John Quincy Adams, from the White House; and Adams had not waited to greet his rival, but had retired to become member of the House of Representatives and to fight unavailingly against one feature of Southwestern life that he knew and hated: the feature of Negro slavery. Neither he, nor any of the later Northern abolitionists, had ever really understood the attitude of the men south of the Missouri or Virginia border concerning slavery. Slavery to them was of the natural order of things. The Negroes had never been anything else but slaves, and the institution, always working well when the slaveowner behaved as every decent man should behave, needed no defenders, and found none till the abolitionists drew attention to its supposed injustices. What these Southerners really hated, and fought against, was not the Negroes but the Indians. From Tennessee to the last southwestern outpost in Texas, they had learned the lesson, in the twenty years following the Revolution, that the Indians had to be exterminated. That five important tribes, at least, were still settled on good Southern land—guaranteed them by foolish treaties—was an outrage. From Jackson down to the half-savage frontiersmen, the feeling ruled that they must go.

In Arkansas the inhabitants lived as they had from the beginning—backed up against Indian territory; and they shared the frontier dislike and contempt for the Indian to the full. Few travellers of the sort able to write books visited them between Nuttall's time and the year of statehood, 1836. The journey to Little Rock still entailed weeks of discomfort on board a steamboat, or an even more hazardous drive along a primitive wilderness road. The most important of these roads, the "military road," which, as we have seen, ran from Saint Louis down through the lead-mining district of southeast Missouri to Little Rock and so on to the Red River, at last had attained the point where, as a traveller who made the trip on it in 1835–1836 states, "the trees were razed close to the ground"—a statement that does not imply by any means that all stumps were uprooted. It crossed many unbridged streams and was also short on ferry conveniences. Along the Missouri border particularly, it was infested with gangs of desperadoes, living in abandoned cabins off the main route or moving about the country in order to lure any travellers who carried money, towards a woodland ambush in some secluded spot. Taverns there were none; and the traveller, if he did not wish to camp out at night—a procedure which was always under risks as to the weather and was sometimes perilous besides because of wild animals, particularly panthers—had to endure an unvarying diet of fried pork, corn dodgers, and bad coffee (sometimes made of parched corn or acorns) sweetened with molasses, or "long sweetenin'." He had also to endure a table service so scanty that knives and forks were given nicknames; and usually he had to sleep in a single room with several other tenants, oftentimes in the same bed with another guest.

South of Little Rock, still a mere village of some ten streets north and south and the same number east and west, with houses widely scattered between, it was usually even worse. The lawyers who rode circuit through this remote Ouachita territory frequently had appalling conditions to endure, and they had to be hardy men. The usual bed in this region was a pallet of rags lying heaped up on the floor; the usual shelter for the night, a doorless and windowless cabin with a roof that leaked incessantly in the rains. We read of one such place, a cabin kept by an old bear-hunter named Shannon, whom the lawyers, since this was the only place they could find to sleep throughout a considerable district of wild forests, had nicknamed "Governor" Shannon. Except for one old Negro woman and a great number of dogs, this Shannon lived alone and spent his nights sleeping in a hollowed-out log. The judges and the lawyers slept as best they might, on the mud floor; and the dogs slept, too, as close to the travellers as they could manage for comfort, rushing out and running over the recumbent guests and passing through the doorless opening, whenever aroused by any unusual sound in the woods. Shannon was protected from all this disturbance by sleeping in his hollow log; but the travellers had no such protection. One night a judge, who had never ridden this circuit before, stopped at Shannon's cabin and, in the words of the narrator of the story, "becoming at length outrageously annoyed with the stench and the filth of the dogs, one of which had acted very irreverently to his Honor," called out that if Shannon did not instantly take this dog away, he would shoot it. Whereupon Shannon remarked, "I'll be gol-danged if the blasted judges and lawyers of Arkansas hain't slept with my dogs for seven years; and if any man touches one on em, I'll send him to sleep with the painters, in less than no time." Whereupon the judge held his peace.

Travel by steamboat was not quite so uncomfortable, but it was equally uncertain because of the difficulties of navigation on the Arkansas River. At the most, two or three steamboats a month managed to reach the capital city, after struggling with sandbars and snags in a channel frequently described as "four feet deep, and falling." Stagecoaches were practically unheard of except for a line which ran from Arkansas Post to Little Rock, at first every two weeks and then weekly, beginning in 1826; the first widespread stagecoach travel came with the year of statehood, in 1836. Yet Texas, despite all these drawbacks, interested and attracted many hundreds of settlers, particularly from the thirties onward. They got through the dreary forests of the lowlands and the Ouachitas somehow, despite the obvious hardships, and emerged on the prairies after having been pursued by legions of wildcats, bears, and panthers.

And as the white settlers steadily moved in, the Indians slowly moved out. In 1824 the dwindling remnant of the Quapaws at last yielded their lands for a price of six thousand dollars and an annuity of a thousand dollars a year for eleven years. Thus a good deal of what is now the finest cotton land in the state changed hands at a figure which has been estimated as totalling one dollar per thousand acres. Insult was added to injury by an order directing the tribe to remove to the Caddo territory on the Texas border and to link their future fortunes with the Caddo tribe. The Caddoans promptly refused to receive them. The only lands they were given proved to be so close to the famous "Great Raft," formed by drifting timbers in the Red River, as to be always subject to floods; and in three years the Quapaws were reduced to utter starvation. Governor Izard, the Second Governor of Arkansas Territory, who succeeded General Miller in 1825, made a visit to them in 1827 and reported that the rumors of their starvation were all too true. There was no possibility that the Quapaws could continue to live on their new lands; and in small bands they began to straggle back into Arkansas, under the leadership of Saracen, a very old and exceedingly friendly Indian, who had succeeded to the leadership after Hekkatton's death from starvation in the Red River country. By this time, there was no land available on which they could settle, though Saracen himself, who had prudently foreseen this contingency, had cannily reserved to himself eighty acres near Pine Bluff, by the treaty of 1824. No one could dispossess Saracen, now become a convert to the Catholic faith and friendly to the French Catholic missionaries.

Governor Pope, a native of Kentucky who was governor in 1829 and who was famous for his plain frontier honesty, as well as for the fact that, like La Salle's lieutenant, Tonti, he had but one hand, wrote thus to John Henry Eaton, the notorious secretary of war in Jackson's first cabinet:

"Saracen called on me and made, I believe, a very sincere and certainly a feeling representation of his sufferings and misfortunes in the Caddean country and the desire of his tribe to remain here in peace with us on some inferior lands; and appealed in a very impressive manner to the justice and humanity of his Great Father the President, and the White People whose blood his nation had never shed. They are a kind and inoffensive people and aid the Whites in picking out their cotton and furnishing them with game. I have heard but one sentiment expressed in this territory with regard to this tribe, that of kindness and a desire that they should be permitted to live among us; I would be particularly gratified to be authorized to assign them a township on this river, in the vicinity of their permanent residence. The residue of this tribe are now on their return from the Caddean to join their friends here—they will all be united shortly on this river and they would prefer death to be driven from the land of their fathers."

Yet, though Saracen, thanks to his land grant and his known friendliness to the whites, remained—he died near Pine Bluff at the age of ninety-seven in 1832—the remaining Quapaws were again forced to go. They disappeared into what is now northeast Oklahoma, the year after Saracen's death. A remnant still survives there, long mingled with other broken tribes.

All that remained of the Quapaws in their native territory was the kindly recollection by some whites, particularly the Catholic missionaries at Pine Bluff, of old Saracen. His partiality to white children was well known and long established. It had been marked in his earlier years by a bold exploit. A French trapper's family living near Pine Bluff had two children kidnapped by a roving band of Chickasaws. The news was brought to Saracen. Going to the mother, he said, "When the sun is so high, Saracen will bring your children. If Saracen do not find them, you will see Saracen no more." Alone, he stalked the marauders to the Arkansas River near the Post, and rushed in among them with his tomahawk, rescuing the children. A memorial window to this event, set up in the Catholic Church at Pine Bluff in 1888, has by now completely disappeared, along with Saracen and the Quapaws.

If the vanishing of the Quapaws was a minor tragedy, what are we to say of the greater tragedy of the Five Great Tribes, the Cherokees, Chickasaws, Choctaws, Creeks, Seminoles, driven en masse from their lands in Tennessee, Alabama, Georgia, Upper and Central Mississippi, and Florida, to the Indian Territory by the operation of the Removal Act of 1830? "About November 1, 1832," the vanguard of this army of fugitives appeared in Little Rock in the shape of "six or seven thousand Choctaw and Chickasaw Indians from North Mississippi and West Tennessee," mounted on ponies, driving their cattle, the males attired in the usual breechcloth, leggings, and beaded moccasins, the women with their papooses slung at their backs. A nephew of Governor Pope, who saw them passing through the village, recalled sixty years later how they were "several days in crossing the river, although hurried out of town as soon as possible. They had a great desire to loiter and spy around, and had to be driven almost like sheep." He also remarked that "two days before this migrating party reached Little Rock, an officer arrived in town and warned the citizens of the thieving propensities of the lower class of the Indians, and advised them to close their stores and dwellings while they were passing through. With all the vigilance that could be displayed, many articles of the utmost uselessness to the Indians disappeared from the yards of private residences." Considering that these Indians once had titles to very much more than "articles of the utmost uselessness," guaranteed them by the United States—titles now completely broken—the only wonder is that they did not "steal" the entire town.

In the spring of 1833, with cholera raging up and down the Mississippi Valley, more Indians appeared. They had been stricken with cholera when they arrived at Memphis and were not allowed to approach Little Rock. Instead, according to Governor Pope's nephew, they "were compelled to cross several miles below town and go out by way of Fourche, where they struck the military road. As soon as they reached the pine-hills southwest of town, the disease began to abate." Since Fourche Bayou was, up to the time of my own boyhood, nothing but a formidable and wildly malarial cypress swamp, one can only imagine what the Indians endured.

But these horrors were as nothing compared to the dreadful epic of the migration of the Eastern Cherokees—an epic involving Arkansas in its tragedy. These Indians, occupying a large district in southeast Tennessee, northern Alabama, western North Carolina, and northwest Georgia, and numbering over sixteen thousand five hundred souls by official count in 1835, many of them living as prosperous farmers, in houses often two-storied, and in the happy possession not only of devoted missionaries but of a written language, with books and journals printed in it since 1828, had never recognized the right of the three thousand Cherokees who had gone west in 1818 to Arkansas, to be counted as full members of their tribe. They had foreseen, and rightly, that this early removal was but part of a deep-laid government plan to force all Indians from the country. Now, their worst fears were realized, and in the worst way.

In 1828 a Negro slave picked up a gold nugget at Dahlonega, in Georgia. As this spot was only fifty miles away from the final Cherokee capital of New Echota, the people remaining in the Cherokee country had really no chance. The State of Georgia, under Governor Gilmer, now declared—despite the solemn treaty that the United States had entered into with the Indians in 1818—that it had a perfect right to seize all the Cherokee lands. Since no Cherokee was accepted as a witness in the courts, this was the beginning of the end. Some of the Indians had already been bribed to sell their lands; others were simply forced out by the violent onrush of the white squatters. Vainly the tribe attempted to revive old laws invoking the death penalty for any Indian who parted with his lands. Then, in 1830, finding the Indians still recalcitrant and unwilling to give up, the Georgia governor issued a proclamation forbidding any Indian to mine gold, since all the land belonged to the State of Georgia by right. This was followed up by another, early in 1831, insisting that every Indian as well as all whites (this meant the Congregational missionaries) must take an oath to be loyal only to the Georgia laws. The missionaries, chief of them Samuel Worcester, of Massachusetts, a very strong and courageous spirit, refused to take the oath. They were promptly sentenced to hard labor in prison for four years.

Prayers, petitions to Congress, meetings of missionary boards, propaganda in the *Cherokee Phoenix*—the newspaper now printed by the missionaries at New Echota—all alike were in vain. Whatever the United States may have declared to be its treaty obligations, to President Jackson "the only good Indian was a dead Indian." By forcing the Cherokees to get out, Georgia had only asserted its statutory right over its own territory. And though the Supreme Court reversed the Georgia decision and ordered the missionaries to be set free, Jackson very promptly remarked, "John Marshall has now made his decision. Let him enforce it."

A great rift had already appeared in the ranks of the Cherokees. Driven from their homes by the force of armed mobs, a party arose which was, at last, in favor of selling their Georgia lands to the state and removing to the Indian Territory, whither the Arkansas Cherokees had preceded them by 1828. Early in 1833, the missionaries, after every attempt that Georgia could make to evade the Supreme Court decision, were at last released and brought home amid wild demonstrations of joy. But by now the whole Cherokee country was under martial law, instituted by the Georgia State Guard, which had been called up. And a party led by John Ridge, the best orator of the tribe—soon joined by Elias Boudinot, the most learned and intelligent man among them, who had given invaluable aid to the missionaries in their enterprise of translating the entire Bible into Cherokee—was actively in favor of coming to terms with Georgia and the United States government, despite the iron resistance of the head chief, John Ross, who lived where stands the present-day city of Chattanooga, and who remarked merely that their lands, for which the United States were ready to pay five million dollars, were worth at least twenty million. All this was in keeping with Ross's character—he was only a quarter Indian, the child of a Scotch trader and a half-breed woman.

But Jackson was determined to satisfy the demands of the Georgians. Through an emissary who was not at all averse to bribery, about five hundred of the tribe were induced to assemble, and on December 29, 1835, they signed a treaty whereby, for the sum originally set, all their lands were sold and they agreed to go westward. By this time the missionaries, denounced in the Georgia press as Northern abolitionists, had thrown up the charge and retreated to the Indian Territory, where Worcester finally died. The press and printing plant had already been seized by the Georgia State Guard. Ross, whose own home was seized by force, vainly protested by getting up a petition to Congress, signed by over twelve thousand, designed to show that the overwhelming majority had never been in favor of removal; but for all that, Congress ratified the treaty, the Senate finally voting it after Jackson had gone out of office, in 1837. Although John Ridge himself, repentant of his part in the treaty, had protested that the five million dollars was never likely to be paid them but would be claimed in large part by Georgia for rent on lands which Georgia had never owned, the Cherokees had to go.

It was impossible, however, to persuade the Cherokees to remove voluntarily. Only a few parties, undertaking the long steamboat journey up the Tennessee River to the Ohio, down the Ohio to the Mississippi, and down the Mississippi to the Arkansas, were induced to depart. The United States Army was called in, and in the winter of 1837–1838 rounded all up but a few hundred who retreated into the inaccessible fastnesses of the Great Smokies, and threw them into what would today be called concentration camps along the Tennessee River. By now, even John Ross realized that nothing further could be done and agreed to depart, if it could be done under their own officers, without further interference by the American Army. But it was not till the close of the summer of 1838—a summer of great heat and dryness—that the armies of the Indians, now about fifteen thousand strong, took to the road, in wagons, ahorse or afoot, over a circuitous route which lay through Nashville northward into Kentucky, crossed the Ohio into Illinois and the Mississippi at Cape Girardeau, Missouri, to strike through northwest Arkansas into the Indian Country. This was the celebrated "Trail of Tears" witnessed by a few white travellers, who marvelled at the Indians' stoicism and discipline, remembered as late as 1932 by one old Cherokee woman who made it when about four years old. It cost the Cherokees about four thousand lives in all; and was not completed till March, 1839. Among the dead were famous old chiefs, buried at the roadside; innumerable infants; and Ross's own Cherokee wife, Quatie, who sickened aboard the steamboat that brought her husband, and was buried at Little Rock among strangers.

A year and more before this—as far as I can gather from his narrative, it was on February 9, 1838—the Hamburg-born German hunter and traveller Friedrich Gerstaecker, who was temperamentally fitted to understand and sympathize with the Indians, approached Little Rock afoot, walking southward across country. What followed is best told in his own words:

"Long after sunset on the 9th I arrived on the Arkansas River; the lights of Little Rock shone from the opposite bank, but a strange fantastic scene presented itself on this side, at which I stared with astonishment. An Indian tribe had pitched its tents close to the river. A number of large crackling fires, formed of whole trunks of fallen trees, which lay about in abundance, offered good shelter against the wind; over the fires were kettles with large pieces of venison, bear, squirrels, and whatever else the chase had given them. Here young men were occupied securing the horses to some of the fallen trees, and supplying them with fodder; there lay others, overcome with fire-water, singing their national songs with a mournful and heavy tongue. I stood for a long time watching the animated scene.

"A tall powerful Indian, decked out with glass beads and silver ornaments, came staggering towards me, with an empty bottle in his left hand and a handsome rifle in his right, and holding them both towards me, gave me to understand that he would give me the rifle if I would fill his bottle. The poor Indians have fallen so low and become so degraded by the base speculations of the palefaces, that they will give all they most value, to procure the body and soul-destroying spirits. Though I had but little money left, only twelve cents, I declined the exchange; he turned sorrowfully away, probably to offer the advantageous bargain to someone else, in which case I thought it best to indulge the poor savage, and save him his handsome rifle; I took the bottle out of his hand, filled it, and gave it back to him. On my refusing to accept his rifle, he laid hold of me, and dragged me almost forcibly to his fire, obliged me to drink with him, to smoke out of his pipe, and eat a large slice of venison, while his wife and three children sat in the tent and looked at the stranger. He then stood up, and in his harmonious language related a long history to me and to some sons of the forest who had assembled round us, of which I did not understand one word. At last, as the noise became annoying, I stole away quietly to seek a berth for the night."

The indifference of the Arkansawyers to such scenes, their general attitude of not caring how many Indians lived or died like flies on the way, may be palliated, if not excused, by saying that here, too, facing the Indian camp of which Gerstaecker spoke, were pioneers making a hazardous living. Already the great currency depression of 1837 was abroad in the land; already the Real Estate Bank of Arkansas was suspending its unfortunate operations, to leave the state burdened with a debt that went on for two generations. Cholera epidemics, since 1833, had taken their toll; smallpox was so common that, by Gerstaecker's own statement, he was offered a room in Little Rock containing a corpse recently dead of the disease. We who are both civilized and aware of the failure of civilization to provide any solution for human want, misery, and injustice, can afford to sympathize with the five civilized tribes who, in their great crisis, bore themselves nobly and shamed the lust of the land-greedy white men. The Arkansawyers of that day thought differently: they wasted but little sympathy.

Seven

BY BRAWLING, ARKANSAS ACHIEVES STATEHOOD

There is in existence a letter, written by an Arkansawyer who had become one of the pioneer gold-seekers in California in 1849, in which he compares the conditions that prevailed in the mining camps of that lawless region to those that existed in the Territory of Arkansas throughout the early thirties. This statement is no exaggeration, as anyone looking through the Arkansas newspapers of the early thirties can testify. Brawls and duels were never more common; they culminated in the furious election campaign of 1833, remembered twenty years after, along with unprecedented floods, a violent epidemic of cholera, and the famous meteor shower of November 13, as having made that year full of portents and of terrors.

In 1829, Miller's successor, the refined and accomplished Izard, descendant of an aristocratic Huguenot family of Charleston, South Carolina, suddenly died. This gave President Andrew Jackson his first opportunity to sway the course of Arkansas politics, and he took it to the full. He appointed as governor John Pope of Kentucky, a tough and blunt frontiersman, who, as we have seen, had but one hand. But the real ruler of the Territory since the summer of 1819, the power behind both Miller and Izard, was the thirty-three-year-old Robert Crittenden, of Kentucky, already known to his intimates by the expressive nickname of "Cardinal Wolsey" to symbolize both his power and his ambition. In 1829 he suddenly found himself thrust by Jackson's administration out of office. And his soul thirsted for revenge.

Crittenden, it will be remembered, had, in 1827, got rid of one opponent, Henry W. Conway, of Tennessee, by shooting him; but a whole host of other Conways—sons of that remarkable pioneer woman, Ann Conway, were ready to take his place. A rising young lawyer, just twenty-seven years of age, Ambrose H. Sevier, of Tennessee, had succeeded in being elected delegate to Congress to replace Conway in 1828. When he came up for reëlection in 1831, Crittenden had promptly decided to oppose him. He had chosen as his henchman Ben Desha, his second in the famous duel; and Desha was instructed to raise against Sevier the issue of possible statehood for the territory.

But in spite of this opposition, Sevier—known as "Don Ambrosia" to his friends, and a tactful, diplomatic sort of man—won out against Desha and Crittenden. And other more deadly opponents of Crittenden's rule were coming into the field. They consisted of the Conway faction, to be known later as the Conway dynasty, who were ready to transform the issue of the famous duel into a family feud. Behind them stood, in close alliance, the crafty Ashley, nicknamed "Talleyrand" by his Arkansas friends, who were good at giving nicknames. Ashley had struck up an alliance with Woodruff, the proprietor of the only newspaper in the territory. The opposition to Crittenden was only waiting for an opportunity to show its strength; and the appointment of Pope gave the opportunity.

Crittenden had, for the moment, chosen to ignore the threat to his power. He had built, in the winter of 1827–1828, the first—and for a long time, the best—brick residence in Little Rock, a handsome one-story affair in the style of the Greek revival, standing on a whole block of land at Cumberland and Chestnut streets, with slave-quarters, kitchen, wellhouse, smokehouse and storehouse adjoining, where he lived in fine style, dispensing wine, cigars, and patronage to his numerous henchmen. But when he was driven from office by Jackson, he found it impossible to go on living at such a rate, and waited for a chance to get even with his opponents. John Pope, in the meantime, lived in no such style; he occupied a simple cabin at the edge of the town, where an English traveller found him still living in the winter of 1835–1836. This traveller did not see the Governor—he was informed by Mrs. Pope that her husband "was out in the woods looking for a sow and pigs belonging to her that were missing." All of which says much concerning the Arkansas of that day, as well as of Pope and Crittenden.

The opportunity that Crittenden had sought soon came; in 1831 Congress set aside ten sections of the best Arkansas land to be sold by the territory, the proceeds to be devoted to the erection of a suitable building for the territorial capitol. Pope had already delivered his inaugural in the leaky shack run up by the Austin Associates and was determined to build something more appropriate and permanent. But Crittenden saw in this move a chance to enrich himself, as well as to reassert his power; he promptly induced the territorial legislature to bring in and vote a bill to exchange the ten sections of land for his own brick house, which was declared entirely suitable for a capitol. Pope vetoed the bill, which Crittenden now recklessly boasted had been obtained by offering to members of the legislature more than thirty fine hams from his own smokehouse. Faced with Pope's stubborn opposition, he went even further. He induced the legislature to vote a petition to Congress, asking for Pope's removal. This was the signal for Ashley and his ally Woodruff and his protegé James Sevier Conway, brother of the Henry Conway who had lost his life in the famous duel, to start action. The *Arkansas Gazette* began to sound loud innuendoes against "Cardinal Wolsey" and his "canvassed hams."

Meantime, Ambrose Sevier's conduct—he was connected with the Conways by the fact that Ann Conway, mother of them all, had been a Sevier before her marriage—was elaborately investigated on the floor of Congress, and he was forced to defend himself in a two-hour speech against a charge of having stood by while one desperate character shot another desperate character in the back, on the very steps of a courthouse; and against another charge of having visited a resort on the banks of the Arkansas where faro was openly played. Pope, however, with frontier tenacity, stood his ground. Jackson had refused to oust him, despite the legislature's action. By January, 1833, enough money had been obtained from the sale of the ten sections of land set aside by Congress, to start construction on the new capitol. Pope obtained a set of plans from Gideon Shyrock, of Kentucky, and decided to start building at once. Ashley had for some time been unobtrusively at work on his old rival, William Russell, of Saint Louis; and both now offered a site for the new building at the foot of Center Street. Crittenden tried to head this off by spreading rumors to the effect that this spot had been the location of an old Indian burial ground, and had been used later, in 1809, by some mysterious French or Spanish gold-seeking expeditions—said to have been headed by Jean Lafitte, the famous Louisiana pirate—for the purpose of burying several of their own deceased members in coffins hollowed out of logs. Pope remained unperturbed. It is said he replied simply, "We will build, then, a monument to their memory."

In the summer of 1833, with the Arkansas River rising to such heights as no white man had ever before seen, Crittenden came out openly against Sevier; he asked the people of the territory to elect him as their delegate to Congress, as a vindication both of himself and of their legislature. The sneers of Woodruff's *Gazette* and the references to the canvassed hams were now redoubled. But Crittenden had taken care to have more than oral support. He had induced his brother-in-law, Charles P. Bertrand, who had been born in New York in 1806, and who was known on account of his citified ways and fine clothes, as "Beau Charley," to come to Little Rock and start a rival newspaper, to be called the *Advocate*. With him was soon associated Charles Fenton Mercer Noland, a bold young gamecock from Kentucky who had an itch for writing and who deserves mention here as being, under the name of "Pete Whetstone," Arkansas's pioneer humorist in the backwoods style later to be immortalized by Mark Twain.

These newspapers, the *Arkansas Gazette* and the *Advocate,* in the spring of 1833 began a series of violent attacks on each other. A number of highly scurrilous letters, signed "Devereux," detailing Pope's incompetence in office and his partiality for the members of his own family, began to appear in the *Advocate*. To these Woodruff retorted, as he best might, in the *Gazette* by referring continually to Crittenden as the "canvassed ham" candidate. Tempers began to run high, and it is said that the adherents of the two factions refused, though members of the same congregation, to take the sacrament together with their opponents. Knifings and stabbings began to be common. Crittenden called on the National Republicans and Sevier on the Democrats for their support. So intense was the contest that Woodruff paid little attention in his pages to the agitation that year in South Carolina over Calhoun's attempt to nullify Jackson's tariff. Woodruff thought that South Carolina's defiance was undesirable from the standpoint of the interests of the newly developed western country where he lived, but that was all.

Crittenden's thoughtless boast that his hams had been successful in getting the members of the legislature to vote for his side was now working against him; the *Gazette* began to brag that "Beau Charley," "Devereux," "Cardinal Wolsey" and all their host were about to meet their Waterloo on election day.

At this juncture, a new recruit, and one of surprising energy and audacity, suddenly emerged from the backwoods and sprang recklessly to Crittenden's side. This was an obscure young schoolteacher named Albert Pike, just over twenty-three years of age. He had been living in a one-room log schoolhouse on Little Piney Creek, in the wilds of Pope County, teaching tow-headed mountaineer children their A.B.C.'s, and being paid—if at all—in hogs. Meanwhile he had, as he later said, been writing heaps of poetry, which he hoped would bring him fame later on. In this summer of 1833, his pen being idle and the school languishing, he impulsively sent off a packet of manuscript to the *Advocate,* Crittenden's newspaper. The packet consisted of a series of quite imaginary "Intercepted Letters" purported to be written by Sevier to Woodruff and to Ashley, and revealing the misdeeds, real and imaginary, of the Democratic party. These letters were signed "Casca," and immediately became so famous that Crittenden himself mounted a horse and sought out, by the obscure bridlepaths of the Ozarks, their schoolmaster author. When he saw Pike he was so impressed by the man's personality that, then and there, he invited him to Little Rock to take a place on the editorial staff of the *Advocate.*

In November the election took place to the accompaniment of the usual duels and challenges to duels. Pike himself said, many years later, that it was after this contest that duelling finally began to go out of fashion in Arkansas. But there are records to show that quite frequently duels were still fought up through the days of the Civil War, and occasionally even later. No doubt Pike was right in believing that duels were far more common during this election period than at any later time.

For instance: About the time of the election, Pope's young nephew inserted a card in the *Gazette* demanding to know who had written the famous and scurrilous "Devereux" Letters. His uncle had advised him to ignore these epistles, which reflected on his own conduct; he had refused to do so. To ignore such a public card would have been considered, in those days, the act of a coward; accordingly, Charles

Fenton Mercer Noland, coeditor of the *Advocate,* promptly replied, admitting his authorship.

A duel was then arranged with young Pope—though his uncle still tried vainly to restrain him—as the challenger. The spot chosen—since duels in the territory were supposed to be still illegal—was a narrow strip of land at the head of Long Prairie, on Red River, which was generally supposed to lie outside the territory of Arkansas in the Mexican province of Texas. The journey to the duelling grounds, undertaken in the depth of the midwinter that followed the election, was tedious and difficult. Both parties travelled together, on horseback, through one of the wildest regions of the territory. At one halting place, Noland, along with the rest of the party, was already in bed when the mail rider, a youth in dripping, mudstained clothes, entered and, throwing off his wet garments, started to get into the bed, naked as he was, with Noland. Not liking the idea of sharing his bed with a naked, wet, and doubtless mud-grimed stranger, Noland remarked, "Look here, my friend, I have the itch," to which the boy promptly retorted, "That nothing; I've got the seven-year itch," and proceeded to enter the bed. As he got into one side, Noland rolled out at the other and sat up all the rest of the night in a chair.*

Farther along the road, at Washington, a village of some four hundred inhabitants in Hempstead County, Pope's second became so ill with an inflamed sore throat that another man had to be found to act as substitute. The duellers finally reached the ground selected, on the fourth of February, 1834. The usual ten paces having been marked off, they took up positions with the pistols in their hands. One of the seconds then gave the words agreed upon: "Gentlemen, are you ready? Fire, one, two, three, four." At the word "two," both pistols were discharged, the ball from Noland's pistol going into Pope's left leg between the knee and the hip. Pope fell to the ground. Pope's substituted second thereupon asked Noland, "Are you satisfied?" to which the answer was, "I am in the hands of my friends." Noland's second then asked Pope's substituted second: "Ask your principal if he is satisfied, since he is the challenging party." But Pope, still lying on the ground, answered, "No; I must have another shot." He was then lifted to his feet and set in position; but before he could fire a second time,

*Noland himself did not fail to make use of this incident, somewhat elaborated and embellished, in one of his "Pete Whetstone" papers. My version is taken from W. F. Pope, *Early Days in Arkansas,* 1895.

he again fell to the ground. The spectators now interposed and stopped the contest; but Pope, with the ball still in his leg, taken on a tedious carriage journey back to Little Rock over rough ground and in bad weather, died slowly from the result, early in June of 1834.

Another duel, happening in October, 1833, soon after the great contest was over, at the corner of Main and Markham streets in Little Rock itself, was for months afterward, we are told, the talk of the town. The parties were Robertson Childers, a Tennessee man prominent in law and in politics, and, as we shall see later, host to Davy Crockett, and one Stewart, a professional gambler. The duel arose out of a quarrel at cards—not uncommon in those days, when a faro-bank, by admission of Sevier himself on the floor of Congress in Washington, was openly running without interference close to the legislative seat of the territory. (As late as 1880, I have been told, the mayor and aldermen of Little Rock, at their sittings, sent out a messenger to ask the "bank next door" to close down its operations while their meeting was in progress.)

Childers and Stewart decided to dispense with all seconds, surgeons, friends, or other paraphernalia, and agreed to meet at opposite sides of the street on a certain hour, armed with double-barreled shotguns loaded with buckshot, pistols, and bowie knives. The shotguns were to be fired first and then the pistols; if neither of these took effect, the two men were to advance to the middle of the street and attack each other with the knives.

A slight flesh wound in the leg for Childers, from the buckshot, was the only result from the gun and pistol shooting; and both men were already moving upon each other with their bowie knives drawn, when a judge of the territorial supreme court, Benjamin S. Johnson, highly respected by all, happened to walk by and stopped the contest by summoning gaping spectators to arrest the two men at once.

Truly, these people, thanks to the advent of the frontier-born Jacksonian democracy on the American scene, were growing up into the breed later made famous as "half-horse, half-alligator" by no less an authority than Davy Crockett himself. That fine frontiersman, who declared, "I can whip my weight in wildcats; I comb myself with the lightning; and I drink up the Mississippi River when I'm dry," characterized them all. Crittenden, though he had so many people of talent working in his favor throughout this campaign, lost it finally by a margin of one thousand nine hundred and thirty-six votes—a blow from which he never recovered, for he died a broken man only a year later. And on December 13 of the same year, Ambrose H. Sevier, victorious candidate for Congress, boldly introduced a bill in that body providing for a census of the Arkansas population preparatory to their admission as a state.

The next year, 1834, was notable chiefly for mass meetings. County after county held demonstrations on behalf of Arkansas's becoming a state. At Little Rock, the Fourth of July was celebrated in the true old-fashioned American style, with a banquet and floods of oratory. A program of this celebration has come down to us. The day was opened with a salute of artillery, fired by a local militia company; later on the people assembled in the Presbyterian Church, the only church building then standing. The exercises were opened by prayer, followed by the reading of the Declaration of Independence and an oration by the young Albert Pike. After the benediction, the audience dispersed. In the evening, the banquet took place—and the following toasts were set down on the program: "The Day We Celebrate," "The President of the United States," "The Memory of Washington, Adams, Jefferson, Monroe and Madison," "The Army and Navy," "The Heroes of 1776," "Lafayette, The Hero of the Revolution," "The West," "The Youth of Our Country," "Ireland, the Country of Emmet, Curran, and Grattan," "Our Honorary Members," "Our Fair Countrywomen." To this proud array were now added, "His Excellency, Honorable John Pope, Governor of Arkansas," "The Little Rock Debating Society, the Nursery of the Future Statesmen and Patriots of Arkansas," "Honorable William S. Fulton, Secretary of Arkansas," "The Rights of the States and of the Union of States, may the heart of every true American be devoted to the preservation of both," "The American People, may they enjoy the same freedom in 1894, as they do at this day." To which a wag added this: "May we be free, but not too free," a toast doubtless demanded by the exalted condition of the audience at this time.

The community in which all this took place was a strange one, uniting the characteristics of a virgin wilderness and an untamed frontier. According to the invaluable letters which young Hiram Whittington, who had come down to assist Woodruff in his printing office, wrote to his brother back in Boston from the fall of 1827 onwards, there were about sixty buildings in Little Rock, six of them made of brick, eight of frame, and the rest log cabins. There was a school, called the Little

Rock Academy, in one log hut, and the territorial capitol building (which Whittington calls, mistakenly, the State House) in another. Governor Pope delivering an address in this building once, during a rainstorm, found the roof so leaky that he was obliged, during his speech, to keep shifting his papers from side to side. Most of the buildings stood near the Rock itself, between Markham and Second, around the foot of Cumberland and Rock streets; there were a straggling few, including Pope's own residence, westward, near the foot of Center and Spring streets, where was a good supply of water, and where the new territorial capitol was now building. Women were notably scarce—perhaps eight or ten married women, and some five or six young girls, for a male population of well over a hundred. Though young female partners were hard to come by, dances were frequently held, and much drinking was indulged in. In the summer there were frequent religious revivals held by evangelists who penetrated this remote region by horseback or on one of the rare steamboats. Whittington himself refers to one such revival, which seems to have touched him; he stayed on in Arkansas, although unable to find any young woman to be his wife; and in 1835 he migrated as pioneer settler to Hot Springs, still writing half humorously and frequently to his brother about his difficulties as a bachelor. At one time he seems to have canvassed the possibility of taking a squaw from the Cherokee Settlements above Dardenelle; but he finally went back to Boston, obtained a wife, and settled down in Arkansas for good. His letters cast a strong, if perhaps sometimes humorously exaggerated light on the characteristics of the period.

While all this was going on in Arkansas, the much-agitated question of Texas independence rose into prominence. Stephen F. Austin, after his father's death in 1820, had become the chief American colonizer in these lands beyond the United States boundary. He had handled, since 1824, the various revolutionary governments of the Mexican Republic with supreme skill, and, ten years later, had under his control eighteen thousand colonists, over whose lives and destinies he ruled as supreme autocrat. The Mexican population, centering around San Antonio, was already outnumbered four to one. Since Austin had discouraged lawlessness from the start, and had shown great diplomatic skill in obtaining concessions from the Mexican Government, his colony had already begun to attract settlers from abroad, notably Germans who now began to make their appearance on the southwestern border in considerable numbers. Vast tracts of fertile black bottom lands were left untenanted in southern Arkansas by settlers eager to take advantage of the favorable terms which Austin offered to all comers. But since the new advent of Santa Anna to power in 1831, further immigration of Protestants had suddenly been strictly forbidden by the government of Mexico; and the Austin colonists had become more and more discontented with the Mexican administration. Plots were now openly hatching to throw off all Mexican control and to proclaim Texan independence, and at the centre of those plots stood a strange man who lived for a time in Arkansas.

This was Sam Houston, ex-Governor of Tennessee, a man six feet six inches tall, engaging and handsome, who had ended a reckless early career as Jacksonian partisan in 1829 by fleeing from his newly-wedded wife and office, and by taking refuge among the Cherokees in the Indian Territory. Here he had acquired a squaw, Talahina, who died a year later, and had lived as an Indian, being known among his tribesmen by two significant Indian names, which were, we are told, "The Raven," and "Big Drunk." On his flight across Arkansas Territory, an episode had taken place which casts much light not only on Houston but on the character of the backwoodsmen then inhabiting the territory.

At Lewisburg, a frontier settlement some twenty-five miles up the Arkansas River from Little Rock, close to the present-day town of Conway, there lived a frontier lawyer by the name of John Linton, apparently an old acquaintance of Houston's, who, like all the old frontier lawyers of that time, was largely self-taught, full of mispronounced Latin quotations, and—in his case, at least—had put a checkered past behind him. He was a fugitive from a jail sentence back in Virginia. To him now came Sam Houston, another fugitive; and Linton was easily persuaded, over tall glasses of corn whisky, to accompany Houston to Fort Smith, a hundred and twenty miles away. So he mounted on his horse Bucephalus (a name which he pronounced "Buck-a-full-os") and escorted Houston to the frontier of the Indian Territory. The rest can be told only in the words of John Hallum, Arkansas historian of 1887, whose magnificent frontier eloquence is inimitable in its own way:

"Here in the face of opportunity, they could no longer restrain themselves; the ardent was plentiful, and they celebrated the orgies of Bacchus in roaring style; tip after tip and cup after cup soon attested their unrivaled accomplishments in that line, at that shrine. They soon became generous rivals for championship at the hilarious shrine of the wine-god. Houston suggested that an offering, meet and appropriate, be made, indicative of the highest regard for Ancient Bacchus; and Linton said: 'If it is anything within the range of human possibilities, I am ready to sacrifice and atone to the God.'

"This sacrifice consisted in pulling off and consigning all their wearing apparel to the flames. Linton heroically followed Houston's lead until his shirt, the last garment, struck the flames; he snatched that out, but Houston chided him for reneging, and he returned it to the flames. There each stood in a log cabin with dirt floor, face to face, in a state of nature. Linton was a stranger, away from home, without friends or money; and was forced to wrap up in a blanket and retire to a straw bed. Houston's servant had another suit for him, and soon repaired the loss and, before his master had recovered from the spree, had him in the saddle on the way to Fort Gibson. When Linton recovered consciousness, Houston was forty miles away. . . . It was several days before succor came. Linton always dreaded mention of this episode, but Madam Linton never 'let up on him' while he lived. She often begged him to be careful and avoid the company of 'big folks,' lest he should become inspired again to sacrifice to heathen gods, and to burn his shirt."

All during this flight from civilization, Houston seems to have preferred nudity to clothing. It has also been stated of him, that he stopped at Little Rock for a time, at a tavern, before reaching Lewisburg, and that the members of the territorial supreme court decided to call upon him. On reaching the tavern, they were asked to go upstairs to ex-Governor Houston's room, which they did, only to find the future hero of the Battle of San Jacinto lying on the bed, without a stitch of clothing on his massive body.

By 1832, the fit of drunken despair which had sent Houston off into the territory of the Cherokees, seems to have burnt itself out; and he was rational enough to visit Washington—it is said in full Indian regalia—where he again found his old hero, Andrew Jackson. Jackson befriended him and insisted on buying him a white man's suit. Houston thereupon returned to white men's ways after long walking the Indian's road. In the fall of 1833, this mysterious man, now aged forty, reëntered Arkansas, apparently possessed of much money and, according to one who then saw him, "riding a splendid bay horse.

His saddle and bridle were of the most exquisite Mexican workmanship, and were elaborately ornamented with solid silver plates and buckles. He was enveloped in a Mexican poncho, which was richly ornamented." Such an attire betokened nothing less than a gambler, in those days; and the word got around that Houston was, in fact, a devotee of cards, spending his waking hours in the study of faro and seven-up.

Houston was indeed a gambler, but for higher stakes than anyone supposed. The object of his gamble was the whole of Texas. Secret meetings were held, in the dead of night, at Washington, the capital seat of Hempstead County, where a persistent legend has it that Houston first met Stephen Austin. Rifles began to appear in southwest Arkansas in even larger numbers than common; and by 1834 a considerable band of individuals, gathering from the states east of the Mississippi, were settled around Washington for the alleged purpose of buying up the government lands; and very soon thereafter public meetings were held in various eastern cities by the "friends of Texan independence" to obtain funds for the furtherance of Houston's new project.

President Jackson, though it is quite likely he had originally started Houston off by lending him money, promptly disavowed the movement. It would not do to provoke an open war with Mexico. But Houston kept on, and in October, 1835, the American settlers, with the aid of his rifles, drove the Mexican forces out of the country in the short space of two and a half months. At the end of that year, Antonio López de Santa Anna, ruler of Mexico and ablest general of the Republic, recrossed the Rio Grande going northward at the head of over five thousand men, bent on reconquering the refractory Anglo-Saxons who had flouted his authority by declaring themselves independent of his rule.

What fired the Arkansawyers more than anything else and caused them finally to make the cause of Texan independence their own was the sudden appearance of the redoubtable David Crockett in Little Rock, with six or eight companions from Tennessee, on November 12, 1835, on his way south to render aid to the uprisen Texans in their fight for independence from Mexico. By this time Crockett, now nearly fifty, had already become a legendary figure everywhere on the western frontier. He was known to thousands in the mountains of Tennessee, Kentucky, the Carolinas, Missouri, and Arkansas, as the backwoodsman par excellence, heir to the great tradition of Daniel Boone. Innumerable tales were told of his prowess in hunting, of the deadliness of his rifle "Betsy," of his amazing exploits which far outrivalled those of other folk-heroes, such as the "King of Keelboatmen," Mike Fink, or that later lumberjack, Paul Bunyan. It was said that he had been cradled in a snapping turtle's shell, with a wildcat's skin for a pillow. A pair of elk horns hung over the cradle, with an alligator-skin atop. It was said that he owned a pet bear, named "Death Hug," and that, mounted on this bear's back, he had often forded rivers and ridden off to hunt buffalo. It was said that he had once wrung the tail off a comet, and that he could stand in front of a tree and, by merely grinning, bring down a raccoon—or even a panther—from it. Now he was here, actually on Arkansas soil, and on his way to Texas, having been decisively defeated for Congress in Tennessee only the year before by the Jacksonian party, whom he had dared to oppose, and by their candidate, the wooden-legged old pioneer, Adam Huntsman, whom he always sardonically referred to as "Adam Timbertoes."

Whether the story be true or not that the delegation of Little Rock citizens, headed by Robertson Childers, who went to call on Davy at his hotel, found him out in the backyard skinning a deer he had just shot a few miles out of town; whether Crockett promptly greeted this delegation with the remark that he had made this animal "turns ends at two hundred yards," is not material. The fact remains that Crockett had to act in character—and this sort of exploit was just what the frontiersmen of Arkansas expected of him. Only the most expert of shots could make a running deer go head over heels in a somersault at two hundred yards. After being assured that "there were no United States marshals about," Davy, it is said, consented to take part in an impromptu banquet to be held that night in his honor; and he delivered himself of a typical Crockett speech, talking freely of his career in politics, his refusal to wear a collar inscribed, "This dog belongs to Andy Jackson." The audience were entranced; even the rigidly Jacksonian *Gazette* unbent the next day to recognize his presence among the Arkansawyers. Then Davy, buckskin hunting-shirt, coonskin cap, rifle and all, rode off to Texas, to meet a heroic death within the walls of the Alamo, along with James Bowie, Barrett Travis, and a hundred and eighty other heroic souls, while Santa Anna's army of five thousand outside the walls blew the call for no quarter on their bugles, late in February, 1836.

By April, while the Arkansawyers watched anxiously and many a frontiersman, oiling his rifle, slipped across the frontier to join in the fight, Sam Houston, at the head of less than a thousand untrained men, retreating across the Texas plains, suddenly turned on his adversary at the Prairie of San Jacinto, close to Buffalo Bayou—and in twenty minutes had Santa Anna's entire army and Santa Anna himself at his mercy. By a miracle, Texas was now free. In the next ten years, it could boast of thirty thousand inhabitants—so great was the rush for the fertile lands of the Lone Star Republic.

Meantime, the fight to make Arkansas a state had gone on. Sevier, during his term in Congress from 1833 to 1835 had not failed to press the matter, but Congress took no action. Sevier stood again for Congress in 1835, unopposed, on the sole platform of making Arkansas a state and of calling a convention to frame a constitution without waiting for Congress to decide upon statehood. Despite the last-minute opposition of Governor Fulton, successor to Pope, his cause won the day.

On June 15, 1836, after an all-night sitting of the House to consider the new constitution, which had been hurriedly transmitted to Sevier, the bill to admit Arkansas as a state was voted and signed by Andrew Jackson. On the following Fourth of July, Sevier returned in triumph from Washington to find the citizens of the small village of Little Rock hanging out their flags and preparing to illuminate the half-constructed streets, in honor of the news they had just received. Arkansas was now a state, with all the proud privileges of statehood. The frontier stage of its history was nearly over and done with; and in another fifteen years tales of big bears, of bowie knives, of enraged buffalo chasing hunters around a lone tree, of frontier brawls, and of travellers on lonely roads looking for some sort of shelter for the night, ceased to be common folklore and became art products. They were replaced by other stories: of California goldfields, of perilous trips over the Santa Fé Trail or across country from Fort Smith, of wild exploits in the Mexican War. But the fury over elections which began with Crittenden's last contest in 1833 went on; it persisted even up to fairly recent years. I have talked with several Arkansawyers, still hale and hearty, who remember clearly seeing the great torchlight procession, held to celebrate Cleveland's victory, which marched through the Little Rock streets on a November night in 1884. That was a rip-roaring occasion. The entire population turned out to see it, hailing as it did the return of the Democratic party to power after twenty-four years in the wilderness. Blaine—Blaine—"that animated liar from the State of Maine," no doubt was given a good Arkansas roasting from a crowd lit up in more ways than one. There was also some excitement later, especially in 1896, as I recall, over Bryan. But when Woodrow Wilson came to be the next Democratic president elected in 1912, torchlight processions, as a means of registering popular joy, were already fading out, along with the horse and buggy, dear to the older generation; and popular enthusiasm since then, in Arkansas as elsewhere, has been manifested most frequently at college football games.

Eight

THE FINE ARKANSAS GENTLEMEN AND THEIR DAY

In 1835 the population of Arkansas, destined the next year to be a state, was 51,809. By 1840 it was nearly double, the national census of that year showing 97,574. Little Rock, chartered as a city since 1835, had, so far, only 1,500 inhabitants; but it was a city nevertheless. The six brick houses which Whittington had seen in it had been supplemented by at least four others, all two-storied affairs with high ceilings and columns in front, lying for the most part—except for Ashley's magnificent mansion which faced the steamboat wharf and the river—out on the southern edge of town, where plenty of acreage was accessible and buildings were not set close together. This was in keeping with the Southern aristocratic tradition of Natchez and elsewhere; and for the twenty-five years from statehood to the Civil War, "the fine Arkansas gentlemen" who had Southern leanings and lived in such houses, largely ruled the state.

In addition to these fine residences, Little Rock had, from 1839 onwards, a theatre (though the original building erected for that purpose blew down in a windstorm after only a year's service), two or three churches, a visiting circus, a Federal arsenal, horse-racing, and occasional fireworks displays. Well might the editor of the *Gazette* declare, "We have now in about the twentieth year of the existence of Little Rock, all the amusements and recreations of an old and settled community." Stagecoaches ran, more or less regularly, to Arkansas Post and to Hot Springs; and in 1841 the whole edifice of civilization was crowned by the building of the Anthony House, a fine two-story structure of brick with "a dining room sixty feet long, two parlors, twenty-eight bedrooms, a bar, baggage and store-rooms, kitchen, laundry, meat house, ice house, servants' quarters, a stable and carriage house," which became—as we shall see—the most famous hotel in Arkansas, till it burned down in 1875.

Notable figures, apart from the Conways, the Seviers, and the Johnsons—all interconnected by marriage—who ruled the state politically, began duly to make their appearance at other places than in Little Rock. Captain Bonneville, early explorer of the remote West, settled down near Fort Smith, to be interviewed and immortalized by Washington Irving. The house he built there is still standing. At Hot Springs, from sufficiently humble beginnings, Hiram Whittington grew into a man of prominence and fortune. At Van Buren, in the summer of 1839, Josiah Gregg, notable historian of the Santa Fé Trail, made a temporary but important appearance, to lead a party of eighteen men and forty wagons straight across the dreaded Comanche country to Santa Fé, and from thence on to Chihuahua. The oldest house now in Helena, still owned by its original family, was put up by 1850. But these were as nothing in comparison with the group of residences of lawyer-politicians living around Little Rock.

The State Capitol building was now finished; and already gone were the days when half a dozen prominent citizens could, for a wager, attempt to ride their horses up its interior spiral staircase. Even more remote were the days when a native could say to one of the territorial governors: "Oh everybody here does about as he pleases, anyway; and we get along just as well when the governor is away as we do when he is here." There was now printed a digest of Arkansas laws and statutes; and politics, as a career to follow, appealed to the most wealthy and the best connected, as in other parts of the South.

Although the scandalous affairs of the Real Estate Bank had culminated in 1839 in the suspension of all specie payments, the whole financial standing of the community had been decently concealed by the directors of that institution, who formed themselves into a committee of trustees to liquidate it, and who successfully staved off all investigations till the later forties. Otherwise the state was prospering. Except for the cotton gin and the steamboat, it operated still on a handicraft economy. Railroads there were none; the first through track between Little Rock and Memphis was not begun till 1854 and not completed till after the Civil War, in 1871—after seventeen years of suspense, as the papers then said. Telegraphs were unknown until the first line came in 1860. The sewing machine appeared as a novelty, in the fifties.

Luxuries, such as fine beaver hats, silk dresses, wines, books, were confined to Little Rock and to a few other places accessible to steamboat and stagecoach travel; they did not penetrate far into the backwoods. In the eastern half of the state, in the rich river bottoms, the one-crop cotton economy of the old Southern planter was gradually built up, staffed by a slave population rising to a hundred and ten thousand by 1860; but in the Ozark section, the population was and has remained white, consisting altogether of independent dirt farmers. Squatters in remote spots were still fairly common; the famous story of the "Arkansas Traveller," first told by Sandford C. Faulkner, who was good at both fiddling and telling a story, sprang from these days. It is said that the finest hotel in New Orleans kept a room which was always reserved for "Colonel" Faulkner whenever he made a visit; and on its door was a silver plate bearing the title "The Arkansas Traveller," so famed was this story. Other rooms in the same hotel were similarly reserved for other notable Arkansawyers; to visit New Orleans, famous for eating, luxury, and culture, was still the goal of almost every native's dream.

Seen in retrospect from the lean and haggard days that followed after the Civil War, this was the golden age in Arkansas, though few of those who survived the War and Reconstruction would, probably, have really cared to live in it. Now was the time when Memphis grew from a keel-boat landing with a few "doggeries" close by, to a flourishing city; when Napoleon, at the mouth of the Arkansas, was equally flourishing, boasting of a large United States Marine hospital before being swept without a trace into the river in a few gigantic nights of flood; when two hunters, in less than an hour, killed nine hundred passenger pigeons on Fourche Bar, a few miles below Little Rock; when passengers who wished to make the trip to the capital city in most comfort and safety took the steamboat from Montgomery's Point up the White River for one hundred and forty miles to Rock Roe (now Clarendon) near the sluggish and swampy Cache River, and then transferred to the easy, thrice-weekly stagecoach that crossed the Grand Prairie, sixty-three miles to Little Rock. The journey was then made in only thirty-six hours. This was, above all, the flood tide of western expansion: when the fields around Van Buren were white with tents of companies organizing to go to California, and when—in the fall of 1850—the keeper of the toll-gate bridge across Bayou Meto, twelve miles northeast of Little Rock, counted no less than fifteen hundred and twenty-nine "waggons, carriages, vehicles, and oxcarts" passing westward between September and January.

The episodes of the Mexican War and of the California gold rush were just exciting enough to stir up the Arkansawyers. These and the continual talk that went on about the Mormons—who had attempted to colonize Missouri as early as 1833 and of whom no one approved—kept the minds of the natives keenly interested in the development of the West. From 1850 onward, the Southern States took the lead in projecting a transcontinental railroad to run to the Pacific. Although nothing practical was done, numerous public meetings were held on the subject and resolutions voted. Mass meetings and railroad conventions were held during the same period in Arkansas; from 1850 onward the tide of western emigration was so great that the hotels at all principal places were crowded to overflowing, and not a single house was unoccupied in Little Rock. The wharves at Little Rock, Pine Bluff, Fort Smith were packed with steamers; as many as twelve boats arrived and departed in a single week; but near the Little Rock landing, Ashley's celebrated band of Negroes no longer played, the "Senator" having died in Washington in 1848. Gone, too, was Ambrose H. Sevier, who died after having well served the United States in the negotiations with Mexico which led to the Treaty of Guadalupe Hidalgo. But the Conways and the Johnsons, who had come into power with Crittenden's early downfall, still ruled the state as the leading Democratic political dynasty, though much disliked by the Whigs. Their final triumph was in 1852, when Elias W. Conway was elected over his "independent" opponent to serve until 1860.

Foremost among the Arkansawyers of the period, for his intellectual attainments no less than for his political and military exploits, must be set the commanding figure of Albert Pike. We have already seen him, as an obscure backwoods schoolteacher, coming to Little Rock to help edit the *Advocate,* at Crittenden's instigation, during the famous campaign of 1833. But before that date Pike already had behind him a career of adventure and excitement. Born at Newburyport, Massachusetts, in the year of 1809, Pike had for a time, it appears, attended Harvard, but had been forced to give up a college career because of poverty and had taught in a primary school. He had left

Boston for the West in the spring of 1831, to arrive in Saint Louis that summer and to join a trading expedition under the leadership of the famous Charles Bent, which with ten ox-wagons set out over the Santa Fé trail in August. In November, the expedition arrived at Taos, where Pike met Bill Williams, one of the most celebrated of the early "mountain men," trader, trapper, Indian scout, and plainsman extraordinary. Pike then went back to Santa Fé, where he remained for ten months, according to the best account, and then left again, from Taos probably, in the company of a considerable number of mounted trappers who proposed to cross the plains directly in the late summer or early fall of the following year, 1832.

About the adventures of this party, Pike himself was disposed to romance in later years; he appears (though undoubtedly he had already felt the itch to write), to have kept no record at the time, and to have relied on an uncertain memory later in writing about what had happened. But there is little reason to doubt that he went, as he says, with some part of the party—others had already turned back or taken a different route—down the Pecos to the Bosque Redondo, about forty miles north of the site of the present city of Roswell, New Mexico, which was reached in sixteen days; and from there struck directly across the Staked Plains to the upper Red River, in a land that to this day is cut deeply by winding canyons and is well equipped with thorny thickets. At that time it was the very heart of the dreaded Comanche country; but Pike's party rode directly across the dangerous territory and, though nearly "rubbed out" by the Indians, reached Fort Smith by December, 1832.

"Falstaff's ragged regiment was nothing to us," Pike wrote later. "I had on a pair of leather pantaloons, scorched and wrinkled by fire, and full of grease; an old grimy jacket and vest; a pair of huge moccasins, in the mending of which I had expended all my skill during the space of two months, and in so doing had disposed upon them a whole shot-pouch; a shirt made of what is commonly called counterpane which had not been washed since I left Santa Fé, and to crown it all, my beard and mustacios had never been trimmed throughout the entire trip." But, doubtless, there were compensations. The packs of valuable beaver "plews" that the party carried set them up for a while, at least; though, as we have already seen, Pike soon enough reverted to the condition of a rural schoolteacher in Pope County, by the summer of the next year. Apparently the hardships and perils of the trip had cured him of too much taste for travel under the hard conditions then prevailing.

In 1834 there was published in Boston the first of his literary works, the now exceedingly rare *Prose Sketches and Poems written in the Western Country,* the preface to which is dated "Arkansas Territory, May 1, 1833." The book, undoubtedly the very first ever written by a man of considerable talent who realized to the full the local color of New Mexican life and scenery, was later supplemented by several articles published in Boston periodicals around 1835 and 1836. *Prose Sketches* is obviously the work of a young man of talent, eager to discover new material and capable of making a good deal out of it when discovered. The prose pieces are, undoubtedly, more interesting than the poems, which betray only too clearly the malign influence of Byron and Shelley. One of them, and that the longest, "Ariel," said to have been written on the prairie itself, is a complete pastiche from several of Shelley's poems, notably "The Witch of Atlas." So deep is the gloomy Byronism of several others, such as "Lines Written on the Rocky Mountains," "Moon in Santa Fé," "Taos," that one is almost led to suppose Pike to have fled from New England as the result of an early love affair which had turned out unfavorably.

It is probable that from the time of his arrival at Fort Smith Pike cultivated the long flaming locks and the uncut beard that distinguished him in later years. A great many of the worthies of the old West (down to the days of Buffalo Bill Cody) had the same habit of wearing their hair long and their beards uncut, since neither could be easily shorn or shaven, while living among the Indians; and some of them seem to have done so deliberately, the better to impress the redskins. Whether Pike actually acquired his flowing locks and his Jove-like beard earlier than the Civil War, I do not know: but there is no doubt that he was a man of commanding physical appearance and that he dominated from the start the frontier community in which his life was henceforth cast.

By 1836 he was already weary of his editorship of the *Advocate* and of partaking in the violent political squabbles of Little Rock; and during that year he retired from this task and obtained a license to practice law. He had already married, in 1834, Mary Ann Hamilton, a vivacious brunette, daughter of an early settler at Arkansas Post and, as it afterwards developed, a woman of violent and ungovernable temper. But his friends back in Boston kept urging him, apparently against his own inclinations, to make further attempts at literary fame; and accordingly, in August, 1838, he sent off to John Wilson, editor of *Blackwood's Magazine* in Edinburgh, Scotland, a man famous then and later as a critic under his pen name of "Christopher North," no less than nine long poems, some six hundred lines in all, entitled "Hymns to the Gods," which he had written between 1829 and 1830 and revised later. These, along with a covering letter, completely disarming in its tone, made their arrival at Edinburgh before the close of the year; and Wilson promptly published in full the strange contributions that had reached him "as a testimonial of respect offered by a resident in southwestern forests," and added to them this brief note: "These fine hymns which entitle their author to take his place in the highest order of his country's poets, reached me only a week or two ago."

This, in itself, should have been enough to encourage Pike to persist; but the fact remains that he did not do so. To the last of his life, he remained only occasionally and sporadically a poet; and the world has not endorsed "Christopher North's" verdict, rendered, it may be, hastily and summarily by a very busy man who was probably quite unaware of what was going on in America, who was, in fact, engaged at the time in weeding out from Tennyson's earliest poems the selfsame influences of Byron and Shelley that betrayed themselves only too clearly in Pike's efforts. The "Hymns to the Gods" reveal that Pike had read very extensively in the romantic poets I have mentioned; and that, like the earliest Keats, he depended far too heavily on Lempriere's *Classical Dictionary*. America—the country to which Pike, after all, belonged—simply appears nowhere in these poems. They are skillful exercises in rhetoric rather than transcripts from actual experience.

As a young lawyer Pike rapidly prospered; and in 1840 we find him, in company with Chester Ashley, Absalom Fowler, and William Woodruff, putting up one of the finest residences in early Little Rock. By 1851 his restless and dissatisfied temperament drove him to announce that he was meditating on settling in New Orleans, which he no doubt thought a better field for his talents; by the winter of 1852–1853 he was already visiting Washington. But even before that date he had done two things which were essential for any Southern gentleman of the old school. He had shown an interest in military affairs and had volunteered for a war; and he had taken part in a famous duel.

Military affairs were familiar to the Arkansawyers from the start, for shortly after the territory became a state in 1836, Andrew Jackson had withdrawn all troops from the Indian Territory in order to fight his long drawn-out war with the Seminoles, who, under their chief Osceola, were being driven by the United States to extermination in the Everglades. As soon as the troops were withdrawn from the Indian Territory, the Comanches, Pawnees, and Kiowas westward attacked the Choctaw, Cherokee, and Chickasaw settlements. Arkansas was requested by Jackson to raise a regiment of mounted volunteers; and this regiment remained in service at Fort Towson, on the Red River, till 1837.

In the fall of that year of statehood, Albert Pike—not to be outdone by his competitor Fowler, who had raised the first company for this service in the Indian Territory—had himself organized another company of Arkansas Artillery. Equipped with two six-pounder field guns, this company, which seems never to have left Little Rock, was in great demand for parades and displays, and became expert at drilling, either ahorse or afoot. To the citizens it was always known as "Pike's Artillery." The uniform worn in winter, we are told, consisted of a full suit of black broadcloth, the coats being of the swallowtailed variety, faced with red. A wide gold band of braid ran down the seams of the trousers; and the headgear were shakos of black beaver, with red pompons. In the summer the company wore gray blouses with red trimmings, white duck trousers, and gray fatigue caps. Guns, sabres, and muskets were all furnished by the state; but the uniforms, as well as the horses, no doubt, are said to have been provided by the members themselves.

At the head of such a company, Albert Pike, with his long hair and beard, must have looked and behaved like a god; and everyone was, quite properly, in ecstasies over him. He was, by this time, in much demand as an orator on important social occasions; he was known as a poet; he was one of the most prominent lawyers in the state; and except for the fact that he seems to have completely eschewed politics after 1833, he was the most eminent man in Arkansas, with a fine house containing a large and extensive library, much borrowed by his neighbors and friends. In 1843, he advertised in the *Gazette* that no less than eighteen of its books were missing—mostly novels. In the same year, the old burying-ground of Mount Holly, at his request, was officially given to Little Rock as its first cemetery.

I do not know whether—though known as a Whig—Pike took any

part in the riotous election campaign of 1840, the famous "log-cabin and hard-cider campaign," when a big canoe, brought down from Batesville in sections, was solemnly paraded through the streets of Little Rock, with a log cabin at the prow, upon the roof of which was perched a live raccoon—all followed by a huge crowd chanting "Tippecanoe and Tyler, too," and "Van, Van is a used-up man." Despite this campaign, the first in which such publicity methods were used, the Arkansawyers remained obstinately Democratic; and Pike apparently did not commit himself too far in support of the Whigs. By 1843, when Woodruff founded the first circulating library in Arkansas, Pike's neighbors may have been finally persuaded to stop rifling his library: so all about him was peace and content.

Three years later, early in 1846, Pike proudly named, in a poem that has come down to us, five oaks that stood on the lawn of his home at Chestnut (later Seventh) and Rock streets, after his five children. The tallest one was named for Hamilton, "our little manly boy," who survived his father; the second, for Walter, a merry, affectionate imp of mischief, who was killed in the Civil War; the third, "for our silent little girl, the quiet Isadore, who sits demurely working at her doll's new pinafore." Isadore died, by her own hand, after she had accompanied her father to Memphis on his last flight from the state, in 1869. The fourth was for "blue-eyed Lilian, the merriest of all," who also survived her father; and the smallest was for the newly-born baby, named Albert. This last, on May 16, 1858, was drowned, at the age of twelve, while swimming in the Arkansas River and is now buried with two later-born infants in Mount Holly Cemetery at Little Rock.

When my father first took me, a child of three, to the "old Pike place," in the late summer of 1889, there were considerably more than five immense oaks on the lawn there, including stumps; and my youthful ingenuity was much taxed to find out which of these magnificent trees, far older than the house itself, were the ones that Pike had named after his five children. The old brick pigeon house, from which the "hundred snowy doves" had emerged "to settle on the grass" in the same poem, was still in existence, though disused; it has long since followed most of the oaks and all of the Pike children into oblivion. Also gone now, though outlasting my own childhood, was the name "Isadore Pike," scratched carefully with a diamond upon the pane of an upstairs window; but the legends of that place are still poignant in my memory. It was said that one of the Pike children had either jumped or fallen into a heap of burning leaves on the lawn and been burned to death; it was said that silver, buried since the Civil War, might still be found somewhere by digging; it was said that Mrs. Pike, in her last years, had once become so angry with a Negro servant who was brushing out her hair, as to drive the girl to leap out of the central window upstairs and break her leg on the downstairs verandah floor; it was said that the old lady's ghost had been frequently seen in the library downstairs, rocking herself in a certain rocking chair. All this, no doubt, served to color my youthful imagination.

This, however, is anticipating my story. In May, 1846, soon after Pike had written this poem, the United States finally went to war with Mexico over the disputed question of the Rio Grande boundary—Texas had been formally annexed in March of the year before—and this event, which stirred Arkansas as it did the nation, directly led to the first of a whole series of events which produced, in the end, Pike's famous duel.

News that the United States was actually at war with the neighbor republic reached Little Rock early in May. On the twenty-seventh of that month, the governor, Thomas S. Drew, an honest backwoods farmer who had come down from Vermont to Batesville, and who lived there in a log cabin before being pitchforked into politics by the reigning Conway-Johnson dynasty, issued a proclamation calling for the formation of a regiment of cavalry to serve in Mexico and for five companies of infantry to take the place of the troops on the Indian border, now all ordered south by old "Rough and Ready," Zachary Taylor. By June 19, eight companies of this mounted regiment had already been formed at Little Rock and supplied with arms from the arsenal built there five years before, by the United States government.

Albert Pike, you may be sure, commanded one of these companies, called "The Little Rock Guards"; Solon Borland—as violent a Democrat as Pike was a Whig—commanded another, also drawn from Pulaski County; and among other companies, the name of John S. Roane, Captain of "The Van Buren Avengers," stood out. Flags—bearing in the case of Pike's company the appropriate motto of "Up Guards and At 'Em"—had already been embroidered by patriotic ladies and presented. And no less a person than Archibald Yell of Fayetteville, the leading Democratic congressman for the state, had resigned his seat in Congress and come south to enlist as a private in Solon Borland's company.

By June 28, four companies took the military road southwest to Washington, which was the point where all were to assemble: by July 10, all ten companies were there, and proceeded to the election of officers. It is noteworthy that, in this election, Pike was passed over. Archibald Yell was chosen colonel, John S. Roane lieutenant colonel, and Solon Borland major. Pike, despite his flowing locks and Jove-like presence, remained a simple captain. The regiment moved on to San Antonio, where it arrived at the end of August. Pike was presumably annoyed at the way his name had been passed over. In any case, after arrival at San Antonio, his company, along with another, was detached from the regiment and put under an independent command.

On October 10 the Arkansas regiment, with other troops, crossed the Rio Grande. Meanwhile the Polk administration in Washington had been having its own troubles. The war was already proving so unpopular over large sections of the country that its tenure of office was threatened. The Whigs, sensing their advantage, were already plotting to nominate no less a person than General Zachary Taylor, who had already taken Monterrey. And Taylor, blunt and tactless as he was, had openly criticized the way the war had been handled and had let it be known that he would not decline the nomination. Moreover, Santa Anna, the most shifty master of intrigue as well as the best general that Mexico had, whom the war had found in exile at Havana, had been allowed to slip back to his country, where he had promptly forgotten all his promises to Polk's agents and was now engaged in raising a really good army. It was decided to detach troops from Taylor and put them under the command of Winfield Scott for an expedition aimed directly at Vera Cruz and Mexico City. Taylor had reluctantly agreed to reduce his army, so that this purpose could be effected.

Santa Anna, knowing that the Scott expedition could not be ready for some months, decided to move his new army—hurriedly drilled and equipped as it was—north against Taylor, who had fallen back to guard Saltillo. Taylor's troops, outnumbered by Santa Anna about three to one, had achieved only a partial concentration, thanks to the casualness of their commanders, when on February 22, 1847, Santa Anna's better disciplined and equipped host fell on them at the hacienda of Buena Vista, four miles south of Saltillo. The first day's fighting was indecisive, as Santa Anna had not yet brought up all his troops; the second day's battle nearly destroyed Taylor's entire army.

Only the vigor and resolution of Arkansas, Kentucky, and Mississippi riflemen managed to hold, in part, the barren mile-high plateau up which the Mexican cavalrymen and artillery charged and thundered. Archibald Yell was killed; even Pike, held in reserve, came up for one wild charge at the close of that desperate day. On the morning of the twenty-fourth, the Americans, exhausted and battered, expected final annihilation; but when they heard that Santa Anna had inexplicably retreated southward in the night, it is said that Taylor and Wool, his subordinate, fell into each other's arms, and hugged each other in delight.

Pike's company had played but a small part in this battle, though six days later he wrote a stirring poem about it; for the most part, he had been kept in reserve, guarding the supplies of the army throughout the decisive day. But Pike was not the sort of man to be cheated out of his share of the glory, as the sequel will show.

The Arkansas Regiment was mustered out in June, and it returned to its native regions. Before that date, as early as March 8, Pike, stung probably by the way he had been overlooked in the choice for officers, stated in a public letter, that "it is a sad thing that brave men, for they were brave, should be so destroyed for want of discipline. In the first place, the companies of our regiment engaged there (at Buena Vista), had been hardly drilled at all, except what the company officers had done. The Colonel and Lieutenant-Colonel had never drilled them since they left San Antonio." This letter stung Roane, who was lieutenant colonel, to the quick; and he promptly retorted that neither Pike nor his company had been part of the regiment after San Antonio, and that Pike had taken no very important part in the battle and was generally disliked by all, as a braggart and a liar. Whereupon Pike promptly challenged Roane to a duel.

The two men met on July 28, 1847, on the agreed duelling grounds: a sandbar in the Arkansas River, opposite Fort Smith, in what was then Indian Territory. News of the duel had got about, and there were a number of people present to witness it, including several Cherokee Indians. Pike stood up stream and Roane down; and while the seconds were loading the pistols, Pike waited coolly, smoking a cigar before the crowd to display his calmness. At the first fire, neither man was hit; Roane, as the party challenged, declared himself unsatisfied, and a second pair of pistols were loaded. At the second fire,

Pike's ball grazed slightly Roane's ear, and Pike's beard was just touched by Roane's ball. Pike now demanded, according to the code, a third shot, saying, "I want one more shot at him and will hit him in a vital part; I believe he has tried to kill me; I have not tried to hit him." This was agreed to by Roane, and by one of his seconds, Robert W. Johnson; but the other second, Henry Massie Rector, strongly dissented. A heated argument now arose among Roane's seconds; and Pike, along with his seconds and surgeon, withdrew and sat down on a cotton-wood log near by. Finally they saw Roane's surgeon approaching, "with slow and dignified step"; he beckoned to Pike's surgeon, and when that worthy doctor got up remarked: "Dibrell, it's a damned shame that these men should stand here and shoot at each other, till one or the other is killed or wounded. They have shown themselves to be brave men, and would fire all day unless prevented. The seconds cannot interfere, because that would be considered a derogation of their own party's honor. So let us surgeons assume the responsibility, and say they shan't fire again; unless they make this quarrel up, we will just go away and leave them to hurt each other as much as they want, and not be on hand to help them. What do you say?"

This novel appeal led to a reconciliation. The two men promptly agreed to bury the past, to forget the quarrel, and never to refer to it again; they shook hands, and became, apparently, good friends. Pike, however, was not altogether a good hand at burying the past, as his quite unjustified attack on Roane at the outset had already shown; and in later years, his habit of sulking and of feeling injured because something or the other had gone wrong with his pet schemes, kept continually getting the better of him. An opportunity for revenge came to Roane later on; and it was taken to the full, as we shall see.

The Roane party travelling to this duel had stopped for two days—during which Roane, it is said, carefully practiced his shooting—at the home of Henry Massie Rector's cousin, Major Elias Rector, one of the most prominent and certainly the most colorful inhabitant of early Fort Smith. As he was immortalized by Pike in a poem which does not deserve to be forgotten, as being "The Fine Arkansas Gentleman" par excellence, more must be said of him, by way of ending this chapter.

Elias Rector was a descendant of John Rector, said to have been born in 1717 in Germany, an early Saxon settler in Virginia, at Germantown, in Fauquier County. The name may have originally been Richter, later anglicised into Rector. His grandfather, Frederick Rector, born in 1750 in Fauquier County, married Elizabeth Wharton, and from this union came thirteen children, nine sons and four daughters—many of them later famous in the Southwest. One of the sons of Frederick Rector moved to Saint Louis sometime around 1800 and was the father of our Elias Rector, who came to Arkansas about 1825 as a young man, soon settled in Fort Smith, and became, under Jackson, first United States marshal for the Indian Territory, and later general Indian Agent for all the tribes settled west of the Mississippi—a position he held for sixteen years. He was so well known as a prosperous planter, famed throughout the Southwest for his lavish hospitality, that a famous hotel in New Orleans permanently bore his name on a silver plate before a door of one of its rooms, which he always retained for his annual visits. Sometimes he chartered an entire steamboat to take his cotton crop down the river. Unschooled, but possessed of a ready wit and courtly manners, he dominated the society of the small frontier garrison-town of Fort Smith. One peculiarity he had which we also find in Pike himself; he wore his hair long, like that of a woman; and tucked it up under his hat with a comb.

This circumstance led indirectly to a lucky escape which was so characteristic that it must here be told. Once at a ball in New Orleans—presumably in the Mardi Gras season—the ballroom was invaded by a drunken mob of rowdies. The lights were rapidly put out and the crowd began to push, shouting and shrieking, toward the doors. Rector, who was present, suddenly bethought him of a way to get out. He carefully let down his long hair; and the crowd, pushing and shoving, supposed that he was a woman and let him pass through. His period of magnificence, of fabulous parties held at his home, of equally fabulous trips made down river to New Orleans, came to an end completely at the time of the Civil War. Not wishing to take up arms against the South, yet being at heart opposed to secession, he fled to Texas and remained there in hiding for four years. He returned to find his fortune gone and his house occupied by the Federal troops. He died finally, a broken man, in 1878.

It was of this worthy that Pike, in the winter of 1852–1853, at Washington, his wits fired by the liquor of a gay party held to celebrate Rector's recovery from an illness, improvised on the spot these lines, said to be a parody of an old English drinking-song, known as "The Fine Old Scottish Gentleman":

"Now all good fellows listen, and a story I will tell
Of a mighty clever gentleman who lives extremely well
In the Western part of Arkansas, close to the Indian line;
Where he gets drunk once a week on whiskey and immediately sobers
himself up completely on the very best of wine,
A fine Arkansas gentleman
Close to the Choctaw line!

"This fine Arkansas gentleman has a mighty fine estate,
Of five or six thousand acres or more of land, that will be worth a great
deal some day or other, if he don't kill himself too soon, and will only
consent to wait;
And four or five dozen negroes that would rather work than not;
And such quantities of horses, and cattle, and pigs, and poultry, that he
never pretends to know how many he has got;
This fine Arkansas gentleman
Close to the Choctaw line!"

In the later verses, Rector goes down to New Orleans, on his annual pilgrimage:

"This fine Arkansas gentleman makes several hundred bales,
Unless from drought or worm, or a bad stand, or some other damned
contingency, his crop is short and fails;
And when it's picked and ginned and baled, he puts it on a boat,
And gets aboard himself likewise, and charters the bar, and has a devil of
a spree, while down to New Orleans he and his cotton float.
This fine Arkansas gentleman
Close to the Choctaw line!

"The last time he was down there, when he thought of going back,
After staying about fifteen days more or less, he discovered that by
lending and by spending, and by being a prey in general to gamblers,
hackmen, loafers, brokers, hosiers, tailors, servants and many other
individuals, white and black,
He had distributed his assets and got rid of all his means;
And had nothing left to show for them, barring two or three headaches,
an invincible thirst, and an extremely general and promiscuous
acquaintance in the aforesaid New Orleans;

This fine Arkansas gentleman,
Close to the Choctaw line!"

After this New Orleans escapade, Rector comes up to Washington, is robbed again, and falls ill:

"So when his moneys were all gone, he took unto his bed,
And Dr. Reyburn physicked him, and the chamber-maid, who had a great affection for him, with her arm held up his head;
And all his friends came weeping 'round, and bidding him adieu,
And two or three dozen preachers whom he didn't know at all, and didn't care a damn if he didn't, came praying for him too;
This fine Arkansas gentleman,
Close to the Choctaw line!

"They closed his eyes, and laid him out all ready for the tomb,
And merely to console themselves they opened the biggest kind of a game of faro right there in his room;
But when he heard the checks, he flung the linen off his face,
And sang out just precisely as he used to do when he was alive, 'Prindle, don't turn! Hold on! I go twenty on the king and copper on the ace!"
That fine Arkansas gentleman,
Close to the Choctaw line!"

Pike stated in his later years that this song was first sung at a party at which Rector himself was present. No doubt Rector was extremely proud of it, and—though he may sometimes have pretended not to be—Pike was, too. They had good reason to be, for in these careless-seeming lines, the typical old Arkansas plantation magnate—Southern and yet Southwestern—lives again, vividly, once and for all. Ten years later, and all was lost for the "fine Arkansas gentlemen" and their kind—all but a desperate and hopeless retreat before the forces that slowly strangled them and brought them down to annihilation.

It is not to be supposed, however, that all prominent Arkansawyers in that day were of Pike's and Rector's kind; nor that these, dominant as they were, were entirely representative of the entire population. Woodruff, for example, was markedly abstemious throughout his life; he never drank, and only occasionally smoked a cigar. Absalom Fowler, Pike's great rival at the law, was—though he too, lived in a superfine house—stern to the point of forbiddingness. The Conways and the Johnsons were all eminently respectable; they had nothing to do with sprees or faro tables. But a quality of open-handed generosity and hospitality prevailed among all; no one really admired a mean man. And all were frank at expressing their opinions. To these qualities, men like Pike and Rector merely added a touch of Western devil-may-care recklessness.

Meanwhile, over a good half of the state, throughout the Ozarks, the population remained independent dirt farmers, knowing little of either cotton or slavery. They had learned, by hard effort, to be self-sustaining; and though they had little control over politics, they preserved their own ways.

Here nearly all the farmers raised sheep, and their wives and daughters carded, spun, and wove the wool into most of their clothing. Corn, garden-truck, sorghum, cattle and pigs provided all the provision necessary for man's needs; and small patches of tobacco were regularly grown—they still are, in the hills—to help in man's comfort. In the woods were venison, wild turkey, wild ducks, opossum and bear meat to be had for the hunting; there were also wild pecans, persimmons, and a curious array of herbs thought to be useful for most human ills. Candles and bullets and moccasins were made at home, and also whiskey; all that men and women required to buy, except for horseshoes and agricultural implements, were hats, shoes for party days, rifles, sugar and coffee, quinine and other articles of the common pharmacopoeia, gunpowder (difficult to manufacture, though often tried), and luxury things such as a fine dress, or ribbons. Men kept themselves in skill as agriculturalists by holding informal plowing contests, cotton-pickings, corn-huskings; cabins were made of logs—it took two men a whole day to square and trim about three twenty-foot logs—and a "log-raising" was a feast to which all must come and be fed. Hunting skills were kept up by prize matches, in which men "shot for a beef"; eight men being usually selected with eleven shots granted to each, and the best six shots out of each eleven counted for the five prizes, which were the four quarters of an ox, and the animal's hide, hoofs, and tallow. Sometimes an extra prize was added in the shape of the bullets used and retrieved from the target. The targets for each man were small square pieces of paper fastened to blackened boards, set up at about forty yards' distance; and it is said that the whole eleven shots of a single marksman could be covered with half-a-dollar. A really good shot could hammer in a nail with his rifle.

All that these independent hill farmers of the Ozark region needed and could not provide for themselves amounted to so little by comparison with what they could, that it is small wonder that a good many of them felt altogether too independent to take much interest in either the causes or the possible consequences of the oncoming war. When it came, many bent their chief energies to standing aloof, unless caught and forced to enlist by Confederate recruiting officers. It was not until the Missouri border was ravaged by jayhawkers and bushwhackers, operating from both sides after the spring of 1862, that most of them felt like fighting anything; it was not until the notorious Reconstruction militia in 1868–1869 ravaged the state, that they suddenly realized they were Southerners after all. Not that they lacked courage. They had courage enough for anything. But they were simply aloof and indifferent. They preferred to let the city folks come their way, rather than to go to theirs.

They were not, like the plantation owners of the eastern half of the state, shackled hand and foot to a one-crop economy. Slavery was, indeed, already breeding the thing that would have eventually destroyed it, had there been no war: the broadcloth-wearing plantation owner, far more than the homespun-clad mountaineer, was frequently drawn by his debts down to the very verge of ruin. Fortunately for him, after the depression of 1837 had died away in the early forties, there were, for a time, no more depressions; and he and his kind sided with Davis and the entire Confederacy in agreeing that cotton was king. But even the plantation owners, so far as Arkansas was concerned, lived in less great state than many of the highly paid lawyers. At Little Rock, Pine Bluff, Helena, Batesville, Fort Smith, Searcy, Camden, Washington—and around the rising watering place of Hot Springs, there were now colorable imitations of a fairly well-settled urban society. Here were hotels, with wines, ales, cigars; here were fine lofty-columned brick or frame houses; here from 1834 onwards were theatricals, amateur or professional; here were churches—not the rude campmeeting grounds of the remote wilderness. Steamboats and stagecoaches visited these places. And the fine Arkansas gentlemen who moved on their streets walked in pomp, attired in broadcloth, rather than linsey-woolsey; while their women had sometimes ribboned bonnets and carriages and silk dresses and fine fans to flaunt before the beholder.

Nine

THE WAR CLOUD LOWERS

In Arkansas in the fifties, the young bride, just married, put on her best clothes, known then as the "infare dress," and the day after the wedding, with the newly made groom, rode off on horseback or drove by wagon to the "infare feast" at the home of the husband's oldest relative. Steamboats tooted for a crossing through the silence of tender-leaved forests; rural camp-meetings were held in early summer, after the cotton had been chopped and laid by, at "brush arbors" by the roadside, with much singing and shouting, much praying and repentance, and with the solemn ducking of a dozen or so white-clad figures in the nearby creek; rural doctors mounted their nags, carrying in their saddlebags huge doses of calomel, quinine, and tartar emetic, and rode here and there on their missions of healing; wagons laden deep with cotton, driven by brawny Negroes and drawn by stout mules, rolled up to the gins in October; and hunters tramping the woodlands in late fall followed the tracks of does, sighted wild turkeys in the underbrush, saw squirrels swarming into cornfields like an army, watched the sky blacken with wild pigeons, noted the gaps in the green canebrakes where the big brown bears had crept through to find a spot for the winter.

Many of these phenomena of Arkansas life in 1860 have survived, in one way or another, down to the threshold of today; but the Arkansas that followed after 1865 was profoundly different from the Arkansas that went out of the Union in 1861. After Appomattox the people of the state, though they succeeded in getting the better of Reconstruction, lived by a myth—the myth of the perfect South, which had never really existed. That myth dissipated slowly after 1900. But the lingering traces of its passing may still be found for the seeking, even today.

For ten years after 1849 the state had been prosperous, with a prosperity never before known. There were, it is true, some fine financial snags still set in the path of its progress. As we have seen, in 1839, both the State Bank and the Real Estate Bank had suspended all specie payments and closed their doors; in 1843, the affairs of the State Bank—over a million and a half dollars in debt—were liquidated; but the Real Estate Bank—in which the Conways were involved—had still opposed every plan of liquidation.

By 1855, after Congress had already reached its last compromise on the subject of slavery, and while Lincoln was carrying on his running political fight with Douglas over the question of slavery in the territories, Governor Elias N. Conway, who held office for a longer time than any other incumbent (1852–1860) had finally attempted a thorough investigation of the Real Estate Bank's affairs. Since 1842 that institution, in order to forestall any such investigation, had been in the hands of fifteen trustees as receivers. The state was forced in the end to bring suit against the trustees to recover its own property. Conway's investigation revealed a dreadful state of affairs. Among other things, $500,000 in state bonds, issued to support a branch bank in Van Buren, had been taken out of the state by the cashier of that bank, around 1840, and sold for $121,366 cash to a trust company in New York—which promptly had resold them for $325,000 to James Holford and Company, of London, England, a private banking house. The $121,000 obtained had been spent by the trustees long before Elias Conway began winding up the bank's affairs—but the Holfords in person had started a suit against the state for principal and interest on their bonds, which had never been met. Their debt had been upheld by the state supreme court; yet it remained uncollected through Civil War and Reconstruction, and was not finally repudiated until 1884. Except for this debt—a legacy from the Jacksonian days of finance—the state was largely prosperous; and the chief topics under discussion during the fifties were the building of new schools and the construction of railroads.

Not a penny of taxes had ever been raised for schools; such free schools as existed were supported by the sale of public lands; but in the fifties a number of paid schools were chartered, including no less than four colleges, not one of which exists today—not to mention St. John's College, planned by the Masons as early as 1850 and finally built next door to the arsenal in Little Rock. It opened its gates on the eve of the Civil War, to represent, with its castellated main building and uniformed cadets, a dream which never came to full fruition. Among the other four colleges, Cane Hill, a once-famous denominational institution, was at first situated, in 1850, at remote Booneville; but it soon moved to Cane Hill itself, west of Fayetteville, then a famous town, from which in 1849 two or three hundred people had volunteered to go to California. Cane Hill had eighty-eight students enrolled in 1859, among them some Cherokees; and it was controlled by the Cumberland Presbyterians. At Fayetteville, in a prosperous apple-growing district colonized by Missourians from across the Ozarks, was Arkansas College, from 1852 onward, controlled by Methodists of a somewhat Northern cast; it became famous for being the first Arkansas institution to grant a master's degree, in 1859; and in its first year it had an enrollment of seven juniors, six seniors, eleven freshmen, twenty-one preparatory students, twenty-four in the English department, and sixty-three primary students—one hundred and thirty-two in all. The other colleges were insignificant. But Female Seminaries abounded at Little Rock, at Cane Hill, and at Fayetteville; and the interest in education was growing.

About one third of the area of the state was still owned by the United States government, and although large public subscriptions had been raised and two million acres of land allotted, the only railroads anywhere near the state were the Cairo and Fulton, which, pushing down from Saint Louis southward, had not yet reached the Arkansas border; and some forty miles of construction on the Memphis, Little Rock and Fort Smith Railroad, which ran only from Memphis to the Saint Francis River. The next section of this road, from Little Rock to De Vall's Bluff on the White River, was not finished till 1862, in the dark days of the war. The record-breaking journey between Little Rock and New York in the fifties took eleven days.

Despite its lack of railroads, the state now had flourishing coal mines up river at Spadra; salt works near Arkadelphia on the Ouachita, a small clothing factory at Murfreesboro in the southwest, and a number of other infant industries. In the months between November 1, 1858, and June 30, 1859, there had arrived at the Little Rock landing no less than three hundred and seventeen steamboats—well over one a day. Little Rock had now risen in population to 3,720 inhabitants, but it was not until the spring of 1860 that it was lighted by gas, the lamps being kindled every evening by two lamplighters, known as Dick and Ben, who carried a lantern and a ladder and were frequently accompanied on their rounds by a crowd of curious small boys. Lest this fact be assumed to display some special primitiveness, let me hasten to assure the reader that I have myself seen the time when many of the outer suburbs of London, England, were lit in much the same way.

Primitive in another sense Little Rock undoubtedly was, for it had few sanitary and drinking conveniences. People still drank from wells and from nearby springs; and modern sewerage was nonexistent. The famous "town branch," a muddy creek apt to be much swollen after rains, ran through the heart of town, coming down West Orange Street (now West Capitol Avenue) to Main, and running down one side of Main Street nearly to the river. It is said that its waters served to turn the wheel of the largest flour mill west of the Mississippi River, at the corner of Orange and Center; but this is scarcely believable, for in dry weather this town branch became a mere gully. At all events, a flour mill did stand there, and next door to it was a market house, a large frame building with latticed doors back and front, where farmers coming into town hitched their teams to posts in adjacent wagon yards and sold their produce. This market house stood till it became a nuisance, many years after the war. The business district proper was five blocks farther down, close to the steamboat landing and the intersection of Main and Markham streets. In 1857 there were thirty firms here in business, including a well-established bookseller and a bookbinder. The town branch threaded its way through this district, spanned by several wooden bridges; and it is said that on warm evenings householders who lived on its borders took their chairs out and sat on the bridges—though one of them, who tilted his chair back too far, fell in. Pigs were not uncommonly seen about the chief streets, and were considered quite useful as destroyers of garbage; and much the same conditions prevailed also in the national capital, up to the days of the Civil War.

As late as 1875, when the Anthony House burned down, the lack of fire-fighting equipment at Little Rock was painfully apparent. A bucket brigade of volunteers was then formed, which poured bucketfuls of water passed from hand to hand to the fire from a well a block away. Pine Bluff, the second city in the state, had about two thousand inhabitants; Fort Smith, the third, had only fifteen hundred. Over ninety per cent of the population in 1860 were still farmers.

How little the people surmised that the greatest conflict to be fought on the North American Continent was about to come upon them is shown by the state and the national elections of 1860. In April, 1860, the Democratic State Convention met; and since it was completely dominated by the Conway-Johnson dynasty, nominated Richard H. Johnson for the governorship and nearly adopted a platform endorsing Douglas for the presidency. Douglas was now generally disliked in the South as an adroit politician apt to blow both hot and cold on the subject of slavery; and the people were also generally tired of the Conway-Johnson faction, which had dominated them ever since statehood. The nomination of Johnson brought a leading newspaper, *The Old Line Democrat,* out in opposition; and at the close of April, another convention held at Helena, a prosperous river-boat town, boldly came out for Bell and Everett, the nominees of the Constitutional Union Party, who were for peace by conciliation, and vigorously denounced the Conway-Johnson party. It urged, particularly, that the Real Estate Bank bonds should be repudiated, as having been imposed on the state by the Conway faction, which was now trying to redeem them; and early in May, as a result of this action, Henry Massie Rector, second to Roane in the famous Pike duel, resigned his post as associate justice of the state supreme court and announced himself as an independent Democratic candidate on a platform favoring actual repudiation.

The state election, hotly contested, was held in August, after the Democratic National Convention, splitting into two factions, had by June nominated Breckinridge and Douglas as opposing candidates of its Southern and Northern wings, and after the youthful Republican party, about which no one in Arkansas knew or cared anything, had put up Lincoln at Chicago in May. Rector and Johnson then met in public debate; and Rector impressed everyone with his frank forthrightness, his boldness, the clear quality of his mind. He carried the election by a margin of two thousand; but the Conways and the Johnsons, biding their time, were waiting to undermine him; and later, during the war, they did.

The national election in November showed how conservative—as befitted a state still emerging from the wilderness—the Arkansawyers could still be. Breckinridge, the nominee of the slaveholders, had 28,730 votes; Bell and Everett got a little over 20,000; Douglas had only 5,227 followers, and Lincoln none. My father, then a young man of twenty-nine, told me, in my boyhood, that he himself had voted for John Bell, of Tennessee, and Edward Everett, of Massachusetts—in the hope, no doubt, that the "irrepressible conflict" following upon the Democratic split could still somehow be stayed. That hope, not uncommon in the upper South, was in vain.

On November 15, with the election of Lincoln an accomplished fact, Rector delivered his inaugural address in the guise of a message to the legislature. It was a first-rate effort. As to the state of the nation, he pointed out that no less than eleven Northern States had already prohibited their officials and citizens from aiding in the execution of the Fugitive Slave Law, though this had been upheld by a Supreme Court decision; that the issue was therefore, "one made up by the North and which we of the South will not be permitted to decline: either the Union without slavery, or slavery without the Union." This being the case, no further justification for secession was, in his view, really necessary; but it was remotely possible that Southern and Northern States might meet in a convention and agree to some sort of compromise; therefore he counseled no "hasty or precipitate action." Still, if "any one of the Southern States, prompted by just resentment towards the North, should deem it necessary to declare her independence and assert a separate nationality, Arkansas, having like grievances and a common purpose to subserve, ought not to withhold her own sympathetic and active support."

In another part of his address, Rector discussed in detail another question upon which he also held advanced views, that of education. He lamented that the state was "without colleges, male or female, suitable for imparting a knowledge of the higher branches." In consequence of this, he declared, many of the youth of the state were now being educated elsewhere, "which might tend to loosen the ties that bind them to the institutions of their native land." This process, too, he said, took thousands of dollars out of the state; and he recommended the establishment of two subsidized colleges. Since Arkansas at this time had 727 institutions listed as "public schools" (there was, however, only a little more than one teacher per school, and only twenty-five of them were entirely free), not to mention 109 private schools, with 168 teachers, and nearly 4,500 pupils, it may be thought that Rector was exaggerating the need for more institutions of learning. However, the five colleges then in the state had between them somewhat less than a thousand students. And there were still 23,640 illiterates in all Arkansas.

Apart from Rector's warnings, few—if any—were disposed to treat the situation of the state seriously in that year of 1860. No doubt, from November onward, there was much loose talk going on about one Southerner's being able to lick ten damn-yankees. The entire state was booming. The white population had more than doubled since 1850, and now stood at 325,000. The whites had come for the most part from the Southeastern States, and among them were but few foreigners, the Irish (1,312) and the Germans (1,143) furnishing the most, with less than a thousand for all others. The Negro population, too, had tremendously increased, from 47,100 in 1850 to over 111,000 in 1860. The value of taxable property had advanced four and a half times. The cotton kingdom, moving steadily westward out of the already exhausted lands of the Carolinas and Georgia, had definitely crossed the Mississippi. Labor was scarce; and good workable slaves, capable of being used or farmed out, were selling for prices well above a thousand dollars apiece. It was known already, thanks to the labors of David Dale Owen, the first state geologist, that Arkansas was rich in minerals; it was believed that silver and gold in considerable quantities lay in the Ozarks.

The region around Fayetteville was much divided in its sentiment on the subject of secession; around Batesville, on the upper White River, was another considerable group of Northern Unionists; but as 1861 dawned signs began to multiply that Arkansas might follow Rector's advice, after all, and get out of the Union. In December South Carolina had seceded; she was rapidly followed by Mississippi, Florida, Alabama, Georgia, Louisiana, and Texas, which, despite Sam Houston's refusal to sign the act, went out on February 1, 1861. On February 22, Jefferson Davis, newly elected provisional president of the Confederacy, took the oath of his office between the beautiful Corinthian columns of the old state-house in Montgomery, Alabama; a new flag, made for the occasion, was lifted to the breezes by a granddaughter of President Tyler; and thus the Confederacy, legally or not, was born even before Lincoln, closely guarded, took the oath in Washington on March 4. In Arkansas, too, things had moved with rapidity.

Rector signed on January 15 a bill just passed by the legislature calling for a convention of representatives of the people, by February 18, to decide whether or not the state should go out of the Union.

It may seem that Arkansas, and all the South, now acted precipitately, but the motives that prompted such action had been operating steadily for years. The South had become more determined than ever, since the discovery of gold in California and the admission of that territory as a free state, to defend—and if possible, to expand—its "peculiar institution." Hence the agitation over "squatter sovereignty" in Kansas and in Nebraska, which set Lincoln against Douglas. Hence the Dred Scott case of 1857, in which the Supreme Court declared not only that a Negro slave was always a slave, no matter where carried, but that the Missouri Compromise had never been constitutional at all. It was in vain for some of the more conservative Southerners, Whigs as they had been in principle, to try to distract attention from this overwhelming issue of slavery or no slavery by allying themselves with the "Know-Nothing" movement, which ran its brief course around 1856 and attempted to turn the crusade against slavery into a crusade against the Pope and against "foreign-born" Catholicism. Pike himself, now a great Freemason, had led that movement; but it got nowhere at all. From 1858, when a mass meeting in Little Rock was held urging the removal of all free Negroes throughout the state (it was believed that free Negroes were being used by Northern abolition agents to incite a slave revolt), the Arkansawyers, like all the rest of the South, were wavering on the crater's edge of actual civil war. The Northern States, through local "liberty laws," refused to obey the verdict of the Supreme Court handed down in the Dred Scott decision. The underground railway, which enabled fugitive slaves to escape to Canada, was more active now than ever in all the regions north of the Ohio River. One half of the Southerners talked about the abstract right of secession (no one had ever seriously questioned that abstract right); the other half were Unionists at heart, but watched anxiously for signs of a slave uprising. After John Brown's famous raid on Harper's Ferry in 1859, tension greatly increased.

In August, 1860, a destructive fire, causing losses of $400,000, broke out in Dallas, Texas, and about the same time similar fires broke out in eight other places. Soon after, a newspaper in Van Buren, Arkansas, carried the following scare headlines:

"Fearful Abolition Raid—Insurrection of Negroes. Ossowatamee Brown Among Us. Northern Texas to be Laid Waste. The Work Already Commenced."

Although John Brown's body was already "mouldering in its grave," this news may have had some basis in fact. To the Texans, now in a state of extreme excitement, living as they did on the far southwestern frontier with their borders unprotected from Comanche invasion, a sudden and destructive fire in Dallas might easily have seemed the warning of an imminent slave uprising. And on September 22, 1860, by coincidence perhaps, came the most destructive fire in the history of Fort Smith, which wiped out property valued at $112,000. Possibly all these fires were really the work of pyromaniacs. Whatever their cause, it was clear that a dangerous spirit was abroad.

Before this, on February 12, 1859, Governor Conway, as one of his last official acts, had signed a bill ordering all free Negroes out of the state by January 1, 1860. As we have seen, the Arkansawyers had made up their minds that these Negroes were dangerous. Thus, when Rector, in his inaugural address in November, 1860, mentioned secession as a strong possibility, he had spoken only what others were thinking and had been thinking for a long time: that the day had come for the South to defend itself. The Conway-Johnson families, though they were Rector's political opponents, agreed with him about this and were at least in favor of a convention to decide upon secession. So too, finally, was Pike, who, despite his Massachusetts ancestry and his Whig antecedents, now suddenly spoke loudly on the subject of Southern rights. One of his closest friends was Robert Toombs, of Georgia, a fellow Mason of the highest standing and a Southern hothead who took an active part in starting the Confederacy.

In February, 1861, Governor Rector again emphasized the secession sentiment expressed in his inaugural speech. Late in the preceding November, a company of some sixty artillerymen, under the command of Captain James Totten, had suddenly been moved by the Federal government from Kansas to the practically disused arsenal in Little Rock. This move, the purpose of which was never disclosed, led to a quickening of feeling. Kansas was well known as being a hotbed of abolitionism; and the citizens of Helena, being strong on the Southern side, promptly offered Governor Rector five hundred men to capture the arsenal. Wild rumors flew about that further reinforcements of Federal troops were already on their way. Rector replied that the arms in the arsenal would not be removed or destroyed if he could prevent it, and that he would see to it that no further reinforcements were sent. But despite this, early in February, a mob—from Helena and Little Rock and the surrounding territory—collected, said to be eight hundred strong, and at a mass meeting voted to lay siege to the arsenal. The mayor and city council of Little Rock, in a panic, begged Rector to intervene; excitement ran high. On February 6, Rector finally demanded the surrender of the arsenal to the state; and Totten and his men marched out with the honors of war on February 8—two months and more before Fort Sumter was fired upon. Since Arkansas was not officially out of the Union, Rector had no legal justification for this act; but no doubt he acted in accordance with his own convictions and with those of most of the citizens.

The State of Arkansas was now preparing to go out of the Union—although the citizens of Carroll County in the remote northwest of the state were still more interested in telling stories about the fifteen children, spared by the Mormons from the Mountain Meadows Massacre in far-away Utah in 1857, who had been ransomed and returned to their kinsfolk by 1859, than they were in secession. What had caused Arkansawyers to hesitate was, first, the fear that the Indians to the west, open as they were to abolition agents from Kansas, might be stirred up somehow to attack them; and, second, the unexpected amount of Unionist sentiment around Fayetteville, Fort Smith, and other northerly quarters. This was reflected in the first meeting of the convention to discuss secession, which assembled with seventy-five delegates present, on March 4, 1861, while Lincoln was delivering his first inaugural in Washington. By a vote of 40 to 35, a strong antisecessionist from Washington County in the northwest was elected president of the convention, though a sop was thrown to the slaveholders and slaveholding Cherokees by electing as secretary of the convention Elias Cornelius Boudinot, brilliant half-breed Cherokee lawyer, whose entire family had been strong upholders of the slaveholding faction among the Indians.

Four days after the secession convention had convened, on March 8, 1861, the telegraph line that was to connect Little Rock with Memphis and so with the outside world, and which had been building all the previous winter, was finally completed; and the people of Arkansas could thereafter learn promptly about the efforts which were being made in Tennessee, North Carolina, Virginia, Kentucky, and Missouri to get these states to follow the seven rebels that had already gone out of the Union—and also concerning President Lincoln's attempts to keep them from doing that very thing. It is doubtful, however, if this news, now available, had any effect on the final result. Living on the frontier had bred independence in the bone of most of the Arkansawyers. For over thirty years—more than a full generation of men—as an outpost of the South, they had become fully determined to settle this issue in their own way. With the acquired caution that the southwestern wilderness had already given them, it was probable that they would move as one man, in the end, but only under the pressure of outside events; they would move only if forced to make a decision. Although the state was mainly Southern, it was also a frontier state and had known prosperous times for only about ten years. The feeling of proximity to the Indian Territory and to Texas, which had governed so much of its early history, still persisted and controlled the issue in the end.

The same characteristic blend of caution and daring which pervaded Arkansas in that spring of 1861 is sometimes to be seen in the state even today. The Arkansawyer of the backwoods is singularly indifferent, as a rule, to what outsiders may say or think about him. Among his close friends and associates, he may usually treat his own failings as a joke; but woe to anyone who, from without, tries to change his characteristics. He then becomes like those wild razorback hogs first left behind in the woods of the state by De Soto—a veritable demon at fighting. So President Lincoln found out to his sorrow in that tragic spring of 1861.

Ten

THE STORM BREAKS

The best story that I have ever heard concerning the part that Arkansas played in the Civil War is about a family. The clan spirit in this state, as in other upland parts of the South, still ruled very strong; and in this particular family—pioneers in the Ouachitas to the southwest of Little Rock—it had been the rule from time immemorial, to hold a family council on the eve of undertaking anything very important. When it became clear that Arkansas was to go out of the Union, a council was held by the six fully grown sons who inherited the family name and property. It was decided to do two things. First, all the available cash—something over a thousand dollars—would be buried under a certain tree on the family plantation. Second, all the Negroes possessed by the family, some eighteen or twenty, would be handed over to the oldest brother, a man over forty, who from his youth on had shown a disposition to grow faint at the sight of blood, and who was therefore considered to be but poor military material. This man lived, as it happened, in a district difficult of access; and he was instructed to stay on his plantation and look after the Negroes and see to it that none ran away. That done, the five other men promptly volunteered to defend their state; and, by implication, the Confederacy.

These men were the descendants of East Tennessee pioneers. All of them had been born in Arkansas, to which their parents had come even before Arkansas was a territory. None of them had done anything noteworthy, anything at all to compare with the exploits of Ashley and

Pike and Crittenden and the Rectors, the Johnsons, and the Conways. But they had sustained themselves in a frontier territory—an effort demanding forty years of toil and vigilance—and had become men of substance. Like many other Southerners, they now owned slaves. Slaves were property, to be looked after like any other property. So, unlike the aristocrats among the planters, who were permitted by the Confederate government to stay at home and look after their Negroes and who buried their silver as the Federal army approached, they saw to it in the first place that their property was put away in a safe spot. Then, without arguing about the abstract rights and wrongs of secession, they prepared to defend themselves by joining the Confederacy.

Much the same attitude was taken here, then, as in Tennessee, Kentucky, Missouri—all Border States where sentiment was evenly divided between slaveholders and nonslaveholders. These states were, at the outset, but little impressed with the convention of seven seceding Southern States, which in February, 1861, elected Jefferson Davis to be the provisional president of the Confederacy. They cared little for Alexander Stephens' extremely legalistic and constitutional arguments concerning the right of secession. Nor were they entirely overcome by the fact that the Northern abolitionists had at last succeeded in electing Lincoln. They were busy with more concrete questions: how to raise log cabins; what was the best kind of religion; how to cure the milk sickness. Their minds were turned rather to the West than the East. And the West—except possibly Kansas—was indifferent to the war.

This explains, if anything is needed to explain, why Arkansas refused to secede until Lincoln, after the attack on Fort Sumter, issued his proclamation for seventy-five thousand volunteers to put down the dawning insurrection. Then, under pressure from without, the people acted promptly. Till then, though that new-fangled toy, the telegraph, had brought them every day new talk of secessions and defections, they were unwilling to make a move. Though Governor Rector—who combined both the pioneer and plantation slaveowner in his own person—had harangued them ably, pointing out that the Union was already dissolved and that secession could be made to pay, a small majority in the convention had voted down all propositions to go out, including a final one on March 17 to submit the issue of secession to popular vote, by a vote of 39 to 35. It is said that the inhabitants of Fort Smith persuaded the Federal garrison at that place to fire off a salute of thirty-nine guns, in honor of those who had thus kept Arkansas in the Union.

The convention finally adjourned on March 21, with no agreement reached except to send delegates to a Border-State convention, now requested by Virginia, Kentucky, and Missouri, set to be held at Frankfort, Kentucky, on May 21. It decided, however, to reconvene on August 19, or even earlier, if David Walker, its nonsecession president, should think that step to be necessary.

But events, rather than their own willingness or unwillingness to act, soon took matters out of their hands. Fort Sumter was fired upon on April 12; and on the fourteenth, it surrendered. Lincoln issued his celebrated call for volunteers to put down the rebellion; and on April 20, Walker signed a proclamation hurriedly reconvening the convention for the sixth of May. Even earlier than this, Rector, on his own responsibility, had acted. On the twenty-second, he had replied thus to Lincoln's secretary of war:

"In answer to your requisition for troops from Arkansas to subjugate the Southern States, I have to say that none will be furnished. The demand is only adding insult to injury. The people of this commonwealth are freemen, not slaves, and will defend to the last extremity their honor, lives, and property against Northern mendacity and usurpation."

A day before this—so fast had been the rush to volunteer—four companies of Arkansas recruits, including an artillery company, hastily drilled and equipped with the four good guns left in the Little Rock arsenal, under the command of William Woodruff's son, left in three steamboats, in response to Rector's call, to go up the river and capture the Federal arsenal at Fort Smith. Though some of these men were not even equipped with uniforms—the ladies of Little Rock, sitting up all night stitching away at gray jackets, had not been able to provide them fast enough—they had little difficulty in taking Fort Smith, for at their approach the commandant there promptly fled into the Indian territory.

On their way down the river, arriving back at Little Rock on the second of May, as one member of the expedition later testified, "Cheering was the order of the day, on shore and aboard. Artillery salutes and brass bands wore out all ears, patience, and 'Dixie.' By order we had two field pieces on the forecastle, firing salutes, which left a stink of sulphur and saltpeter, and a ribbon of smoke, from Belle Pointe to Petit Rocher." Arkansas had begun its little war with high good spirits, without even waiting for a decision upon secession; and the result of the convention was already a foregone conclusion. When it reassembled, on a magnificent May day, in a hall packed to suffocation with spectators, it promptly proceeded to vote on an ordinance of secession drawn up that very morning. The vote came at three in the afternoon, and out of the seventy delegates present, there were only five who had the temerity to vote "No." Isaac Murphy, a tough old frontiersman from the Missouri border, who had put behind him a varied career as pioneer farmer, backwoods schoolteacher, and unsuccessful gold seeker in California in 1849, was one of these dissentients. The four others all came from the same Ozark mountain region as he did himself.

At the announcement of the result, a great burst of applause—the first that day—roared through the room; and the president of the convention arose and requested the five men to withdraw their votes, and to make the result unanimous. Murphy alone dissented. His second emphatic "No," coming after the other four had all yielded, brought a sudden awkward silence, punctuated by a bouquet of flowers, suddenly flung by a woman sitting in the gallery, which fell at his feet. Arkansas was now out of the Union, but one Arkansawyer had abided by his frontier convictions. It is significant that Murphy did not resign, or even quit the convention. He remained in his seat, though his "No" was written into the record; and he boldly supported the convention during its further sessions.

The convention, emboldened perhaps by its own rashness, would not quit its post after once voting for rebellion. It remained in session till the close of May, passing numerous other acts, which included the adoption of a new—and badly drafted—Constitution, the raising of an "Arkansas Army," to be commanded by two brigadier generals, the subscribing of an "Arkansas War Loan" of two million dollars, and the confiscation of all public lands and moneys in the state. These actions, intensely imbued with the spirit of local independence, considerably embarrassed not only Rector but also the young Confederacy, which had appointed a Texas general to the command of the Southwest frontier, with instructions to stand on the defensive.

This decision for defensive warfare was an initial blunder on the part of the Confederacy, and it was dearly paid for. From the day that he had been inaugurated into office, Lincoln had set himself the task of holding the Border States to their loyalty to the Union. Virginia, Tennessee, Kentucky, Missouri were now all trembling in the balance; and in Missouri particularly, the same situation was repeating itself which had already occurred in Arkansas, between a secessionist governor and a loyalist convention. Had the Confederacy been willing to take the offensive at the outset, Missouri almost certainly could have been won; but it preferred to wait for an ordinance of secession, and none came. The chance for the Confederacy was to strike rapidly in all directions, before Lincoln had organized the North; but it was Lincoln, trained to political tactics in a state which had its own considerable minority of slaveowners and Southern sympathizers, who acted first in every instance.

Though the State of Arkansas was now spoiling for a fight, and ready to make one, the tragic fact remained that there were no arms to fight with—beyond the "squirrel guns" that these frontiersmen already had. By September of that year twenty thousand of the natives had gone into service. But Rector, soon after secession, had, that spring, frankly informed the convention that the state possessed only "ten thousand stand of arms for infantry, cavalry service for one regiment, with thirty pieces of artillery all told; the latter generally of small calibre, with many pieces unfit for service." Lead mines capable of producing bullets lay no nearer than Granby, Missouri, in doubtful territory; there was not an iron foundry in all of Arkansas; a small clothing factory in the southwest, near Nashville, was the only establishment of that sort; another, improvised at Little Rock about 1862, succeeded in producing some harness and a few wagons; but that was all.

The troops that invaded Missouri that summer and fought the battle of Oak Hill on August 10 were but half armed. Everyone had to bring his own clothes—uniforms there were none. Wagons were lacking, shoes were scarce, harness was made of rope—but there were plenty of mules and horses till close to the end. That, and spirit, were all the Confederacy in Arkansas ever had. In the opening weeks of July, a man standing at the corner of Main and Markham streets, in the heart of Little Rock, could discover no one walking in any direction for seventeen minutes by his watch. All men under sixty had gone off to the wars.

In the state capitol at Little Rock, the present Arkansas History

Commission has already listed the names of 58,000 Confederate soldiers. Granting that one out of three may be a duplication, this still leaves nearly 40,000; surely an astounding number for a state that in 1860 had a white population of only 325,000. Also, the State History Commission has listed the names of about 6,000 others, coming from Arkansas, who served in the Federal Army. Truly, there were few pacifists or shirkers among the frontiersmen.

In addition to all this, the Confederacy had at least secured one important diplomatic victory to itself, by insuring the tacit support of most of the Indian tribes settled west of its territory. In May, at Robert Toombs's insistence, Davis had sent Albert Pike to the Indian Territory as special commissioner to all the tribes, to negotiate treaties with them. And in this mission, Pike had the greatest success of his entire career. He had, though somewhat belatedly, thrown himself into the Southern cause that spring, having revised the words of the Negro-minstrel tune of "Dixie," now sweeping the South, to make it more full of patriotic sentiment; and his knowledge of the frontier, drawn from his own early experiences, stood him in good stead. All that summer he camped and travelled in the territory with a small mounted escort, displaying the Confederate flag openly and making no concealment whatever of his purposes. His portly figure, gross from too much good living, his Jove-like locks and beard, his knowledge of many languages, his stately formality, even his addiction to a long meerschaum pipe, were alike irresistible. As one observer put it, "As he sat before his tent, smoking and reading, the Indians, dismounting, looked on him in awe, as a God." By the end of August he had won the Creeks, the Choctaws, the Chickasaws, the Seminoles, the Cherokees, the Osages, the Shawnees, the Senecas, and the Quapaws to declare for the Confederacy. And even the wild Comanches, feared alike by the civilized tribes and the white men, had ridden in and promised "to hold the Confederate States by the hand, and to be of one heart with them always."

Unfortunately, the Cherokees, the most numerous and powerful of all the Indian tribes in the Indian Territory, had held out till the last; until, in fact, John Ross, the wily old chief who had come to the Territory with his people along the Trail of Tears, became convinced that the Confederacy was capable of winning victories. On August 10, the battle of Oak Hill—or, as the Federals called it, Wilson's Creek—was fought in Missouri, resulting in a defeat for the Federals and the death of their commander, the Connecticut-born Nathaniel Lyon. Ten days later Ross, who up to now had refused to negotiate, sent for Pike himself and asked for a treaty. And in that treaty—remarkable like all the others for granting to the Indians all they had ever claimed and failed to obtain from the Federal government for fifty years—there was written the stipulation that any military force the Cherokees might raise for the Confederacy should be used only as a home guard to protect their own lands, and should be stiffened with white troops. Whether Pike—who after some show of reluctance, agreed to command all the Indians—was actually sincere in accepting this concession wrung from him by Ross, nobody knows, or knew; and whether he meant to abide by it, was still anyone's guess.

The Confederacy in Arkansas—unaided as it was by the government, which moved to Richmond that summer to fight Bull Run and to fail to take advantage of its first victory—was at cross-purposes both politically and militarily. The ablest military man anywhere on the near horizon was Sterling Price, who as a Missourian and a slaveholder had been steadily forced by Lincoln and his aides, the Blairs, from a position of compromising neutrality to open alliance with the Confederacy. Fifty-one years old, with a distinguished career of service behind him, he was a Welsh Celt, with an unusual fund of expansive good nature, immense personal courage, and an irresistible charm for the Missouri backwoodsmen. It is said that he wore a high plug hat and a frock coat into battle at Oak Hill, since Missouri had not seceded; and it is certain that his men, largely unarmed and without uniform, called him "Old Pap Price" around their roaring campfires. He soon had about twenty thousand of them at his back, but the Confederacy, legalistic as it was, refused even to acknowledge that fact. Davis, who much disliked him, called him simply "the vainest man I ever met" and never troubled to give him a chance. His superior, McCulloch, had been a Texas ranger. He was coarse in speech, obstinate and tactless. Price handed over his entire army to him before Oak Hill was fought, only to see that victory thrown away. In an effort to compose the quarrel between the two men, the Davis government in November finally attempted to coördinate all commands by setting over everyone the young and ambitious Mississippi-born Van Dorn. But Van Dorn, unable to make anything out of the situation he found in Arkansas, only moved in time to meet a Federal invasion of northwest Arkansas at the end of February, 1862; and at the fiercely contested field of Pea Ridge, fought in bitterly cold weather on the seventh and eighth of March, the last chance to advance into Missouri was thrown away. Pike, in command of the Indians, disgraced himself by his general unsoldierliness; McCulloch was killed by a Federal sharpshooter in the early stages of the fight; and Price saw his Missourians cut to pieces and dispersed, never again to reassemble except as guerrillas and bushwhackers. Van Dorn, who had led them all to this supreme disaster, had now nothing to do but to retreat; and this he promptly did, following it up by moving all the Arkansas troops—twenty thousand of them—out of the state by the end of April, off to Tennessee, where Fort Donelson had already fallen earlier in February, where Nashville had been lost and Albert Sidney Johnston killed in the violently inconclusive battle of Shiloh on the sixth and seventh of April. The evil days of divided responsibility had already come for the Confederacy; and Arkansas, off on the western border and remote from Richmond, which was now threatened by McClellan's first great army, was naturally the first to feel the blow.

Eleven

ABANDONED AND BETRAYED

With the battle of Pea Ridge and the defeat at Shiloh, where the best hope of a victory over the still untried Grant was lost, the war, which had begun as a picnic to most Arkansawyers only a year before, had turned into a disaster. From this time on, it was every man for himself; and certain Arkansas characteristics, still familiar today, were greatly accentuated in the months that followed.

The mountaineers, in particular, became at this time both aloof and suspicious in their dealings with the world outside. Many of them had not wanted to fight at all, for few of them had been slaveholders. Their attitude toward both sides had been that of the squatter to the Arkansas Traveller in the celebrated story—"Ye kin git to go to hell." They resented being bothered with the issue which divided the country. They had controlled the convention which had refused to do Rector's bidding; and they did not vote an ordinance of secession until it was forced upon them. Many of them refused to enlist till recruiting agents rode through the outland districts telling them the war was on and they must take sides. By this time, the Confederate Congress at Richmond had voted conscription—but owners of twenty slaves or more were exempt, and it was possible to avoid personal service by hiring a substitute. In the eyes of the Ozark people, that made the war frankly "a rich man's war but a poor man's fight." And it bred in them a tendency towards suspicious isolationism, combined with lawlessness, which has persisted, and which contrasts very strongly with their free and easy indifference of "The Arkansas Traveller" days.

Governor Rector had fully foreseen the consequences of one lost battle and had summoned his legislature as early as the last week of February, 1862, to meet in extraordinary session on March 5. He knew that the rush to volunteer, of the previous summer, which had brought almost half the male population to the colors, would lead to nothing permanent in the event of a long war. Most of these volunteers had already been mustered out without ever having been armed or equipped, or having seen battle. Now the question arose whether they would rejoin the Confederacy unless compelled to do so by conscription. Van Dorn, after the débâcle of Pea Ridge, had got back at last to Van Buren, with little more than half his army—the rest were dispersed or scattered. Price, a commander without a command, went with him; but all that Van Dorn could do was to announce that he intended to make his headquarters henceforth in the northeast part of the state near the Mississippi. This meant that the northwest part was abandoned—except to Pike who had moved back into the Indian Territory, reinforced with two companies of infantry and Woodruff's battery—and to the desperate Missourians, now turned guerrillas and bushwhackers.

Rector, no doubt, was increasingly bitter at the thought that the legislature called for March 5 did not assemble till March 17, when Pea Ridge had been fought and lost, and St. John's College, turned into a hospital, was so full of sick and wounded that four or five other houses in the city had to be commandeered to take care of the overflow. But neither Rector nor anyone else could control the vagaries of the climate, which that month turned out sleet and bad weather in such profusion as to make all travel nearly impossible. Van Dorn, at Van Buren, did not move towards his new base at Pocahontas till the close of March; and his opponent, Curtis, at Fayetteville, which had been ravaged by both armies, did not move at all.

When the legislature finally got together, it was of one mind with Rector. The extraordinary session lasted only six days, but it produced an astonishing amount of really first-rate law-making. Acts were passed which prohibited the further distillation of all grain into spirituous liquors; the further sale of public lands was prohibited till the close of the war, and these lands were pledged to the redemption of the state war bonds already floated; the families of all volunteers were to be provided for; and there was also passed an act defining and punishing sedition. Anyone henceforward who discouraged volunteering was to be given not less than three or more than five years' imprisonment. Further, it was also voted that anyone found cultivating cotton to the extent of more than two acres per field hand would be indicted for misdemeanor, and if proven guilty would be fined not less than five hundred or more than five thousand dollars. All this came at a time when Davis's secretary of the treasury, hopelessly wrong, was encouraging everyone to subscribe their cotton to the Confederate War Loans—in the hope of eventually shipping it abroad to Europe despite the blockade! Truly these backwoodsmen showed grim common sense, although their actions were somewhat in the nature of locking the stable door after the steed had been stolen.

Rector, who must have been momentarily proud of their accomplishments, was not permitted to stay in peace for long. The only Confederate army in the state now lay on the northeast border, around Jacksonport and Pocahontas, and was in command of Earl Van Dorn. That soldier, whether rightly or wrongly, decided that it was his business to transport his entire army to the threatened east bank of the Mississippi and take part in the desperate fight now raging to hold some part of Tennessee against the advancing Federals. Price, as always far too easy-going, apparently did not disagree with him; and so, at the close of March, Van Dorn began to prepare for this step by appointing subordinates (including Pike) to take his place in Arkansas. By the end of April, Van Dorn had succeeded in moving his entire army, twenty thousand strong, by road and steamboat out of Arkansas; and the state was practically without defenders of any sort.

At this news, Rector fairly exploded; he had been frank enough in the past, and he was far franker now. General Samuel Curtis, the victor of Pea Ridge, still lay with his army around Fayetteville, but the entire state was open to him. Rector at first threatened to set up the capital at Hot Springs—a course from which he was barely dissuaded. On May 5, in a proclamation calling for more volunteers, he let it be known that Arkansas had been used by the Confederacy to the point of what, in his opinion, was betrayal into the hands of the enemy; that the state must very shortly "build a new ark and seek its own safety"; that, in brief, secession was again in order! This was too strong a medicine for the Johnsons, the Conways, and their factions, who were still smarting under the defeat that Rector had administered to them back in 1860; they recalled that the new Constitution of 1861, voted by the convention, had called for a new election to state offices in 1862, and they bided their time.

By this time, about six hundred sick and wounded Confederates, wreckage of Pea Ridge and Shiloh, were overcrowding the halls of Saint John's College. Others were in six or eight buildings—including Christ Episcopal Church, built since 1843—scattered about town. On May 15 the city council of Little Rock bought, chiefly from William Woodruff, a plot of land on the southeast border of the city, forested mainly in oaks, as a cemetery for soldiers. That cemetery, known as Oakland, exists today, and Federals and Confederates are mingled in the democracy of death within it. Rector, indifferent to the fact that such acts were unpopular, now put all the state under martial law; and under his orders more than three hundred thousand bales of cotton on the Arkansas River were burned to prevent them from falling into the hands of the Federals, whose gunboats had already appeared on the Mississippi, both north and south of the Arkansas. Thus the crop of 1861, a very good one, was almost completely lost. The early summer of 1862 brought heavy floods, and a poor crop to take its place.

Meanwhile, General Curtis, whose skill at choosing his own ground and standing on it at Pea Ridge, was equalled only by his later caution in advancing, had moved his army so slowly that it was not till May 4 that they again reestablished themselves. Curtis had ignored Little Rock completely and, moving leisurely southeast, went off to Batesville on the upper White River. Here he could be reached by gunboat from the Mississippi and could also keep up a line of communications by road and by telegraph with Missouri; he could also threaten the entire country as far east as the Mississippi, as far south and west as the low ridge that guards Little Rock northward of the city. Fayetteville and the whole northwest were now abandoned to the jayhawkers and the bushwhackers; it lay as a no-man's land between bands of armed ruffians, fighting under the black flag, until August of that year. Only the line of railroad, which had been rushed to completion at the end of January, from Little Rock to De Vall's Bluff, on the White River, afforded Little Rock any protection; and it, too, might soon be cut by Curtis's cavalry.

The city was, however, soon protected, and that by as remarkable a man as Arkansas had ever seen. Thomas Carmichael Hindman, a young Scot who had been born at Knoxville, Tennessee, and who had lived in Mississippi before coming to Arkansas in 1856, had, before he was twenty, once before distinguished himself for gallantry, in the Mexican War. At Helena, where he had settled down to an active life as lawyer and politician, he had been elected as one of Arkansas's congressmen in 1858. In 1860, he had been reelected by throwing his support to the side of Rector and by touring the state in the anti-Johnson interest. He was an able and forceful speaker, as hot a secessionist as was Rector himself, and a soldier, as it proved, of daring and resource. At Shiloh, where 3,500 Confederates had been killed and more than 16,000 wounded, he had made himself conspicuous for his gallantry, and had been promoted to the post of brigadier general by Pierre Gustave Toutant Beauregard, the Louisiana creole who had to finish the battle begun by Albert Sidney Johnston.

Beauregard, uneasily aware that Van Dorn had quitted his command in Arkansas to join with him in guarding the all-important railroad junction of Corinth, Mississippi, which linked Richmond with Chattanooga and Vicksburg, and aware also of the growing despair in Arkansas, was persuaded, perhaps by Hindman himself, to send Hindman back to Arkansas with positive directions to take charge of that entire region as well as the Indian Territory, and to reorganize both for defense. Without waiting for the Confederate Congress or for Davis himself to endorse Beauregard's decision, Hindman swung into action.

His success was astounding, and must have surprised even Hindman himself. Before Memphis could capitulate to the attack of the Federal gunboats—which it did on June 6—Hindman, dark-bearded, tough, and magnetically resolute, was back in Arkansas, having raised the then enormous sum of over a million dollars from the bankers of Memphis to outfit a prospective army. This Helena lawyer-politician who, unlike his famous fellow-townsmen, Patrick Ronayne Cleburne, had not come up the hard way and had no mean opinion of his own abilities, had taken good care to obtain medical supplies, blankets, and much ammunition by denuding every shop in Memphis and Helena, as well as the United States marine hospital at Napoleon. He had brought with him no less than twenty-six guns, including a sixty-four-pound siege gun, brought up river by the gunboat *Pontchartrain,* which was duly unloaded at Little Rock and set there on the south bank, with its nose pointing to the enemy. He proclaimed martial law, and declared he would enforce it—and he was as good as his word.

Further, he ordered that any citizens who wished to do so could organize themselves into companies and operate independently of any command—a mode of war that the backwoodsmen enjoyed and understood. Curtis, off at Batesville, was soon enough quaking in his shoes. He affected to believe, and probably did believe, that Hindman was bringing back into Arkansas the entire army of Van Dorn.

Curtis had found at Batesville a warm welcome from the Unionist section of the population—what slaveholders there were in his district soon packed up and moved off, in wagons, to Texas. Old Isaac Murphy, with his blue eyes that looked as if they were forever watering, and with his unshakable convictions, went around urging all the mountaineers he could find to join a brigade that was forming in the far northwest of the state. Elisha Baxter, of Batesville, whom we shall see later playing a great part in Arkansas's next bad crisis, helped to raise a Federal regiment at Batesville, and was offered the colonelcy, which he refused because, as he said, he did not wish, after all, to make war on his own people. This lame excuse left people wondering whether he was not a coward.

Hindman, on his arrival at Little Rock, found only some three or four regiments of Texas cavalry, eight companies, all unarmed, of Arkansas infantry, and six guns without any artillerymen. Nevertheless, from his arrival, armies seemed fairly to sprout from the ground. In particular the Arkansas cavalry and the Missouri cavalry, under the command of those picturesque daredevils, J. S. Marmaduke and Jo Shelby, were intensely active. They fairly rode around Curtis's army of occupation at Batesville, cutting off his line of communications through Missouri once for ten days, and capturing wagons and supplies and even his telegraphic correspondence with his superiors in Missouri. An old gunboat, the *Maurepas,* was ordered up the White River from the Mississippi, and successfully destroyed supplies under the very noses of Curtis's outlying camps.

It was a magnificent effort, akin in its daring onrush and power of improvisation, to the speed with which Arkansas had been opened to immigration in 1819, the impetuosity of the gold rush in 1849, the outbreak of the Civil War. But it could not last. Memphis had fallen on June 6; and the Federal gunboats held the line of the Mississippi clear down to Vicksburg. At the middle of June, in answer to Curtis's frantic appeals for help over his newly-repaired telegraph line, four big ironclads suddenly appeared at the mouth of the White River, the

Saint Louis, the *Mound City,* the *Conestoga* and the *Lexington.* The old *Maurepas* was still in the river, but its captain, Joseph Fry, a man to be remembered by all Arkansawyers, knew that his single unarmored boat could offer no resistance. Thirty miles up stream from the mouth of the river was, and is still, the now much-decayed old river-boat town of Saint Charles, with some low sandy bluffs, about twenty feet high, on the west bank of the river. Here Fry—he was to be caught and executed by the Spaniards eleven years later as the leader of an American filibustering expedition into Cuba—ordered a halt. He had all his guns—two rifled thirty-two-pounders and four field pieces—brought ashore, and posted them with the one hundred and fifteen men he commanded, as a battery along the bluff, to overlook the river. Then he boldly sank the *Maurepas,* along with two small steamboats, as an obstacle, in the very midst of the channel, and sat down to await the attack.

When the Federal ironclads appeared with several companies of infantry in their wake on steamboats, Fry's batteries opened fire. At first their shots bounced off the leading two ironclads like hailstones on a slate roof. But Fry himself suddenly noted a porthole left open on the *Mound City,* and fired a single shot, which went through the porthole and hit the steam-condenser of the engine. The *Mound City* stopped, steam filling it rapidly from stem to stern; the crew swarmed out on deck to escape the scalding vapor; and they all were promptly picked off by Fry's sharpshooters ashore. In all, one hundred and fifty men were thus killed by a single lucky shot, and the *Mound City* sank close to the barrier of the other boats. Up to a few years ago, its wreckage at low water was still clearly visible. The Federal infantry, which had landed below the town, finally silenced the battery, wounded and captured Fry; but the important railway junction of De Vall's Bluff farther up the river, and only sixty brief miles across the open prairie from Little Rock, was saved for a time, though the railway tracks leading from it were soon after torn up. In fact, the four gunboats might never have reached Batesville at all, nor Curtis kept open his communications, had not another officer, who was utterly incompetent, soon after thrown completely away a pitched battle at Des Arc.

But Hindman, though he had done everything that a man could do, had reckoned without one whom he was to turn into his greatest enemy. Off in the Indian Territory, General Albert Pike, who had perhaps done more to produce the disaster at Pea Ridge than any other man on that field, still held his independent command. Van Dorn, in his report on that battle, had said nothing at all about the blunders and incompetencies committed by Pike; but had, on his retirement from Arkansas, graciously allowed that worthy to take with him two regiments of Arkansas troops and a six-gun battery commanded by young Woodruff. With these as a guard and as his assistants, Pike, smarting as he was at the libellous criticism levelled at him by the *New York Tribune* and other Northern papers (for his Indians had scalped some Federal dead), now proceeded to build for himself a fort, two hundred and fifty miles from the northern border, down near Texas, on the Red River, and there sat down to read through Napier's *Peninsular War.* And all the while another old army post, Fort Gibson, lay at the junction of the Arkansas and the Grand, just fifty miles from Fort Smith and close to Tahlequah, the important Cherokee capital!

On his arrival in Arkansas, Hindman had promptly sent a peremptory note to Pike, demanding the return of the two regiments and of Woodruff's battery to Arkansas. Pike sent off one regiment and the battery, with instructions not to waste a single cartridge, or shell, till they reached Little Rock. But Pike took good care also to send a long letter to Davis's secretary of war in Richmond complaining of the way he was being treated. The troops he had forwarded had not yet reached Little Rock when Hindman sent him another letter, again demanding them and pointing out that, inasmuch as Pike had been left in charge of Fort Smith and Van Buren by Van Dorn, he should now move north and occupy Fort Gibson. This infuriated Pike, who, like Hindman, had no mean opinion of his abilities. He immediately dispatched another long letter to Richmond, questioning the validity of Hindman's appointment to command.

The Richmond government was at that moment fully engaged in the life-or-death enterprise of driving, with Lee's and Jackson's assistance, McClellan's invading army away from Richmond and down the Peninsula; the distracted Davis, "a throbbing mass of nerves" and dyspepsia, was busy saving his almost-doomed capital; and all that Davis's secretary of war, the able and intelligent George W. Randolph, could do was to write to Pike and say that his complaints would soon be considered. But Hindman, carried away by his impetuosity, would not stop. He knew that a great "Indian expedition," urged upon Lincoln by Senator Lane, of Kansas, since the preceding winter, and composed of Pawnees, Osages, and other plains tribes, commanded by white officers, was already on its way south from Fort Leavenworth, not only with the avowed purpose of breaking the alliance of the Oklahoma tribes with the Confederacy, but also aiming at capturing Fayetteville and Fort Smith. On July 14, some of its cavalry—disorderly and blundering as they were, and little better than bushwhackers—occupied Fayetteville almost without resistance. Pike was still doing nothing whatever, and had left the entire Cherokee country without any defenders except for old Stand Waitie, that most faithful full-blooded Cherokee Confederate, and his Indian cavalry. So Hindman, twenty years younger than Pike, kept after his adversary; and his notes, each more and more peremptory, soon became insulting reprimands.

But Pike still had friends at Richmond, and he knew it. His Masonic connections—he was the highest ranking Mason in the United States—and his long association with prominent ruling factions in Arkansas served him in good stead. The delegation of Arkansas's congressmen at Richmond was persuaded to call upon Davis and to point out to him that Hindman's appointment had been quite irregularly made by Beauregard, and had never been completely agreed upon by the Secretary of War. They begged the haggard and exhausted Davis to appoint another officer to command over both Hindman and Pike.

Davis's answer was characteristic. An old classmate of his at West Point, Theophilus Hunter Holmes, born back in 1804, had been mistakenly made a brigadier general in June of 1861, before Bull Run, by Davis himself. Except for a typically martinet tendency to drill his troops, engaging them in sham battles, marching and countermarching them, he had done, so far, absolutely nothing. At Bull Run he had commanded a reserve battalion and had taken no part. At the Peninsula, he had stubbornly refused to move his troops against McClellan, even when the sound of the guns had grown so loud as to rouse every officer but himself (after all, he was quite deaf) into the mood for moving forward. This was the man whom Davis—who ran his own War Department—now had to offer the Arkansawyers. Sterling Price, chafing down in Mississippi, could come back and see what he could do with the Missourians who still remained loyal to the Confederacy. Pike could remain in the Indian Territory. Hindman, who had already saved Arkansas once, could still remain in that state; but Holmes, and none other, would command the entire Trans-Mississippi Department, and all would be subject to his orders.

Pike, thoroughly infuriated at Hindman's criticism, had already sent in his resignation. This fact might have been overlooked had Pike not chosen to follow it up by a really amazing public address to the Indians, announcing in flamboyant style, "to the chiefs and people of the Cherokees, Creeks, Seminoles, Chickasaws, and Choctaws" that the neglect of their needs had been entirely Van Dorn's fault, not his; that "I have resigned in order to go to Richmond and make known to the President the manner in which you have been treated"; that the Indians should "remain true to the Confederate States and to themselves. Do not listen to any men who say that the Southern States will abandon you." Considering that old John Ross, the head Cherokee chief, had already pointed out recently, in a personal letter to Davis himself, that he had practically nothing to defend himself with but two hundred guards set around his house at Park Hill, while the "great Indian expedition" was closing around his capital and his territory, Pike's truculent bombast was so futile as to arouse the suspicion, voiced by one of his own subordinate commanders, that Pike himself must have been either drunk or insane when he wrote it.

Holmes, though urged to make all speed to his new post, did not actually arrive in Little Rock till the twelfth of August, as he had to be routed through Vicksburg. Everything in the West was now going wrong for the Confederacy. In Tennessee, Beauregard had given place to Bragg, whom Davis considered a military genius and who invaded Kentucky late that summer, only to throw away his entire campaign. In Arkansas, Curtis was still at Batesville, and he now commanded the entire line of the White River: while still another Federal army, composed of farm boys from Kansas and Iowa, was soon to occupy Fayetteville. The "great Indian expedition" which had been, in reality, nothing but a glorified plundering and looting excursion, came to an ignominious end, suddenly and disastrously, on July 18, when one of its white "officers" attacked another white officer; but it left John Ross a not unwilling hostage in the hands of the Federals and devastated the entire Cherokee region for many years to come.

Pike was on hand to meet Holmes on his arrival at Little Rock; but Holmes had already read Pike's Farewell Address to the Indians. All that the "fine Arkansas gentleman," with his white locks and Jove-like head, was able to obtain from the precise, pedantic, dry little North Carolinian—who went back after the war to live on the same upland plantation he had come from, to admire Davis to the last as the "real hero of the Confederacy"—was a cold leave of absence while the little matter of his resignation from the army was being considered. And so the flamboyant Pike—later hailed as "Albertus Magnus" by one of his Arkansas admirers—did not go off to Richmond to bother Davis, after all.

Instead, he drifted off to Texas. Holmes had promptly given Hindman the job of reorganizing the Indian Territory as well as the command of western Arkansas; and Pike, no doubt, was furious at that. He had earlier shown a disposition to cherish old grudges—as witness his duel with Roane—and when once stung into action, nothing would stop him. He settled down in Grayson County, just across the Texas border from his old stamping-ground and fort on the Red River. And then, that September and October, something strange happened. A secret organization was discovered among the Texas ranchers of that very county, engaged in smuggling rifles and agitating for an uprising against the Confederacy. Wholesale arrests were made, and some of the arrested swore that Pike was engaged in actively helping this underground conspiracy.

Whether this testimony was true or not, very soon thereafter it was reported back to Holmes that Pike was behaving very queerly—in fact, that he was acting precisely as if he had never handed in his resignation at all. Ammunition trains had been stopped on the open prairie at his orders. This state of affairs could not go on for long—and on November 3, Holmes learned that Pike had suddenly and dramatically started again for the Oklahoma border. Holmes now, at last, had enough. He immediately sat down and wrote out an order for Roane (now in the Confederate service and Pike's old enemy) to arrest Pike. Two hundred picked men from Shelby's and Marmaduke's cavalry were to execute the order forthwith. As much courtesy as possible should be shown to Pike, but the order was to be carried out "to the extent of taking life, should resistance be offered." Pike was run to earth at Tishimingo in the Chickasaw Country, on November 14, and brought back to face his superior. As Holmes had already found out that the Secretary of War was now ready to confirm Pike's resignation, he let his captive go. But Pike's pen was not to be restrained; and he burst forth in Holmes's face in a torrent of verbal denunciation, which he actually had printed and which stands to this day as a dreadful monument of its kind. Thenceforward he practically disappeared from Arkansas life, to devote himself solely to his work for Masonry.

Rector, too, a better man than Pike, had already followed him into oblivion. The Constitution drawn up in 1861 by the secession convention had provided for another election in 1862; and the Johnsons, still clamoring for Rector's scalp, demanded that the election be held. They already had their hand-picked candidate, a good soldier named Harris Flanagin, who would do as they said. Rector was too bitter, too actively preoccupied with his duties to campaign actively—and most of the soldiers (who certainly would have voted for him) were out of Arkansas. So Flanagin won, in an election that was pure farce, to have the barren honor of surrendering three years later. But there were plenty like him, even then, to put party above patriotism, though few to reap the just reward.

The authorities at Richmond had effectually, thanks to Pike's vanity and rancorous hatred, turned their backs on Arkansas. Holmes—a man who had no conception or intention of fighting, and who knew nothing about battles or about the spirit of the people who had to do the fighting—now commanded. He obtained arms (though much had already been done in that direction by Hindman) and saw that his troops were well-drilled; but for the rest he was dilatory and ineffectual, much divided in his mind between the requests of Davis and the demands of Hindman. Secretly, no doubt, many people now quoted scorching parts of Pike's diatribe against him:

"Twenty-six pieces of artillery, a fixed supply of ammunition, and other trifles on hand, with one million three hundred and fifty thousand dollars in money, and over six thousand suits of clothing in prospect, were the booty Hindman had to tempt you withal; and for it you sold your soul, as Faust sold his to Mephistopheles. Your lieutenant became your master; you found it convenient to believe his version of everything, and you ended by making all his devilments your own; and by adopting the whole infernal spawn and brood, with additions of your own, to the family."

Others, such as several of the excellent Texas regiments now hurriedly summoned up by Hindman to defend Arkansas that summer, thought of Holmes quite frankly as merely a good general for the parade-ground.

Off at Fort Smith, early in September, Hindman had whipped together another army, fifteen thousand strong and equipped—God knows how—with a pitifully meagre supply of guns and ammunition for at least a short campaign. The Indians, reorganized and more disciplined than they had been under Pike, were in that army; the Missouri cavalry under Marmaduke and Shelby, the Arkansawyers along with the Texans; even Louisiana had contributed artillery and cavalry. Though there were few uniforms and almost no shoes, this was the best, as it proved to be nearly the last effective army Arkansas ever had. Hindman had made no secret of his plan to Holmes. He intended to advance from his base at Fort Smith and to fall on the two Federal armies now covering a great stretch of territory in both Arkansas and the Indian Territory, separately. Though outnumbered, he felt sure he could beat the Federals out of the state. Curtis, off at Batesville still, was no longer a real danger; he was harassed by cavalry continually, and the Missouri authorities were urging him to withdraw.

Holmes at first agreed to Hindman's plan; and then, in September, disagreed; he ordered Hindman to come to Little Rock and see him. Hindman discovered a troubled soul. Randolph, Davis's secretary of war in Richmond, had been really making life too bothersome to poor Holmes. He had insisted that all men available be sent off to defend Vicksburg, which was gravely threatened. Holmes had promised to comply with Randolph's order, but at the last moment Davis himself had countermanded it. Now Randolph was threatening to resign. He—Holmes—was really sure that Pemberton, at Vicksburg, with only about three thousand to oppose to the vast numbers gathered there by Grant, was badly off. At the same time, it would not do to strip Arkansas again of all its defenders, as had been done, unfortunately, that spring before he took command. Would it not be possible for Hindman to reduce somewhat his force at Van Buren, and send part of them east, where they could be shipped to Vicksburg if it actually was shown to be necessary?

Hindman reassured him. Behind his steely gray eyes and his dark beard, his pale face and grim demeanor, Hindman's mind was working furiously, egging him on to speak the truth: that he, and he alone, had created an army capable of defending the state, and that he intended to defend it. What, in truth, did Vicksburg matter to him? His business was to drive the Federals out and to recover the valuable lead-mines in Missouri, as well as the rich Cherokee country, now plundered and ravaged. But it is probable that he said none of these things. He knew his man. Since Davis himself had countermanded Randolph's order, was it not possible that the President had, after studying the situation, come to the conclusion that Vicksburg was in no immediate danger? He—Hindman—had two armies now north and west of him: Blunt's, off in southwest Missouri, and Herron's, inactive at Fayetteville. Would it not be better to defeat each separately before they made a junction and so outnumbered him? He could always turn back then towards Little Rock, if the order to relieve Vicksburg ever came.

It took him a long time to convince Holmes. Finally the deaf old man gave in to the younger and more daring one, merely exacting a promise that Hindman would turn back at once if the order should come again from Richmond to relieve Vicksburg. Hindman rejoined his army. In November, soon after learning that the Cherokees, off to the northwest, had been routed by Blunt at Cowskin Prairie near the deserted old Fort Wayne, and that Blunt had scattered his men in pursuit, he sent off five thousand cavalrymen to keep Blunt's scattered forces in play around Cane Hill. And then on December 3 he got his whole army into motion in the direction of Herron and Fayetteville.

It is said that he had in his pocket a dispatch from Holmes, sent about the middle of November, warning him that Seddon, Davis's newly appointed secretary of war, had ordered him to detach ten thousand men immediately to relieve Vicksburg. But Hindman had deliberately chosen not to heed that warning. His plans had been made a long time in advance, and the time had now come to spring the trap on his enemy. Like Rector, he was fighting for Arkansas, not for Jeff Davis. Let Holmes fume. It would not take him, Hindman, long to complete an inevitable victory. Such a victory as he had planned was worth some technical disobedience to his superiors.

He left Van Buren at midnight, and with his small force soon got himself completely between the two Federal commanders. At daybreak on the morning of Sunday, December 7, his cavalry literally drove Herron's cavalry back on Herron's own army, just starting out from Fayetteville. It is true that the day before, while his cavalry skilfully had held Blunt in play before Cane Hill and his main army moved relentlessly down on Herron, he had openly sent his ammunition train of wagons far to the rear, as if planning a retreat, or as if fearing it might be captured. It is also true, as he stated later, that his men had marched practically without anything to eat for the last four days, and that his battery horses "were literally dying of starvation." But he now had a unique opportunity before him: to defeat Herron and retake Fayetteville, before Blunt, twenty-five miles away to westward, could even advance.

In this juncture, Hindman hesitated. It may be that he actually did have in his pocket newly arrived and precipitate orders from Holmes to return to Little Rock at once or to face the consequences. If so, neither he nor Holmes later ever admitted that fact. It may be that he was afraid to advance farther, having left Blunt in a good position to westward, able to threaten his rear. At all events, he carefully picked out a good position, a little grove of trees on a low horseshoe-shaped ridge lying out on the open prairie, with a small mountain stream in front, some twelve miles away from Fayetteville, midway between Blunt's army and Herron's, and there he waited calmly for his enemy to attack.

Herron attacked at first, having brought up his artillery by noon; the first Federal charge was permitted to approach within sixty yards, and then was literally mown down. A second charge met with the same fate; but by two o'clock, Blunt, in a furious temper, had managed to move up, and attacked on the left flank of the Confederate position. There the undergrowth was denser, making the advance easier; but Blunt, too, was shaken off. Now for an hour, the full fire of the superior Federal batteries was turned loose upon Hindman; and it was followed by an infantry attack all along the line, together with an attempt by the Federal cavalry to turn both flanks of the position. All this utterly failed, and the Federals were now thrown back to the edges of the prairie, leaving both flags and prisoners behind. Their artillery thereupon recommenced; and it pounded Hindman till close to sunset; a last charge just before dusk swept across the open prairie—to fail as all others had failed.

Arkansas had made its last stand, in fact as well as in fame. During that night, Hindman began cautiously to retreat; his artillerymen had wrapped the wheels of their guns with their blankets to make no sound. By morning, all had started south from as complete a victory, which resulted in nothing, as ever was fought in any war. The Federals had lost heavily, nearly two thousand killed and wounded, as well as two hundred and seventy-five taken prisoners; five flags captured, as well as five hundred small arms and twenty-three supply wagons. The Confederate loss, by Hindman's official statement, was 164 killed,

817 wounded, and 336 missing—a total of 1,317! Expecting nothing less than a renewal of the battle the next day, Blunt, who had been in a towering rage ever since he discovered that Hindman had outgeneraled him, sent forward at dawn a flag of truce with a request that the dead be buried. He found only Hindman and some cavalry, under a similar flag, alone in possession of the field, engaged in that same grim business. Then Blunt exploded, and insultingly charged Hindman with abusing the flag of truce to cover his own retreat.

The fact remains, however, that Blunt and Herron had both been beaten by an inferior force. To do this, Hindman had undoubtedly disobeyed Holmes's orders. However, Holmes let him do so, when a stronger general would have insisted on complete obedience. The responsibility for the final disposition of the troops rests entirely on Holmes's shoulders; the glory of having beaten, with an ill-equipped, almost shoeless army, a force nearly twice its size, rests on the shoulders of Thomas Carmichael Hindman. Henceforward, the defense of Arkansas—vital as it was still, in every sense, to the Confederacy—had become very much like the apparent defense provided by that great siege gun which Hindman had brought to Little Rock by steamboat in the dark days of June, and which still stood there, close to the Rock itself, pointing its muzzle northward. No one either could or would fire that gun; it was spiked at last, abandoned, and not again resurrected until fired for the first time, a long twelve years later, in June of 1874.

No lasting glory had been reaped by anyone from Prairie Grove, as none had been reaped from Pea Ridge. The state which had made its choice to stand by the Confederacy, would be given no credit by anyone for defending itself. The next year Hindman, at his own request, was to be transferred east of the Mississippi—he had accompanied this request with a threat of resignation. To him Arkansas was already a "grave of ambition, energy, and system." To this day, not a single statue of any Confederate general stands before the state capitol at Little Rock. It was the people of the state who had to make this war, abandoned and betrayed and alone. And they fought with a grin of pain on their faces, as if to say to all beholders: "We know we are nothing but backwoods trash, inferior to everybody. It does not matter to anyone. We will still fight on."

Twelve

GLORY AT SUNSET

Of the five colleges listed as being in the state by 1860, not a single one opened its doors after 1862. Saint John's College at Little Rock was, as we have seen, a vast military hospital; Cane Hill had become a barracks for Federal troops; Arkansas College at Fayetteville, was a roofless ruin, having been burnt along with the Female Seminary and the stagecoach stables, as the Federals and the Confederates contended for the prize of northwest Arkansas in the campaign that culminated at Pea Ridge. Its faculty, Unionists of the Northern Methodist denomination, had all fled north; one of them, a few years later, was to give a vivid picture of Fayetteville under the ravages of war. It must have been in those years that the legend arose that a governor of Arkansas had once said, "I will not give any money to public education. The people do not deserve to be educated."

Faculty and students alike were now learning bitter lessons drawn from ghastly experience—lessons of the battlefield that cost many lives and ended in inevitable defeat for the South. Twenty-five thousand Arkansawyers were in the unlucky and consistently misled army that was fighting to hold the vital railway lines and mountain gaps in Tennessee. They made and fought the battles of Stone's River, of Chickamauga, of Chattanooga; and if they had been led by either Patrick Cleburne, of Arkansas, who was too selfless in his devotion to duty, or Nathan Bedford Forrest, of Tennessee, who was too much of the tough, outspoken old freebooter, instead of by the incapable Bragg, they might, despite the blockade, have actually kept the Confederacy alive for a long, long time. Another twenty-five thousand, poorly armed and equally misled, stood guard in Arkansas. Sterling Price, J. S. Marmaduke, and Jo Shelby—all of Missouri—did everything they could for them. As late as August, 1864, Price led a daring cavalry raid about seven hundred miles northward to fight a battle on the outskirts of Kansas City and to attempt to recruit yet another army for the Confederacy. But the sands were running out, and no more men or equipment came.

The crops of 1862 had been poor; those of 1863 were good. No one in Arkansas suffered from such conditions of semistarvation as, by 1864, affected both the population of Richmond and Lee's armies alike. Coffee, of course, was almost nonexistent, and there was a great lack of needful medicines and of clothing materials. A bad shortage of both cotton and wool cards, for distribution among the people, appears and reappears in successive reports from Arkansas during the years 1863 and 1864. The winter that lay between those years was long famous for its bitter cold. For weeks around Christmas the thermometer never arose above freezing point; several below-zero temperatures were recorded; and the Arkansas River was so deeply frozen over that Federal artillery, it is said, crossed over it on the ice.

Vicksburg had fallen on July 4, 1863—a disaster which perhaps might have been prevented by Holmes, had not that officer kept on temporizing and delaying. Memphis, New Orleans, Helena, and Arkansas Post had preceded it in falling, and the Mississippi now lay open from its source to the sea. To the inhabitants of Arkansas—and even to the Cherokees, still keeping up, under that invincible old Indian, Stand Waitie, some sort of resistance along the line of the Arkansas River—the fall of Vicksburg was like the end of the world.

Yet it was not until early September, two months after Vicksburg's fall, that the Federals occupied Little Rock. Curtis, harassed as he had been at Batesville by the cavalry raids started by Hindman, retreated into Missouri early in 1863; and Elisha Baxter, the Batesville civilian who had helped raise Union troops for him, was captured and brought to Little Rock, where he was thrown into jail under a charge of treason. Aided by friends (there were fifth columnists even then) he escaped from jail and went off into hiding. Except for a force at Helena, there were no Union armies of any size left in eastern Arkansas; and after Prairie Grove, the two Federal commanders, Blunt and Herron in the West, found the country too difficult to hold and retreated into

Missouri. The advance on Little Rock was, in the end, directly ordered by Grant, who, after Vicksburg, was the idol of the North and the man who commanded Lincoln's confidence. It started off from Helena on August 8, and on September 10, without a single pitched battle, Little Rock fell to the veterans from Kansas and Iowa, whom Steele commanded. Later on, in view of the last-ditch resistance which, throughout 1864, went on from around Arkadelphia and Camden, and from the line of the Ouachita River south, Minnesota troops were ordered to reinforce Steele in Arkansas; they lie today in droves in the military cemetery at Little Rock, and have a bronze monument set up there in their memory.

Sterling Price, whom we have seen retransferred to Arkansas at the close of July, 1862 (at the same time that Holmes took command of the Trans-Mississippi Department), had not actually made his reappearance in the state till the close of March, 1863, when Hindman's complete refusal to serve any longer under Holmes had forced Davis and his latest tool, the cadaverous old dyspeptic, Seddon, to do something. Holmes had then been eased out of the headship of the Department in favor of the far abler Kirby Smith, of Tennessee; but he had still been allowed to keep his command of all the armies in Arkansas. Hindman had already gone off to Tennessee, to be wounded so desperately at Chickamauga, where he lost an eye, as to be of no further service; and Davis had finally been persuaded to relax from his rancorous hatred of Price sufficiently to let him return. But Price was still under Holmes's orders. His only hope to save Little Rock from being eventually taken lay in attempting to drive the Federal army from Helena; and so a scant seven thousand, out of the more than twenty thousand men left, made the attempt on July 4, the very day that Grant entered Vicksburg. Outnumbered and outgunned as they were—for Helena was now a fortress—they were bound to fail; and the last advancing Confederate flag was duly planted—appropriately—on Graveyard Hill, to fall a few minutes later. After this, Holmes took to his bed, "a-chillin' and a-feverin'," as the Arkansawyers say; and the defense of Little Rock before Steele's advance was left to Price.

Ten miles northeast of the city lies a long even ridge of clay and rock, the last outpost of the Ozark region; in front of it the sluggish and swampy Bayou Meto, descending into the Grand Prairie, cuts its way. Here were, and are still, to be traced in many places, the line of rifle pits and trenches which Hindman had prepared over a year before to defend the capital city. Here Price placed his army. Many of them were the rawest kind of recruits, farm boys of sixteen and seventeen in butternut-dyed homespun, who had seen no action in the war. The main body of Arkansas veterans were already fighting and dying in Tennessee, around Chattanooga. But the line which Price occupied was formidably equipped for defense, although Steele far outnumbered him. It was supposed that Steele would have to break Price's line, before being able to take the city.

But all was not well now within Price's army. The thought of the futile and hopeless attempt to take Helena still rankled among them. Many of the officers were now free in offering blame and criticism. Marmaduke, of Missouri, had been especially outspoken in some of his remarks against Walker, of Tennessee. He had declared that Walker's regiment, that day at Graveyard Hill, had been ordered to advance and had not advanced, and that Walker was a coward. Hearing this, Walker had, at first, merely laughed; but when he heard again that Marmaduke was asserting that another, unnamed, officer had reprimanded Walker for his cowardice, he grew angry. He appointed Colonel Bob Crockett, son of the immortal Davy, to seek out Marmaduke and demand an apology or a duel. Marmaduke refused the apology, but accepted the duel.

On the morning of September 6, 1863, with Steele's army manoeuvering to get into position south and east of Little Rock along the line of Arkansas, the two officers met, in the approved fashion, at the edge of Lost Prairie, ten miles northeast of Little Rock. At the first fire, Walker fell, mortally wounded. His body, borne on a stretcher improvised from a window shutter, was carried into the city, where it was at last bundled into a waiting hack and taken to Saint John's Hospital. I have myself seen and talked with people who saw that grisly procession. The city, already half-deserted since Flanagin and his state government had fled, five days before, south to Washington, was filled with rumors and loud talk; and much of it was directed against Price, who seems to have heard of the duel too late to stop it, and who let Marmaduke go with only a reprimand. The tragic uselessness of the whole proceeding—a duel fought by two men over a question of personal honor when everything material was already lost, only heightened the horror that hung over Little Rock.

On the afternoon of the ninth, after two days of reconnoitering south and east of the city, Steele decided to throw about five thousand of his fifteen thousand men boldly across the river on a pontoon bridge, thus outflanking Little Rock from the south, while he himself marched directly against Price's lines. On the morning of the tenth, the weak and scattered forces which Price had left to the south discovered a pontoon bridge already in position across the Arkansas, and attempted, by firing a gun or so, to stop the Federals from crossing—meantime sending off a hurried courier to take the news to Price. But Price decided not to let himself be trapped, as had Pemberton at Vicksburg, and ordered a general retreat. So at eleven in the morning, across the pontoon bridge which he himself had constructed at the foot of Main Street, his tired and dusty infantry duly appeared in Little Rock even before the inhabitants were aware that their day to yield had come.

Realizing that they were being abandoned for the last time, though for no reason that they knew, the citizens of Little Rock set out buckets of water and dippers—a thoughtful touch in the parching heat of that September day—for the ragged, sweaty ranks of grimy, unshaven men and boys in gray, who advanced into the doomed city. The men eagerly broke ranks as they saw the standing buckets, picked up the dippers, and took big mouth-filling swigs: then laughed at some girls standing near one of those buckets, and said, "Well, goodbye girls. We've got to be going on, but we're coming back soon to fight for you," and so ran on. I have reason to recall that incident, for one of the girls was my mother, who later told me.

Not a shot had yet been fired, though the Confederate cavalry and some artillery were now holding the final line of muddy, sluggish Fourche Bayou, four miles east and south, to keep the advancing Federals from closing in till Price's main body could pass across the river. Steele's idea, since he now was master of the situation, was to save his ammunition, and let the Confederates depart: a decision which won for him in advance golden opinions from the people, weary as they were of war. About four o'clock, his batteries, mounted on the heights to the north (near the present-day Camp Robinson), threw a few rounds of shots in the direction of the old arsenal, which Price was already preparing to blow up or burn. By this time the warehouses along the river bank were already blazing fiercely, with fifty thousand bales of cotton in them; the pontoon bridge was rapidly being demolished; and Hindman's big siege gun on the south bank had been spiked and dismounted. None of the shells, as they came over for some five or ten minutes, ever hit anything; but some citizens, cowering in the only cellar available, the one beneath Pike's old residence, heard them whiz overhead; and one lay unexploded in the street nearby till some boys carried it off to an adjoining backyard, where it lay, up to a few years ago.

At five o'clock, General Steele, over the easily repaired pontoon bridge, rode into Little Rock to receive the city's submission from the hands of an old man, since Woodruff and others had fled south, the oldest living inhabitant of the half-empty city. He told Steele that his name was Charles P. Bertrand, "a Crittenden Union man." "Beau Charley" had come a long way from the days when he strode, a dashing young buck in his beaver hat, through the streets of a primitive village to sling ink at his rival Woodruff, in the columns of his *Advocate.* His memoirs, if he had only consented to write them, would have provided the world with some interesting reading; but he wrote no more now, and he died two years later.

Five days after this, the old weak-eyed but die-hard antisecessionist, Isaac Murphy, was informed by Lincoln that he was now provisional governor of the state; and thus he reaped his reward for his persistent efforts on behalf of the Union. The people of the little town, after their days of uncertainty, settled down to the occupation calmly, and were generally surprised at the moderation displayed by Steele and his men. No houses, so far as I know, were burnt, and none was plundered, though Federals were soon billeted in every available locality. In Saint John's College as well as in the arsenal young Minnesotans and Iowans died in increasing numbers from the unfamiliar malaria.

Yet it was a full year and seven months before the Confederacy, still tenaciously holding to the line of the lower Ouachita through Arkadelphia and Camden, finally gave out. And during all this time dogged and desperate battles were fought in all that rough region, while Price and Marmaduke and Shelby still rode northwards on long, destructive, and daring cavalry raids. One such raid, in 1864, went as far as the outskirts of present-day Kansas City and a pitched battle was fought on that spot. The Arkansawyers and Missourians and Texans, though completely outnumbered and cut off from everything but what they could make for themselves, outgeneraled Steele and his lieutenants completely. They still showed the desperate mettle which characterized them.

Three incidents in their story stand out. None of them is well known to anyone living outside the state. All reveal something of the characteristics of the people who lived there at the time—the characteristics of backwoods pride and frontier determination which were later destined to pass almost entirely away.

When the Federals took Little Rock, a young woman named Susan Bricelin Fletcher was living on a farm some twenty miles west of Little Rock, in that Maumelle region that, to this day, provides such an abrupt transition to the Ozark backwoods. This woman was as yet under thirty; she had been married some ten years; and she was now living there with a few Negro slaves, a niece of her husband, and one child, a son, aged four years. The farm abounded in chickens, cattle, hogs, and mules; and there was much on it for a woman to do. But the location was unhealthy—in these often-overflowed bottom lands bordered by rocky ridges malaria was rife—and the young boy had already become badly "salivated," because of vast doses of calomel prescribed by local doctors. These doctors lived as far away as Benton, some forty miles distant; but there were other and better doctors to be had in Little Rock, as this woman knew; but the Yankee scouts had already come her way, had driven off many of her cattle and looted the smokehouse, and had left her thoroughly frightened. It was known, she reflected, that her husband, along with three of his brothers, was in the service of the Confederacy southward, and was now, at this moment, still holding the southwestern corner of the state, around the new capital at Washington, against all invaders. If she went on to Little Rock, she did not know what might happen to her.

Still, her child was very ill. A doctor was sent for from Benton, and he came. He prescribed more calomel, which left the boy only worse. Sent for again, through the "no man's land" of pinewood, he informed her that he was now out of all drugs; that her only hope of obtaining any remedy lay in going to Little Rock. So the mules were hitched to the farm wagon, and the day-long journey was made to the Federal headquarters. There a blue-uniformed officer informed her that medicines could be obtained only if she would be willing to sign the oath of allegiance to the United States government. Guarded by two sentries with rifles, her child in her arms, she was marched out to the main building of the old arsenal, still standing in the Little Rock of today. Here she took the oath, and was provided with medicines, as well as a permit enabling her to spend a hundred and seventy five dollars (she still had Federal money, carefully hoarded, in her possession) for supplies, mostly goods to make clothing. A few days later, she was sent back to her plantation.

That same week, another Yankee scout officer came, with some more men, to see whether there was enough left "to keep a crow flying over in his rations," as General Phil Sheridan had remarked of the Shenandoah Valley. The young woman met him calmly. She said that he could not legally disturb her now, as she was a loyal American citizen and had the legally attested oath in the pocket of her dress. "Yes, Madam," the officer answered. "You have the oath in your pocket, and a lie in your mouth." And he moved in to ransack the house, to thrust a bayonet through the top of a locked trunk, in which she had just put away some newly sewn shirts for her husband, to scare her Negroes thoroughly, to take from them some quilts they had just pieced together and to commit other petty nuisances, like taking out her carefully saved hats and sticking them, ripped of their trimming, to the tops of the fence posts. After this frolic, he too rode away.

Apparently the oath provided no security so long as she lived in the back country. She began to wonder whether it would not be better to go to Little Rock, take with her the five thousand dollars in gold she had left buried in a safe place, and buy herself there another piece of property. She was still debating this when some more bluecoats arrived—it was now in the early spring of 1864 and nothing had as yet been planted. These men, finding nothing worth taking, told her that if she didn't move, her house was likely to be burned; so the day after they left, she did. The money was dug up and hidden in the wagon, the furniture was loaded on top; the niece, child, and Negroes added, and the wagon duly started for "the Rock," as it was still called.

They arrived on May 12, 1864, and on the twenty-fourth the young woman paid her five thousand dollars down in gold for a new home in a desirable location. But living on in Little Rock proved to be frightfully expensive. As the railroad tracks had all been destroyed, the only communication was by boat; and most of the supplies of the town went to the Federal army of occupation. The entire town was, in fact, only a military base camp, with an immense hospital and a military prison for captured Confederates, which had formerly been the penitentiary. The only people left, apart from a few Southern sympathizers already afraid of losing their last property, were a host of speculators who had just followed the Federal army south. Even the banks in which Susan Fletcher had put her little remaining capital, were no longer safe.

She soon decided to move south again, to Washington, the provisional Confederate capital. But how to get there through the Federal lines was the great problem. The new property was resold to a speculator, for six thousand dollars, and another thousand was added, in twenty-dollar gold pieces from the bank. Then this woman and her niece set to work. Strong linen was bought and made into two "corset waists," set around with pockets, each large enough to hold two twenty-dollar gold pieces. There were, in all, over eighty pockets in each waist, sufficient to hold the entire seven thousand dollars—but the weight was so great that for weeks beforehand the two women wore the waists constantly, so as to be able to walk around without anyone's taking notice of anything unusual in their gait or appearance. They even slept in them.

Finally, in the late summer of 1864, another wagon was procured, an old man engaged to drive it, and all preparations made for departure southward. At the advice of friends, Mrs. Fletcher boldly went to General Frederick Steele, now in command at Little Rock, and asked for a permit to go south, as her husband was in the Confederate part of the state near Washington. As she spoke to General Steele, her voice trembled and almost broke; but he apparently liked her frankness, and offered her a pass, together with an escort, to pass through the Federal lines. The old man who had agreed to drive the wagon, however, backed out of his part of the bargain; so the two women were left to shift for themselves.

As they were leaving, determined to drive on, though neither knew anything of the way, numerous neighbors, who had heard of the venture brought them bundles of the now worthless Confederate money to take to their friends outside; so, at the last, they had a trunkful. They started south, dressed in plain gingham dresses and wearing sunbonnets, and taking turns in driving. They had been allowed to take no food, but had managed to procure some twenty pounds of coffee, which they readily exchanged for food outside the city. Somewhere beyond the bounds of Pulaski County, after the Federal escort had departed, they ran into a Confederate cavalry detachment scouting through the deep woods. These guided them into Washington at last. As they entered the little town, after the dusty hundred-mile, five-day journey, a band organized among the Confederate troops there, was playing "Dixie" in the streets, and the Stars and Bars flapped gaily. It seemed to them that they had reached heaven. And after they took off the "corset waists," it seemed to them that a considerable part of themselves had somehow disappeared altogether.

At about the same time that this young lady regained her kin, a young man—not more than a boy—was parted forever from his. David Owen Dodd, second child and only son of humble parents who had previously lived in the country south of Little Rock on the Benton road, but who had emigrated to Texas, was born there on November 10, 1846. He grew up to be a frail but active sort of boy, with a great eagerness and inquisitiveness about life, and an open, clear, and frank power of expression. In 1858, his parents—obviously his father was not very successful as a farmer—came back to Benton, and finally to Little Rock, where they lived at the time of the outbreak of the war. There they strove to give their son—the boy was bright—even precocious—as good an education as could be had. He was sent for a time to Saint John's College, but had to give up because of a bout of malaria. When the illness was over, the college had already closed on account of the war; and David, being eager to be in touch with the big events pending, took a post as telegraph clerk on the newly built Little Rock-Pine Bluff telegraph line.

In the late summer of 1862, his father moved off down south, leaving his mother and sister behind in Little Rock but taking David with him. Although the boy was as yet scarcely recovered from the attack of fever, he found no difficulty in obtaining a post as telegraph clerk at Monroe, Louisiana. Here he stayed till early in January, 1863, obviously enjoying the responsibilities of his position very much and helping his mother out with part of his salary, while writing long, chatty letters back to his sister. Finally, sometime early in 1863, his father obtained a job as army sutler to the Confederates camped near Grenada, Mississippi; he purchased tobacco and other supplies wholesale at Mobile, and resold them to the soldiers. This job was not a very desirable one, but he wanted David to help him in it; and David consented. He was, apparently, eager to see something of army life. He resigned his job as telegraph clerk—he was still under age for the army—and went to Grenada to help his father.

After the fall of Little Rock, the father, now operating near Jackson, Mississippi, decided that his son should go back to Little Rock and arrange for his mother and sister to leave the place. David agreed, and reached Little Rock openly, sometime early in October. But for some reason, the mother and sister would not go. Though they did take a steamboat as far as De Vall's Bluff, the rest of the trip was suddenly called off. Early in December, the father arrived on the scene, slipping apparently through the Federal lines unobserved. This was bad; but worse still was to follow. Apparently the father was aware that, if found, he would be arrested; so the family were hurriedly bundled into a wagon, and got back somehow into Camden, to the Confederate headquarters there, with David's active assistance.

All might still have been well with young David, had not his father (in reading this story one really grows tired of the older man's irresponsibility) decided that since he had left some "business" unfinished in Little Rock he must send David back to that city. So David came, with at least two letters, as well as a pass signed by the Confederate officer in command at Camden and a birth certificate, on December 22, 1863. Equipped with all this, David set out, riding on a mule, and had no difficulty whatever in passing through the Federal lines. He stayed in Little Rock till the morning of December 29, visiting with an aunt, meeting one of his sister's girl friends, and even attending a dance or two during the Christmas season. On the twenty-ninth he set out again, the Federals having now given him a pass. Eight miles from the city he was stopped by a cavalry picket, a private of one of the Missouri German regiments, who later testified that he took the pass, kept it for a time, and finally tore it up when relieved of his duty.

Just before dusk, about two miles farther on at a point near which stands today a famous brick house long used as a stagecoach halt on the main road to Benton and Hot Springs, another private of the same Federal cavalry regiment, a German like the first, was scouting where the main road was crossed by another running southeast. This soldier suddenly saw a mounted man riding by and ordered him to stop. It turned out to be David, without a pass, and with a pistol in his possession. The pistol, he insisted, had been obtained at the home of his uncle, who lived some miles farther on, in the direction of Hot Springs, on another old side road; but as David had no pass on him, the officer to whom he was turned over (his headquarters was at the Stage-Coach House) insisted on going through all his papers.

Among these was discovered a memorandum book, with some dot-and-dash writing in the Morse code. This aroused suspicion; and the next day, David, under armed escort, went back to Little Rock to a military trial.

At the trial, the officer in charge of the Military Telegraph Station at Little Rock swore that the words in Morse code in the telegraph book gave definite information as to the Federal troops now on service in the captive city. The trial ended on the fifth of January, 1864, with a verdict of guilty. David was sentenced to death by hanging, and General Steele ordered the sentence to be carried out on January 8. It is said that Steele, realizing the boy's age (just over seventeen years) went to him personally and begged him to reveal the names of his informants, but David firmly refused. In any case, Steele decided—probably because the boy had been in Little Rock for some months—to make this execution a public affair as a warning to all others, and ordered all the troops to be turned out for it.

The morning of January 8 dawned intensely clear and cold. Snow lay thick on the ground—since the end of the previous year, temperatures had gone to zero and the Arkansas river had been frozen over. At three o'clock in the afternoon, the troops of the Little Rock garrison were drawn up under arms in a hollow square facing a gallows erected on the level ground lying in front of Saint John's College. Numerous citizens had also collected. Some of them had already begged Steele to let the boy off, but in vain. David now passed through the lines in an open ambulance, sitting on his own coffin; he surprised everyone present with his coolness. The provost-marshal and the attendants were obviously nervous, and apparently the provost-marshal had forgotten to provide a bandage for the prisoner's eyes. David remarked coolly, "You will find a handkerchief in my coat," and mounted the scaffold. When the noose was adjusted and the trap sprung, the body, light as it was, hung writhing, choking slowly to death—and the assistants had to pull at it to break the neck. At this horrible sight, at least one soldier standing in the front rank fell over in a dead faint, in the deathlike stillness, with a clang as his rifle struck the ground. Grieving friends later claimed the body and buried it under a stone, marked only with the dates of David's birth and death, in old Mount Holly Cemetery in Little Rock. Since then, it has become the most famous grave in Arkansas.

On July 22, 1864, a good white saddle-horse, saddled and bridled, and "burdened with a pretty heavy pair of saddlebags," stood at the door of a home in the little southwestern town of Washington, Arkansas. Inside the house, U. M. Rose, a man then just over thirty and chancellor of the Arkansas chancery courts since 1860, was bidding farewell to his family. He was about to ride off to Richmond, Virginia, on a hazardous and difficult mission.

Rose had been born in Kentucky, and after being left an orphan at thirteen had largely educated himself, graduating as lawyer from Transylvania College at Lexington, Kentucky, in 1853. He had then moved to Arkansas, where he had established himself at Batesville. A moderate Unionist, like many Arkansawyers, he had at first opposed secession. He was, like all Arkansawyers, to be equally bitter against Reconstruction later on. Upon the fall of Little Rock, he had followed the Confederate state government down to Washington; and the Confederate Congress having only recently voted an act to appoint a state historian from every state engaged in the struggle, Rose, who had little to do in the disordered and divided condition of the state, volunteered for the appointment. He was determined to proceed to Richmond and collect, in the War Department, records of every Arkansas soldier engaged on the Southern side. To make the trip from Washington, Arkansas, to Winona, Mississippi, which was the nearest railway point out of Federal hands, in a location some eighty miles inland, Rose would have to cross the entire lower part of the state, get across the river somehow, and proceed through the swampy Yazoo Delta inland—a journey, as it happened, of a week. But Rose had become an Arkansawyer in his natural reactions; he was now able to do the most difficult things if left to himself, but was not so good when doing things at the suggestion of others. He was genuinely interested in the new task he had undertaken; to accomplish it, he took with him the sum of six thousand dollars—the amount of his salary as historian, paid in worthless "state scrip," but exchangeable for Confederate currency nearly at par; and he took also an almost equal amount, which had been paid him as salary for his chancellorship. He had as a travelling companion a soldier named Barksdale, who was used by the government as a sort of travelling postoffice, carrying letters and dispatches from one side of the divided Confederacy to the other.

War is the great leveller. Along the roads on which Rose and Barksdale travelled—it took them over three days to reach the Mississippi—few people were encountered except old men and boys, afoot or on horseback. Stagecoaches had ceased to exist, and private conveyances were unknown. Crops were laid by, schools were closed for the summer or for "the duration"—and everywhere refugees from those parts of Arkansas already abandoned to the invaders were living in derelict cabins or abandoned homesteads, the women doing their own housework while the men were away with the army. As Rose himself said quaintly, "Carriages containing fair ladies and brave men were no longer encountered." While the Arkansas armies were still stubbornly holding the southern part of the state, and were even deciding upon a daring cavalry raid into Missouri that summer, to be led by Price and Shelby; and while Jefferson Davis—abetted by the sinister Bragg—was attempting to persuade them all to move east and defend doomed Atlanta, the people of the state who were not fighting were living as best they could, sorely in need of cotton and wool cards for their home weaving, lacking in all medicines, wearing old clothes repatched and remade, and consuming a diet, as Rose says, of "a dull uniformity." Food was fairly plentiful still, but it lacked variety; and coffee had long since disappeared. But hospitality—the boundless hospitality of a people united by common suffering—made up for all.

On the morning of the twenty-sixth, Rose and his companion reached the Mississippi at Catfish Point, ten miles below the mouth of the Arkansas, where apparently there was a ferry—though this was actually invisible as they rode up. The ferryman stood, however, in the willow thickets lining the shore and, shifting the cud of tobacco in his cheek, silently pointed upstream. There, below a dark cloud of smoke, could be seen the hulls of two iron-clad Federal gunboats. To cross now would be impossible, though the ferryman remarked philosophically that the gunboats usually shifted their positions later in the afternoon. So hours went by, while the sun beat more and more hotly on the water. Finally, at three o'clock, the gunboats moved and passed on up the river.

By tugging violently at a rope fastened to a stump on the bank, the three men lifted to the surface a large, completely sunken boat. A tin can was fetched from the thicket to bail it, and a tow sack to wipe off its seats. The horses would be swum alongside, while the ferryman held the boat, with a pole, in the current. All was ready to start.

Although the river was low, it took them a good three quarters of an hour to get across. Then they mounted again, to reach the first

Mississippi settlement at nightfall, where Rose, suddenly discovering a small rent in one of his saddlebags, paid twenty-five dollars to have it repaired. Two days of further travel through the dense swamps of the Sunflower and the Yazoo, along a road which was but a track cut through an endless swamp, "with mud up to the saddle skirts for many long weary miles," brought them at last to Greenwood, to Carrolton, to Winona at last. There after a day's rest Rose parted from Barksdale, who took the faithful saddle-horse that had carried Rose back into Arkansas.

The war had by now left its strong mark on all the South's railroads. Rolling stock was increasingly scarce, and all trains were overcrowded. The tracks were much out of repair at many points; so trains rarely travelled faster than fifteen or twenty miles per hour. As seats were frequently not to be had, some passengers usually climbed up the sides of the cars and roosted on the top—Rose himself travelled "many, many miles that way." It added to the hazards; but everyone was growing used to dangers. Changes of trains were very common. There were neither sleeping nor dining cars to be had; and a post on the roof was often preferable to a seat in the overcrowded, ill-smelling interior, where soldiers, coming or going on furlough or returning home wounded, with their free manners and open ways caught from campaigning, were very common. At night all passengers descended from the roofs, and tried to find seats within.

Rose travelled through Jackson, Mississippi, and Meridian, to Selma, Alabama, where a steamboat took him to Montgomery; then on through Opelika, Columbus, Macon, Milledgeville, Augusta, Georgia, to Columbia, South Carolina; and then through Charlotte, Salisbury, Greensboro, North Carolina, to that famous Richmond and Danville Railway down which Davis was to flee from Richmond in defeat the next April. It was a tedious journey, which took several days. It skirted, be it noted, Atlanta to the east, where William Tecumseh Sherman had already opened his celebrated siege, and where the over-cautious Johnston had been replaced by the over-rash and headstrong Hood. (The Arkansawyers have always believed, ever since, that Pat Cleburne, the Irish-born, former drug-store clerk from Helena, who had saved the entire Confederate Army the previous fall from complete defeat after Chattanooga, by holding Ringgold Gap with twelve thousand men, while Bragg retreated south to Dalton, would have been given this job, had he not imprudently advised Davis beforehand to emancipate and arm all the Negroes—advice Davis did not dare to take.) In the midst of such stirring events, Rose finally reached Richmond—to find the city under siege and suffering from famine.

The South had made its last great throw at Chickamauga and had lost. Lee was being more and more attenuated in his lines by Grant, who was determined to "fight it out on this line if it takes all summer." Davis's position was already hopeless—Europe would have none of him, because neither Louis Napoleon nor Victoria, nor their ministers, wanted to have any truck with slavery. Under the circumstances, it is rather pathetic to see Rose, able and conscientious as he was, establishing himself in Richmond, sending to Charleston for extra large paper, hiring girl clerks, and settling down to the dreary copying of muster rolls, in order to preserve details of a history that so soon would be lost. But Rose had a determination to carry through any task embarked upon and a good, well-trained and disciplined mind. He set about the task with a will. And as far as is known, he was the only Southern state historian even to have made the attempt.

Living in Richmond had become a matter of existing from day to day. After a stay of less than two days at the best hotel, Rose took humbler lodgings with a respectable family and arranged to take his meals at a boarding house, for which he paid down two hundred dollars a week—which was at a considerably cheaper rate than the hotel had charged him. Tea, coffee, milk, cream, sugar had all disappeared. The food was exceedingly scant; but apples were plentiful, at a dollar apiece, and everyone ate them—including Mr. Benjamin, Jefferson Davis's secretary of state, who was cheerfully munching at one as Rose entered his office. Davis, tall, distinguished-looking, and well-dressed, received him with grave courtesy. The entire city had become, after the terrible fighting of the summer, a vast hospital. It was ill-lit and without amusements of any sort—though the churches were overcrowded with people desperately praying for the Confederacy—and it was dangerous to go out on the streets after dark, for robberies had grown exceedingly common. As the summer faded towards the last fall, a deeper pall of gloom descended. Few realized that, not many miles away, Lincoln in the White House was scarcely expecting to be reëlected; that thousands throughout the Middle West, which had lost so many of its sons, were shocked and horrified by the terrific slaughter of Grant's troops and Sherman's month-long pause before Atlanta;

that the copperhead societies were actively at work, stronger than ever, striving to elect their candidate, McClellan. Could the South have made a single advance now (there were none left but Forrest in Tennessee and Price in Arkansas to dare dream of such a thing) the war might yet have been won by the side that had been losing, hour after hour.

But while Rose was still in Richmond, each day copying painstakingly the records of enlistment in Arkansas regiments, Atlanta fell; and Hood, left stranded off to the South, moved up past the familiar mountains around Chattanooga, where the war had already been won, to try to retake Nashville. Sherman, even more daring, cut loose from his base at Atlanta and set out for Savannah and the sea. Close to the very day that Rose left Richmond, December 15, 1864, the last battle around Nashville opened, in desperate icy weather, following on a great sleet storm—a battle which only the bravest inhabitants of Nashville would later speak about, so inhuman and so horrible it was. A few days later, Hood, for the last time, had failed.

In Richmond, as Rose recalled, it was a bleak, black day, with torrents of cold rain descending and whole streets flooded. The documents which had been copied so carefully for the last four and a half months had been all stowed away in a tin box and shipped on to Jackson, Mississippi; now Rose was to have some difficulty in getting even a cab to take him to the railroad station. "My horse was apparently composed of a fortuitous collection of bones which a starving vulture might have disowned; my cab was an antediluvian buggy held together precariously by countless ropes and strings; my charioteer, a gaunt and aged African, a model for any painting representing the extreme effects of famine, set off with such an assortment of rags as never could have been matched. We had not gone very far when . . . this equine skeleton slipped on the wet and rough cobblestones, and fell prone on his side with his head down hill, on a steep descent, flat and motionless on the cold and uneven pavement; and there he lay, with his white teeth displayed, without any sign of life. Fortunately I soon found another carrier, an African who took up my baggage; and we two trudged on through the rain, and arrived in time to catch the outgoing train."

Rose unfortunately left no clear and exact record of what the return trip through the South must have been like. As Sherman had moved on towards Savannah, and his army had taken Milledgeville in

Georgia, the journey must have been largely of the hairbreadth-escape variety. All that Rose tells us is that he missed a train connection at Augusta, Georgia, and was forced to buy a new suit there—apparently riding on the tops of trains had its disadvantages, for he paid nine hundred dollars cash down for his new clothing. Somehow, over the ravaged railway, he managed to reach Selma, and was then sent on a detour north, to Hood's army, already refitting and reassembling, north of the railway terminal, at Blue Mountain. Here he had to acquire another horse, as he was expected to visit Hood's headquarters; perhaps he had been asked to give the desperate Arkansas troops, grieving for the futile sacrifice at Franklin of their best leader, Pat Cleburne, some sort of assurance and comfort. The horse he acquired had no other gait than a racking trot; yet he succeeded in visiting the army and staying there two days, only escaping the Federals in time by jolting day and night with the Federal cavalry directly at his heels, to the railhead, where the last train on the line took him safely back into Selma.

From there he went, by a more peaceful route, down to Mobile; having left the horse with the racking trot in the hands of a Confederate captain, who promised to return him to Selma in four or five days. At Mobile smuggled supplies were still to be had; and Rose was able to buy with his dwindling funds ten yards of common calico as a present for his wife, as well as four ounces of precious quinine (another most useful article!) for which he paid $400. He then returned to Selma, but his horse was not there as the captain had promised.

Fortunately, he was able to get in touch with two other Arkansawyers: one a civilian who had also been to Richmond, and the other a furloughed soldier who had been in a Federal military prison, and was on his way to visit his mother in Texas. Both had good horses; and the civilian pointed out to Rose the advantages in the present situation, with good horses getting more scarce, of having a reserve fund in Federal gold. However, Rose had no gold and there was nothing for him to do but accept another sorry nag, which he did. The ride to Jackson, Mississippi, along the line of the broken-down railroad line now commenced; it rapidly jolted Rose's bones into a jelly. Another horse-trade resulted, leaving Rose no better off than before. The new horse was a completely broken-down animal and could barely summon up a walk if beaten continually. Thus the caravan crawled into Jackson, where Rose found his documents safe in an army warehouse, but was told that they could not be transported across the river, and that he himself must go miles to the southwest, towards Port Gibson, before finding any safe place where he could cross.

There, with his two Arkansas-born companions and an aged Texas farmer riding on a mule, he again embarked in a boat, dragged like the other up from the bottom, but they were fired upon by a Federal gunboat before reaching the opposite shore. The shots did not hit them; but the aged Texan's mule suddenly and mysteriously sank while swimming alongside, hit probably by a stray bullet; and when they reached the sandbar on the opposite side (their hundred-dollar fare being hurriedly paid en route) they skipped pell-mell across open territory into the woods, without stopping. Fortunately Rose and his two friends, riding on, reached a fine well-kept Louisiana plantation home at sunset, where music played and sung by the daughters of the house made the scanty supper more pleasant. About ten o'clock, the old Texan, who had lost his mule, turned up resolutely afoot (he was fully three score years and ten), and demanded that the daughters play "The Yellow Rose of Texas" as being the "best music I ever heered in all my born days"—but the daughters could not do it, for they did not recall the tune.

It was now the end of December, but the rains common to that season had fortunately held off. The last part of the trip, at a slow walk, was accomplished in perfect weather. In the southwest corner of Arkansas the Confederates were still holding out, ten thousand strong at least, along the line of the Red River; they were not to surrender till well past the next cotton-planting time, at the close of May. Rose's work had been done to the best of his ability; but the records, last seen by him safely stowed in the warehouse at Jackson, never reached Arkansas. They were burned soon after, along with the warehouse, in a Federal cavalry raid. The originals from which they were taken were lost, too, by April, in fallen Richmond. The Confederacy was disintegrating to its close, with Lincoln reseated safely as President and Grant closing around the Confederate capital—though Davis, hoping to the last to gain something, insisted on a futile conference with his adversaries as late as February. In Arkansas, the final army, well handled to the end—though some of its men went off on furloughs at last to try to do some planting and so failed to surrender their arms—was finally yielded by agreement, despite Kirby Smith's objections, on May 26, 1865. At the last minute about five hundred of its men, who had been plotting to continue the struggle, rode off across Texas into Mexico; among them were Kirby Smith himself, Price, Jo Shelby, of Missouri, and Hindman, who had been invalided out of service in Tennessee for longer than a year, and had retired to Arkansas again. Many of these men, it is said, carried their bullet-ridden battle flags with them across Texas, burying them finally on Mexican soil; many others, less desperate perhaps, or less violently and picturesquely heroic, soon after rode out of the state far northward, to join "the left wing of Price's army," as it pushed on through the sagebrush of the dangerous Sioux country into even wilder territory, that of new-born and remote Montana.

Thirteen

THE FIRST SHARECROPPER AND THE SECOND CIVIL WAR

When the last Confederate force had surrendered at the close of May, 1865—though old Stand Waitie, steadfast to the last, kept up some sort of resistance in the Indian Territory and did not come in till June—the Arkansawyers, or most of them, were probably relieved at last. Few of them suspected that it would require their utmost strength, courage, cunning, and determination to survive for the next ten years.

The bitterness felt by the people of Virginia, the Carolinas, Georgia, Alabama, Mississippi, and Louisiana was apparently not shared by the people of Arkansas till Reconstruction in 1867 taught them what they must expect. Except along the northern and western borders, in the mountain region, there had been singularly little destruction of property, and a good deal of that destruction had been done by roving bands of irregular jayhawkers and bushwhackers. Some of it had been deliberately done by the Confederates themselves, in the spring and summer of 1862, to prevent their cotton from falling into Federal hands. But there had been nothing to compare with Sherman's policy of devastation in Georgia.

Armies, both Confederate and Federal, had, of course, lived off the country; and since the land was still sparsely settled and most agriculturalists were away fighting, it grew harder, from the winter of 1863–1864 on, to keep an army subsisting. Throughout 1864 the final Confederate army, operating from around Camden and Washington, had beaten back large forces which had come up the Red

River from south and other forces coming down from Little Rock. It had the advantage of living in a fertile region well protected by surrounding swamps, forests, and hills; and it made full use of that advantage.

Kirby Smith's surrender found a Unionist government already installed at Little Rock, through Lincoln's actions and Steele's consent to them. It had been made as legal as possible under the circumstances, by calling a convention in the spring of 1864, which—though not at all representing the people as a whole—had rewritten the old Constitution of 1836 so as to abolish slavery, but had not granted the Negroes any power to vote in elections. The thirteenth amendment had been ratified; and Isaac Murphy had been declared elected as governor without any opposition to serve for four years from the spring of 1864. But there was not a dollar in the state treasury; and the Confederate debt was, naturally, repudiated. Heavy tax penalties were laid on those remaining disloyal, in order to produce some revenue.

Most of the manhood of the state was in other regions, surrendering at last under Joseph E. Johnston in North Carolina. When they returned finally, a good many of them must have felt like one cavalry officer I have heard of, who came back on the same horse with which he had set out, and who remarked as he sold it: "Well, all that is over now. I don't intend ever again to talk or think about it." Most of them, in short, were willing to let bygones be bygones and to start afresh, like the president of the Secession Convention, who was among the first to take an oath of allegiance.

But their present poverty, as compared with their former prosperity, must have often galled them. I know of at least one living man, now prominent outside the state, who recalls how as a youth he tramped along the newly constructed railroad tracks in midwinter, at the edge of Little Rock, looking for stray lumps of coal to heat the desolate home where his parents still lived. Education was altogether lacking, though the restored loyalist government soon attempted to introduce a public school system. But there was little enough revenue for this, or for anything else, till after Reconstruction got under way.

Meanwhile the Freedmen's Bureau was active throughout the state, making the offer familiar to every Southerner, of "forty acres and a mule" to all the ex-slaves, opening Negro schools, and, from first to last, spending a great deal of Northern money. In 1865 the money had largely to be spent in feeding an enormous army of the starving. The Confederacy had given up too late in Arkansas to enable a crop to be planted; and in May of that year the Bureau reported to its headquarters that it had served out seventy-five thousand rations to refugees, as well as forty-six thousand to the Negroes. And from June, 1865, to September, 1866, the enormous number of 1,705,000 rations were actually issued in Arkansas and Missouri, Missouri taking none of these after the end of 1865.

The Murphy government was honest and well-intentioned, but could do nothing to check the ravages of famine, brought on by four full years of destructive war. Ex-jayhawkers and ex-bushwhackers, now turned into open bandits, still prevailed through the northern and western part of the state, while off in the Indian Territory the tribes had begun to revert to savagery. All that Murphy could do was to govern with economy; and this he did, having a surplus to report as early as November, 1866, of some $153,540, though the state was, and had been for a long time past, under an enormous bonded debt of some $3,363,000—a debt largely incurred on behalf of the long defunct and fraudulent Real Estate Bank, and one on which no interest whatever had ever been paid.

Nothing could really be done to ease the common destitution till after the crop of 1866 went into the ground. Though, in the effort to get cheap labor, "immigration aid societies" were organized as early as the end of 1865, few immigrants came. The plantation section was prostrate, and what advances were made came first in the fruit and grain growing and mountain section around Fayetteville. Stagecoaches came back, making the trip to Hot Springs in twelve hours for a fare of ten dollars, and steamboats also; but people were far more interested in the railroads as a new possibility.

But above all arose this question: What would Congress do about readmitting Arkansas and the other seceded states back into the Union? In 1864 the Murphy government, while the southern part of the state was still holding out, had duly elected two senators to go to Washington. The Senate had refused to seat them. A resolution of January 27, 1865, declaring Arkansas to be now restored to the Union, was promptly tabled in Congress.

Following Lincoln's assassination, the Radicals, led by Fessenden, of

Maine, and Grimes, of Iowa, in the Senate, and by Thaddeus Stevens, of Pennsylvania, in the House, took charge of Congress. Against them stood one man—Andrew Johnson, of Tennessee, mistrusted by both North and South, whose vindication in history took fifty full years to establish. In February, 1866, Congress adopted the notorious resolution that no senator or representative from any of the insurrectionary states should be admitted till Congress itself should have declared them entitled to admission. This knocked the props out from under any conciliation policy. And in June the committee on reconstruction reported that the South was not ready to be brought back until properly chastised by its conquerors.

Meanwhile, in Arkansas, two distinct social and political movements soon manifested themselves, both prophetic of the future. It was already apparent that the Freedmen's Bureau was utterly unable to provide the Negro population, now free but utterly without economic status of any sort, with the "forty acres and a mule" that had been offered. During the latter stages of the war, with the Federal troops in occupation of most of the state, many Federal officers had themselves taken over abandoned plantations and had devoted themselves to growing cotton, encouraging the ex-slaves to return and settle in their former occupations on the mere promise of housing and feeding them. In 1865–1866, the practice spread more widely. Plantation owners who had served the Confederacy but who had taken the oath of allegiance had been permitted—though in some cases the matter had to be contested in the courts—to return and repossess themselves of their estates. They found that cotton, in the markets of Liverpool and New York, was selling at fantastic prices, while they themselves were faced with acres largely uncultivated for two years past and with a starving army of unemployed Negroes. The easiest way out was to give the Negroes cabins, to agree to furnish them and their families with food and necessities through the winter, to let them have twenty acres apiece to till, and to take half the crop when harvested, plus the cost of feeding them. In this way, new plantation fortunes were rapidly made and the sharecropper system became fastened upon the lowland area of the state. What was most remarkable about it was the fact that the Negroes readjusted themselves without protest to it; nor did the Freedmen's Bureau, which soon became merely a tool for winning elections in the hands of Reconstruction politicians, register any protest. The same sharecropper system, which had worked so successfully with the Negroes, later was applied to the whites, as we shall see—with abidingly bad results.

Advertisements therefore appeared in the newspapers, such as the following, from the *Arkansas Gazette* of May 9, 1867:

"One hundred laborers wanted to work on a plantation on the Arkansas River. Proprietors to bear all expenses and will pay one-fourth of the crops; or will give number one hands $240.00 a year with provisions, good comfortable houses and firewood."

Labor was indeed so scarce, with cotton reaching unheard-of prices, that it was solemnly proposed for a time to import Chinese labor into the state. The proposal did not succeed, and probably could not have succeeded. There is no evidence whatever to show that any of the former Federal soldiers or supporters now established in the State, soon to be known as "carpetbaggers" to distinguish them from the "scalawags," the native sons who pretended to be loyal, objected in the least to the coming or the spread of the sharecropper system.

The other movement was purely political. In December, 1865, the state supreme court decided that the law passed by the Murphy legislature that each elector before voting should be required to take an oath that he had not voluntarily borne arms against the United States and had not aided, directly or indirectly, the Confederacy since April, 1864, was void as being unconstitutional. The ex-Confederates now took new hope, and in the election of August, 1866, swept the legislature in their favor. They dubbed themselves the "Conservatives" as opposed to the "Unionists," and with true Arkansas invective assailed Murphy as "Old Imbecility." When the new legislature assembled in November, it was openly hostile to Murphy and went so far as to propose a vote of thanks to Jefferson Davis, now a prisoner of the Federal government, for "the noble and patriotic manner in which he conducted the affairs of the government while President of the Confederacy"; and it also voted a law providing pensions for ex-Confederate soldiers, and firmly rejected the Fourteenth Amendment to the United States Constitution. Murphy boldly vetoed the act providing for the Confederate pensions, but it was repassed over his veto. The Arkansawyers, in characteristic razorback spirit, were defiantly coming forth from the canebrakes into which they had been driven by the Federal conquest.

Murphy fought this movement, but he could not prevent a delegation of Arkansas citizens, appointed by the legislature, from proceeding to Washington on January 7, 1867, and being entertained there by Andrew Johnson and all his cabinet while they expressed freely the view that the "supreme court would be the umpire in the controversy" between the governor and the lawmakers of the state. They were utterly mistaken in such optimism. The decision rested rather with Congress, and Congress, dominated by the radical Republicans, was ready to act. On March 2 the blow fell. Thaddeus Stevens, of Pennsylvania, introduced into Congress on that day the first Reconstruction Act.

This declared boldly that no legal state government existed in Arkansas or anywhere else in the South. It divided the Southern states into five military districts, Arkansas and Mississippi being the fourth district, under the command of a Federal general; it empowered this military commander to substitute, for the civil courts, trials before a military commission; it forbade any Southern state to reenter the Union until it had voted a new constitution in conformity in all respects to that of the United States, as already amended; and it insisted that Congress must first approve any such constitution; further it proposed as a fresh condition for readmission, the ratification of the Fourteenth Amendment; and last, it stipulated that the voters in every state should be "all male citizens of whatever race, color, or previous condition," who were at least twenty-one years of age, had resided in the state for one year at the time of the election, and were not already disfranchised for having participated in rebellion, or for having committed any felony. All such voters must register with the military authorities. Such was the law, which, despite Johnson's veto, now passed rapidly through Congress.

By April, 1867, Murphy told the legislature that they could not, as they had fondly hoped, reassemble in July. The Confederate pension act was voided by order in October. Reconstruction was on, not to disappear till May, 1874—seven long and lean and remarkable years.

Had Congress been known to be determined and ready to force this policy of reprisal on the people of Arkansas, as soon as their surrender had taken place, the Civil War might have gone on far longer than it actually did. Desperation makes for resistance, even if that resistance be only one of sporadic bandit and guerrilla uprisings. But the people of Arkansas, on account of the circumstances of their own situation, as well as on account of the support given them by Richmond, had long found no particular confidence in anything but themselves. They were willing to forget the past and to come back into the Union, so long as their independence as a body could be maintained. And Lincoln, as long as he lived, had encouraged them to believe that the process of restoration would be easy. Although from 1864 onwards the radical majority in Congress had gone as far as they dared in opposing him, he had wisely avoided forcing on the South the dreaded alternative of a military occupation and a forced submission.

Thaddeus Stevens and his associates, writhing with embittered hate directed towards Lincoln's successor, Johnson, did not. And so Arkansas, like all the rest of the South, was forced through Reconstruction. Only this consoling thought remained: that something a little less bad had, for a time, been attempted. Since Stevens and his associates did not dare to move towards their scheme till some time after the surrender, it was certain from the outset that Reconstruction could not last; but not certain what way the various Southern States must take to overcome it.

Coming as it did on the top of Lincoln's policy of conciliation, Reconstruction created the "Solid South," the South that every Southerner born between 1865 and 1933 fully knew; an area of passive resistance, firm in its faith, but inevitably degenerating spiritually, since its only progress was material progress brought to it from without. This period fastened upon Arkansas, no less than upon other Southern States, the system of one-party government, where the choice has to be made between well-meaning inertia or "progressive" corruption; the scheme of social discriminations against the Negro; the unaltered and unalterable tenant-farmer system. With all these, it left the Southerner passive, ready to fight again in conflicts not of his own choosing, least ready of all Americans to find remedies for his complete economic subservience. It ended by dividing, all over again, the upland South and the lowland area in a breach that even now is not altogether healed. It made "the nation's number one economic problem" out of a territory owning half the productive resources of the entire country.

In these respects, Arkansas went through the same process that the other Southern States endured, the only difference being that in getting out of Reconstruction Arkansas had to adopt a way of her own. The way was eminently characteristic. It amounted, in the end, to a threat of waging anew the Civil War.

On March 2, 1867, the Reconstruction Act was passed, over Johnson's veto; and General Ord, commander of the new military district, entered on his duties. The first of these was to examine into the state's finances. They were eminently satisfactory. Ord contented himself with ousting the acting state treasurer, a man of known Confederate sympathies, and appointing a henchman of his own choosing. The second act was to start the registration of qualified voters, as required by the law. In Memphis, Albert Pike, who had chosen exile and whose application to be restored to full civil rights, though made even before the Confederacy collapsed, had so far produced no result from the Johnson government, was now editing a leading newspaper; and he violently opposed the idea of registration, with his familiar eloquence. All that he could counsel the Arkansawyers to follow was a course of passive resistance to Negro suffrage. In Arkansas, however, Hindman, who had but recently returned to his home in Helena from voluntary exile as a coffee planter in Mexico, came out surprisingly for registration. He pointed out that radical Republicans in Congress could now be undermined only step by step.

The election to decide on a new constitution was held in November; by December, the results were given out. Of the registered voters of the state, numbering 66,800, only a little over 41,000 had voted; there was a majority of 14,000 for the convention to make a new constitution, in accordance with the policy just adopted by Congress. On January 7, 1868, the convention assembled at Little Rock in an atmosphere qualified by the exhortations of the radical press to the voters of Arkansas to support the party that stood for "progress and reform." "Good roads, free bridges, free schools, arts and manufactures," and all other such dubious benefits were abundantly promised. The ex-Democrats, now dubbed "Conservatives," had no clear policy. Most of them had objected to registering at all. The *Gazette,* as well as several other opposition papers, was violent in its denunciation.

The convention was a sufficiently motley assemblage. Only eight Negro delegates were actually seated in it, and their conduct was so much better than that of the whites as to absolve them altogether from what followed. Twenty-three of its members were of the kind already contemptuously known as "carpetbaggers" or "carpet-sack men"; that is to say, they had followed the Federal army south, with all their possessions packed up in one carpetbag, on the quest for good jobs and easy fortunes. Their leader was Joseph Brooks, a black-bearded, heavy-set, sullen-looking former exhorter and evangelist from Iowa, who had come down with the Federal army as chaplain to a Negro regiment and was active in the Freedmen's Bureau; a man with a huge, bellowing voice, a choice ability to make campaign denunciations, and a reckless fury against his opponents, not easily to be matched. Aiding him was James Hinds, a shrewd, not-too-scrupulous lawyer from New York. And prominent among their number was John McClure, a tall rawboned midwestern lawyer from Ohio, known to all his friends as "Poker Jack" from his fondness for that game; he wore a wide-brimmed wool hat, a black frock coat reaching down to his knees, smoked cigars perpetually, and was cynically profane in his conversation.

Among the thirty members who were "scalawags"—native sons who had gone over to the radicals—there was no one particularly prominent; but the "Conservatives" had succeeded in electing about a dozen, their chief man being J. N. Cypert, a slight, frail-looking individual with an unruly shock of black hair and beard, and the remote and dreamy eyes of the frontiersman. He was from White County, fifty miles northeast of Little Rock, where the pretty little town of Searcy still lies, just at the point where the flat-bottom lowlands are first cut into by the rocky, flat-topped Ozark ridges. Cypert managed to obtain the chairmanship of the unimportant committee on revising the journal, and from that obscure post aided mightily in impeding the convention's progress. Cypert had actually been a member of the secession convention in 1861; and he had also served as major in the Confederate army; but was now believed to be Unionist by all his neighbors, and so had had no difficulty in registering and being elected as delegate to the convention.

Six days after it met, Cypert arose and moved that the Constitution of 1864 be readopted. This was the very Constitution that Lincoln himself had presumably already accepted; under it, although the Negro had full property rights, he was not given the franchise, nor did it disfranchise any white citizens. This motion was immediately countered by Hinds, who moved that the matter be referred to a special committee of Negroes already set up to investigate the affairs of the penitentiary. Cypert protested at this attempt to ridicule a serious matter, and a great debate was on. It continued for days, Brooks making perhaps the most violent of the speeches, in which he taunted Cypert's arguments as being "of a piece" with the violent denunciations now going on in the *Gazette,* the opposition organ. He read the *Gazette's* description of the convention, as follows:

"The bastard collocation whose putridity stinks in the nostrils of all decency, now in session at the capitol, has very conceited ideas of its importance and pretentious opinions of the scope of its powers. As a matter of some trifling interest to those who have not witnessed the exhibition of the menagerie, we would state that the Negro members, eight in number, occupy seats on the western side of the hall." He declared, over Cypert's protests, that Cypert held precisely the same opinion as this, of the Negroes. And he wound up with this peroration: "I can say that loyal men have now left their homes in Arkansas for the last time! We claim the right to be here. They may confront us here and elsewhere with such slang as that which has been employed in regard to the odor of our members and our constituents. I have only to say, sir, if I am to elect between the two, if I am to choose between the odor of my constituents and the smell of treason, which 'smells to heaven,' then I affiliate over this way to all eternity!" Cypert in vain protested that he had said no such thing: that he did not object to Negroes' sitting near him; but that he thought they were being misled. He closed the debate by defending his original resolution; but it was rejected by a vote of 63 to 10.

The convention went on to minor but no less important matters. Provision had to be made for the payment of its members and for the printing of its proceedings. In regard to the latter, it was decided that no bids for printing were to be made. One John G. Price, who had formerly been a member of a minstrel troupe, was to be the public printer, and the president of the Convention was allowed to fix his fee. The provision concerning members' payment was lavish. Each member of the "menagerie," as the *Gazette* had called it, was to receive eight dollars a day, plus mileage. In addition, he was to be given, free of charge, no less than ten daily newspapers (of course, these papers were all ardent supporters of the official party) to read. They must have done a great deal of reading in the convention, to get through so many newspapers; despite the fact that, as the proceedings went on, debate was carried far beyond daylight and the final sittings were prolonged all through the night, under a Southern sky charged with February cloud and sleet; with smoky oil lamps fizzling all around the room, and the galleries framed with eager faces of Negroes, come to gape and to listen at the wild debate that broke out below.

A financial committee headed by "Poker Jack" McClure turned in, at a point in the convention's proceedings, a long report denouncing the state officials of the antebellum days as having promoted "a system of financiering known only to thieves and robbers without conscience." This touched off a new flood of oratory, in which shone one Bradley, like Brooks an ex-preacher, from Bradley County, a border district in the southeastern section, whose political principles had embraced both support of the Confederacy and, since then, strong Unionism. He said, as a sample of the supreme Arkansas eloquence of the period, in reply to an equally denunciatory outburst by Brooks:

"Sir, I have travelled over the mountains of Arkansas; I know her people—the most generous, hospitable, noble hearted people I ever saw, in any country, lived here within her borders and live here today. Society has been slightly adulterated I confess, but we cannot help that. (Laughter.) We are told, sir, in this report that the system of financing pursued in this State has been one that could be known only to thieves and robbers. Well, it was never known until that committee found it out! That is all that I have to say on that point.

"I have almost given up my hopes, for this country. As I have sat here and listened to the debates, I have sometimes been ready to go to the water's edge, and have felt like exclaiming: 'Oh that my head were waters, and mine eyes a fountain of tears that I might weep day and night for the slain of the daughters of my people!'"

Here Brooks interposed with a question: "Who slew them? As the gentleman is going to weep for the slain, I would ask him who slew them?"

Bradley (pointing to Brooks): "They were slain by the same instrument that the Philistines fell by! And sir, their ranks are still falling today as the weapon sweeps."

This produced a roar of laughter, in which even Brooks was forced, half-heartedly, to join. Both men went on taunting each other. Both men were taunted by members—sleepy, no doubt, and weary of the bad atmosphere of the ill-ventilated hall.

It was only after one of the most able Negro members had arisen and complained that a debate on vital and important issues was being made into an opportunity for the display of personal venom, that the constitution was finally voted upon. The last vote, taken in the small hours of the morning, showed that forty-five members were for the new instrument, and twenty-two against; and so the Reconstruction Constitution of 1868 duly passed. A roar of applause from the galleries, packed with Negroes, went through the hall.

Cypert, fully aware of the fact that his minority had risen from ten votes to twenty-two, was determined to resist to the last. He had skilfully conducted the debate on the issue of whether the new law was to give the Negroes—who were uneducated, and known to be under the influence of unscrupulous political leaders—complete domination. Now, as the applause subsided, he arose, and boldly remarked:

"I have had a little experience in revolutionary movements. Six years ago, I heard just such a clamor from those galleries as I heard a while ago. It shocked me then—it shocks me now."

But Brooks, who had all along dominated the convention with his presence, was contemptuous. He retorted: "I am sorry for the gentleman's nerves, but I think he will feel better, pretty shortly." However, Brooks was mistaken. It was he whose nerves were soon to be shaken. Cypert, and the entire minority, firmly refused even to sign the new Constitution.

The Democrats, completely routed by the turn of events, had not dared to nominate candidates for state offices under the new Constitution; they had merely advised voters to vote against it; but the Republican state convention, though dominated by Brooks, had surprisingly passed him over in its selection of candidates. Its chosen nominees were Powell Clayton for governor, J. M. Johnson for lieutenant-governor; Lafayette Gregg, John McClure, and Thomas M. Bowen as state supreme court justices; James R. Berry, auditor; R. J. T. White, secretary of state; Thomas Smith, superintendent of schools; and J. R. Montgomery, attorney-general. Of this list, none was uncorrupt except the superintendent of schools, who unobtrusively began to put into effect the laws establishing an efficient system of free public education.

Two elections were now held; the first, on March 13, for the vote on the new constitution, being supervised by the military; the second for state officials and congressional delegates, not being supervised—though in this last election there was no opposition. The result of the first election, not given out till April 22, showed a majority of only 1,316 votes for the constitution; and an actual majority of the qualified and registered electors of the state had not voted for it. Congress had, however, already provided for this contingency by decreeing that a bare majority of votes cast would be sufficient to pass any new constitution imposed on the states which had been defeated in the war. Negro domination was now a reality; and so was carpetbag rule. Brooks, however, who had done so much to obtain this result, was left out; but he was content, for the moment, to bide his time.

On June 20, Congress, deeply engaged in impeachment proceedings against Andrew Johnson, voted that Arkansas was a state in the Union again. And on July 2, an open carriage, accompanied by mounted soldiers and drawn by six black horses, conducted the outgoing and the incoming governors of Arkansas to the old State House in Little Rock. The stands in front of the white-columned building were full of fashionable women in summer dress, waving fans and chatting, and with well-dressed carpetbaggers and scalawags near by. Farther off, under the shade of the sycamores and the oaks, stood ex-Confederates, suspiciously ragged and hungry, looking on with proud contempt and also with a touch of agony. Still further away stood the Negroes, humble and silent, wondering if the Day of Jubilee had dawned for them at last.

Powell Clayton, the new Reconstruction governor, was, at this time, just under thirty-five years of age. Born, like Thaddeus Stevens, in Pennsylvania, he had gone while young to Kansas, and there had acquired much knowledge of the violent political movements that had marked the birth of that divided state. As an officer of a Kansas regiment he had come down to Arkansas in 1862–1863, and had shown himself to have considerable courage and resource as a commander; his defense of Pine Bluff, by means of cotton-bale barricades, against a violent Confederate cavalry and artillery attack at the close of 1863 was well known. In 1865, like many other Northern men, he had married a Southern woman and, with cotton selling at fantastic prices, soon became a wealthy planter.

His entry into politics had come only with Reconstruction. He was an able speaker, not possessed of the ranting invective employed by Brooks, but capable of coherent and forcefully apt argument. It may have been for this reason that the Republicans, led by such men as Hinds, Logan H. Roots (builder of a large carpetbag fortune) and other shrewdly unscrupulous men, had chosen him as their candidate. In making him governor they had not only ignored Brooks, but also J. M. Johnson, an old Loyal Unionist from the Fayetteville region, who had hoped for that post.

Within two days of the Fourth of July, 1868, Clayton sat in the same carriage as Isaac Murphy, close to seventy, with the mild blue eyes, tangled beard, and long wavy locks of the mountaineer. Murphy was wearing for the occasion a suit of plain homespun. Clayton had put on, to set off his determined jutting jaw, a suit of full broadcloth, with frock coat and wide wing collar; and he was wearing fine kid gloves. As he got into the carriage, Murphy—according to Clayton's own statement—took a long look at the gloves and drawled, "Well, I reckon I never saw anyone but you wearing gloves in July! Only dudes do that!" To this Clayton retorted, "Governor, it's not the garb that makes the man; but in deference to you and especially in view of the character of the work I am about to enter upon today, which will require handling without gloves, I will now remove mine." Whereupon, Murphy shook hands and, when the inauguration was over, invited Clayton to his office, where stood, according to Clayton's memoirs, "a barrel filled with straw. From it Governor Murphy fished out a gallon stone jug, removed the cork, and politely presented the jug to me. After proposing his good health, and future prosperity, I partook of its contents. It was the real 'mountain dew' as the Governor had characterised it." The old mountaineer had saluted his successor; had made the carpetbagger welcome, in his own way. Clayton recalled the incident later, at eighty; but he never understood, in all his long life, why this was the only expression of good will the mountaineers ever gave him.

He had good reasons, and many of them, for taking off his gloves before entering into the duties of his office. His nomination for the important post had stirred up dangerous animosities in his own party. Moreover, a secret organization, which was generally known throughout the South as the Ku Klux Klan, and which patient historians have now traced back to a little harmless fun indulged in by some bored young men in Pulaski, Tennessee, in the "Dying Month" of December, 1865, was already on the loose and was making converts among the Southerners, hour by hour. Its officers, known by the mysterious names of "Wizard," "Titan," "Cyclops," "Magi," and "Monk," held their secret meetings at places known as "dens." Its members gathered in the dead of night, clad in shrouds and hooded masks, and rode around the country, terrifying Negroes, warning carpetbaggers to depart, and in some cases, actually shooting or drowning their victims. The organization had already been openly referred to in various Southern newspapers. In March, 1868, a Memphis newspaper had printed what, in its way, was a remarkable poem. The paper stated that the poem had "very mysteriously found its way upon our table yesterday. The writer is evidently a man of genius, and certainly knows something about the 'Klan.' We wish some member of the organization would tell us when, where, and how to join this mysterious order, as from one to three hundred applications are made to us each day." Some stanzas from the poem follow:

The wolf is in the desert,
And the panther in the brake.
The fox is on his rambles,
And the owl is wide awake;
For now 'tis noon of darkness,
And the world is all asleep;
And some shall wake to glory,
And some shall wake to weep.
Ku Klux.

Thrice hath the lone owl hooted,
And thrice the panther cried;
And swifter through the darkness,
The Pale Brigade shall ride.
No trumpet sounds its coming,
And no drum-beat stirs the air;
But noiseless in their vengeance,
They wreak it everywhere.
Ku Klux.

The misty gray is hanging
On the tresses of the East,
And morn shall tell the story
Of the revel and the feast.
The ghostly troop shall vanish
Like the night in constant cloud,
But where they rode shall gather
The coffin and the shroud.
Ku Klux.

This poem has been attributed to Albert Pike, who was at the time in Memphis, editor of another newspaper and still anxiously awaiting his pardon from Andrew Johnson for his part in the Confederacy. There is little doubt that Pike had already evinced a strong sympathy for the Ku Klux and their methods; and there is a persistent tradition that he had already met and had a conference with General Nathan Bedford Forrest, the reputed "Grand Wizard" of the order. Its method of passive resistance and of working underground to obtain its object was of a sort likely to appeal to his temperament. But whether Pike, author of "Morals and Dogma," a moralized prose allegory of life conceived under the symbols of Freemasonry, and published in 1871, really had so much poetic power as this poem shows, may perhaps be doubted.

The next month, in the midst of a sudden wave of sporadic disorders already sweeping over the state, the Republican newspaper of Pine Bluff published the following notice, said to have been found posted up in that city:

K.K.K.

Corinth Division,
Pine Bluff Retreat
Special Order No. 2.

Spirit brothers; Shadows of Martyrs; Phantoms from gory fields; Followers of Brutus!!!!! Rally, Rally, Rally. When shadows gather, moons grow dim, and stars tremble, glide to the Council Hall, and wash your hands in tyrant's blood; and gaze upon the list of condemned traitors. The time has arrived. Blood must flow. The true must be saved.

Work in Darkness
Bury in waters
Make no sound
Trust not the air
Strike high and sure
Vengeance! Vengeance! Vengeance!

Tried, condemned. Execute well. Fear is dead. Every man is a judge and this executes!!!!!! Fail not!!

Mandate of the
M G. C. D.

By D. M. G. C. 12 m. p. 2

Clayton knew well that something serious might develop from this strange rant. Thousands of the Arkansawyers were seeking for ways and means of revolting from Reconstruction. As Confederate soldiers, in the last months of Arkansas resistance, they had departed from the ranks and had slipped off home, taking with them their rifles; others had obtained furloughs in that spring of 1865, before the surrender, and had gone home with their arms, not actually surrendering; still others had actually surrendered but had been carelessly permitted to depart without turning in their favorite "squirrel guns." Evidences now were accumulating for Clayton that the people of the state would never endure him as governor. They still had weapons and ammunition, and the wit to use them. The Ku Klux Klan was abroad. Bandits and desperadoes were more active than ever; and up in Missouri, the James Boys had already commenced their headlong career as robbers of the Bank at Liberty on a February morning in 1866. They had taken seventy-two thousand dollars in cash from the tellers' counter, amid shots and rebel yells. Clayton's own hard early experience, bred in Kansas border wars, had hardened him. He was no sentimentalist. He must counterattack.

In his inaugural message, he had recommended and promised the organization of a militia; he now proceeded to try and make good on that promise. To a man of his military background, force was the only remedy for the state of affairs in which Arkansas now stood. The great majority of the people had never even voted in the election that gave him the governorship. In their eyes he was a usurper, knowing nothing and caring less about their wants and needs. The old flame of local independence, which had been sufficiently manifested at the time of the Civil War, was burning up again stronger than ever among them.

Early in September, an agent of the Freedmen's Bureau was filled with buckshot as he sat at a window of his office in Crittenden County. Disorders had already become rampant in this region, bordering on the Mississippi, where lived many Negroes; once the disorders started, they went on. In the same month, at Helena, General Hindman who—be it remembered—had advised his neighbors to register for the election that had brought in Clayton, was also shot while sitting at his window, only living long enough to forgive his unknown assassins. And in the same month, according to Clayton's own statement, made more than forty years later however, a certain "mysterious stranger" whose name was never given but who was promptly furnished with three hundred dollars to enable him to disappear from Arkansas, called on Clayton in the dead of night and revealed to him the oaths and prescripts, as well as the names, of the officers of the dreaded Ku Klux Klan.

A new national presidential election was due to be held in November; and though the Democrats had put up candidates, it was quite obvious that nothing was likely to stop the swing of the tide to Grant, that idol with feet of clay. Arkansas, however, as a state duly "reconstructed," was, in part at least, able to vote; and in that fall, great demonstrations were organized in favor of the Republican party. One of them, a night torchlight procession of Negroes into Little Rock from the plantations below, was, it is said, rapidly dispersed, because of two or three shots casually fired from a nearby window; the fear of Ku Klux reprisals against Clayton's rule was now growing every hour among the freedmen. In October, on their way to a Republican rally near Clarendon, James Hinds and Joseph Brooks, riding together through the dense swamps of the White River, were fired at from the underbrush. Hinds was killed instantly, and Brooks was severely wounded. Whether all these signs of an incipient revolt were enough to justify Clayton in his steps taken to fix martial law on the state, is still a matter for dispute; but there is no doubt that lawlessness was daily increasing. He felt he must do something. An agent whom he had sent to Searcy to spy on the doings of certain Ku Klux "dens" said to be active there, also had suddenly and mysteriously disappeared; long later his body was found, drowned, in a well on the outskirts.

Since he had first come into office, Clayton had begun to write long letters to the War Department at Washington asking for rifles and ammunition wherewith he proposed to keep subdued the rebellious population of the state. The head of the War Department at first frankly favored the request, but it has been said that one of his staff officers advised him not to listen to such wild appeals. Clayton thereupon made fresh requests for arms to certain Northern governors but did not get any response. He finally sent off an agent, north to Detroit, who succeeded in buying four thousand secondhand Belgian muskets, one hundred pounds of cartridges for each gun, a million five hundred thousand percussion caps, and powder to match, and shipped this entire consignment down to Memphis by the last of September.

Arrived at Memphis (since the railroad between Memphis and Little Rock was not yet completed) the entire cargo was put on the wharf for boat shipment; but not a single steamboat captain there would agree to transport it to Arkansas. Accordingly, on October 12, 1868, Clayton chartered the steamboat *Hesper,* waiting at the wharf at Little Rock, and ordered it to proceed to Memphis, and to pick up his invaluable cargo. The word, however, about the nature of the consignment had already been well passed around; and on the night of October 15, having loaded the munitions and steamed some twenty miles down river, the *Hesper* was suddenly challenged, while taking on wood, by a steam tug, the *Nettie Jones,* which was seen in the darkness to contain a considerable party of masked and armed men. A few harmless shots were fired; the masked party swarmed aboard the *Hesper* and dumped the entire cargo over the side into the muddy Mississippi; and the *Hesper,* without her cargo, was then allowed to proceed, while the *Nettie Jones* steamed back to Memphis.

It is said that there was a ball given in Memphis that night, and that an astonishing number of young gentlemen arrived late for it; that their boots were observed to be flecked with Mississippi mud when they did arrive; but that the ball was, nevertheless, a great success. Clayton, when he learned of the raid, promptly memorialized Congress to put an end to all such high-handed acts, which he qualified as sheer piracy; but though the *Nettie Jones* was actually captured in Arkansas waters four months later and its commander and crew duly arrested, nothing could be elicited from them as to who the persons were who had organized and carried out the daring raid. The *New York Tribune* declared vociferously that behind this act had stood no less a person than General Nathan Bedford Forrest, alleged leader of the Ku Klux Klan, and famous for his die-hard Southern sentiments, as well as for his ability "to git there fustest with the mostest men"; but no one now paid much attention to old Horace Greeley, who had committed the crowning eccentricity of going on the bond of no less a person than Jefferson Davis, when that worthy was brought to trial. Clayton finally obtained a fresh supply of arms from various private sources but was never able to equip more than about two thousand men in all.

Because of the upset given to his plans by the *Hesper* affair, he did not actually proclaim martial law till the day of the presidential election, and then only in ten specified counties. But now, at last, he was able to divide the entire state into four military districts and to appoint a military commander for each district, while he prepared to send his troops wherever the inhabitants should show any signs of armed opposition.

Throughout the rest of 1868, and well into the spring of 1869, large areas of the state were therefore at the mercy of this militia, which was composed almost entirely of Negroes and officered by men who in many cases were little better than the outlaws who had infested the mountain districts since the days of the Civil War. It was generally believed throughout my boyhood, at least, that, in many places, this Clayton militia tortured various inhabitants by sticking their feet into fires, to get them to reveal where money and valuables were hidden. This had undoubtedly been done by some particularly lawless Federal soldiers in 1862 at Clarksville, and there was nothing to prevent a revival of the practice. Shootings and robberies and burnings were fairly common. Clayton himself later listed a large number accomplished also by his opponents. He frankly admitted that in some cases, white women were violated by Negro militiamen.

At Center Point, an insignificant village amid the pinewoods and clay ridges of the southwestern quarter of the state, the most sensational incident occurred in the shape of a battle between Clayton's militia and the inhabitants. One of Clayton's commanders, a redheaded frontier bully named Catterson, heard that the villagers had a large supply of arms concealed there and were preparing for some sort of uprising; so by three roads, he and his men, about three hundred and sixty strong, converged on the settlement. The outlying inhabitants, hearing of the proposed invasion, gathered in some force and fired off a few shots at Catterson's approach; whereupon the village was taken by storm, a Ku Klux den discovered, with altar and Confederate flag in place, and sixty prisoners captured to be paraded through the streets of Little Rock. In Crittenden County, the lawlessness that another of Clayton's "generals," named Upham, promoted roused such strong fury that here martial law persisted long after it was gone elsewhere; and in Pope County, a mountaineer region without Negroes to the northwest, a veritable guerrilla war broke out in 1871, because Clayton had attempted to back up some resisted arrests by calling in the militia to reinforce the sheriff. This last outbreak is significant as showing that the mountaineers were getting ready to make common cause with the lowlanders; their feeling for the South during the war had never been strong, but they were not going to be ruled by the methods of Powell Clayton.

Meantime at Little Rock, which had tripled its population between 1860 and 1870—rising now to a city of 12,380 inhabitants in that latter year—people, though terrified at the excesses Clayton and his gang were prepared to commit, struggled valiantly to repair their lost fortunes. Some, too proud or too sensitive, could not submit and sank into proud and utter insignificance; others maintained a no less stubborn pride, insisting on celebrating the bygone glories of the Confederacy's stand, but engaged in the menial occupations of storekeeper and cotton-buyer, standing behind ill-equipped counters, elbow to elbow with the Negroes in the muddy streets while the bales, more valuable than ever now that Lawrence and Lowell and other New England towns were filling up with imported foreign mill labor, were lowered down from the clay-flecked drays and lifted on to the steelyard scales. For those who could stand the pace, the South was booming, despite mountains of debt amassed by carpetbag legislatures and despite loss of effective political power. The boom was temporarily halted by the panic of 1873; but it resumed again after Reconstruction had finally vanished.

For the moment, Arkansas, like all the rest of the South, having sown the wind of war in 1861–1865, was reaping, with Powell Clayton's help, the whirlwind of Reconstruction.

Fourteen

A HUMBLE MAN DECIDES THE ISSUE IN HIS OWN WAY

Governor Elisha Baxter, of Arkansas, sat in his office upstairs in the west wing of the State House at Little Rock. Nothing in particular was happening at that moment; and for this Governor Baxter was deeply and sincerely grateful, as he had always had an appreciation of peace, quiet, and contentment and had found little enough of all three in his own life. Except for his son, a frail-looking young man about twenty years of age, who was sitting in the office along with him reading a newspaper, Governor Baxter was alone. Through the windows there came the sounds of some boys playing in the street beyond the State House grounds. They were engaged in a game of this new-fangled thing called baseball, now sweeping over the country. A mocking-bird was singing, loudly and insistently, in the fresh-leafing oaks, and a Carolina wren called challengingly to another, some distance away. Robins were fluting from somewhere; the sky was clouding over fast, and it probably would rain that afternoon. The growing smell of spring earth, sun-warmed and soon to be freshly sprinkled, drifted through the half-open windows. The falling petals of a flowering tree slid past the casement. A bee, caught and attempting escape, droned heavily on the pane. Governor Baxter's face, broad, heavy, fleshy, with its great mass of coarse dark hair above black eyebrows, beneath which gleamed dark eyes that revealed his Scotch-Irish ancestry, relaxed somewhat. His heavy, sturdy body settled deeper in its chair. The creased lines around his stern mouth softened, and he smiled towards his son. It was the morning of April 15, 1874.

His mind went back to the time, twenty-two years ago, when he had come to Arkansas. People were moving out of the older eastern states, and Governor Baxter had but followed the example of thousands in going from North Carolina to the Trans-Mississippi region. He had been a young man then, barely turned twenty-five, with a wife married only three years before. They had made their way, along with thousands of others, in a canvas-hooped wagon, through a country still largely without railroads, happy if they could drive twenty miles in a day. Now the new railroads were already running through Little Rock from Memphis to Fort Smith and from Saint Louis to Texarkana. Governor Baxter stared at the wall, with the faded print of Washington upon it, and wondered what that Founder of the Republic would have thought of a railroad train. For himself, he frankly admitted, the sight of one still overawed him.

He had chosen, as a spot to settle, Batesville, a pretty village, lying at the point where the sparkling, steady White River broke out from the long, densely wooded Ozarks and there took to the plain: a land of limestone ridges, cedars and hickories, and wide bottomlands good alike for cattle and for corn. He had opened a store there, at first, with the funds he had brought with him, but it had not prospered. Within two years he was penniless, a bankrupt. There were children to feed now; and Elisha Baxter had set himself to study the law, sitting up late at night after a day's hard work, poring over much-thumbed law books frequently borrowed from his wealthier neighbors. These neighbors had helped—he often wondered whether there were any better people anywhere in the world than the hill people of Arkansas—and in a few years he was on his feet again. He had insisted on paying off all the debts left by that first venture into storekeeping, though he was sure that his Arkansas neighbors would have readily forgiven them. And he had become, at length, a man of substance, owner of a fine old home not far out from Batesville, known as "Catalpa Hall."

The law, at which he had prospered, had led to politics naturally, and he had not needed much urging by his friends to stand for the state legislature and to take part in two sessions of that body. But he had not—he admitted to himself—been much of a success as a politician. Somehow he could never make the sort of speech that would get other people all excited—what he had to say was too simple, too plain. When he saw how the wild secession talk was beginning to sweep over the country, he had retired and had taken no part in the movement that had carried Arkansas out of the Union. The war had found him a private citizen, with six children, and the respect of all his neighbors—many of them Unionists at heart—at Batesville.

Following on the battle of Pea Ridge, when General Curtis—a man, he thought, not unlike himself—had occupied Batesville, he had come out strongly in favor of a restoration of the Union. He had helped to recruit a volunteer regiment, had made speeches in his slow, precise, stolid way, had even been offered the command of the regiment at last. But he had not cared—had never cared—for fighting. Early in the following year a Confederate cavalry raid, led by that fire-eater, Marmaduke, of Missouri, had swept around Batesville, and cut Curtis's line of communications, forcing the ever-cautious Curtis to abandon his post and start a retreat. He, Baxter, had reluctantly followed Curtis north into Missouri, not wishing to have an open war with his Batesville neighbors on his hands.

This decision—like so many others forced on him by circumstances—had nearly cost him his life. In April of sixty-three, Marmaduke, from his new headquarters at Batesville, had pushed up into Missouri. At Patterson, a small town north of the border, Marmaduke's scouts, under the command of Colonel "Bob" Newton—a friend of Baxter's in Little Rock—had discovered him living peaceably, as a private citizen and had promptly arrested him and sent him back to Little Rock under guard. Here he had been indicted for treason to the Confederacy. Thanks to his friends, he had escaped from the common jail and had fled north to the familiar district around Batesville, where plenty of other people lived who had never wanted to choose sides and who had never expected to be drafted for a war not of their seeking. Here he had lived, practically as an outlaw, till, upon General Steele's coming to Little Rock, he had at last become a Federal colonel; and after the Murphy government had taken office, he had naturally been elected United States senator, but had never been allowed to take his seat in that body.

This was a time about which he did not want to think much, and yet it was always present in his mind, like an uninvited guest at the table. Who had made that miserable war, anyway? Not he, or any people of his sort. They had hoped to the last that if slavery was to be allowed to remain—since the lowlanders had insisted over and over again that it was guaranteed them by the Constitution and that they could not raise cotton without it—the government would proceed to gradual emancipation by offering the slaveholders compensation for what was, after all, their property. Even he, Baxter, had found it difficult to run one of the largest plantations near Batesville without some slaves. That did not mean that slavery was right. He and thousands of other hill people did not think so. It would be better to give up slavery altogether than to go on raising "bumblebee-cotton"—cotton so small that a bumblebee, by stretching its legs, could reach from the bolls to the ground—as so many of his neighbors had already done, simply because cotton was the "money crop" of the South. If nothing better than that was possible, then indeed the South was in a hopeless way! . . . In Congress and out of it, from Fort Sumter to Appomattox, the South had been led by a minority of hotheads to a war that was sheer madness. The hill people whom they had ignored had no particular objection to fighting, but had only demanded to know what all the fighting was for.

He had even been branded as a coward because he had not wanted, after all, to fight at Batesville. What some, including one or two of his five strong-minded brothers, had said of him did not really matter—but it had rankled just the same. He would not make a war on people who had been his neighbors for more than ten years. Not only that—he would not make war on people who had given him a fresh start, who had raised him up from a penniless bankruptcy to a proud and an honorable position. However misled they were, he cared too much for them to make war on them. So he had preferred to be a fugitive rather than to commit an injustice. Curtis was all right; but many of his men had done nothing but loot and plunder at will. He preferred to be thought of as a coward, rather than to stand alongside such soldiers. . . . Governor Baxter shifted uneasily in his chair as his mind ran over the past.

Men who knew nothing of Arkansas, whose only merit was that they had been Republicans, were now considered fit to sit in the convention and to make the new laws. Men like Isaac Murphy—who had tried to restore the credit of the state and had fought the attempt to pledge a nonexistent credit in order to aid the incoming Northern railroads—had been relegated to poverty and obscurity. The newly arrived speculators and bond-jobbers had already begun to build their magnificent new houses on Lincoln Avenue, "Robbers' Roost," as the citizens of Little Rock called it, overlooking the new Union Depot, the Arkansas River, and the penitentiary; while Clayton, one of their own sort but even more ruthless, was ready to sacrifice anything to gain and keep power. And he, Elisha Baxter, had been given, for all his efforts to keep the Union together, a miserable circuit judgeship, entailing much hard work and open-air exercise, up along the sparsely settled Missouri border.

Here he had come into conflict at the start with Clayton's martial law and Clayton's militia commanders. There were now two conceptions of law abroad, the one of the courts and the juries, and the other of armed gangs; and Clayton had openly favored the latter. He had been in terror of the Ku Klux Klan, not realizing that the mountaineers, as such, would not and did not join that organization. In the winter of 1868, in Fulton County, the clash had come. A troop of armed men under the command of William Monks, who was no better than a border outlaw, had turned up, under authority from Clayton, and had started to arrest peaceable citizens, to loot and plunder their homes, and to commit other outrages. As the judge responsible for the district, he had, by writ of habeas corpus, forced them, finally, to turn over to the legally-appointed sheriff, all their prisoners for trial. He had written, then, a letter which his enemies had long used against him:

"Colonel William Monks:—

"We ask you most earnestly, as officially representing the judiciary of Arkansas, to turn over your prisoners to the sheriff. We beg of you as citizens to allow the majesty of the law to be vindicated in this matter, and not to imperil the lives and homes and property of all good citizens of this State.

"Respectfully and truly yours,
"Elisha Baxter."

People had actually sneered loudly at that letter—his face flushed heavily—as if that, too, had been the action of a coward. Was he a coward? Did a man have to brag and bluster and threaten his way through life in order not to be called a coward? He had done what he thought to be his plain duty, but had tried to be polite even to Monks, because, after all, Governor Clayton had trusted such fellows. Clayton, he was sure—he was Senator Clayton now, and much in demand among the lobbies of Washington—had been utterly mistaken as regards the methods to be used. He, Baxter, had at least called a halt to Monks's lawlessness. What was more, he had been in favor of removing the disabilities which under the Reconstruction Law had kept all ex-Confederates from registering as voters; and as judge he had openly said so.

Why had Clayton, who had carried everything along with him with so high a hand, gone out of his way to snub and offend Joe Brooks? Did he not know that the black-bearded, bull-voiced preacher from Fairfield, Iowa, was never likely to forgive an injury? Did he not realize that all the colored people, without exception, who could vote, would vote for Brooks and do exactly as he said? It was to be feared that Clayton, at bottom, was a dude and a snob, as Murphy had laughingly said. Brooks had forced through the new Constitution, had loyally campaigned for Clayton, and then had been completely ignored. Then, in his anger, he had come out in 1870 for state senator on a platform repudiating Clayton and, what was worse, had nearly been elected. Johnson, the lieutenant governor, had declared that Brooks was, in fact, elected; and a contested election case revealed that Brooks had an even more dangerous ally in the shape of that old bushy-bearded rascal with his frock coat down to his knees, "Poker Jack" McClure. Clayton had planned to go from the governorship to the United States Senate; but faced with this new kind of revolt he had been forced to shift his policy and recommend that the disabilities on voters be removed. So great had been the split in the ranks of his own followers that Clayton himself had narrowly escaped impeachment and had warded it off only by offering the secretaryship of the state to Johnson and by insisting that Brooks remain unseated.

In March, 1871, three years before, Clayton had finally felt it safe to go off to the Senate, leaving the governorship in the hands of his old friend Hadley; while Brooks, unseated, still remained in outer darkness. But at that point the whole disastrous result of martial law had exploded in Hadley's face—up in Pope County, of all places. The mountaineers of that independent region had never owned, nor wanted, Negro slaves; they had had nothing whatever to do with the Ku Klux Klan; but a feud between two families had led to a murder, and the sheriff had made some arrests. While the alleged murderers were being transported to the county seat of Dover, a town which had been much damaged by bushwhackers during the war, they had escaped and taken refuge with some of their own people; then the sheriff had called together the militia to aid him in re-arresting them, and had moved on Dover with two hundred and fifty armed men at his back. They had been fired upon from the fence corners and the windows of houses, for the distance of a quarter of a mile and the space of several hours, with the result that they had to withdraw without ever finding the fugitives. Violent methods had only bred violence—and this among a people who had shown no enthusiasm at all for rebellion of the Jefferson Davis brand.

Then Brooks, in that spring of three years ago, had finally come out for the governorship, fighting like a wild beast! It was not for nothing that one of his colored supporters had compared him to an old brindle-tailed bull he had known as a boy, which had bellowed so loud that it scared all the other cattle half to death. The phrase had stuck, and Brooks's followers became known as the "Brindle-tails," while Clayton's crowd were called the "Minstrels," perhaps because they sang more sweetly to Clayton's ears. Anyway, Brooks had come out for the governorship and had made a bid for the votes of the Democrats. Many of them had been willing enough to give their votes to anyone who offered to beat Clayton. In five years, the people of the state had paid over six and a half million dollars in taxes, and still the state debt had risen from four millions to nineteen millions. Railroad-aid bonds and "levee bonds" had been floated right and left; and more and more "Robbers' Roosts" had arisen in Little Rock, but no one was a penny the better. The best railroad that Little Rock had, had gone from Saint Louis to Texarkana without being granted a penny of aid, and everyone knew it.

Baxter had at least pledged himself as being opposed to all further grants, and everyone knew that fact. He had been offered the nomination in order to head Brooks off, and he was well aware of it. Brooks had declared that, if elected, he would fill Pulaski County Jail so full of Clayton's followers that their arms and legs would stick out of the windows; and the Democrats had refused to name any candidates, had backed instead Brooks's candidacy. Under these circumstances it was up to Clayton to find someone believed to be honest. Baxter hoped, indeed, that he was honest. He had tried all his life to be so.

The nomination had been his, and he felt he could not decline it, though he had scarcely asked to have it. There followed the campaign. His own speeches had been so cold and so dull that Clayton had come down from Washington to run his campaign for him and to defend the Regular Republican record. Clayton had had a hard time justifying himself, while Brooks had flailed him mercilessly. Not a speech had gone by without its allusions to the Bible. Brooks had quoted, "The sabbath is not made for man, but man for the sabbath" to prove that people were not made for the party, but the party was made for the people; he had said that "beating their swords into plowshares and their spears into pruning hooks" was impossible as long as the militia was not disbanded, and while the militia generals, those "seven-by-nine bobtails," kept their posts; he had heaped denunciation on denunciation. And the people had cheered him to the echo with cries of "Go it, old Brindle!" "Give 'em fits, parson!" Things went so badly, in fact, that Baxter had regretted having taken the nomination at all.

On the election day, Clayton, through his henchman Hadley, had ordered out the militia to guard the polls. This had resulted in so many known Brooks supporters' being turned back, that "side polls" had been opened, and there were two sets of election returns. The official return showed that he, Baxter, had been elected; the unofficial return was for Brooks. Since the unofficial return had been irregularly obtained and showed also a majority against Grant, there was no doubt that neither Clayton nor Hadley would ever accept it. But the manner of his installation was a supreme irony, the bitterest pill of all. He had been inducted into office by a legislature carefully picked beforehand to represent none but Clayton's supporters and guarded by Clayton's militia under that scoundrel Upham. The people, as represented by the Brindle-tails, who had made their will known by holding an indignation meeting at Fletcher and Hotze's Hall, had no part in the proceedings.

All this had happened to him, a year and three months ago. He had been determined, from the first, to serve out his term, whatever happened, and to keep his election pledges. He had refused any further grants-in-aid to the railroads. Forces led by "Poker Jack" McClure had repeatedly tried to bribe him; and Clayton himself had sent down an emissary from Washington to persuade him to soften, but to no purpose. To all he had but one answer: he did not mind making money, but he was going to do so honestly. The credit of the state was not going to be pledged again, so long as he was in office. An attempt had been made to unseat him, by bringing on an action in the state supreme court, which demanded that Brooks be proclaimed lawful governor. Just before adjourning, the court had expressed—"with some delicacy"—an opinion that the question was not for them, but for the legislature. John McClure had, of course, vigorously dissented to that—but Brooks was determined to go on. The Pulaski County chancery court had issued a *quo warranto* writ against him. His attorneys had postponed action on that, perhaps only temporarily. Open threats had been made that he might be assassinated. He had been forced to go to the Democrats to ask for a small guard. All this he had done, without wishing to do so, such things being contrary to the traditions of the American people—but he now saw that it was very likely he would be thrown out by force. Clayton himself was getting restless in Washington and urging him to tolerate certain things which were no better than robbery. But in spite of Clayton, only a month ago he had announced finally, and in the teeth of the legislature, that under no conditions would any further railroad-aid bonds be issued by him, the debt of the state being what it was. That had brought Clayton himself hurrying down from Washington by train. Midnight conferences had taken place. Angry words had passed. Clayton had tried to force him into line, but he had shaken his head. Finally he had been threatened openly with a reversal of Clayton's former policy and with support thrown to Brooks. Well, he would not change his position, nor would he yield the office, unless it were on account of armed force.

God knew that he had not sought this office of governor. Clayton himself had urged, almost besought him to take it. He would gladly have resigned long ago and gone back to his judgeship, but honor forbade. All his life he had fought against obstacles, taken unpopular sides. His own relatives were now calling him a fool, but he would go on doing exactly as he had promised, even though none but the Democrats thought him right in doing so. They did not care so much for Brooks now. And Clayton would scarcely dare act as he had threatened, considering the long story of bad blood between him and Brooks. Clayton, in fact, up to the time he discovered that the Governor could not be "managed," had urged him to stand firm in his post. The eyes, not alone of Arkansas, but of all men were on him; their eyes were turned on the South. The South! Yes, the South, betrayed as it had been by the greed of men who had used the defeat of the Confederacy to further their own ends. The Confederacy had been wrong; but the South must again be made master of its own destiny.

He was Southern now, as Southern as an Arkansas oak which had gone on growing though the windstorms had broken off its top and twisted its branches. He thought of Catalpa Hall, up at Batesville, with the date 1846 clearly stamped on its gutters, its tall-ceilinged rooms, its air of quiet peace, the great cedars in its dooryard. Would he ever go back there again? Or would he be killed here, assassinated even before his term closed, done to death because he had tried hard to be honest? He soon would know.

The door was suddenly flung open. Governor Baxter, his big head bowed over his ruffled shirt, had scarcely noticed the interruption to the course of his thoughts, till an exclamation from his son brought him to himself. Standing before the desk was Joseph Brooks, grimmer and hairier than ever, and behind him were the red-faced Catterson, the oily Hodges, the monstrous fat man, "Toot" Dillon, three or four others, all armed. The tramp of feet without told Governor Baxter that other men were already filing into his anteroom. Governor Baxter raised his head and looked squarely into the somber eyes of Joseph Brooks. Brooks spoke, harshly and sternly, waving a paper in his hand.

"This memorandum of the decision of the Pulaski County chancery court, rendered only this morning, makes me governor of Arkansas. I have just taken the oath of my office before the chief justice of the supreme court." With a gesture of his thick, hairy hand, Brooks flung the paper boldly on the desk. "All books and papers here are now mine, and you are forbidden to take anything away from this building without my permission." His dark, passionate, hairy face glared grimly.

Governor Baxter rose heavily to his feet. His glance inquiringly sought out the tall, lank, red-faced Catterson, in full militia uniform, fingering a rifle as he stood at the side of Brooks.

Catterson spoke: "You will be left at liberty to leave this office unmolested, unless you offer us resistance. If you do, force will be employed to expel you. We have other men ready near by." He nodded off in the direction of the open door.

Governor Baxter steadied himself for a moment by resting his hand on his desk. In a voice firm and steady, and rather loud, he replied, "Very well, gentlemen. As you see, I am alone here, without any means of resistance. I must, however, protest against this lawless invasion of my office." (Here he paused for a moment, while Catterson took a step forward.) "There is now nothing left to me but to submit to force. I wish, however, to remind you" (here his voice rose again till it filled the room) "that I have already been guaranteed against the employment of such means by the very men who are now putting forward your candidate for this office. I am willing to submit to this for the present, but to the usurpation of my lawful office, I will never submit willingly."

Brooks's face scowled at that. But Catterson grinned slyly and nodded: "You are willing to go, then, if we force you?"

"Only if forced." Baxter's face was sternly composed.

"Very well, Governor." Catterson's face flushed, and Brooks openly glared at him in protest over the misplaced title. "Two of my men will now escort you out through our lines to the street." Two armed men moved lightly through the doorway and touched Governor Baxter on the shoulders. "You may take your son and clear out. Here is your hat. But remember, we've got plenty of others outside, if you want to try any funny business." He grinned again cheerfully.

"I am going, gentlemen," said Governor Baxter firmly. "Come, son." And then, to Brooks and Catterson, "You will hear from me soon again."

Fifteen

THE MINSTRELS OUTSING THE BRINDLE-TAILS

By the next night, Thursday, April 16, 1874, the people of Little Rock were thoroughly aroused. The city had taken on the aspect of an armed camp. After leaving the State House, Governor Baxter had walked calmly across Main Street to the Anthony House three blocks away, where he sent off a telegram to Grant asking for the aid of United States troops to reinstate him in office and then drove off in a hack to Saint John's College. There he had been greeted by the heads of the College, by the one hundred and fifty cadets assembled, who made themselves into an honor guard, by a representative of a New York newspaper who happened to be in town and scored a good scoop in interviewing him, and by a number of citizens calling—despite the heavy rain that afternoon—to offer him their support. Brooks, in the meantime, settled down in the State House, with two or three hundred men, mostly Negroes, as a guard; they were commanded by two of the most notorious of Clayton's militia leaders, Catterson and Upham.

The Baxter forces had one advantage from the outset. They were in command of most of the city, including the telegraph office, though for the first two days emissaries from Brooks were still allowed to use this. But Baxter, that afternoon, received from Grant the discouraging reply that the Federal government was not going to interfere in the struggle. The Brindle-tails, holding at first only the State House and its immediate approaches, were engaged from the start in throwing up barricades of timber around the old building, placing two field guns found in the State Arsenal, organizing and drilling. Brooks had already received telegraphed reassurance from Clayton and Dorsey, the two Arkansas senators, that he need only hold his post, leaving them to explain matters to Grant, and all would be well. This was rapidly followed by telegrams supporting him from three out of the four state congressmen. He therefore issued a proclamation, declaring that he would abide by the decision of the courts, that he would resist all efforts of Baxter to dislodge him, that he needed no further support. He counselled all the citizens to pursue their usual occupations. This left the city open to Baxter recruiting, which went forward actively throughout the sixteenth and seventeenth.

The Baxter forces commanded the approaches to the city by railroad and by steamboat. If the Brindle-tails, immediately after throwing Baxter from the State House, had seized the railroad station of the Cairo and Fulton, on the site of the present Union Station, or the iron bridge, named for the London banking house of Baring Brothers and just finished, which led across the river, or the Fort Smith and Memphis Station across on the north bank, they would have soon put their Minstrel opponents into a great difficulty. But they made no move. Apparently Brooks was over-confident from the start. His coup had been delivered and he now held the State House, by virtue of a writ in a minor court. This he thought sufficient. Any attempt of Baxter to repossess the State House would be merely the action of an illegal mob.

Neither side, at the outset, was able to obtain sufficient arms to support its claims by force. There were a few hundred rifles and two field guns in the small arsenal at the State House; these Brooks now had. The commandant of the United States Arsenal next door to Saint John's College, Brevet-Colonel T. E. Rose, who had only a partly-filled regiment under his orders, had been here at this post ever since the disputed election in 1872. At first he did not take the situation seriously. During the afternoon of the sixteenth, he received requests from both sides to deliver to them the fifteen hundred stand of arms he had, but being advised by Grant that he must take no part, he refused. Brooks, no doubt advised by Catterson and Upham and supported by the state treasurer and auditor, was the first to take action to obtain weapons.

Immediately after possessing himself of the State House, he caused an appropriation of fifty thousand dollars to be made out in his favor;

and he sent off a well-known supporter, George W. McDiarmid, "a quiet, unassuming, little gentleman," to Saint Louis by the very first train out of Little Rock. This gentleman immediately proceeded to ship down, in various consignments, through the channel of a well-known Saint Louis printing office, no less than two thousand Springfield rifles, in plain cases, consigned to the "Honorable Joseph Brooks, Governor of Arkansas," and marked "Arkansas State Reports." These cases were duly delivered at the State House, before the Baxter party were even aware of what was going on. Thirteen thousand rounds of ammunition were also sent, shipped in cases marked "Whiskey" and consigned to Joseph Garibaldi & Company—the said firm occupying a well-known saloon just opposite the State House, in the Benjamin Block already occupied by the Brooks forces. Provisions—it is said as many as five carloads—were also sent down by freight and were carelessly allowed to pass on to the hungry Brindle-tails encamped within the State House grounds or in the rooms of the building. So from the first day of the contest, Brooks had made provision for enduring a long siege; while the Baxter men, though not lacking in provisions, found it difficult to obtain arms and were forced to seize upon the stocks of the three or four locksmiths and vendors of guns in the town.

At dusk on the sixteenth, after issuing a proclamation of martial law in Pulaski County, Baxter, attended by a small volunteer company of young men of Little Rock, in an open carriage along with R. C. ("Bob") Newton (the ex-Confederate officer who had captured him in 1863 up in Missouri and who was now appointed to command his forces), returned to the Anthony House, henceforward his headquarters. A large body of citizens afoot followed him. Though the rainstorm of the previous afternoon had been followed by a steady drizzle all day, excitement ran high. Circulars were on the point of being issued, signed by leading citizens and calling for support to Baxter; the Little Rock bar had met and passed resolutions declaring the decision of the circuit court in Brooks's favor null and void. By the time Baxter reached his new headquarters, cheers for him were being raised loudly from the streets amid shouts of "Good-bye, old Brindle!" "Down with Clayton!" "Thieves to the rear!"

The morning of the seventeenth found the Baxter forces established either in the Anthony House or in other important buildings within a radius of two blocks distant. The Brooksites were now rapidly building barricades around the State House and commanded its approaches with their two guns, front and rear. Between the two factions lay exactly one block of neutral ground, stretching between Main and Louisiana, and Markham and Second streets, a narrow margin. Colonel Rose, having received orders from Grant in Washington to take no part in the collision, moved his troops out to various points—such as Third and Center two blocks away from the State House, Fourth and Main within three blocks of Baxter's headquarters—and also took possession of the City Hall, midway between the State House and Main Street on Markham. Here and all the way up to the Metropolitan Hotel on the northeast corner of Main and Markham streets, lay ground nominally neutral but occupied mainly by forces sympathetic to Brooks. Meantime, partisans of the ex-parson were busy fortifying and receiving supplies from the North all that day.

By Saturday, the eighteenth, the lines were drawn that were to persist throughout the ensuing "war." And war it was, if a city under siege, with armed guards patrolling the streets and men enlisting and business houses closing down (though all the saloons were open and did good business), could produce war. The postmaster-general of Grant's administration had now recognized the fact that there were two governors installed and active, by ordering that "letters addressed to Governor E. Baxter or Elisha Baxter, Governor, should be delivered to said Baxter. Letters addressed to Governor Brooks, or Joseph Brooks, Governor, should be delivered to Brooks. Letters addressed to Governor of Arkansas you will hold till further orders." And the German-born mayor of Little Rock, Frederick Kramer, who had appealed to Grant for the assistance of United States troops in maintaining order, was told bluntly that the troops would attempt to prevent bloodshed—as they did, by standing between both armies—but that no further aid could be rendered under any circumstances. Grant's administration already had enough troubles on its hands without adding a local war to them.

And yet it was not war. Beyond his original force of some three hundred Negroes under white command, Brooks had received no reinforcements. But offers of support had poured into Baxter's headquarters in the Anthony House, where a spick and span United States flag floated from the wrought-iron balcony of the dignified, two-story brick hotel, with its long, green shutters protecting tall French windows. And to one of these offers, Baxter had listened. H. King White, of Pine Bluff, a raw-boned, freckled, redhaired Kentuckian of some thirty years, who had once ridden with Morgan in the War Between the States, but who had been prominent since then in the ranks of Clayton's party, had completely switched his allegiance to Baxter. He had offered to recruit any number of Negroes, since Brooks's troops were mostly of that sort. And his offer had been accepted.

At daybreak on Saturday, the steamboat *Mary Boyd* arrived at the Little Rock landing from Pine Bluff, her decks covered with three hundred Negroes which King White, by combing all the plantations around, had enlisted in Baxter's army. They were accompanied by the mayor of Pine Bluff, a representative of the press, and various leading citizens, as well as by a brass band. They disembarked at the wharf at the foot of Commerce Street and marched the three and a half blocks west to Baxter's headquarters, with the bands playing and colors flying. The Negroes sang what later became famous as the "Baxter Song":

Do you see that boat come around the bend?
Goodbye, my lover, goodbye;
It's loaded down with Baxter men.
Goodbye, my lover, goodbye!

Baxter came out on the balcony of the hotel to greet them and waved to King White as he rode past on a fine coffee-colored "claybank" horse with full cavalry accoutrements, at the head of the strawhatted, coatless, and largely un-armed mob of Negro field hands. As all the stock of the three gun-merchants in Little Rock had been forcibly seized by Baxter agents, these "troops" were armed, if not drilled, upon their arrival in Little Rock. And with this reinforcement swelling his army to about six hundred men, Baxter thought he could easily retake the State House, from which he had been ejected for four days.

Brooks, however, was not to be beaten. Though the telegraph office was now in Baxter's hands—it was situated next door to the Anthony House—he had already obtained another telegraph instrument, which he set up in the State House; and his men were busy that day in leading out wires to the nearest poles at the back of the State House, along the banks of the Arkansas River. He had also sent agents up to the University at Fayetteville, which had been established there since 1872, to obtain two field guns which were known to be in the armory. Baxter had also sent young William E. Woodruff, now on his side, and famed since Oak Hill, off to Texas to obtain guns and other munitions.

On that same Saturday Brooks issued his second proclamation to the people of Arkansas, in which he said, "I desire to avoid bloodshed and destruction of private property; but while this is so, I cannot sit idly by and see the private property of the citizens of the state taken without compensation by an armed mob, and peaceful citizens halted and maltreated within sight of the capitol. In the interest of peace and good order, I request and command all persons who may have been deluded into rallying to the standard of a pretender, to lay down their arms and return to their homes within twenty-four hours."

So things wore on for the day, with merchants everywhere closing their doors and the streets rapidly filling with irregular troops on both sides. By nightfall the mayor had given up all hope of restoring order. The United States troops, skillfully placed by their commander between the contestants, alone served to prevent an armed clash. But the Brooks forces during the day attempted to extend their territory by practically taking possession of the Metropolitan Hotel, at the northwest corner of Main and Markham, within a block just opposite the Anthony House. They arrested and put into their guardhouse for the day Captain Sam Houston, now in command of the steamboat *Hallie,* the same man who had been in command of the *Nettie Jones* in 1869, when the *Hesper* had been despoiled of Clayton's arms. Captain Houston, who had come out violently for Baxter, had wandered too close to the Brooks outposts, but he was released by Saturday night. Apparently even the Brooksites wanted to avoid an open battle.

The next day being Sunday, the two rival governors, from their respective headquarters, began to besiege Grant with further telegrams, though it was known that under pressure from Clayton, Dorsey and all the Arkansas delegation but one man, W. W. Wilshire, Grant now favored Brooks as governor. Brooks persuaded all the state officers with the exception of three who had gone over to Baxter, to telegraph Grant declaring that Brooks was rightfully governor. And Baxter, more confident because of his reinforcement, also sent off a telegram to the President:

"The people are coming to my aid, and are ready to restore me at once. In making this organization I am obstructed by the interference of the United States in displacing my guards from the telegraph office, and now it is apprehended that there will be further interference. Such interference breaks me down, and prevents any effort on my part to restore the State government and to protect the people of their right. I beg of you to remove the United States troops back to the arsenal, and permit me to restore the legislative government."

There was no reply to this. On the next day, Monday, the twentieth, Brooks received more field hands recruited from their tenant cabins in the region south of the city. They were marched up from the south and had no difficulty in getting to the State House through the loosely held Baxter lines. Baxter also had a train load of reinforcements which came down on the Fort Smith railroad from Pope and Johnson counties, including many who had already had some taste of resistance to Clayton's militia in the Pope County war. As they disembarked on the north bank, one of their number was thrown under the wheels of the train and was killed. This was the first casualty of the conflict.

Grant had already ordered a company of soldiers from Humboldt, Tennessee, to take the train to Saint Louis and report to Rose in Little Rock immediately. They were due to arrive at noon on Tuesday, the twenty-first. Meanwhile Rose, who had on Saturday sent some of his men to take possession of the telegraph office, next door to Baxter's headquarters, began to show signs of growing more nervous. He abandoned the telegraph office, and moved his men to the foot of Louisiana Street, a block east of the State House itself, and also moved two more pieces of artillery from the arsenal to Louisiana and Second streets (there were already two of his guns in position at Fourth and Main). At this move, made about five in the evening, the Baxter men suddenly betrayed considerable excitement. A line of armed troops rapidly formed across the eastern side of Markham, facing Main; King White, mounted on his coffee-colored "claybank" horse, rode here and there, mustering his colored followers, yelling wildly, to the foot of East Second Street; Bob Newton and Churchill, organized for Baxter, were soon on the ground posting other men into position. The Brooks troops also, it is to be presumed, placed themselves rapidly into position to repel an attack. But by seven o'clock a truce was agreed on by both sides till nine o'clock the next morning. Both sides kept their sentries on the alert all that night.

Tuesday, April 21, dawned fair; fair for those farmers of the state who were as yet taking no part in the tumult in large numbers; and fair also for battle. The *Hallie,* under its commander, Sam Houston, returned with five hundred fresh field-hand recruits for Baxter. These swelled the Baxter forces to about two thousand men, billeted as they best could be along Markham and Second streets, in close proximity to Baxter's headquarters. Brooks also had ready an equal number. A band of Negro musicians having joined his army, it was proposed to hold a dress parade that afternoon on the State House grounds. A large crowd of citizens gathered in front to view the scene, but it was said the next day, in the sole paper remaining favorable to Brooks, that the parade soon broke ranks at a rumor that Baxter's men were coming and ran back to their breastworks. There were ludicrous incidents in connection with this scene, and it may be that Brooks's troops, undisciplined as they were, were largely in liquor, furnished them by nearby saloons. They were scarcely a fighting force, though Brooks may have thought them so. At any rate, the Baxter leaders felt confident of success, and were ready to take the State House, if permitted by Colonel Rose, as quickly as possible.

They had recruited, as had the Brooks side, as many Negroes as they could gather from all the surrounding territory. Thus the race liberated only nine years before was being asked to decide, by sacrifice of blood, whom they wanted as the governor of the state in which they lived. Brooks's appeal to them had been very powerful in the past, but the fact that he had been unsupported in his claim to the office by Clayton and by all the official leaders till only a few days ago, had left them irresolute. It is doubtful if they actually wanted to fight in either army. The greater part of the respectable white citizens, including all the newly-come Germans, certainly did not, and had hoped up to a day or so ago that the excitement would somehow die down. But King White, on the Baxter side, was determined to force a decision if possible; he had whipped up the Negroes just recruited for him into wild enthusiasm, and though Baxter had carefully refrained from proclaiming martial law anywhere except within Pulaski County, White was ready to carry the war into other regions of the state.

About five o'clock, with all the men just disembarked from the *Hallie* at his back, King White decided to outwit Brooks's attempted dress parade of that afternoon and hold one of his own. He mustered all his men out into the street. At least two hundred of them were still unarmed. They gathered at the Ditter Block at the foot of Markham and Rock streets just east of where the old Ashley mansion stood, deserted and desolate, on its lawn. Thence they moved on to Scott, within half a block of the Anthony House and a block from the Brooks outposts on Main. Then they turned on Scott, all the way to Ninth, and went east two blocks to Rock again. The blaring of the band, the loud trampling of feet, the singing of the "Baxter song" brought the inhabitants to their doors and windows. King White led, mounted on his coffee-colored horse. Arrived at Ninth and Rock, they all turned north again and marched back to Markham; but there turned west, reaching the Anthony House, where they faced about, fronting the building and its balcony. The head of the column, the band and its musicians, was but ten steps away from the corner of Main Street, and a few steps further was Colonel Rose, sitting on his horse in the middle of the street. Just beyond, a half block away, at the corner of the Metropolitan Hotel, a three-story building, armed supporters of Brooks lined the open windows.

When the troops halted, loud cheers were given for Baxter, and voices were raised in insistent calls for his appearance. No doubt Baxter had been aware for hours past that a great demonstration was being made in his favor. He had, as we have seen, telegraphed Grant two days before, urging him to remove the troops, so that he could get at his opponent. Grant had not replied, and Baxter displayed the same unwillingness to force an issue that he had shown as governor. He must say something. What King White obviously wanted him to do was to give a command to take the State House forthwith. This he was not ready to do. So he pleaded illness:

"Soldiers, I am in point of fact, too unwell to address an audience. My health, for a number of weeks, has been such as to almost disqualify me for business.

"But there is an emergency; there is an insurrection; the government has been seized; the archives are in the hands of the insurgents. I have called you here for the purpose of asserting, not the rights of Elisha Baxter, but the rights of the sovereign citizens of the State of Arkansas. [Great cheering.] The seizure of the archives was effected without my ever having been served with process of court. I am making preparations. I intend to assert my right, so far as respects the governmental functions of the executive, to govern the State of Arkansas. [Renewed cheers and cries of "Hurrah for Baxter!" "Thieves to the rear!"]

"I have however to say that it is a well-known fact, in military service, that officers and commanders cannot give in advance to the troops of the country, a detailed account of their proposed operations. They are necessarily military secrets, they are matters which must necessarily be kept quiet; and you will not expect of me, on an occasion as public as this, to detail my plan of operations."

At this point, King White, no doubt thinking this speech both cold and dull, shouted: "Just tell us whether you are going to have us take the State House, or not."

Baxter gripped the iron railing of the balcony and replied slowly and gravely: "I ask you, gentlemen, be patient and quiet, conduct yourselves orderly as good soldiers, such as I know you to be; and in due time, proper orders will be given you, to assert the rights of the State." And with fresh excuses about the state of his health, Baxter started to withdraw from the balcony. But one of his own officers requested him to return—King White still had something to say.

When King White spoke, the attitude of the crowd changed in an instant. He began by remarking that it had been said the colored men under his command would prove treacherous. He asked them publicly if they would all stand firm for Baxter. The roar of "Yes!" in response was mingled with shrill yelling. He went on, addressing Baxter directly: "Furnish us simply with the means—give us the authority, pronounce the order—and I will guarantee to you, sir, that in twenty five minutes from the time the order is written, Joseph Brooks will either be in hell or the archives"—and the rest of his sentence was lost in furious and exulting cheering. He wound up by saying again "All that we ask is, that the time and the orders will soon come."

Baxter in reply could say no more than this: "In consequence of the condition of my health, I must be permitted simply to exhort you, in conclusion: be patient, conduct yourselves orderly, and have no fear of the consequences." He then retired from the balcony to his inner room.

The Negro band at the head of King White's column now struck up and began playing a lively tune. White turned his horse from the balcony, in the direction of Main Street and the head of the column. As he did so, Colonel Rose, who had been sitting on his horse in the middle of Main Street, watching the extraordinary scene, suddenly rode up towards White, his horse—no doubt excited by the bursts of cheering that had swept through the street—knocking aside one or two of the musicians and interrupting the music as it began to play.

What happened then passed in a flash. With Baxter's Negroes, partly armed, staring on from the street, Brooks's armed followers lining the upstairs windows of the Metropolitan Hotel opposite, and the sidewalks packed with citizens gazing, Colonel Rose's white horse suddenly was halted by King White's coffee-colored one. An angry remark or two was exchanged. We may suppose that Rose said: "Do you intend to march your men up this street towards the State House?" to which White replied, "I had not so intended, sir; but I want to warn you that I won't permit you to ride over the men of my command, even if you are an officer of the United States."

Rose retorted hotly, "You must keep your place then, and your men must keep their place." To which White remarked, "You are an officer and should be a gentleman. Whether you are or not, I am; I'll not permit you to ride over my men, nor over me!"

Rose's free hand now made a threatening gesture towards White, and White, it is said, knocked it up in the air. At that moment, someone on the sidewalk, probably one of White's Negroes, fired point blank at Rose. At the sound of the report, firing became suddenly general. A volley from the Brooks men in the Metropolitan Hotel, raked the balcony on which Baxter had just been standing. The United States flag, above the balcony, was pierced in several places. D. Y. Shall, an old and respected citizen of Little Rock, owner of a large estate, was standing at a window. A bullet struck the side of his skull and he died an hour later. One of Brooks's "colonels," Dan O'Sullivan, got a bullet through both of his legs, and it was at first thought both would have to be amputated. A chambermaid jumped from an upstairs window in the Anthony House and broke her leg. Windows were shattered, and people were cut by flying glass. Many of King White's colored followers ran away. The firing went on for five minutes.

At the first fire, Rose wheeled his horse away from King White and rode back hurriedly over Main Street to the City Hall. He ordered his men out, with the fire ladders of the city fire department, and in a few minutes had a barricade hurriedly set up. Members of Baxter's army, veterans from Pope County, advanced under cover of the river bank towards the State House, expecting a battle. General Newton, Baxter's chief of staff, rode up and down the lines, giving directions. A half hour passed and darkness came. The unarmed citizens, who had held off to this hour, again appeared on the streets and walked around, looking at broken windowpanes and new-made bullet marks on buildings. Apparently there would be no fight that night. But blood had been shed, and everyone expected a fight the next day.

Not so Governor Baxter. For a man who had just made the excuse of illness, he acted with considerable vigor. That night a telegram in his name went forward to Grant. He said that as he could not move his troops without coming to a collision with the United States Army, which he would not do under any circumstances, he proposed to call the legislature as soon as possible to decide who was legally governor. Grant replied in kind the next morning: "I hereby approve any adjustment, peaceably, of the difficulty in Arkansas—by means of the legislative assembly, the courts or otherwise—and I will give all the assistance and protection I can under the constitution. I hope that the military forces on both sides will now disband."

This news was not made public till the following day, which was Wednesday. But on that Wednesday afternoon, the river news recorded that the steamboat *Clarksville* had left for Memphis, "taking with her to Pine Bluff, Col. H. King White's colored troops." Apparently the project for capturing the State House from Brooks in one wild smash had quietly subsided.

Both sides, however, continued to receive reinforcements. The Brooks forces strengthened their barricades around the State House and began to excavate the ground for a powder magazine. On Thursday the proclamation by Baxter summoning the legislature for May 11, duly appeared in the newspapers. It was countersigned by J. M. Johnson, as secretary of state. That gentleman, whom we have met before in these pages, had been visiting his mountaineer friends and relatives up in Madison County. He had at last returned to Little Rock, and he duly signed Baxter's proclamation. He also attempted to get into his own office at the State House that afternoon but was refused admittance on the plea of "military necessity" by Brooks, Catterson, and Upham.

After Baxter's proclamation, the war languished in Little Rock, though peaceable citizens kept their windows barricaded with mattresses against stray bullets, and took other precautions. D. Y. Shall's body was given a fine funeral. Business houses kept their doors closed. On Friday, the twenty-fourth, nine days after Baxter had been forced from the State House, he approached Brooks through "Poker Jack" McClure and his own attorneys, attempting to get Brooks to agree to withdraw all forces on both sides until the question of the governorship could be settled by a competent tribunal. In his reply, Brooks stated that he undoubtedly was governor and therefore could not withdraw his forces until Baxter disbanded his. So the matter rested, with the United States troops, now reinforced, keeping the ground that lay between the combatants.

But King White was not to be beaten. He was determined on a fight, and he made it. Having barely arrived in Pine Bluff, he proclaimed martial law on the twenty-fifth. As the next day was Sunday, things quieted down somewhat; but King White was left in possession of the post office, the telegraph office, and the sheriff's office. Whether Baxter agreed or not to this move, history does not say. Later, under sworn testimony, he declared that a proclamation of martial law for the entire state had been made out by his officers while he was sick in bed, but that he had refused to sign it. It is quite likely that White, chafing in inactivity, simply took the law into his own hands.

The results were not long in coming. The Negroes of the back country were still strongly for Brooks. They had not forgotten the bellowing voice, the coal-black beard, or the biblical promises of salvation. And Brooks had white supporters in Pine Bluff. One of them, an Irishman named Murphy, a former friend of White, was determined to force White's hand. For White had begun arresting citizens under warrants drawn up by himself.

Murphy began to recruit a company of Negroes for Brooks at New Gascony, some fifteen miles down river and on the opposite side from Pine Bluff. It was soon rumored that he had two hundred men under him; he intended to take and sack the town. On the morning of the thirtieth, with two hundred of his men, all mounted and armed, King White descended on New Gascony, aboard the inevitable *Hallie.*

Murphy's men were at a church near by, having assembled there for parade and drill; and White, landing unseen, charged down on them. The Murphy company retreated behind a fence and returned a hot fire till their ammunition ran out. Murphy himself, hit in the head, was taken prisoner by White and lodged in the jail at Pine Bluff. His troops were routed, and it is said that nine of them were killed and twenty wounded. This was, as it proved, the hottest fight of the entire war.

Meanwhile in Little Rock, preparations on both sides—in which a considerable number of the citizens seem to have taken no part—went on. Baxter, after the second Sunday truce had been declared and observed on the twenty-sixth, telegraphed Grant again, asking his aid in preserving the peace until the legislature could assemble. It was known by now that U. M. Rose, whom we have met previously, had gone to Washington to argue Baxter's case before Grant, and that Albert Pike and Robert W. Johnson, former Confederate senator, in law partnership together at Washington, were active on the same side; but Grant remained obstinately mute. His troops, still stationed along Main Street and showing no signs of withdrawal, seemed determined "to fight it out on this line, if it took all summer." And so did Colonel "Bob" Newton, in command of Baxter's men. On the twenty-sixth, after days of hard work, the Baxter forces had succeeded in unearthing and unspiking the large sixty-four-pounder siege gun which had lain abandoned on the river bank since the fall of the Confederacy. It was solemnly taken, on a dray pulled by four strong horses, up to Markham and Scott, and there set in front of the Anthony House, its muzzle pointing off in the direction of the besieged Brooks and his men. And so another week began, with nothing to report in it except that on the last day of April, several of Baxter's officers, hearing that large reinforcements for Brooks were arriving from the South by railroad, rode over to the depot at the west end of town to investigate, only to find themselves suddenly surrounded and cut off in a saloon. They were, with one exception, captured after a brief fight; but the next day, it was informally agreed upon by both sides to release all prisoners. It was also agreed that no further arrests should be made unless of persons actually found engaging in hostilities or breach of the peace; that all persons arrested should be turned over to their own side for punishment; and that the streets should be opened to all people. This agreement, which could be terminated only by giving six hours' notice, is a clear indication that the war, as far as the people of Little Rock were concerned, had now become comic opera. They were willing to let it run on as long as no actual damage was done or blood was shed.

Brooks, off in the State House, had known for days that he must do something. He had rashly supposed that the people—especially the Negroes—would rise up in his favor, but they had not risen. Even Grant in Washington had remained obstinately silent, had given no hint of his intentions beyond that encouraging telegram to Baxter. His time and his provisions were running short. The State House had become a militia barracks in an indescribable stage of disorder. A group of citizens, all in Little Rock, were giving him advice, but he still had not dislodged Baxter or Baxter's recruits. And King White's recent actions had warned him that the conflict might soon spread to the rest of the state.

So on the thirtieth, Brooks officially appointed, over the heads of the hated Catterson and Upham and the rest, James F. Fagan, a brave Arkansas officer who had fought for the Confederacy to the end. And on the same day this fact came out, a public address, signed by several respected Little Rock citizens, was circulated in Brooks's favor. It was said later that Fagan and his friends had already struck up a bargain with Brooks, that in exchange for their support, he had agreed to call for a new election under a new constitution. That may have been true. The brindle-tailed bull, in his trap, was growing desperate. Except for his private wire to Washington, and the efforts of the "Republican" newspaper, he had as yet little signs of support turning in his favor.

Neither side now wanted an actual fight; the town was too evenly divided. But Brooks knew he could not stand an indefinite siege. He therefore attempted to legalize his position. He was determined to reinforce the decision rendered in his favor by the circuit court, by a decision of the supreme court. He ordered his auditor to draw out a warrant on the state treasury, which the treasurer was to refuse on the grounds that Brooks was not legally governor. Then Brooks applied to the state supreme court for a writ ordering the amount to be paid. The court, consisting of McClure (known to be a supporter of Brooks) Lafayette Gregg (in favor of Baxter) and three other judges, Bennett, Searle, and Stephenson, was to meet on Monday, May 4, and render their decision. Since these judges were known as good carpetbag Republicans, it was feared their decision would go in favor of Brooks.

Two of the judges, Bennett and Searle, were due to arrive in Little Rock on Sunday night, the third of May, by train from Memphis. When the train arrived on the north bank opposite Little Rock, a party of armed men boarded it, hustled the two judges off, and in skiffs ferried them across the river. They were taken to Saint John's College, but all further trace was then lost. The next morning, the son of one of them learned, through a note in his father's hand, that he had been captured, was alive, and well treated. But no one knew where they were.

The next day, Monday, the fourth of May, the war suddenly threatened to flare up all over again. Reinforcements suddenly rushed in from everywhere, and most of them were for Brooks rather than

Baxter. The people of Little Rock were uncommonly willing to express their indignation over the fact that members of the state supreme court had been kidnapped! The "majesty of the law" must be upheld. Excitement ran high all that day, while the missing men were intensively sought for; that night the Baxter guards were doubled. Rose ordered out his men to stand at their arms all night, and the people thronged the streets in crowds till far past midnight. But on the morning of the fifth, the missing judges turned up, safe at a Benton hotel; they were released that night, to ride into Little Rock the next day and deliver their verdict. The verdict, as might have been foreseen, completely reversed their stand of 1873 in favor of Baxter; it declared that the verdict of the Pulaski circuit court must stand. One might add, in view of the record of these same judges—two of them elected on Baxter's own ticket—that their verdict could do nothing but leave confusion twice confounded. They might as well have stayed kidnapped, for all the good their decision did.

But the excitement engendered by the kidnapping of the two justices would not down. The press of various cities, far from the scene of conflict, were already taking up the case, and comment unfavorable to Brooks—and also to Grant, who by letting the soldiers under Rose remain where they were, was still preventing Baxter from getting at Brooks—appeared, as far away as Saint Louis and Chicago. Brooks in the meantime was attempting to consolidate his position by digging trenches and throwing up breastworks for a block around, and by seizing the Jewish-owned Concordia Club nearby as a hospital for his sick and wounded. One of the Brooks soldiers died and was buried on the State House grounds on Wednesday.

It was now learned by the Baxter men that the arms and ammunition which Brooks's agents had demanded from the State University armory at Fayetteville had left Fort Smith on a flatboat early Wednesday morning. They would arrive and reinforce Brooks by Friday morning unless intercepted. The *Hallie,* back again at the Little Rock wharf, was pressed into service, its bow protected by two-inch planking, and its stern by a barricade of cotton bales. Thus fortified, at three o'clock on the morning of Friday, May 8, the *Hallie,* still commanded by Captain Sam Houston, with John Myers pilot, and a company of twenty-eight men and two officers aboard, all Little Rock volunteers for Baxter's cause from the start, started upstream.

That same morning, at nine, there occurred the most famous fight of the war. The *Hallie* had slipped past the back of the besieged State House and Brooks's army unobserved; but somebody—probably someone passing from one army camp to another—presumably tattled and by six the same morning, about one hundred of Brooks men, all well armed with the rifles from Saint Louis, arrived on the north bank, to board the Fort Smith train. Sixteen miles further on, where Palarm Creek runs into the Arkansas, these men got out of the train and scattered themselves along the north bank amid the rocks and woods, observing at two miles distance the *Hallie* stopping at Natural Steps, just beyond the magnificent truncated cone of Maumelle Mountain, to take on wood. Twenty minutes passed, and the *Hallie* again started upstream. An officer of the Brooks forces, standing on the north bank a little below his men, at the point where the *Hallie,* by keeping to the current, veered over to that side, shouted loudly, "Turn back your boat!" Houston, in reply, signalled to his enginemen, "Full steam ahead," while his men took such cover as they could behind the bales and planking. The shout was repeated, but there was no further response. The Brooks troops then fired a well-directed volley, which shattered all the windows on the side of the pilot house. A steam pipe was pierced by a bullet, and clouds of scalding steam arose from near the engines. The Baxter men aboard—ever after known as the "Hallie Rifles"—kept up a scattered fire, but the steamboat was disabled.

On the floor of the pilot house lay Captain Sam Houston, shot in the breast with a bullet that pierced the lung. He died an hour or so later. The pilot, still holding the wheel but unable to do more than let the *Hallie* drift, was badly wounded by three balls in knee, calf, and breast. Frank Tunis, one of the "Hallie Rifles" was lying dead close to the engines. Bascomb Leigh, another, was so severely shot through the knee that it was thought his leg would have to be amputated. He survived for sixty years, a dignified old gentleman with a limp and a cane, often seen in Little Rock. All of the crew, with but one exception, were wounded.

The *Hallie,* at the mercy of the wind, helplessly drifted over to the other side of the river; the Brooks men sent another volley; and the Baxterites, leaving their surgeon on board to care for the wounded, abandoned her and took to the woods, after raising the white flag to signify to the Brooksites that the *Hallie* was now theirs. The Brooksites sent over a small detail of troops in a skiff to take charge of the ill-fated steamboat. The *Hallie* returned, patched up, at three o'clock that afternoon and was tied up at the back of the State House. The wounded men were taken off and returned to their homes. The Baxter forces, after retreating into the piney woods some five miles, returned to the river near Natural Steps and remained there until dark, hoping that the flatboat with Brooks's ammunition would appear. It did not, and they marched back to Little Rock, crossing in a log dugout to the north side, by White Oak Bayou, under cover of darkness, and not reaching Little Rock till past noon the next day.

This famous naval engagement, the only one of its kind ever fought in Arkansas waters west of Little Rock, lasted for some fifteen or twenty minutes. Two of Brooks's men, both colored, had been killed, and only two of Baxter's, for Myers, the pilot, like Bascomb Leigh, recovered. But the echoes of that furious volley at Palarm Creek were "heard around the world" as far as Little Rock was concerned. Bascomb Leigh became a hero for life; and for forty years and more afterwards the "Hallie Rifles" were famous in Arkansas history, along with David O. Dodd and Hindman.

On Saturday, at the time that the weary veterans of the famous river fight were returning to their barracks, and while the *Hallie* herself, her decks riddled and spattered with blood, her broken steam pipe tied up, was resting below Brooks's guns, which were trained towards Argenta opposite, King White rode back into town with a company and with news that others were following. Members of the legislature, summoned by Baxter for the morning of Monday, the eleventh, and due to meet at the Ditter Block, at Markham and Rock streets, well within Baxter's lines, were on their way to the capital. Colonel Rose was determined to nip further fighting in the bud, and on Saturday night ordered the Brooks forces to return the *Hallie* to her owners by seven Sunday morning. Under cover of darkness the *Hallie* was scuttled and sunk in the river—by which side, no one could ever later learn.

The Baxterites spent a good part of that Saturday in building trenches along the river bank near Main. The siege gun, christened "Lady Baxter," was dragged up to the corner of Main and Markham, where it directly commanded the State House. All was in readiness for a fight on the next day, though that day was Sunday.

At eight o'clock Sunday morning, about two hundred men from Brooks's forces were hustled across the river by bridge and boat to take possession of the roundhouse at Baring Cross, belonging to the Cairo and Fulton Railroad, and also the Fort Smith and Little Rock depot near by. Seeing this, King White, who had just received two hundred recruits from the south, crossed his entire force, including a cavalry company, by ferry and landed on the north bank. The citizens of Little Rock, sitting down to their Sunday breakfasts, heard that a fight was afoot. Instantly the housetops were covered with people craning their necks and staring. Little puffs of white smoke were developing rapidly on the opposite side of the river. White and his cavalry were seen to rush in a wild charge at the roundhouse—and then, suddenly, Rose sent out a company in a steamboat under flag of truce demanding cessation of hostilities. He had already notified commanders of both sides that if they fired across his lines, he would return their fire; now he took steps to stop a fight on his doorstep. King White, who had practically surrounded the entire Brooks force in the roundhouse, withdrew in surly fashion. Three or four of the Brooks men had been killed. By two o'clock, White was back in Little Rock, and the region around Argenta was quiet. The workman in the railroad machine shops, no longer in danger from bullets, had gotten up from the floor.

One other attempt to "shoot it out" occurred, though the next day, Monday, the legislature summoned by Baxter met. A quorum was not present, but the members who assembled sent a telegram to Grant asking for the protection of the Federal troops. Those still attached to Brooks did not even attempt to come—including the lieutenant governor, Volney Voltaire Smith, and John M. Clayton, Powell's brother. They were still holding out at the State House, unwilling even to listen to a call coming from Baxter.

Grant, on the ninth, through his attorney general, who had been listening to arguments on both sides, had pronounced his verdict. It was that both governors should issue a call to a special session of the state legislature, which should be held May 25, and which, after hearing Brooks's claims, should finally decide who had been legally elected. This session should be held at the State House, and all armed bodies should therefore immediately disband. The President had been severely criticized in papers both North and South for his interference in the affairs of "reconstructed" Louisiana, and he was determined not to risk further criticism—hence this decision. Up in Washington,

Powell Clayton knew well that Grant would go no further than this; so he telegraphed Brooks to accept the offer at once.

Brooks did, on May 11. He issued a proclamation—the last of his career as governor, calling together the legislature on May 25, in accordance with the attorney general's plan. But Baxter now would not accept. He pointed out, in a telegram to Grant, that the legislature had already met but had adjourned as lacking a quorum. He was willing to let them go on adjourning from day to day, "till every supposed Brooks adherent is present." He was willing to disband his troops in proportion as Brooks disbanded his. But to hold the session in the State House was impossible unless Brooks moved out as far west as he, Baxter, was east, and gave up the building.

Grant thought this proposition reasonable enough and telegraphed it to Brooks. But Brooks now declined. He insisted that the legislature called by Baxter was one having no legal authority. There must be a joint call for the session, as first proposed by the attorney general. The courts of the state, he pointed out, had supported his claim. He had the recognition of every branch of the state government, except that of J. M. Johnson, the secretary of state. He insisted that the judgement of the courts had already deprived Baxter's pretended legislature, held within his own military lines, of every shadow of authority.

It was becoming obvious, even to Grant's slow-moving mind, that Rose and his regiment of troops would soon be inadequate to maintain any semblance of order. The disorders in Little Rock had inevitably spread to other parts of the state; and attempts to establish martial law had been made by others beside King White. One leading citizen of Little Rock had publicly let it be known that he had subscribed twenty thousand dollars to aid Baxter. He declared he intended to subscribe two hundred thousand or, if necessary, all he possessed. The sands were running out for Brooks, and the people of Arkansas were determined to see him go. He had damaged his position by refusing to listen to Grant's final telegram.

On the afternoon of Tuesday, May 12, with the legislature still adjourned as not being able to obtain a quorum of its members, a steamboat arrived from up river, loaded down with Baxter adherents. With the fate of the *Hallie* fresh in mind, the steamboat did not attempt to run past the railroad bridge west of the capital, nor past Brooks's stronghold itself, but halted somewhat above the bridge, near where the great curve of the river runs southward past Big Rock and the present-day "Squatter's Island." Here the Baxter men started to disembark; and King White, with his white cavalry, rode out to the hills around the present-day reservoir to guard their disembarkation. The Brooks militia were ordered to go out and capture the steamboat. They were hard pressed by White's cavalry and were forced to take refuge in old rifle pits surrounding the railroad station. Firing became lively, and the housetops of the city, as on the previous Sunday, soon became crammed with eager spectators. The Brooks men were rapidly reinforced from the State House, till nearly the entire Brooks army became engaged. Baxter's main forces now moved out, in the direction of the Union Station; but at the corner of Fifth and Arch streets, they met a large party of Brooks men, and forced them back to Broadway and Spring in the direction of the State House. Residents in that neighborhood who had not yet barricaded their windows, soon did so, and the whine of bullets cut the air around. Wounded from both sides were given refuge in nearby houses. The fight went on for two hours and was developing into a general mêlée when at four o'clock Rose ordered his men out at a double-quick charge to occupy the neutral ground. The fight then stopped, as by magic. No one was killed, but eight or ten were wounded. And the steamboat, guarded by King White, disembarked its recruits for Baxter in perfect safety.

The next day the legislature met again and found at last a quorum present. They appointed a joint committee to draft resolutions to be sent to Grant and then adjourned till the fourteenth. And on May thirteenth, just a month from the time Baxter had been forced from the State House, two excellent field guns for Baxter—privately subscribed for—arrived from Galveston under the charge of Major William E. Woodruff of Oak Hill fame. They were placed close to the "Lady Baxter" at the foot of Markham Street, and the ladies of Little Rock, vying with each other in attentions to Baxter men, wreathed the muzzles of the guns with flowers. But sentries still walked the streets, and street fights and sniping still went on.

On the fourteenth, the legislature passed its joint resolution calling on the President of the United States to put them again into possession of the State House. Baxter addressed them briefly, urging the calling of a convention to draft a new constitution in place of the one forced on the state by Reconstruction. This move made Baxter champion of the people, finally and irrevocably; and former supporters now began to desert Brooks in large numbers. From Washington, since his last telegram to Grant, had come no hint of further support for the Brindle-tail cause. Brooks's position was becoming desperate. He was forced to take what consolation he could from the arrival of some reinforcements in the early morning of the fifteenth from Fort Smith and Dardanelle, up river.

May 15 dawned fair, a magnificent spring day. There was still a little shooting going on back and forth between parties of Baxter's supporters on the north bank opposite the State House and the Brooksites at the back of the besieged capitol. The legislature met that morning but, having as yet received no message from Grant concerning its resolution of the preceding day, adjourned till three that afternoon. When it reconvened the president of the senate and the speaker of the house informed them that a communication had at last been received from Grant.

The communication was in the form of a proclamation, declaring Baxter to be governor and ordering Brooks and his troops to disperse within ten days. The news ran like wildfire through the city. Men and women, white and colored, cheering and yelling, gathered around the *Gazette* office, the Ditter Block, the Anthony House. The *Gazette* hurriedly printed an extra, containing the text of Grant's proclamation, and passed it out, gratis, to the crowd. Such roars of cheering arose between four and five that afternoon, that Brooks's troops clearly heard it in the State House. At 6:00 P.M., two officers from Brooks's troops having now learned the worst, rode under a flag of truce to Baxter's headquarters at the Anthony House to arrange for the disbandment of their men. So dense was the crowd at the doors and so loud and furious the cheering, that at first they could not even get in; but that night a commission was formed to arrange for the terms of surrender.

On Saturday the *Gazette* used its biggest type and a cut of a crowing rooster to express its sense of triumph. It bade ironical "goodbye to Brooks, Fagan, Upham and Catterson; farewell to Clayton and Dorsey." Baxter publicly congratulated his soldiers. The chaplain of the state senate offered up that morning a special prayer of thanksgiving to God.

Six members of the legislature, all followers of Brooks and including John M. Clayton, brother to Powell, who had held out against Baxter to the last, attempted on that morning of the sixteenth, to pass through Baxter's lines and enter the building where the legislature was sitting. Colonel "Bob" Newton, in command of Baxter's troops, turned them back in a furious mood. But the six men persisted, and were at last permitted by Baxter to pass, though Newton's sullen troops were quite ready to take them out and hang them. Newton protested and issued a public address, in which he stated that these men had been known to be in arms against the lawful government and were therefore plotters of treason; that he hoped his men would still observe customary discipline and continue to be good soldiers as before; but that he hoped that "those to whom is committed the gathering of the fruits of your triumph will not, through sentimentality, throw away all the results of your victory." This was a nasty slap for Baxter, who probably, for the moment, was overwhelmed with the news of a complete victory, without further bloodshed. Newton was already threatening to resign, and the Brooks forces were still discussing the terms of their surrender. That morning, however, the final terms were agreed upon, and it was arranged to send the Brooks men from Fort Smith home that very day. Excitement over Newton's action was quickly quelled; and though the six members were allowed to take their seats over Newton's protest, the legislature was even then rushing through a bill providing for a special election by the end of June to decide whether a constitutional convention should be called.

That night celebration held the streets of Little Rock as the people fully realized what had happened. The first Brooks troops had already gone and others were to follow in the next days, Sunday and Monday. Baxter, standing on the same balcony from which he had addressed King White on the day of the Anthony House fight, needed no longer the plea of illness to prevent him from speaking. Brass bands played without further interruptions from Colonel Rose; and King White's Negroes sang loudly, "We'll hang Joe Brooks to a sour apple tree."

The next day, Sunday, prayers of thanksgiving arose from the churches of Little Rock, and a grand review of Baxter's troops took place at five that afternoon. The men, nearly two thousand of them, were no longer the undisciplined mob that King White had brought up from Pine Bluff. Their experiences during the past thirty days had given them a soldierly appearance and bearing. And the sound of the "Baxter Song" meant much now, at last, to the people of Little Rock.

At the conclusion of the parade, crowds flocked to the Anthony House to congratulate Baxter.

It was not until early in the morning of the nineteenth, Tuesday, that Joseph Brooks left the State House, slipping out at dawn for a destination no one knew. As Secretary of State Johnson, who had already taken his office there, was proceeding with the cleaning up of the rooms—all of them in most filthy condition—Baxter, in an open carriage, attended by Newton, rode to the State House, amid rounds from the Galveston field guns. Several ladies of Little Rock helped to fire the salutes by pulling the lanyard. Everybody, even the disgruntled Newton, was happy at last, and every Baxter man was a hero. Those who had stood by Brooks to the last and did not quit the state, were at great pains to explain that they had done so only on the understanding—reached when Fagan took the command—that Brooks would resign and permit another election to be held. At the close of the "war," as the Arkansawyers chose to call it, the *Gazette* estimated the losses at more than twenty killed and twice as many wounded. Since no one had kept any statistics on the point, the *Gazette's* estimate may be allowed to stand.

On Tuesday night the streets of Little Rock were gayly illuminated, and everybody went out and celebrated. A great wave of laughter and relief rolled over the state, not to vanish for years to come. Getting rid of the carpetbaggers had been, after all, an easy thing to do. The "embattled farmers" had simply sprung up to arms as at Lexington, and the thing was over. Baxter, who had never wanted to make war on his fellow Arkansawyers, had had his wish in a war which was no war. The Negroes had taken up arms to defend two white governors, neither of whom had been legally elected, and the result had been that the Negroes lost all their own political power. Grant, of all persons the most successful fighter of his day, had failed to hold two fighting factions from getting—occasionally—at each other's throats. Clayton, adept at schemes for keeping himself in power, was discredited for all time to come. And a second threat of renewed civil war had led, not to fresh conflict, but to enduring peace.

Sixteen

SUBTLE CHANGES

Since Elisha Baxter sat in the governor's chair, immovable against both Brooks and Clayton, not a single Republican has ever been the governor of Arkansas. The net result of the Reconstruction Era was to fasten the one-party system on Arkansas, as in the other states of the South. The "old guard" of Conservative Democrats came back into power, not to lose it till the twentieth century. Baxter himself, as a sole exception, might have had the Democratic nomination had he wished to take it. At the close of his one term, in the fall of 1874, he preferred to return to private life.

Following upon Reconstruction, the state grew faster than ever. The hated carpetbagger regime had given the people two things they wanted: education and a system of railroads. As regards the first, Powell Clayton had himself, as governor, persuaded the legislature to pass, in the spring of 1871, an act establishing a state university, on the lines laid down for such institutions by the Morrill Act, voted by Lincoln's Congress in the summer of 1862. This act, largely intended to hold the Western States in line for the Republican party, had already established many universities, which, though not possessing the facilities for higher learning granted by Harvard, Yale, or Princeton, were capable of teaching at least the agricultural and mechanical arts appropriate to outlying populations. Little Rock, in that summer of 1871, in a county election, refused to vote bonds for the sum of two hundred thousand dollars to locate the new university of Clayton's planning in Pulaski County. There is good reason to think that not more than one third the registered vote was actually polled at this election: people were so generally disgusted with Clayton's government as to refuse to vote at all. But Fayetteville, true to its tradition, voted one hundred thousand dollars, and guaranteed a number of buildings. So, early in 1872, the State University opened its doors there, where it has remained ever since.

Apart from the establishment of the State University, other institutions of learning rapidly sprang up. The Clayton government carried into effect the provisions of the act passed under Murphy, establishing public school systems throughout the state. The Institute for the Blind, which had known a precarious existence at Arkadelphia before the Civil War, was moved to Little Rock, where it occupied buildings still standing at the south end of Center Street. Clayton established also a Deaf-Mute Institute. Other institutions offering education for small payment, on the old lines, sprang up. Saint John's College at Little Rock was reopened, to play its role in the Brooks-Baxter war but to burn down in 1879. A flourishing small college serving many of the brightest boys of the Ozark region was established at Quitman in Van Buren County, a place "the health and quietude" of which, we are assured by its advertisement "are proverbial. Board can be had at the rate of $9.00 to $12.00 per month." And more interesting still, Mrs. Pike, wife of the great Albert (now more than ever declining into the Masonic grandeur of his "Every Year" phase at Washington) was persuaded to give up her splendid home at Seventh and Rock streets, and went to live with humbler people, while the old house became the "Arkansas Female College," to remain as such till the summer of 1889. The back verandah, with its balcony, was torn down; new rooms were added, upstairs and down, by running up walls and partitions; and education for misses was given for a sum not exceeding one hundred and thirty-two dollars per term of five months, including board, tuition, fuel, lights, room, and washing; though music lessons on piano or guitar came to thirty dollars extra.

Railroads had been built, after much hesitancy and delay. And it was now possible to travel from Memphis to Little Rock and so on to Fort Smith by train; and from Saint Louis also to Texarkana. But these roads, managed and financed as they had been mostly by carpetbaggers, had helped to drain the state of its last resources. The cost at which they had been built was terrific. Augustus Garland, who succeeded Baxter as governor under the new and final Constitution voted in 1874, found the state again completely bankrupt. It was estimated that the total indebtedness had reached nearly twenty millions. Of that huge sum, about two millions had been issued in state treasurers' certificates and auditors' warrants during the troubles of 1873–1874. These certificates and warrants, backed as they were by nothing whatever but a promise to pay, were now selling at a price below twenty-five cents on the dollar. Further, there was much "county scrip" in circulation, which was quoted early in 1875 at the price of sixteen cents on the dollar. Garland's new government had no choice but to issue fresh bonds, leaving the vast mass of indebtedness untouched, much of it to be repudiated only at a later date.

At last the state was flourishing. In the wake of Reconstruction German settlers in larger numbers than ever descended on Little Rock, to establish a Lutheran church at last and to hold, in May, 1872, their fourth annual *Mai-fest* of the local *Turn-Verein.* They had all been organized for Baxter in the last days of the great contest. They brought with them a greater thriftiness and possibly a deeper respect for culture and learning than had been possessed by the primitive Arkansawyers. Their *Turn-Verein* celebrations went on through my boyhood and so did the open-air beer gardens established by such local figures as "Papa" Geyer; and the Germans controlled also all bakeries and groceries. The Irish, too, came, though in smaller numbers than the Germans, and the Catholic community obtained its second bishop, the Right Reverend Edward Fitzgerald, who was installed in 1867 and was destined to make Little Rock momentarily world-famous by being one of the two refusing to vote for papal infallibility at the Vatican Council of 1870. These influxes from without did little, however, but reinforce the state's inborn conservatism.

The population steadily grew, from 484,471 in 1870 to 802,525 in 1880. A good deal of that growth was the result of the astounding success of America's Centennial Year, 1876, when, despite the Tilden-Hayes disputed election, the United States showed such signs of vigorous flourishing as prompted Walt Whitman to urge the muse to "Migrate from Greece and Ionia" and reestablish herself in Philadelphia "amid the kitchen ware." Arkansas fairly outdid itself at the Centennial by erecting a separate state building, under the direction of Henry Lewis Fletcher, son of a pioneer settler and husband of the Susan Bricelin Fletcher we have met before in these pages; and it received as a prize a cast-iron fountain still standing in front of the old State Capitol building, and a group of ugly statuary long since vanished from its roof.

Old landmarks and customs were going; and new ones steadily coming in. On the night of September 21, 1875, the old Anthony House burned down to the ground—though the citizens tried to save it to the last by supplementing the work of the inadequate fire brigade with a line of buckets passed from hand to hand. Christ Church, the first Episcopal church building, a small brick structure, calcimined blue, with two yellow doors and a wooden tower with a sweet-toned bell in it, vanished nearly two years earlier, in the midst of a violent storm of wind and lightning, on the night of September 28–29, 1873; and the Metropolitan Hotel, which had figured so largely in the Brooks-Baxter struggle, went too, destroyed by fire, on December 14, 1876.

Truly, the "Lady Baxter," firing its last salute at midnight on January 1, 1876, to be followed up by twelve guns from the fieldpieces at the Arsenal, thirteen more for the original colonies, thirty-seven for the states, and eleven for the territories, was booming out the death of one era and the birth of another. And yet this new era contained much of the old—especially in Arkansas. The comings and goings of such hallowed figures as Jefferson Davis were more than ever the occasion of civic celebrations; Grant, too, rated a celebration when he appeared in Little Rock in the spring of 1880; and much was made of the visits of all Confederate and a few Federal generals. Growth, though apparent on the surface, did not change the heart. Arkansas, like the rest of the South, lived through its period of arrested development; it thought, dreamed, and worked in terms of the great days before the war, grown respectable in retrospect.

The Confederacy remained as a haunting memory, to begin disappearing at last in the fierce spirit of violent partisan feeling caused by the war with Spain in the spring of 1898. Thus the Confederacy, or what people were assured had been such, outlived its own demise for more than thirty years. Firecrackers were still set off, not on the Fourth of July, but at Christmas; and ex-slaves visited former masters on that date and requested their never-refused Christmas gifts. Mardi Gras, which may have been unofficially celebrated even earlier, became an official day of masked-ball and street-parade celebration in 1875, to survive until well within the first decade of the twentieth century. The old South became the traditional South, in which men made the best of both worlds—an older world of agrarian feudalism and a newer one of laissez-faire industrialism.

The Republicans, led by Clayton, had gone down fighting. They refused to the last to admit that Baxter was even legally governor when he summoned the legislature of May 11, 1874, which decided the contest. They held firmly to the opinion that the new constitution of that year, voted for by the same legislature, was utterly illegal. Clayton had the boldness to come back to Little Rock and attempted to live there, on completing his term in the United States Senate in 1877; but he soon gave it up because of complete ostracism and emigrated with his wife and family to the new-rising watering place of Eureka Springs, a stagecoach journey of some eighty-four miles through the wildest and remotest part of the Ozarks.

Underneath the placid surface of respectable one-party rule, old hatreds still smouldered, and bold attempts to do something for the agricultural underprivileged were still renewed. The process had begun as early as January, 1866, when Oliver Hudson Kelley, an obscure clerk in Andrew Johnson's Department of Agriculture, slipped out of Washington on a tour of inspection of the war-devastated South. Out of that trip emerged, in 1867, the once-famous "National Grange of the Patrons of Husbandry," a secret order on the lines of Freemasonry, admitting men and women on equal membership, with seven degrees, the last three of which were known as "Pomona, or Hope," "Flora, or Charity," and "Ceres, or Faith."

In 1872, after capturing several midwestern states, the Grangers invaded Arkansas in the person of a shaggy-bearded sixty-year-old pioneer, John Thompson Jones, who had come from the state of Virginia in 1836 and had long lived the life of a respectable cotton-planter near Helena. The objects for which the new association was organized were such as to appeal to many independent farmers in Arkansas. Members of the new body were pledged to work together for the betterment of their farm homes, the reduction of expenses, the maintenance of laws, the diversification of crops, the systematization of work, the discontinuance of the credit system, the avoidance of litigation, and the suppression of national prejudices. Coöperation in both buying and selling among farmers was urged on the members. Education was to be widespread. Women were to stand on a footing of equality with men. Railroads were asked to discontinue inequitable freight rates, and monopolies were firmly frowned upon. But the Grange, as such, was nonpartisan, and sternly refused as a body to support either side in national politics. All of its efforts were directed instead to the amelioration of the conditions surrounding the farmer's daily life: its members were asked only to support competent, honest candidates for office and put down corruption.

Undoubtedly all this appealed to many other Arkansas farmers, as well as to John Thompson Jones. In 1872, about three million acres—nearly an eleventh part of the whole area of the state—had been forfeited because of nonpayment of taxes. While various Reconstruction legislatures voted enormous sums to legendary railroads and mythical levee boards to aid them in "developing the state," while Brooks ranted and Clayton sat secure in the United States Senate and the Pope County farmers were plotting open war, the legislature of 1872 had been forced to pass an act "to prevent sheriffs and collectors from selling land, or returning persons and property as delinquent, when the taxes have been paid."

So rapidly did the Granger movement grow in Arkansas after an enthusiastic state-wide meeting at Little Rock in January, 1875, attended by delegates from forty counties, that the total membership was increased by the October following to no less a figure than 20,470. Jones, in fact, had done so well that in November that year he was elected master of the National Grange, and served one term of two years. But the decline of the order was equally rapid. Less than a year from its peak, the Grange reported—on July 1, 1876—membership of only 11,340. In January, 1876, only twenty-nine counties sent delegates to the state convention. Salaries of the officials were cut soon after. The last state meeting seems to have been held around 1880; and after that date, the Granger movement disappeared from Arkansas history, to merge imperceptibly with the Agricultural Wheel and the Farmer's Alliance.

The reason for the rapid decline of the Grange in Arkansas (which was paralleled by an equally rapid decline in other states) has been variously given by Grange historians and apologists. It seems evident that in other states, particularly Nebraska, the Grangers hazardously risked their funds in many ill-advised coöperative schemes, such as the purchase of grain elevators, flour mills, warehouses, steamboat lines, and the like. The West at that time was surely no very favorable field for coöperative effort; and the result was disastrous. There is reason, however, to think that the decline in Arkansas had other causes. Whatever their good intentions may have been from the beginning, the Arkansas Grangers could not avoid taking part in politics.

The *Arkansas Gazette,* for the last time resuming its former position as the most influential newspaper in the state, had been friendly to the Grange from its inception and had warned it to steer clear of political controversy. But the period was the time of the Brooks-Baxter controversy; and no group of Arkansas citizens, least of all the Grange, could avoid that issue. Some years later it was publicly asserted that John Thompson Jones, as master of Arkansas Granges, had drafted a circular letter in the spring of 1874 and had sent it out to all the Granges of the North, urging them to use their influence on Grant's administration to support Baxter. Whether this was actually so, we do not know; but in the state election of 1876, as in local elections previously, the Granges had been amazingly active, no less than four of their members being candidates for the Democratic nomination for the governorship that year. And in 1878, John Thompson Jones himself tacitly admitted to political ambitions by attempting to get himself elected for the United States Senate.

It is possible, indeed probable, that the Grangers failed as a national movement because of the violent passions raised anew all over the United States by the disputed Tilden-Hayes election of 1876, which marked the end of Reconstruction in the South. An organization which had both Republicans and Democrats in its ranks could not stand neutral in such days, with the newly-built transcontinental railroads plundering the United States right and left, and the big eastern industrialists, gorged with the spoils of protective tariffs, exploiting the farmers as a class throughout the country. It was impossible for the Grange, with all its good and wholesome intentions, to avoid taking up issues with which it could not actually grapple. So the organization faded from memory almost as fast as it came. But the smouldering fire of agrarian discontent, which it had attempted to fan into flame, remained alive, after all.

Throughout the seventies, eighties, and nineties, in remote and isolated districts, lawlessness went on. Up in Missouri, the two James boys, Frank and Jesse, together with the good-humored giant, Cole Younger and his brother Bob, had made names for themselves, not to be forgotten in future legend, by holding up banks since the dark days of 1866. They had graduated into banditry after a hard early training under Missouri guerrilla leaders, and were known as being sympathetic to the South. In the early morning of January 15, 1874, they made their presence known in Arkansas by holding up the incoming stage from Little Rock, a few miles north of Hot Springs. Five men, wearing long blue overcoats, the lower part of their faces masked with handkerchiefs, had stopped in Hot Springs the night before, but rode out on their horses, going north at dawn. An hour later, the driver of the stagecoach pulled up his horses at a command to halt from the nearby rocks. The fourteen passengers on the coach were ordered to turn over their money and valuables. One of them, a goateed gentleman with a slight limp, remarked that he had been in the Confederate cavalry service, and that he had never seen better horses than those ridden by the band. Whereupon, the good-natured giant, Cole Younger, with a courtly bow, had promptly handed his watch and purse back to him; the James boys would not rob anyone who had fought for the Confederacy.

It was generally believed, in the Ozark Mountains, that the James boys had helped a poor widow pay off the mortgage on her lands with some of the money they had recently taken from a rich financial institution. The story is purely apocryphal and has no basis in fact. It was known, however, and is unquestionably true, that the James boys were good church members of the Baptist faith; that Jesse himself—blue-eyed, sandy-haired, and with a tendency to blink his eyelids—always carried a Bible on him, prayed frequently, and was exceptionally good to his mother, whose right arm had to be amputated as the result of a bomb thrown by Pinkerton detectives at their old homestead, up in Missouri. This was soon after the Hot Springs affair and the inevitable bank robbery that followed. Forces were at work, too strong to be denied, to transform the James boys into Robin Hoods of the backwoods. They plundered the rich to help the poor; and in more than one mountain homestead it was felt theirs was the right way out, the right example to be followed.

The spectacular career of the James boys really ended on September 7, 1876, when a well-organized attempt to rob a bank up in Minnesota miserably failed and led to a vast manhunt which concluded with the running to earth of the Youngers, two weeks later. Jesse and Frank, his brother, escaped, to assume other names and try to be respectable. Six years later, Jesse—with a reward still out for his capture—was shot by a former associate, and that in the back, while he was straightening a picture on the wall of his home. Frank James rode in, was granted a pardon, and lived to be an extremely old man, pious to the last, and full of platitudinous good advice. But the passing of the James boys did not mean that disorders were ended in Arkansas.

Governor Churchill, for example, after his honorable service for the Confederacy and for Baxter, found he had fresh trouble on his hands in the summer of 1881 from a serious disturbance that suddenly broke out in the wilds of Perry County. Several of the local hill men there had long spoken sharply and bitterly about the way a county judge had attempted to enforce the law against them. An editor at Perryville, the county seat, who had publicly supported this judge's actions, had had his newspaper office burned down by an angry mob; and thereupon the judge had appealed to the governor, declaring that he could not, under any circumstances, continue in his functions. Churchill sent out General "Bob" Newton, famed for his leadership in the Brooks-Baxter fight, to investigate. Newton reported that a special term of court should be held to try all those suspected of destroying the newspaper office. But suddenly the offending editor, too, was killed; and the sheriff promptly refused even to look for the assassins. Churchill, on August 1, ordered the Quapaw Guards, a local militia company of Little Rock, out to Perry County. They stayed there three weeks, and the agitation was smoothed over. But local sheriffs there, and in next-door Yell County, have remained, since then, the final court of last resort, above the law.

One might also cite the vivid and violently picturesque story of that strange organization known as the "Bald Knobbers," which flourished as late as 1885–1889, in the remote hill-fastnesses of Taney and Christian counties, north of Arkansas in Missouri. Its history, however, belongs rather to Missouri than to Arkansas; but here again an organization attempting to go too far in enforcing the law in a mountain community was itself destroyed. The Ozark mountaineer, by this time, was determined to tolerate no further interference by self-appointed lawmakers. The Civil War and Reconstruction had taught him that he could sustain his independence only by the hard-won price of passive resistance to all outside influences, however respectable they might be.

The situation along the Oklahoma border was even more symptomatic. In 1875, President Grant had appointed Isaac Parker, the famed "hanging judge," to rule over the Federal court at Fort Smith. From that time to Judge Parker's death in 1896, the court that Grant's appointee directed became the terror of the lawless old West. It tried, in the end, nearly ten thousand persons in its twenty-one years of continuance, and 168 of these were put to death on the celebrated scaffold, which after Judge Parker's death, was torn down and burnt by order of the Fort Smith city council. It was a gallows so constructed as to be capable of hanging no less than twelve men at one time; on two occasions George Maledon, Judge Parker's hangman, had sprung six of its traps and used six of its nooses, at one mass-hanging.

Judge Parker's court—it had no jurisdiction over crimes occurring in Arkansas, but functioned only for those committed in the Indian Territory and other no-man's lands westward—was unique in the history of United States jurisprudence, inasmuch as no appeals could be taken from its verdicts for the first fourteen years of its existence; and its jurors could be selected by the famed "hanging judge" himself, a mild-mannered, soft-spoken person in private life, but, on the bench, insistent on the business of juries either to hang or acquit. The roster of the cases in his court is in itself a history of the bad and wild old West, from the beginnings of white settlement.

That Judge Parker's court stood on Arkansas soil and that Arkansas farmers near Fort Smith turned out in droves to witness Judge Parker's public hangings, are facts in accord with all that has already been said about the state in previous pages of this story. As in the thirties, Arkansas remained close to the frontier till the opening of the twentieth century. Then "progress," long delayed, swept aside the time-honored landmarks.

This was the period, then, of the Daltons and of Bill Doolin, of "Cattle Annie" and Belle Starr, of a long, desperate fight going on into the nineties, between the settlers and the incoming railroads. All this is part of the history of Oklahoma; but many a bandit there, close pursued, learned that it was possible to take refuge for a time in the wild hill country of the Ozarks. The last of them all, "Pretty Boy Floyd," of Sallisaw, Oklahoma, was finally run to earth in the Razorback State, dying near Texarkana, in 1935.

It seemed to the Ozark hill man, as the seventies became the eighties, and these in turn faded out into the last decade of the dying century, that there was much more to be said for the outlaw than appeared on the surface. Elsewhere in the state, there were elaborate Confederate reunions, and the memory of the "lost cause" annually awakened floods of reminiscent oratory. There were, in fact, two different decoration days; the earlier for the Confederates, the later for the Federals, held in that Federal cemetery on the eastern edge of Little Rock, full of Minnesota farm boys who had fallen victim to the fevers of the South more than to Southern bullets. The descendants of the Confederacy at Little Rock, ever since Baxter's triumph, had struck a tacit bargain with the remaining carpetbaggers. Bygones could be bygones henceforth, and the evils of the past could be forgotten. Had not Ulysses S. Grant, on the fifteenth of April, 1880, sat at the head table in the Concordia Club, at a banquet for two hundred and fifty guests, with thirteen other men alongside him, almost equally divided between carpetbaggers and ex-Confederates? Had not the mayor of Little Rock, ex-Confederate as he was, as well as General "Bob" Newton of Baxter fame, done Grant honor? The State of Arkansas was providing the best cotton, corn, apples, hogs, and humans in the world. The North was spending its capital in railways and corporations to develop the state's resources. Though freight rates inequitably favored the North, it was known that the railroads granted substantial rebates to the largest shippers of cotton. More economically subservient than it ever had been before, the South was now far more united than ever before in sentiment. And things, in the long run, were going to let themselves be governed by sentiment—by that "rule of the people" proclaimed on the seal of the State of Arkansas and vocally courted by the leading politicians.

But the hill man, the backwoodsman, the Ozarker, still was not happy. He had been here for a long time—as long as the state itself—and had got little out of it. The good schools were all in the cities, the fine shops, the evidences of culture and luxury. Once a year he hitched up his scrawny mules—or in some cases he yoked up his oxen—to the wagon, put on it the bale or two of cotton he had been able to scratch out of his ten or half-dozen stony acres, piled his wife and anything from six to a dozen towheaded youngsters atop, and started off to the city. There he bought shoes, clothes, perhaps even candy or other small luxuries for his people. Also—it is likely—much-needed medicine for some sick member, who was "feelin' porely" after another bout of "a-feverin' and a-chillin'." For all these he paid ruinous prices, returning with nothing in his pockets again. The people in the cities—smart as steel traps, one could see, one and all—stared at him, his uncouth ways, his blue jeans, his wife's calico, his limp and spiritless children. He was nothing but an old hayseed, a "rube," a yokel. Small boys gathered on street corners and mocked at him, as his wagon creaked drearily past. He warn't getting nowheres, with most of the land worthless and the rest of it wearing out. Them politician fellers in Little Rock, the high-stovepipe-hat, silk-stocking crowd, had never done a danged thing for him or his kind. He still had his rare moments of ecstasy, at a camp meeting when the preacher's voice rolled out over the kneeling crowd, or at a night-long square dance where there were secret drinks of fiery moonshine swallowed outside, to be followed by furtive kisses, and fierce embraces down by the creek, under the bushes. Sometimes there were babies, unwanted babies, afterwards—and it was noised about that another girl had gone wrong. If her folks protected her, it was all right; and many a woods-colt had grown up to be a fine man.

The preacher fellers, always talking about how sinful it was for either a man or woman to go wrong, were maybe mistaken about that. Usually the feller wouldn't even marry the girl afterwards, because she had tempted him in the first place. Women were sinful, as the old ballad said:

All the ancient historians we do understand
And the Bible we have to believe,
That woman is sensual and the downfall of man,
Since Adam was beguiled by old Eve.

Now his wife had just written off for one of those newfangled things, a mail-order catalogue. One of the neighbors had told her about that, and the catalogue, when it came, looked wonderful. There were prettier things in it, and at cheaper prices, than he had ever seen on his last visit to the county seat town. Them Yankees were the beatinest fellers, ever since the first clock-peddler came to the state. There warn't nothing they couldn't make and sell you. He didn't mind his woman writing off to the folks who got out the catalogue, for some new dresses, but he sure did wish he could buy him a new gun. That old squirrel rifle his father had owned, warn't much good.

Game was already getting pretty scarce. As late as 1885 there were still a few flocks of wild pigeons and a man could kill two or three hundred of them in an hour, salt them down, and drive off to a town near by and sell them for six or seven cents apiece. But in the last few years they had taken to disappearing. Even deer were scarcer now, and people were talking about game laws. Game laws! Why his folks had always just had to live off game—this land had never raised enough for big families—just as they had always made their own whisky. The sheriffs had enough sense to let them alone. But maybe the city fellers would start enforcing the game laws, and then there would be a pretty lookout!

He just didn't like those city fellers, with their fine hair parted in the middle, and their dudish manners. They smoked cigarettes and they read yellow-back novels, and they made love to mor'n one woman. They had ways of stealing a feller's land, too, by their lawsuits over taxes. They were wuss than a hull passel of painters. He had seen a painter once, when he was ridin' his hoss through a remote district. There was an abandoned cabin thar—just another half-tumbled down log house—and since it was a gittin' mighty dark, he thought he might sleep in it. When he tied his hoss up to the door, the critter began suddenly shakin' and sweatin'. He didn't know what was the matter, but the door stood open, and off in one corner there was a big pile of hay. Just as he started to get into the door, a big yellow animal jumped out of the hay and started for the door. It mighty nigh plum knocked him down. That was the only painter he ever seed, but he'd rather see that than a lot of these city politicians.

So—because the vote of the mountain region counted for a great deal—the leading politicians set themselves the task of drawing the fire of this undercover radicalism. Something had already been done to mitigate the crushing load of state debt, left as the heritage of Reconstruction. The state supreme court had decided in the spring of 1877 that the railroad-aid bonds, amounting to more than three million dollars issued by the Clayton government, had been unconstitutional, and that the state need not pay them. This had been followed the next year by a similar decision in regard to the levee bonds. But the old Holford bonds of the Real Estate Bank, on which no interest whatever had been paid since the forties, remained to plague the state. William M. Fishback, a dapper, dandified-looking lawyer from Fort Smith, who had settled there in 1858, had known Abraham Lincoln in his early years, and had even gone so far in his early days as to propose to Lincoln a law partnership, had crowned his career as a strong Union man by sitting in the state legislature, and by championing an amendment repudiating these bonds altogether. From 1878 onwards, the question of repudiating the entire state debt altogether—though the Holford bonds were, in part at least, just—had been a live issue. Repudiation was finally voted in September, 1884, by a vote of nearly eight to one. But as late as 1917, the banks of New York were instructed not to handle any state securities of Arkansas, inasmuch as the state had voted for repudiation and had refused to levy a tax to cover its own deficit.

Meanwhile, the flame of agrarian discontent, fanned by the high tariffs of successive Republican presidents, went on. The Grange had died, with the chief achievements to its credit being the encouragement of immigration and some amelioration of the farmers' hard lot through coöperation. Immigrants began to appear in ever larger numbers: one of the first important parties was a group of twenty-six Polish families who came down, having bought lands off the railroad in 1870, and who settled at Marche, on the borders of Pulaski and Faulkner counties—where their descendants live still. Two hundred more families, all Polish, came to join them in 1880; and German Catholics also came, as a result of Bismarck's *Kulturkampf* back in the old country, establishing themselves prominently at Morrilton, Conway, Altus, and Subiaco. Thus, despite the anti-Catholic prejudices of the average Arkansawyer, more likely to be Baptist than not, the state began to change subtly and slightly in its social constitution.

But all this was as nothing in comparison with the growth of the Agricultural Wheel, the successor to the Grange; it was first organized in Arkansas itself and by 1885 boasted of forty thousand members; and in 1886 boldly called for a state convention and a separate ticket. Two years before, in 1884, a candidate for the Democratic nomination for the governorship, who had the convention much in his favor but was suspected of too much conservatism, was passed over at the last moment by a piece of typical political trickery in favor of Simon P. Hughes, who had in his favor his former record as a Granger. This was obviously done in order to head the Wheel off from capturing the state. In 1886 this disappointed candidate at first agreed, and later declined to run as the Wheel candidate for governor, a bad mistake on his part, fatal, for the time, to the best chances for the Wheel's survival. But the flame of agrarian discontent had been too well lit to be put out. Following the depression of 1893, the Populist movement began sweeping the West like wildfire. It took the place that the Grangers, the Agricultural Wheel, the Farmer's Alliance had already held in the state. It formed an active opposition, contemptuous of the working compromise between Southern individualism and Northern finance-capitalism that had been achieved; and the Democrats were forced, despite their conservatism, to pay it some attention.

In agrarian discontent lies also the true explanation for the amazing career of William E. ("Coin") Harvey, who appeared in Arkansas somewhere around the year 1900 (on June 7, of that year he addressed a large audience at Eureka Springs on the subject of "free silver") and died at the obscure mountain resort he had founded, at Monte Ne in Benton County on February 11, 1936. He had been born in Virginia as far back as 1851—and so his boyhood had been darkened, presumably, by the collapse of the agrarian South in the years following the Civil War. In his early years he had done notable service as a railroad engineer on the Union Pacific—the first transcontinental railroad. Later, he became an eminently successful business man, and at the same time, a perpetual theorist concerning money: something akin to England's Major Douglas of the present day. The type is rare, for it combines both shrewdness and naïveté in really extraordinary proportions; men of this sort have not only to possess complete confidence in the most harebrained ideas but to be able to inspire others with the same confidence; and this Harvey was remarkably able to do, as his later career shows. As early as 1894 he had entered the lists of currency reformers with the famous pamphlet of "Coin's Financial School," which, distributed in vast numbers throughout the West and the South, not only helped to make Bryan the logical contender for the presidency that he was in 1896, but is also supposed to have partly inspired the Nebraskan's famous "Cross of Gold" speech before the Democratic Convention. In the same year he wrote a queer, unreadable novel, also propagandizing his theories about currency, called *A Tale of Two Nations* and dedicated "to the people of this age—and ages yet to come." The copy in my possession is a reprint of 1931 and bears on its cover this bait to the public: "With a sufficient number of copies of this book read by the people of the United States, this civilization will be saved from perishing and in a reasonable time there will be a perfected civilization."

Sometime soon after his debut as a pamphleteer, this lean, distinguished-looking man, wearing a pince-nez and looking not unlike a prosperous college professor, turned up in Arkansas and established himself in the northwest corner of the state, following upon the coming of the Frisco Railway system to that section. He brought with him a son, William Hazelton, born in 1879; but his first wife was left behind in Virginia, to be divorced in the end as late as 1927. Somehow, by what means I cannot discover, he persuaded the Frisco Railway to build a spur track connecting with the outside world a large tract of mountain land which he had bought; and then in that region he proceeded to build for himself a miniature kingdom. The two-story frame-built Frances Hotel, still functioning rather fitfully, came first, and was followed by a host of others, the ruins of which go far to establish "Coin" Harvey as the premier builder of the Ozarks.

The traveller of the present day who approaches Harvey's mountain retreat from the Fayetteville-Springdale-Rogers road, may come down from the plateau by a poor road into the hollow itself, flat-bottomed, with dense wooded ridges bordering it, and travel northeast for some five miles toward the upper valley of the White River, within a mile of Monte Ne itself. Here, just before the settlement itself is reached, rises the south spur of another mountain, which culminates three or four more miles beyond the settlement in an amazing panorama of the entire upper White River valley. Here along this spur runs a small creek, straightened and widened, by Harvey's efforts, to a canal running for about half a mile from the railroad station, now vanished, to the main Harvey property. It is said that in the heyday of the place, around 1920, Harvey imported Venetian gondolas and gondoliers to ply on this canal, to take guests from the railroad station to their quarters in the "club houses." These are two enormous log structures about one hundred feet long at least, built facing each other along the main road which runs south from Rogers; the one nearest the west has at its end facing the canal a three-floored stone-built tower in which Harvey, abandoning a simpler log cottage built earlier, lived during his declining years. Closer to the intersection of the two roads lies the main village, consisting of the disused bank and store and two or three other buildings, all put up by Harvey—all now, except for the store, completely abandoned; and behind the Frances Hotel is another colossal structure of stone and of cement, never finished.

But the gem of the entire collection and something which when once seen, can never be forgotten, is undoubtedly the "Pyramid," begun by Harvey in the 1920s and completed, except for the "Pyramid" itself, by November, 1928. Here is an amphitheatre of gray concrete, rising in five high terraces of vaguely Egyptian or Mayan appearance, around the lagoon which terminates the canal. In the center of this lagoon is a rectangular-shaped island, fifteen by thirty feet, containing—for sole decoration—a solid concrete sofa, flanked by two solid concrete armchairs and facing the tortuous extravagance of the semicircular terraces. The whole, according to the plan that flitted through "Coin" Harvey's aging brain, was to be crowned with the "Pyramid" itself, a structure one hundred and thirty feet tall, rising from a base sixty feet square, and containing three rooms or vaults one above another, to be filled with the records of this present-day civilization "from the size of a needle or safety pin up to a victrola," and containing also three copies of a specially prepared book "giving the rise and growth of this civilization, dangers threatening its overthrow, and a symposium of opinions on the cause of its threatened impending death." These books placed in "heavy glass containers, sealed up hermetically," would be placed in the three chambers of the completed structure, after a year during which the whole structure would be given time to dry; the "three entrances would then be closed with reinforced concrete, and the plates securely bolted thereon. During which process the air will be taken from the vaults. On plates of the most enduring metal known," would be this inscription "moulded in the plate": "When this can be read, go below and find a record of the cause of the death of a former civilization."

Harvey had been convinced, by the time this project was born, that our present civilization would inevitably perish of its greed; and that a new civilization would "rise slowly, as this one has, . . . and that it must arrive at a period when steel and dynamite have been discovered by them before they can break into the Pyramid. Which presupposes an intelligence for appreciation of what they find in the Pyramid." And what the future civilization would find there, would be the revelation of past financial and monetary folly described by "Coin" Harvey. That the future age might readily read the discredited wisdom of this age, a "key book to the English language, that will aid in translation no matter what language is spoken at the time the Pyramid is opened, will be placed in a glass container on the pedestal in the center of the room." Unfortunately, though Harvey succeeded, as he had for many years, in getting all sorts of people interested, the final structure was never begun, though I have talked with one Monte Ne resident who told me that as late as November, 1933, most of the inhabitants of the town were mustered out from their homes by the insistent Harvey, who had them pose with picks, shovels, and wheelbarrows on the spot, in order that a motion picture company might make a film showing work still in progress. And as long as "Coin" Harvey lived, the grandiose idea seems to have been kept alive in his mind, to make of his mountain resort not only a home for the chosen spirits of this age but a final monument to the memory of an age doomed to extinction. The ancientness of the Ozarks themselves, he well might claim, had caused him, in the first instance, to select this spot for his memorial to an age already doomed.

Of all "Coin" Harvey's empire, nothing today remains but the decaying buildings and ruins, guarded by a worried manager and the aging widow of Harvey's second marriage. But there was a time, of which this vast and unbelievable project stands as a symbol, when it seemed that such a retreat into remote fastness as "Coin" Harvey dreamed, was the only cure for the ills that afflicted the country. The financial and industrial development of America had outstripped the agricultural development; and Harvey, campaigning for free silver or building his empire in the Ozarks was merely seeking for a way out. His sickness of soul, of which Monte Ne—a name equally Italian and Cherokee, meaning Water Mountain—became the outward expression, corresponded to some deep-rooted sickness in America itself.

In the State of Arkansas, as it developed from 1875 to 1900, it was certain that, sooner or later, some local politician was bound to arise who would capture all the discontent aroused in the backwoods agrarians by the spectacle of the bargain struck between the Northern industrialists and the conservative Democrats. Such a man need have but a single idea, the idea that the Northern corporations were bleeding Arkansas white and that the thing to do was to get rid of all corporations. The man in question did arrive, and his career, while it lasted, provided the most edifying, and also the most disillusioning episode by way of revealing the true backwardness of the population, in the entire history of Arkansas.

Seventeen

A PEOPLE'S CHAMPION IN A NEW CENTURY

The glittering panorama of the World's Columbian Exposition at Chicago in the summer of 1893 faded into the stark reality of the greatest economic depression the United States had seen since the late sixties. People like William Hope Harvey had openly condemned the banking powers; the Populists out West were clamoring for the free coinage of silver. The Southern and the Western States at last began to realize that they had become the victims of the railroad barons and the Eastern industrialists since the Civil War, and that if they wanted to regain their lost heritage they must find some common ground and fight on that. Competition was giving way to monopoly. The thousand-acre cotton field—staffed by sharecropper labor, which was already being sought as far afield as Italy—had conquered the independent hillside farm, whose owner did his own plowing and harvesting. From January, 1899, men began to speak the name of an obscure young lawyer of Russellville, who was named Jeff Davis, now the victorious candidate for the attorney-generalship of the state. The hour and the man had met.

Although the conservative Democracy of the state had fought a long rear-guard battle, culminating in the adoption of a poll-tax amendment to the state Constitution in 1892, excluding all from voting who could not pay for that privilege, the fierce agrarian discontent among the more independent farmers not only continued but increased after the financial depression of 1893. As early as 1890, the Republicans, despite Clayton's attempts to restrain them, made common cause with labor by seeking fusion with the Union Labor party and thus greatly increased their vote for the governorship; early in 1896, with the depth of the depression staring him in the face, the victorious old-guard Democratic candidate for governor finally declared he would not support a gold candidate for the presidency—and from that time on, the fate of the old guard was sealed. It had existed only because of a tacit bargain between the Northern railroads, manufacturers and bankers and the Southern cotton planters. The bargain had assumed high tariffs and the gold standard as the normal order of things. Now that the gold standard and the tariff alike were being abandoned, the bankers and the industrialists would no longer finance the Cotton Kingdom. That summer at Saint Louis, William Jennings Bryan, the Populist candidate, got the vote of the assembled Democrats on the basis of a single electrifying speech. Cleveland's last attempt to make the Democratic party conservative had failed.

Jeff Davis was born in Little River County, in the extreme southwest of the state, on May 6, 1862; but as a boy he moved with his father to Pope County, famed for its mountaineer independence of spirit. There his father had practiced as a small-town lawyer and a local judge. There is a tradition to the effect that as early as 1878 young Davis had sought an appointment to West Point but failed to pass the examination; there is also a tradition that he attended both the University of Arkansas and Vanderbilt University at Nashville, but graduated from neither. The circumstances under which his family lived were doubtless those of considerable poverty, though we may discount the story, told by Davis himself on the platform, that a bacon rind was kept hanging from a string in the kitchen and that the children at meal times were allowed to jump up from the table and smell it or gnaw at it.

At nineteen Jeff passed an examination for the local bar at Russellville, and it is an attested fact that his father, on being asked what the firm's future name would be, replied, in a low voice, "Jeff Davis and Father." The young man was masterful in his ways and a leader in much youthful mischief. A look at his later portrait, revealing a bull-necked, broad-faced man with obstinately determined mouth and challenging eyes, goes far to establish this point.

In 1890 young Davis succeeded in his first ambition—to be elected prosecuting attorney for his district. This job was much sought after by ambitious young lawyers, for it commanded a fixed salary and assured the winner of considerable practice in arguing cases. Davis won the coveted position only after a very close contest. Immediately after, he married, and his wife bore him—after the usual fecund mountaineer fashion—no less than twelve children, eight of whom survived their earliest years.

In 1898, having retired from the office of prosecuting attorney, he decided to run for attorney general of the state. Apparently he was doubtful at the start as to whether he could succeed in winning this election. Against him as chief candidate, stood F. M. Goar, an old professor of law and head of the law school at the University, who was entirely acceptable to the conservative old guard, and deeply respected. It is possible that Davis made this attempt largely because he had become a close student of the speeches of William Jennings Bryan. Bryan's bold and almost successful bid for the presidency two years before must have convinced him that the time had come to make the Democratic party the people's party.

The contest opened inauspiciously enough for Davis. His opening speech at Eureka Springs, coming as it did on top of a recent illness, had to be delivered while he was seated in a chair; it was read from manuscript and lacked all the improvised touches of backwoods humor he was able to give so copiously later. The audience responded coldly. At that time every county held its primary election to choose the Democratic candidate, at a different date; and Goar easily carried the first four counties. Davis was already anticipating defeat by planning to leave the state and take up residence in Oklahoma—since 1896 booming with oil—when suddenly fate intervened dramatically, in his favor. Goar suddenly fell dead on the platform while delivering a speech on April 7, 1898; and Davis automatically became the victorious nominee of the state Democratic convention.

The United States went to war with Spain, over Cuba, on April 19, 1898. Thus—whether the people willed it or not—the United States, thanks to William McKinley, had embarked on a career of imperial world power. Off in Arkansas an unknown hill-country lawyer, poorly educated, hard-working, and ambitious, was plotting a course that—had it succeeded—would have made all American imperialism impossible. The movement that this man (named after the revered President of the Confederacy and always wearing a gray frock coat, a wide-brimmed gray hat, and a "Baptist" black string-tie), invented and championed, amounted to secession in the economic sphere, as the

Civil War contest had revolved around secession in the political sphere. It raised again the old issue, first fought out in the Civil War, refought in Baxter's day, of Arkansas independence.

Just what the newly-elected Attorney General was plotting came to light on March 6, 1898, when a legislature already far more radical than the "plumed knight," Governor "Dan" Jones, who had respectable old-guard connections, was willing to admit, passed an act known as the Rector Anti-Trust Law, which provided that all persons or corporations having any agreement to control prices could not do business in Arkansas. The act, designed mainly to check the Standard Oil Company in its price-cutting wars with its independent competitors, gave Davis an issue on which to fight. He promptly declared the act meant exactly what it said, and openly stated that if any company were organized to fix prices anywhere in the world without reference to Arkansas, but still attempted to do business in that state, he would prosecute it to the utmost of his powers.

The leading fire insurance and life insurance companies were all organized outside the state, and all were members of rating bureaus organized to fix their rates and premiums; so they knew they were doomed. They promptly attempted to influence Governor Jones and the legislature to amend the law. Jones, who had carelessly signed the act, took alarm but could do nothing more than refuse to speak to his upstart Attorney General. A bill to amend the law was immediately tabled by the legislature. Davis, gaining in courage and recklessness, promptly brought one hundred and twenty-six test suits against the insurance companies. The fight was on; and the insurance companies, to the despair of their policy holders and the bankers alike, threatened to withdraw from the state.

On April 11, the Attorney General, as if in response to the frenzied appeal of all the business interests to stop him in his headlong course, brought other suits against express companies, tobacco companies, and cotton-seed oil companies. Once again—as in the days of the Brooks-Baxter War—the Eastern newspapers had wakened to the fact that something unprecedented was brewing down in Arkansas; and they sent their correspondents to look into this strange situation. Here in this backwoods state, one man with the legislature at his back was threatening to undermine the whole ordered progress of American finance-capitalism by driving out all "foreign-born" corporations from the state. And this man had never even heard of the dangerous word "socialism." He was not, like Governor Altgeld, of Illinois, before him, a wealthy man, too much the idealist to endure the thought of sending in United States troopers to break a great industrial strike. His sole contact had been with leathery-faced, gangling hillside farmers, their drab wives, their innumerable towheaded children. The correspondents saw him as a heavy-set but well-muscled and thick-necked man in a suit of Confederate gray, with a sweaty, rather coarse-looking skin, and a deep-flushed complexion, challenging light blue eyes, and thinning, plastered-down straight hair of a reddish-brown color, over a bold, broad forehead. He was now thirty-six years old, and the *Helena World,* a conservative paper published in the plantation-ridden lowlands, had already started vilifying him by calling him a "carrot-headed, red-faced, loud-mouthed, strong-limbed, ox-driving mountaineer lawyer, and a friend to the fellow who brews forty-rod bug-juice back in the mountains."

On April 12, a day after Davis had filed suit against the express companies, a monster mass meeting, prepared by the Little Rock board of trade well in advance, was called at Glenwood Park, in Little Rock, to petition the legislature to amend the Anti-Trust Law to enable the insurance companies to carry on. The railroads had already announced half-fare rates to all persons outside of Little Rock who wished to attend; and about five or six thousand people from the city, as well as another thousand from without, were present. The proceedings were hilarious. A sort of mock-trial of Davis was held; and he was adjudged as having done something really indecent, not to say boorish, by demanding that the law be enforced. At the close of the proceedings James P. Clarke, a shrewd lawyer who had come from the lowland district but who belonged to the post-Civil-War generation, who had been once governor and was believed to aspire to a seat in the United States Senate, was called on to say something. To everyone's surprise, he declared bluntly that Davis was quite right in opposing the trusts. The trusts would have to be curbed, but in a business-like way and through Federal action. This took the wind out of the sails of some of the fun-makers. Someone spied Davis himself in the audience and asked him to say something. He strode boldly up to the platform. In his opinion, he said, the law was a good one. The legislature had acted as brave and true men in passing it. He now called on them to "stand by their guns." He needed their financial assistance to prosecute all the test suits he had brought.

A day or so after, the legislature appropriated the rather insignificant sum of five thousand dollars to enable Davis to hire more assistants to prepare his briefs and help prosecute his test suits. Already their mood of enthusiasm was changing. But the Attorney General pushed on. Fresh suits were brought on April 28. By the close of May, however, the state supreme court decided against Davis, though he had personally argued his case before them for several days, becoming so hot in the process that he had started to take off his coat, whereupon the Chief Justice had reproved him and ordered him to keep it on. As soon as the decision of the state supreme court was rendered, the Attorney General gave out a public statement. He stated he would now dismiss all pending suits and would not prosecute another trust "even if it organized in the State House yard with a brass band." But he declared that the court's decision was wrong; and he proposed, at the proper time and place, to criticize it, just as he would any other decision of a tribunal he knew to be opposed to the interests of the people.

If the conservatives, now assured by the courts of an insecure tenure, thought they had done with the fiery Attorney General, they were greatly mistaken. The self-same legislature that had passed the Anti-Trust Law, had passed another on April 14, urged on them by Jones this time, to provide for the erection of a new state capitol building, not to exceed in cost one million dollars. This act set up a board of six commissioners to procure complete plans and specifications, appropriated fifty thousand dollars to have the new site (that of the old penitentiary) cleared, and directed the penitentiary commission to procure a new location for their building. Davis immediately charged that this law was a barefaced fraud, an organized attempt to steal from the people an enormous sum, and he asserted that the state could not afford a new capitol building, without paying for it in ruinous taxes. On May 17, insisting that the whole law was unconstitutional, he brought *quo warranto* proceedings in court, to oust the entire new capitol commission, just set up by Governor Jones. The Little Rock newspapers were again reminded of Brooks fighting Baxter; but the hill farmers, plowing their stony acres and cussing against the government and high taxes, again pricked up their ears.

The attempt to stop the new state capitol from being built got no further with the state supreme court than did the attempt to halt the trusts; but Davis's fight could not now be halted by such means. In

July of that year, six months after his installation as attorney general, he became an avowed candidate for governor. In a Fourth of July speech at an obscure village in Sharp County, he defended his record, stating that he had intended to retire after one term as attorney general, but now had a fight forced upon him, by the interests of the business community at Little Rock, whom he referred to as "the high-collared roosters" and the "silk stocking crowd." He stated that the editors of the leading papers of Little Rock, "a lot of squirrel-heads who could not buy on credit five cents worth of beefsteak in the town in which they lived, and yet undertook to tell the people how to vote," had already called him a maniac and a drunkard. Well, did he look like a maniac; or like the people's champion? He declared positively that the state could not afford a new state capitol building. That plan was a gigantic steal, solely intended to impose taxes upon the sons of toil for generations. It was associated with another steal, to remove the penitentiary and to buy a new site for it. The state could not afford that either. And the beautiful historic old building, first erected by John Pope, would revert, inevitably, to the original Ashley heirs in the process. Or so, Davis declared, he believed.

During that summer, the Attorney General spoke frequently in defense of his record; and the Little Rock press, which had at first affected to consider him and his ideas as a great joke, now began to pay him more serious attention. On July 13, he delivered another address at Conway, which the papers, scenting danger, printed in full. Here the mode of attack and the style of presentation were what the public later came to expect of Jeff Davis—that is to say, both were utterly Arkansas. None of the pale flowers of Southern sentiment, dear to the old guard, were used: instead there was blunt attack. Davis declared roundly that at Little Rock a conspiracy had been formed to bulldoze him out of town. The hotel where he lodged had already raised his board from twenty-five to fifty dollars a month, in order to force him out; the telephone company had refused him service, the leading bank refused to cash his checks. All this because he had construed the Anti-Trust Law to mean exactly what it said. "If you are a member of any pool or trust, you can't do business in Arkansas." That is what it meant—"any pool or trust that aimed to fix rates or prices, at any place or at any time." For that, they—the "silk-stockinged, high-hatted" gang were trying to run him out!

Here the Attorney General paused and asked the audience's permission to unbutton his collar. The supreme court had already, he said, decided during his argument over the anti-trust suits brought before it, that he could not legally take off his coat. He therefore requested their permission to unbutton his collar. The crowd roared and applauded. Continuing, he declared that he intended to put up a bed in his office, install a cooking stove there, and do his own cooking. He was too poor to rent a room, but he would stand by his guns, as he had already charged the legislature to do. He would not be run out.

This speech not only proclaimed him a master at making a stump speech, but it served notice on all the opposition—still entrenched at Little Rock and in the eastern, the plantation section of the state—that henceforward the Attorney General was determined to represent himself as a martyr to the popular cause. Let his opponents go on criticizing him as a demagogue, whose speeches were filled with lies and misrepresentations. All that they said in this vein would be turned against them, as part of a gigantic conspiracy on their part to discredit an honest man. William Jennings Bryan, though commanding a vast popular vote, had already gone down in defeat before McKinley. Democracy thus had one martyr; and Davis offered himself as another.

By January, 1900, the campaign for the governorship started; and against Davis stood out three candidates: A. F. Vandeventer, a lumber merchant from Morrilton, who had been a member of the House of Representatives of the very legislature that had brought in the Anti-Trust Law; Judge Edgar S. Bryant, of Fort Smith, a well-meaning sentimental conservative past middle age, known as the "silver-tongued orator" of the state; and John G. Fletcher of Little Rock, a man already sixty-nine years old, prominent as a banker, Confederate veteran, local philanthropist, and leading citizen, who had put behind him a long career from the day when he had been born in a log cabin on the North Fork of the Saline River, five years before Arkansas became a state. Fletcher was too old to be out campaigning, and did not wish to do so: but his friends, mistrusting Vandeventer and feeling that Bryant was a light-weight, had picked on him as the kind of conservative likely to stop the Attorney General. The candidates agreed to meet at Center Point in Howard County on February 12 and start the campaign. This was the very village which Powell Clayton's militia had attacked and taken, back in 1869. Davis's speech on that day, made at the beginning of a new century, after a year which had seen the deaths of Elisha Baxter and Henry M. Rector, stands as a landmark in Arkansas's cultural and social history. It was, later, reprinted in pamphlet form and scattered broadcast throughout the state as Davis's greatest effort. Its phrases are unforgettable to this day.

What were his opponents to say in answer to such statements as these, for example?

"Ah, gentlemen, the war is on. Not a battle between my opponents and me—they are too much gentlemen—but the war is on, knife to knife, hilt to hilt, foot to foot, knee to knee between the corporations of Arkansas and the people. The 'Helena World' says that I am a carrot-haired, red-faced, loud-mouthed, strong-limbed, ox-driving mountaineer lawyer who has come to Little Rock to get a reputation; that I am a friend to the fellow who brews forty-rod bug juice back in the mountains and all that sort of stuff. I have a little boy at home, God bless him, a little pale-faced, white-haired fellow. I love him better than anybody on earth except his mother. If I find that boy is a smart boy, Judge Bryant, I will go and make a preacher out of him; if I find he is not so smart a boy, I am going to make a lawyer out of him, and if I find he has not a bit of sense on earth, I am going to make an editor out of him and send him to Little Rock.

"Public sentiment is the most fickle thing on earth. Today she fondles and caresses; tomorrow she scorns and scoffs. But I am a sort of hard-shelled Baptist in my faith. I believe in foot-washing, I believe in baptism by immersion, and I believe in using the straight edge. What is the straight edge? The law. I sued them all. The business men's meeting met. That wasn't enough. They must have some public sentiment manufactured. They had a mock trial out there at Glenwood Park. Some of the judges were there, I am told. All the elite of the city were there. What was the result? Why, the law was crucified at the very foot of the temple of Justice, and its mangled corpse left dead and helpless.

"I did not start this row, but I am going to keep it up. They went out the other day on the Nineteenth Street Pike and bought fifteen acres of land upon which to build a new penitentiary. What did they give for it? Five thousand dollars. That land is so poor that two drunken men could not raise a difficulty upon it. It is so poor, you could not raise an umbrella upon it. It is so poor, you have to manure it to make brick out of it.

"I am not trying to array the country against Little Rock. There are many noble men and women living there, God bless them. But there is a gang down there that needs clearing out, and needs it awful bad. I would give ten years of my life in jail, if it were possible, to be Governor of Arkansas for only two years, to clean out some of the things down there; I will drive out that gang so clean if I am elected, that it will be like the Red River had run through the town.

"Mr. Vandeventer will tell you that I have not, as Attorney General, attended the Penitentiary Board meetings. They have been held in the private office of Governor Jones. Governor Jones does not speak to me. I told the president of the board that so long as they met in Governor Jones' private office, I would not be with them. When I fight a man upon principles, I want to fight him beside the clear waters, under the blue sky, in open, noble combat. I don't want to get shot in the back. I want to die with my face to the rising sun, with my windows open to Jerusalem. As long as they hold their meetings there, in the Governor's private office, I will not be present."

All this may seem to the present-day reader mostly rant and fustian—the last passage particularly so. Davis had not attended the meetings of the penitentiary board, though by virtue of his office he should have done so, solely on account of the fact that Jones, conservative as he was, hated him to the death. But this, as Davis knew, was the stuff to give the backwoods folks, who still had the majority voting power so long as their poll-taxes were paid. The gist of this speech was a skillful attack on the city—and on Little Rock in particular—addressed to a backwoods audience. Little Rock's lawyers were all corrupt. Its courts had made themselves the tools of the "interests." Its business men had leagued themselves against an honest man. Its editors were "squirrel heads," who could be bought, five for a nickel. Its legislators were nothing but a gang of thieves. He was determined to destroy this conspiracy, and to give back to the backwoods their heritage.

He now examined, scathingly, the record of his opponents. Vandeventer had been formerly a goldbug, but now pretended to be all for free silver. He was in league with the crowd that were plotting to put over the steal of the State Capitol! Fletcher was an honorable, distinguished gentleman who had been persuaded to stand as a Conservative; but who, back in 1886, had actually accepted the nomination of the Agricultural Wheel for the governorship, saying to them, "Thank God, I was never born a Democrat!" And then, the very next day, he had declared that he did not after all want their nomination. Could such a man be said to be honest in his principles? He was the president of a National Bank—one of those institutions that had defeated Bryan, one of those people of whom it was known that "they get bonds from the Government; put up ten per cent in money and get ninety per cent bonds, and issue money. They get the interest on the bonds and loan the money to the people at ten per cent again, so the candle is burning at both ends!" How could such a person as he, juggling with money every day, say—as he had said—that he was in favor of declaring it to be a felony for any official of any corporation to issue more stock than the actual amount of the capital paid in? Judge Bryant—ah, Judge Bryant!—hadn't he just made a speech to a Yankee audience up at Chicago, in which he said he didn't regret that the Confederacy had lost the Civil War? "The victorious finger-touch of God rested upon the banner of the Union"—pretty stuff that, but what did it actually mean? That Judge Bryant was glad the South lost, after holding out for four long, weary years! It may have been for the best, after all, that the South did lose—"but you will never get me to say that I don't regret it. God bless you, I am not built that way!"

The audience were by now sitting silent in their seats, gasping and staring at the figure in Confederate gray, while he launched forth into the famous peroration, containing as it did everything that Arkansas oratory had said for years, but giving it all a daring new twist:

"Gentlemen, I may never see you again. I hope that I will hold out physically in this race, if God will only give me strength. That is all I ask. When you present a thing to the people and they see it, they will always do right. I love my native state; I love its hills and its valleys; I love its bright waters. From the health-giving waters of Eureka Springs on the north to the great Father of Waters on the east that finally loses itself in the tepid waters of the Gulf, from the pine-lands and prairies upon our west to our eastern borders, all up and down the hills and valleys of Arkansas there lives as noble, as brave, as generous, as gentle a race of people as ever sunned themselves in the smile of omnipotent God. The papers may say that nobody will vote for me except the fellow who wears patched breeches and one gallus and who lives up the forks of the creek and don't pay anything except his poll tax. I don't know how true that is, but I want to tell you that there is no great reformation that originated on earth that did not come from the ranks of the humble and lowly. Jesus Christ, when he went out and started the greatest reformation that ever blessed mankind, went to the humble and lowly. He went to the fisherman's cot, the stonecutter's bench. He did not have but one smart man in the crowd and he had to knock the stuffing out of him before he could use him."

After such a speech—and some others in which the Attorney General said that he was fighting "the five hundred and twenty-five insurance agents scattered all over the state, as well as every bank, every railroad, two-thirds of the lawyers, and most of the big politicians," and ridiculed also his opponents by asking Fletcher how many gallons of buttermilk he had drunk while running on the Wheel ticket—and ridiculed Vandeventer, who was in the lumber business, by saying that he had spent his time "just lumbering around town," Davis had no difficulty in carrying every county in the state but one in the Democratic primary. The opposition to him had, in fact, disintegrated rapidly. On February 22, ten days after the Center Point meeting, Fletcher had the misfortune to lose his eldest brother, a man who had shown his unimpeachable integrity throughout life by espousing the unpopular Grange, the Agricultural Wheel, and the Populist movement in turn, and who had been altogether skeptical of Fletcher's wisdom in letting himself be made into a candidate by the conservative element. Davis now openly taunted Fletcher with driving his brother (aged eighty-one) to death by refusing to stand out honestly as a radical; an insult which Fletcher felt he could no longer brook, and so withdrew. Bryant too, succumbed to the stream of ridicule and got out; which left Vandeventer alone to contest. The Republicans—now that Clayton, marplot of the party, had been gotten rid of by persuading McKinley to appoint him as ambassador to Mexico—were determined to make a race of it by nominating H. L. Remmel, an able, popular, and likeable life insurance agent who was a novice in politics. The tireless Davis, in midsummer heat, started campaigning the state again against this "tool of the interests"; and in September, 1900, the verdict stood: for Davis, 88,637; for Remmel, 40,741.

The people, the remote backwoodsmen of the Ozarks, the "one gallus democracy," as Arkansas's ablest historian has called them, had found a champion and had backed him with their votes to victory. The only question was, how far would he dare to go?

Eighteen

JEFF DAVIS RIDES TO HIS FALL

Two aged Arkansawyers now represented the state in the United States Senate—James K. Jones and James H. Berry. Both were relics of the Confederacy. Berry had travelled through life on a wooden leg since the Civil War—an honorable if somewhat ineffectual gentleman. These two men—since both had been in the Senate for many years—controlled Arkansas politically through their hosts of friends. Davis was perfectly aware of this, and also aware that James P. Clarke, a rising lawyer of the post-Civil War generation who had served a term as governor just before Davis's day, had hoped to unseat the aged Jones in the Senate. Clarke had declared himself in favor of curbing the trusts, and that, to Davis, was sufficient incentive to go on.

His walk-over victory as governor had filled the Attorney General with supreme confidence. He had ended his whirlwind campaign by remarking, "If you red-necks or hillbillies ever come to Little Rock, be sure to come to see me—come to my house. Don't go to the hotel or the wagon-yards, but come to my house and make it your home while you are in the Capital City. If I am not at home, tell my wife who you are; tell her you are my friend, and that you belong to the sun-burnt sons of toil. Tell her to give you some hog jowl and turnip greens. She may be out in the backyard making soap, but that will be all right; you will be properly cared for, and it will save you a hotel bill. The word 'Welcome' is written on the outside of the door, for my friends." But there is actually no record of anyone's taking advantage of this invitation. Perhaps they lived too far away. And if Mrs. Davis ever actually made soap, I am unaware of the day when it happened. It is indeed said that when Davis became governor, Mrs. Davis for a time kept a cow tethered on the lawn of her Little Rock home. It was a decorative touch, no doubt appealing to hillbilly supporters.

However, his audacity had won a great result; and he was determined to show his strength from the start. His first legislature, of 1901, refused, though he urged it on them, to amend the Anti-Trust Law of 1899 in such a way that the supreme court could not again upset it. A swing back to conservatism was preparing; a determination on the part of the old guard to regain control and prevent his serving even a second term (usually granted, by courtesy, to most successful candidates). Davis was determined to defeat their plans.

As the election of 1902 approached, he became aware that Clarke, whose chief political strength lay in the very section where he himself was weakest, the lowlands plantation section, would come out once more for senator, against Jones. Accordingly, he threw his weight against Jones. He caused to be published a pamphlet showing that Jones had been mixed up in some rather unsavory bankruptcy proceedings, declared that his Confederate record was worthless, accused him of "pumping morphine into the anti-trust bill," and wound up by saying that James P. Clarke was the "White Plumed Knight of Arkansas, the Henry of Navarre of the state." Jones, infuriated that the governor of the state while still in office should interfere in a contest over the senatorship, remarked that Davis must be crazy. He did not realize that the new governor had a method in his madness. The alliance with the shrewd and ambitious Clarke would prove, as Davis now foresaw, the surest guarantee, not only of a second term—but, if he wanted it, of a third.

As governor he had done nothing remarkable except pardon a great number of people who had been convicted of various offenses, and had opposed the state penitentiary board, which was proposing to buy a state prison farm on the lower Arkansas River. He charged them bitterly and violently with mistreatment of convicts and with the wasting of the taxpayers' money. The new state capitol issue he allowed to lapse, as the people in general had shown themselves too much in favor of it. He had therefore continued the state capitol commission. As to his pardoning record, Davis said later in the campaign that he had pardoned people, while his opponents had pardoned the railroads. He pointed out with pride that during his first term the assessment value of the state's railroads had been raised by more than five million dollars. The railroads were thus being made to pay for state improvements, such as a new deaf-mute school, and were being forced to disgorge some of the high freight rates they had forced on the farmers of Arkansas.

Jones, a man of over sixty, refused to meet Davis in public debate; but the opposition, inspired by all the old-guard elements, did not fail to find a candidate to put up against Davis. This was Colonel E. W. Rector, son of that Henry Massie Rector who had been Arkansas's Civil War governor, who, as speaker of the House of Representatives, had given his name to the first Anti-Trust Law. He was a man over six feet tall, of distinguished appearance and good cultural attainments. Rector announced his candidacy on January 2, 1902. The county primaries were being held as usual, around the end of March; and Davis, the younger man, was likely to prove the better campaigner in the remoter districts in the bad season. But Rector's political record was known to have been on the popular side.

Davis, with his customary canniness, had discovered early in the campaign a quite simple issue on which to beat Rector. The superintendent of schools at Hot Springs, where Rector lived, had boldly refused to graduate one of Rector's sons. This superintendent now wrote to the local papers declaring that Rector had said to him, "Why, dammit, my children do not receive any better consideration at your hands than do the children of common woodchoppers." Rector denied saying this precisely, asserting over and over that all he had said was that his children were being discriminated against simply because they were his. But Davis did not fail to raise this issue in every speech he made during the campaign.

It may seem strange that so small an issue as this could have weighed much during the campaign. Davis had done nothing in his two years as governor except pardon a great many convicts, accuse the state penitentiary board of numberless offenses, let the capitol issue go by default, and talk about a new anti-trust law. Rector might have replied to the attack upon him that his personal quarrel with a school superintendent had nothing to do with his ability to administer the affairs of Arkansas; but unfortunately, if he had done so, he would not have been believed. The people had learned, ever since Baxter's day, that between two or three Democratic candidates for office, it all came down to a question of personal likeability. Davis was a good, kind man. Had he not pardoned poor people caught at crimes? Were not his manners democratic? Rector was a villain. The same logic still sways elections in Arkansas to this day.

Rector struck back feebly by frankly discussing Davis's rather notorious drinking habits and declaring that the Governor was in the habit, in order to appear sober, of drenching his skin with a patent-medicine decoction known as "Wizard Oil."

Davis pointed out in his reply that his health had been none of the best and that Rector, whom he supposed to be a gentleman, should be above trying to make capital from another man's infirmities. Rector, however, was so furiously angered at Davis's making use of what he considered false statements about him that he frankly refused to meet Davis face to face on the platform. Since Rector was unable to end his opponent's vilifications by means of the time-honored duel, the result was as might have been foreseen. Davis won all but five of the state's seventy-five counties. He had already built up a great machine in his favor.

A week before the campaign closed, he actually wired some of his henchmen confidently: "Save Clarke; all hell can't beat me." He was quite right in his estimate. Clarke won the senatorial contest, by only a small majority; Davis's majority was, as before, enormous. The fact that he had, as governor, pardoned so many of the poor, that he still stood out against the trusts, that he could talk the people's language—as Rector could not—that he could speak of the state supreme court, as well as of the newspapers which had opposed him, with supreme contempt, counted for everything. Anyone who could say of the supreme court judges: "These judges are an awfully overworked set of fellows. They come down to their offices about ten in the morning, leave at noon, come back at two, and leave at four. They must be worked to death to stand such a constant strain. Upon what meat do they feed, that they are enabled to do such heavy work?"—anyone who could do this was bound to have the crowd forever on his side. All that was needed was for him to go on doing exactly what he had already been doing for two years.

His first act as governor for a second term showed him prepared to throw caution to the winds. He had appointed as a member of the new capitol commission James P. Eagle, a respectable ex-governor of the state, who was also president of the State Baptist Association. This man had made speeches on behalf of Jones and had helped him to fight Davis, on account of his own opposition to that worthy. Davis now demanded Eagle's resignation and, when Eagle refused, published a proclamation removing him. As a result, the board of deacons of the Baptist denomination boldly threw Davis out of the church altogether—an action at which Davis serenely laughed, declaring that he was only a "pint Baptist," while others were "quart Baptists." He had tasted power so fully that it now made him cynical.

In conjunction with the victorious Clarke, he had made himself head of a powerful political machine, but the legislature, thoroughly frightened, refused to give him another inch of advantage. Over his veto, they passed a bill providing for the completion of the new state capitol and they appointed a new commission of their own to supervise it. Davis attempted to fight against this in the courts, but was utterly unsuccessful. The penitentiary board, as well as the new attorney general, a celebrated Irish law-pleader of the day, who could always sway any jury to tears and who had been on Davis's side at first, were now out fighting him to the death. Davis had declared during the campaign that white convicts had been bullied by Negro guards; that one prisoner had been starved and beaten to death; that the new prison farm just purchased was a pesthole of a swamp, full of marsh and malaria and covered with Johnson grass; that convicts could not live there. The Attorney General, fiery Irishman that he was, had retorted that he meant to get the legislature to impeach the Governor. And the legislature had no sooner convened in January, 1903, than a committee was set up to investigate Davis's conduct.

The specific charges investigated revolved mainly around the Governor's use or misuse of the state funds. It was alleged that he had drawn from the state funds sums of money to make trips to look for a suitable site for the new penitentiary farm, money to go to Fayetteville and attend commencement exercises at the University; that he had received free coal from a firm holding the contract to supply various state institutions, and the like. The charges in themselves were insignificant; what really mattered was the spirit that prompted them. All the old guard, as well as a good many other people who had at first supposed they would find the Governor amenable, were now against him. As one of them said, "We had a great deal to endure from Governor Davis. He has endeavored to force his will upon us, right or wrong, without consideration, and regardless of others' feelings if they refused to agree with him. It is his nature; it is his disposition."

During the long investigation that followed, Davis was at his best. He had not yet acquired the later pomp and display that belied his earlier promises, and he still lived simply, without ostentation. Except for occasional hunting and fishing trips, paid for out of state funds, and a rabid attendance at baseball games, he had shown no particular disposition to be extravagant with money that was not his. He still wore his one suit of Confederate gray—indeed, he wore it to the end of his life—and in his private office his eldest daughter was installed as secretary. He could, and did, represent himself as still a poor man persecuted by all the rich; and he obviously enjoyed that position. To a member of the committee who asked him why he had drawn out state money before making the trip to Fayetteville, whether he had not known that his expenses would be met later, he replied, "Yes, sir, but I did not have any money. I haven't got my car fare to go home tonight; and if you will lend me five cents I will be obliged to you."

This was in keeping with the Davis the people loved, the Davis who on his campaigns would stop farmers along the road and ask them for a chew of "hillside navy," the Davis who had declared, "I would rather eat turnip greens, hog jowl, and cornbread with you fellows around the wagons, than go into the hotel and eat with the high-collared crowd." He had not yet begun to abuse his power, to soften up under high living. Small wonder, then, that the committee, after collecting eight hundred pages of testimony, could not agree on any report. The legislature, however, remained determinedly hostile and toward the close of the session passed more than a hundred bills of a sort the Governor would not like, and then adjourned. The Governor waited for twenty days, as the constitution allowed him to do, and then vetoed them all. It is said that he procured a wheelbarrow, loaded it with the vetoed bills, and ordered his clerk to wheel it along to the office of the secretary of the state and there dump the entire barrow-load of bills on the floor.

By the end of 1903 he surprised nobody, except those who still refused to take him seriously or who thought of him, mistakenly, as a coward, by declaring that he intended to run for a third term as governor—a thing seldom before done in the annals of Arkansas politics. He declared the reason to be that he wanted a final vindication at the hands of the people at the polls for the treatment he had now received both from the supreme court and the penitentiary board, and from the legislature. And he electrified everybody, including even his own followers, by declaring that if elected he would in 1905 seek for the seat in the United States Senate, now filled by James H. Berry, the one-legged Confederate, who was immensely popular and who, like the senator Clarke had defeated, had sat there since around 1885.

The question now was, who could beat Davis? With the aid of Clarke's supporters, the state was altogether his. He was entrenched in power, having forged the support of the "one-gallus democracy" into a perfect instrument to reëlect him and his followers indefinitely. After much canvassing, the opposition set up as their candidate an associate justice of the state supreme court, Carroll D. Wood, who had actually been elected along with Davis, on his first campaign in 1900, but who had grown increasingly hostile. Wood was a good speaker, was known as a prominent Baptist, was physically fearless and able to make an active campaign. But Vandeventer whom Davis contemptuously referred to throughout the campaign, as the "Gazette Yankee from Morrilton," was still rankling because of his defeat in 1900; and he came out also as an independent candidate.

The campaign, held like the previous one in the wet and chill winter months of 1904, later became famous as marking the extreme flood-water point in backwoods invective. As was the custom at the time, Davis travelled about the state with his two opponents for company; the leading rallies were held at remote points, along muddy backcountry roads, the candidates frequently riding in buggies to reach them and travelling also by the slow and uncomfortable method of local trains—sometimes consisting only of a single car hitched on to the back of a freight train. Every effort was made to provide Wood with a state-wide organization. "Wood Clubs" were organized everywhere; their members wore big wooden buttons. A giant "Wood rally" was staged in March at Little Rock. The *Gazette,* which fought Davis bitterly, and which he referred to as "that old red harlot," sent along a representative to distribute free copies of its most scathing editorials. But Davis was secure, and he knew it. He had roused the countryside against Little Rock now, and all he need do was to turn on a stream of personal invective against his opponents. Moreover, if his supporters could not pay their poll taxes, he would pay them, in order to gain their votes.

Wood was the chief object of the savage attack. The fact that he had sung in the Baptist Church choir at Little Rock was repeatedly referred to as a cause for ridicule. "When Judge Wood gets up there to speak, I want you farmers to call on him for one of his songs. He is the singing candidate in this race. I can't sing. I ruined my voice crying for gravy when I was little. Judge Wood makes more racket singing in the choir in Little Rock than one of you farmers would calling your hogs home." The fact that Wood, as an abstainer, had also the support of the Prohibitionists, drew an extra round of typical Davis ammunition: "My campaign against my opponents is going to be as easy as taking candy from a baby. I want all of you fellows who ever took a drink to vote for me, and all those who haven't, may vote for Judge Wood. I can stay at home and sleep and beat Judge Wood, or this Yankee from Morrilton. I am depending on the horny-handed sons of toil, the men that pull the bell-cord over old Beck, to help me fight this battle."

Small wonder that the "wool-hat brigade," as Davis himself loved to call them, cheered themselves hoarse and threw their old hats up into the trees at every rally. Here was a real dog-fight of a campaign! It was getting as hot as a cooking stove, as Davis said, from the very start. Davis taunted Wood repeatedly by nicknaming him "Aunt Puss" or "Aunt Julie." As for Vandeventer, he was merely a "Gazette Yankee," travelling, like Wood, on free passes provided by the railroads. "A committee of you farmers can take Judge Wood and Vandeventer—that Gazette Yankee—out back of the smokehouse, take off their vests, shake them around like a dog would shake a two-year-old possum, and you can put skates on a nigger boy and have him skating around on railroad passes for ten feet. If you lack a foot or two of having enough to plaster on the railroad tickets, go down into the Judge's pockets and get a few street-car tickets." And further, "I am going to put knee-britches on Judge Wood and run him for a page when the legislature meets. I will also try to get Vandeventer some kind of a job, even if I have to put him in as a chambermaid around the State House."

Rain or shine, the mad buffoonery went on. At Redfield it rained heavily. The next day, at another rally, Davis said: "I am sorry that my friends all got mad at me yesterday at Redfield; but I couldn't help it. They all got as wet as drowned rats. Just before the speaking began, the winds blew, and the floods came. Judge Wood had his wife's parasol and he got all his friends under it and kept them dry. Vandeventer bought a dollar and a half umbrella, and kept all his friends dry. My friends stayed out in the rain and got wet. Women with babies got so wet, they slipped out of their mothers' arms, just like eels." At another rally, the weather was warmer, and Davis, as was his custom, began pulling off his coat. Instantly a violent fight broke out between two dogs close to the audience, and the crowd began to shift in their seats. Davis instantly remarked, "Keep your seats. It is just one dog walloping another, like I am walloping my opponents. I didn't know I was going to have a row among the dogs or I would not have taken off my coat."

This—as he knew—was the stuff to give "the high-collared crowd that wear collars so high they can't see the sun except at high noon over the tops of their collars; the crowd that, when they shake hands with you, only give you the tips of their fingers; the crowd that you can't tell from their backs whether they are going, or coming back." He stood squarely on his record, as one who had been indeed the people's champion, but had been made the victim of a conspiracy. Now he was out to destroy the opposition, finally and irrevocably, with contempt:

"The other day an old farmer caught Judge Wood by the nape of his coat-tail, took him off to one side as if he was going to ask about a horse thief, and said: 'Judge, who got you into this race?' The Judge said, 'Oh, for God's sake don't ask me who got me into it; ask me who is going to get me out of it.' I will tell you who is going to get the judge out of it. It is the farmers, the mechanics, the wood-haulers, the rednecks, and the patched-britches brigade. They are going to put the judge out on dry land. If the boys in the hills will only touch hands with the boys in the valleys, we will win one more victory for good government. We will whip these Yankees out on dry land and let them stink themselves to death."

The climax of the campaign came at Hope, where Wood, infuriated with such taunts, struck openly at Davis with his fists while the Governor—who was carrying a gold-headed cane presented to him by his admirers and inscribed with "Stick to your guns"—hit Wood over the head with it and dented its top. From that day on, Davis refused to sit on the same platform as his opponents, declaring that his life was in danger. He claimed the right to speak first at all meetings, and when he had finished, usually left, carrying most of the crowd with him.

Again he was victorious. And he was now absolute master of the state. Soon after, he had little difficulty in becoming the candidate for the United States Senate over the aged Berry, whom he began attacking as early as December, 1904. Berry refused to campaign, urging his poor health; and though others campaigned for him, he succeeded in carrying only twenty-four out of seventy-five counties. At last, Davis was ready to pass on to Washington, having in January, 1905, finally set his signature to an anti-trust bill, with "teeth in it," which absolutely prohibited any pool or combination from doing business in the state. But since no prosecuting attorney would dare to prosecute, the law remained a complete dead letter until in 1911 the legislature rescinded it.

The rest of Davis's career was a long anticlimax. Though he caused a ripple of sensation in the United States Senate by making, soon after his arrival, one speech against the trusts, which, as he said, "swept the cobwebs off the ceiling of the Senate Chamber," and which still is—for all its backwoods awkwardness and blunders of phrase—a creditable effort, he soon became only an amusing clown. He attacked President Roosevelt for hobnobbing with the Negroes, and then made himself ridiculous by meeting Roosevelt, who promptly took hold of the lapels of his coat and cried, "Didn't you pardon a great many criminals, when governor? A soft heart makes for a soft head," while Davis could only lapse into a moody silence. It was useless for him to go on saying in Washington that the only things Arkansas ever had on the free tariff list were possums, sweet potatoes, and acorns. The Senate merely laughed at him once and then tired of the joke. He had none of the dangerous ammunition later possessed by the greatest of his followers, the late Huey Long. His mind seemed empty. And in Little Rock his family were living in state, and his sons were going to college in other regions.

His final speeches, probably written for him by others, were turgid with heavy rhetoric. It was only when back on his native soil, campaigning for some of his later henchmen, that he could sometimes fall into the old vein. Despite his attacks, the new state capitol was built and occupied by 1911. Nothing had been done to stop the trusts, to curb the railroads. He had become only an unremovable fixture in the Senate, where his speeches emptied the Senate chamber rapidly. He died suddenly in January, 1913. Between five and ten thousand faithful believers saw their champion's body lowered to earth in old Mount Holly Cemetery in Little Rock, on an afternoon dark with midwinter rain.

Jeff Davis had been an anachronism. When he came to power as attorney general, there had been no automobiles in the state. Now the silent revolution of the "horseless carriage" had spread over the face of the land. The Wright brothers had flown at Kitty Hawk, and man's conquest of the air was secure. Wireless telegraphy had spanned space. Motion pictures had progressed from "The Great Train Robbery" to Charlie Chaplin. But throughout all this, Jeff Davis had survived his own usefulness, had outlived the age that produced him, had even been laughed at in the end by many Arkansawyers who read the accounts of the elaborate balls he gave at his home, and who recalled the bacon-rind that he said had once hung from the ceiling of his boyhood home for the children to smell. His mind had never grown beyond his early years. The reason for his success and his failure alike lay in the fact that, then as now, the State of Arkansas spent less for teachers' salaries, less per school pupil, than any other state in the Union. He had never been fully educated. His mother wit, at first serving him well, had run itself out. In his strength and in his weakness, he had been a living paradox: a combination of brute force and low cunning, of headlong idealism and great grossness, of monstrous sentimentality and equally monstrous cynicism, of crude poetry and cruder buffoonery. In all this, he had stood as a vivid example of the Southern backwoods politician; and his mission, if mission it was, had been to reveal to his own people—and to a generation that had far more complex problems than his to face—the still-unused and long-wasted human ability of the Ozarks.

Nineteen

THE WORLD OF THE MOUNTAINEER

It was the mountain people who had produced Jeff Davis; from the beginning of his career to its end, he was their spokesman and their champion. His coming to power focused attention for the first time on the Ozarks; until then, the mountain region had largely been a no-man's land. It had been peopled with mute, inglorious Miltons in homespun, who were born, who fished and hunted, engaged in brawls, got religion, courted, raised log cabins and large families, passed on to their graves unnoticed by the outside world. Since the day when Davis made their protest real, though he was unable to sustain it against chronic pressure from without, they and their tradition have alike decayed. But the underlying character of the Ozark mountaineer is the same as it ever was.

Two great characteristics the mountaineers possess in common with the peasantry of other lands—their dignity and their homogeneity. The former quality comes naturally from man's hard struggle with the soil; the latter is revealed by the fact that neither Negroes nor any considerable number of the foreign-born whites, even of the second generation, are to be seen among them. Still a third characteristic, that of loyalty, is strikingly manifest, though it has not, in recent years, prevented those individuals who still feel the pioneer urge from going to the automobile factories of Detroit or the fruit ranches of California. The Ozarkers, under the free conditions of what was still a frontier up to the twentieth century, display today many of the characteristics of the peasant yeomanry of England. Seeing them, one might think oneself in the presence of English agricultural laborers from Dorset, Somerset, Gloucestershire, or Devon. Despite the American costume of jumper and overalls, despite the faces baked by the sun and lined by the wind of a more severe climate than that of England, some of these people recall the characters of Thomas Hardy. Many, if not most of them, are blonds—slim, light, easy, with wide, fine foreheads above the steady, cool blue or gray eyes. They have straight, determined mouths and firm, obstinate chins and an air of aloofness and gravity. Strong influxes of Celtic blood, from Scotland and Northern Ireland alike, have made many heads dark; but the eyes are still, nearly always, either gray or blue; here and there one sees hair of a vivid red—the mountain-ash berry color. It might be expected that these people, who, unlike their remote English kinsmen, have lived here for more than a century, untouched for the most part by modern industrialism, would display the contrasting qualities of social conservatism and individual daring, generosity and narrowness, adaptability to circumstances and freedom from outside influence, matter-of-factness and mysticism, that the English, Scotch, North Irish peasantry also have displayed. And indeed this is the fact. They are probably the most independent and yet the most hidebound of all people, these Puritans of the Upper South.

In one respect they differ profoundly from the English yeomanry of the present day. Thanks to their remoteness—broken down only in the last forty years—or to their lack of formal education, which is still manifest, they live and act largely upon impulse, as the Englishmen of Shakespeare's day must have done. It was upon an impulse, caught perhaps from William Jennings Bryan and his rhetoric, that Jeff Davis acted when he made his historic race for the attorney general's office. It is upon impulse that the young men act today when they move off to Detroit or California or rush to volunteer for the American army. They lack—and one is grateful for this lack—the fixed complacency of the English peasantry. Yet, unlike the mountaineers of Tennessee and of Kentucky, whom they otherwise resemble most nearly, the Ozark people are not much given to private quarrels. Hot-temperedness has been left to the aristocratic gentlemen of the lowlands. The Gulf of Mexico climate, stealing up into the hills from Texas and the lower Mississippi Valley, may have something to do with their slowness, their deliberate hesitation, and their dislike for direct action. As was pointed out in the chapter dealing with the causes of the Civil War, these people do not really fight well unless cornered, and then they resist to the death. Theirs is the true razorback spirit. In other ways their mode of living is in many respects wilder than that of the dweller in the Appalachians and the Cumberlands. The proximity of the Western plains—the traditional land of the cowboy, the outlaw, the Indian—is very manifest in the Ozarker's life and in his customs. Or as an old emigrant song I have heard there has it:

Rise up to me, my dearest dear, and present to me your hand,
For I long to take a journey to a far and distant land;
And it's ladies to the center, and it's gents around the row;
We'll rally around the canebrake, and shoot the buffalo!

Shoot the buffalo! That is precisely what the Ozarker is still after. For him the spirit of the West, symbolized by the buffalo, is still present somewhere on his mental horizon, beyond the flat-topped, wooded hills, and the steep hollows of his lonely land.

When one looks from a height in remote Van Buren or Searcy counties over the incredibly unpeopled and winding valley of the Little Red or of the Buffalo River, one can still picture the shaggy herds browsing on the river plain beneath and the hunters gathering on horseback for the kill. This land is neither Eastern nor Western: it has much of both in its contrasts, its alternations of stony, dense-forested ridge and windswept, watered valley. And like the land, its people are both mountaineers and frontiersmen. Theirs is the Southern gateway to the West, which they have held against all comers.

The lives of the Ozarkers, which to an outsider so often seem stark and hard, are in reality richer by far than the lives of the sharecroppers, white or black, in the plantation region. The thing which they hate most is to be compared, in any way, to the Negro; they feel an innate superiority not only towards all dark skins but to the few foreigners and Jews who have come among them. Towards most town dwellers they are indifferent; they are not, and do not care to be, townspeople—and this in itself makes them difficult for outsiders to know. One may see the ugly dusty Main Streets of the small mountain towns full of hill men and their seemingly innumerable trucks and children, on Saturday afternoons, particularly around Christmas and Easter; but on the Sunday following, these same Main Streets are deserted and empty. The Ozarkers prefer to go to church, as they prefer to live, among certain well-known and familiar landmarks and neighbors, chosen from a radius of probably not more than ten miles. They do not, unless they are either ambitious or notoriously "trifling," change their places of abode with great readiness; and this has led to an undoubted amount of interbreeding. Whether this fact is responsible for the not infrequent cases of idiocy to be found, is a question I must leave to the biologists. Except for these cases, and except for the fact that they tend to lose their teeth rather early and that their women age rapidly from overwork and frequent childbearing, they are a magnificent race, tending most frequently to graceful leanness. Tuberculosis is rather too common to be missed; so, too, are the after effects of malaria caught from the mosquitos that swarm every summer out of the river valleys. It is to be feared that the automobile, which has helped to put them into closer touch with the towns, has also helped to spread venereal disease. But apart from this, man for man, woman for woman, they are of a finer type than the present-day New Englanders of the backwoods—closer to the land and its spirit than the vanishing Yankees, now giving way all over New England to Finnish or Polish or Portuguese or French Canadian newcomers.

What they represent is largely an unrealized possibility. Their quickness at learning, their ability to adjust themselves to new and untried conditions, are very marked. In this respect, they have no competitors among the people of the state, except possibly the Negroes; and they often display a greater degree of individual initiative than the Negroes. But most of those who have remained in close touch with their mountain environment are—as regards their minds—like sheets of paper on which little as yet has been written. Lacking, as they do, anything but the rudiments of an education, they live on the accumulations of a folk instinct, an unwritten body of traditional observances which varies hardly at all from age to age. This is their culture; and in regard to it they are conservatives. Unfortunately many of the younger people among them—those born since 1918—have finally grown indifferent to its persistence. The great and last "boom age" of the twenties set before them only too clearly the cities as shining goals of endeavor—and they have, as a result, increasingly tended to minimize their heritage. As the population has been drained off, people from without have come in; to them the Ozark lore is only cute and quaint. The radio, with its commercialized substitute for art, has given them jazz for folk music, cowboy yodeling for folk ballad, and Bob Burns and

Lum and Abner for folk humor. Thus for the first time in their history they are becoming, in this generation, the unconscious agents and witnesses of the degradation of their own folk culture.

The inaccessibility and the lack of response manifest in their minds are the results of their remoteness from any sources of information except the misinformation provided them by the motion pictures (they prefer Western films to all others, as these still emphasize qualities of heroism), and the radio. Over and over again, those who have lived among them have loudly complained of the complete absence of reading matter. Public libraries, bookstores, anything but the occasional magazine which passes from hand to hand, are almost unheard of. Recently there have been attempts to supply this lack, the most important of which was the establishment of county libraries, an activity sanctioned for the entire state by popular vote. More picturesque, perhaps, but not less striking, are the private activities of such a man as Theodore Richmond, who lives in a remote region outside Jasper and who raises goats. By begging among his neighbors and among the people of the state at large, he has amassed a respectable number of books, to be borrowed by his mountain neighbors at his Wilderness Library.

One vividly recalls that story of a school inspector who came from Little Rock into the stark bareness of a backwoods school full of pupils of all ages from six to seventeen. "How many of you here have ever read a book except your schoolbooks?" he asked. Not a hand went up. "How many of you have ever read a magazine?" he went on. One hand—a girl's—went up. "What is the name of the magazine?" he asked. "Ace Detective," she replied, shyly.

This inaccessibility to culture is undoubtedly regretted by a great many of the mountain people themselves, and they honestly do their best to overcome it by every means they may. Even Jeff Davis must have read avidly through the speeches of William Jennings Bryan and possibly through the pamphlets of "Coin" Harvey, in his early manhood. There does not exist in the whole United States any body of people more sensitive to their own supposed intellectual failings than the Arkansas mountaineers. Anyone who refers to them openly as being lazy or shiftless, as perpetual users of snuff and tobacco, as personally uncleanly or lacking in culture, is likely to find out how deeply they resent such slurs. Any person who, after having lived among them, refers to them disparagingly outside, is likely to be greeted on his or her return with a stony silence which implies far more condemnation than an outright contradiction. The suspicion of all "foreigners" so manifest in the Ozarks continues because they do not want to be thought of by anyone as "backward." In fact, they are not. Anyone who comes to live among them from without and who still commands something like a regular income is likely to find out through the acquisition of bad land and worthless animals that the Ozark people are not lacking in shrewdness. From the pioneer point of view, they are still, through the use of mother wit and meagre resources, ahead of the commercialized civilization that surrounds and threatens daily to engulf them. Yet they are extremely poor as regards fresh intellectual currents.

The all-prevailing Baptist Church, as well as its direct descendant, the Pentecostal, has unfortunately tended to keep their minds narrow rather than to open them. This is not the place to assess critically the influence of evangelical and puritanic protestantism on the mind of the South—particularly the upper South. That has been done over and over again in other books and novels. Undoubtedly the early Baptists and Methodists, through the medium of the campmeeting revival and of the far-travelling early preachers, did a great work in keeping these people somehow Christian—which any other sects were unable to do. These sects encouraged, and still do encourage, continued reading and study of the Bible as interpreted in the fundamentally literal sense recommended by the guardians of the faith. But the philosophy of these teachers of the backwoods creed is, none the less, fatal to all intellectual advancement. The theory on which they operate is simple, and at bottom unanswerable. The Bible is the Word of God, and the Word of God will be carried out to the letter; everything else is worldly distraction. Since mankind is going to be universally judged by God at no distant date, everyone who prefers any form of worldly distraction to the sole means of salvation to be found in the Bible, will inevitably go to hell. Moreover, the attractions of the world—which include the stimulation of human interest by reading anything but the Bible—are to be eschewed for yet another reason: the harder one's life is here on earth, the more it keeps to the straight and narrow way, the greater shall be one's future reward.

The mountaineers, compelled, as they have been, to improvise some normal and healthy fun in their lives, have discovered at least one way of circumventing the taboos of their religion. Dancing to fiddle music has for so long been considered sinful that a way has been found to dance without such aid. This is the celebrated "play party," about which at least one Doctor's thesis has been written. Couples weave in and out in regular dance steps, while one sings:

We'll all go down to Rowser's,
To Rowser's, to Rowser's.
We'll all go down to Rowser's,
And drink some lager beer.

Rowser, he's a jolly boy,
Rowser, he's a jolly boy,
Rowser, he's a jolly boy,
And has a jolly time.

Never mind the old folks,
The old folks, the old folks,
Never mind the old folks,
They're all away from home.

Thus some unknown German saloon keeper, whose name may have been Rauser and who probably lived at Cincinnati or Saint Louis or some forgotten river port in the remote early days, is appropriately commemorated.

Even stronger means of distraction from the accepted code are not entirely unfamiliar to these people. Square dances are still sometimes held; and at them almost invariably the "mountain dew" brought along in fruit jars, and always drunk secretly outside the house, is in evidence. This may lead to fights or to primitive explosions of sex during the course of the night. "Log-raisings" at new homes or "setting up with the sick" are still occasionally practiced. And there are also, usually in summer, the "singing schools," where the hymns are learned all over again, and the frequent revivals. These are held, significantly enough, usually at a time when there is little hunting, fishing, or farming to be had; they represent efforts to break down isolation into a pattern of greater coalescence.

The mountaineer—hemmed in as he has been by restrictions of space imposed on him by his environment, as well as by restrictions of thought imposed on him by his creed—is by no means lacking in curiosity concerning the outer world. He will read, if he can manage it, somehow and anyhow. This usually means that popular and easily readable trash is more frequently devoured than good literature. Many of them in the past read such things as *Peck's Bad Boy* or *On a Slow Train through Arkansas,* usually ascribing the latter to the late Opie Read—who, whatever his failings, was not guilty. "Rib-ticklers," and the cruder the better, are popular. Most of the spoken folklore, on the other hand, is not especially funny. Tales of ghosts, of murders, of mysterious caves and buried treasures, of melodramatic escapes from tornadoes or wild animals abound. It has been said that in a society which is not industrial the usual folk tale is one of the physical prowess, and it is true that such are extremely common in the Ozarks.

Superstition, as is natural enough among a people who are still strongly under the Celtic influence, is common. Beans are invariably planted on Good Friday. Almanacs, in the spring, are thumbed through to look for "twin days" and "flowerpot days"—the former being the sign of the constellation of Gemini, the latter the sign of Virgo—the first, good for planting vegetables; the second, producing only flowers without fruit. Certain women are still reputed to be witches and are able to get rid of warts and other ailments through the mumbling of spells; but the tolerance of the South forbids that they should be persecuted for these accomplishments. Tales of ghosts usually make their appearance whenever a party gathers to "set up" with some sick person. There are certain things of which all are equally afraid: thunderstorms, tornadoes, snakebite, panthers, and mad dogs. Even the humblest mountain cabin frequently has its well-constructed "potato house"—in reality a buried cyclone cellar—next door. And a horseshoe, with the points pointing upward, is still set over the doorjamb inside.

Except for certain traditional usages of herbs employed as medicines, now vanishing rapidly, little interest is taken in the local flora. Most trees have their names—trees are, after all, useful; but flowers go unnoticed. Birds and animals, too, unless useful for food, or openly noxious, are not particularly noted. The common superstition that when you hear the first mourning dove in the spring, you will travel off in the direction the sound comes from, may have arisen from the fact that spring was once the reopening of the hunting season. Why the whippoorwill, if it calls from the roof, should signalize a death in the house, I do not know—unless it is that there is something sinister in the bird's nocturnal habits and an ominous quality of sound in its cry. The cry of the screech-owl is also believed to be an omen of death;

and when it occurs, the thing to do is to turn your pockets and wring them out so that the bird's neck is wrung and it must cease its crying. If you are undressed and in bed when you hear the cry, you must get up and turn your shoes over, bottoms upward. This has a similar effect. On the other hand, the song of the cardinal, it is said, brings luck and happiness to every home.

When a death does occur, after the long "setting-up" parties with the sick person are over, if there is a mirror in the room where the dead person is, it is always carefully shrouded—perhaps to discourage the dead person's spirit from looking in the glass. The burial usually occurs soon after; but there is a belief, natural enough in a people so firmly convinced of ghosts, that the spirit of the dead stays around for a time to see if everything goes on all right upon earth. Ghosts, as such, are usually associated with certain places thought to be haunted, usually some old deserted farmhouse, half-ruined.

Wedding feasts, Fourth of July barbecues, and church sociables held out in the open air with plenty of "vittles" piled on a long trestle table, are still fairly common. But the "infare" feast, following the wedding, has long since gone, a casualty of the machine age. Quilting parties are sometimes still given, but none of the other crafts are much practiced today. This is a distinct loss, for apart from their training in skill, the practice of these crafts had some economic value for a people who—except during the brief crop season—have normally little that can lift them from a deep rut of poverty.

The cotton economy of the Delta South, as was fitting in a section which developed so late, took final hold upon Arkansas only in the two decades before the Civil War. Up to that time corn was the crop usually raised in the uplands, and it was supplemented by the raising of hogs, sheep, sorghum, tobacco, rice, and even wheat—a large list. For this skillful diversification practiced by the pioneers, the cotton economy substituted a single crop to be turned annually into cash; and in place of community self-aid, it substituted the sharecropper system. Cotton soon came to be generally grown in highland as in lowland throughout many areas which are not really suitable to its cultivation. In the upper White River region, one may see today hundreds of fields of suspicious, pale yellow clay, rocky and unprofitable, plowed and brought under cotton. This cotton often happens to be of the "bumblebee" variety, already explained, or else of the "dogtail" variety, so called because it is no bigger than the tip of hair on the end of a dog's tail. Yet many of the hill men think of it as the crop that causes them the least trouble. It may bring in enough money at the year's end to buy new clothes and shoes and some food for a large brood of towheaded children, or it may not.

Fruit- and berry-raising has been, for the past forty years at least, a far more profitable source of revenue for those who would turn to it. The last period of extremely high cotton prices before 1944–1946 came around 1918–1922, at the close of the First World War. A few years before the Civil War, apple-growing for profit had started around Fayetteville in a region which is frankly out of the cotton belt; and there is a poetic irony and justice in the fact that the profitable cultivation of the grape in the same area was effected largely through the efforts of Italian Catholic laborers who, being introduced into far Southern plantations to take the place of Negro sharecroppers as early as 1900–1902, migrated northwest and founded the flourishing grape settlement at Tontitown. Other efforts at fruit- and grape-growing were made early by German-Swiss Catholic settlers. During the seventies there was, indeed, a great German Catholic migration, beginning around Subiaco—where stands still a great German-Swiss-built Benedictine Abbey—which spread vigorously to Altus, Morrilton, and on through the upper Arkansas valley. Strawberry culture began around Fayetteville; but its chief field today is around Searcy in White County in the clay upland between the Little Red and the White River. Youngberries are still more modern; and cattle raising in the modern style, more recent still. All unfenced country remains legally open range; and it is only of very recent date, in fact in the last four to six years, that the prejudice of the mountaineer against allowing his cattle—which are always turned loose in the woods—to be rid of their ticks periodically through state dippings, has shown some signs of breaking down.

Sheep are far less common than they probably were a century ago; the Ozarker with a good flock of sheep is an exceptionally active and exceptionally enterprising sort of person. Goats, which can live anywhere and require less care, are probably on the increase. Apart from a large field of cotton and a small plot of corn, some vegetable truck, a cow or two, and a few chickens and pigs (which often stray off into the woods like their forebears, the razorbacks), there is nothing that the average conservative Ozarker raises except small private patches of what Jess Davis called "hillside navy," in other words, tobacco. A few "hands" of drying tobacco are still to be found hanging from the roof poles of most mountain cabins. A gun is also usually present, but is little needed except in the spring or in the fall. Accordingly, the native mountaineer, once his crops are laid by and the hot days of summer come, is in much the same case as the lowland sharecropper. He has little to do except to sit on his splint-bottomed chair on the porch and stare off into vacancy. The house behind him is usually built of rough, unpainted lumber, showing considerably less structural ability than the decaying log cabins of older days.

Around about 1910, that is, the time that Jeff Davis passed on into the United States Senate and to a much-visited grave in Mount Holly Cemetery in Little Rock, the lure of the cities and their ways became more and more insistent for the Ozarkers. Since all the hill girls marry early—at fifteen or sixteen—and since there is a strong preponderance of male births over female, the ambitious young men tend, more and more, to get out to Detroit or to Chicago or to some other big industrial city, where the wages offered by such employers as Henry Ford have been a strong bait, or, more recently, since the terrible drouth summer of 1930, to the fruit ranches of California. The effect of the dust bowl on the Oklahoman has thus had a corresponding echo on the mountain-bred Arkansawyers. But the "Arkies" of recent years have been possibly the only natives of the backwoods who have made any special efforts to return once they found out that California was not, after all, a land of gold.

Thus the Ozarks to this day have been a pool of fecund and valuable human material, used only if taken outside the state, for purposes entirely unconnected with the state's economy. There is irony in the fact that Arkansas, with untouched and undeveloped mineral resources in its hills, beggared itself from 1927 onward to construct great modern motor highway systems for the cars built by Tennessee, Kentucky, and Arkansas mountaineer labor in Detroit to run much of the surplus white population out of the state.

These mineral resources—aluminum, cinnabar, manganese, zinc, lead—have been developed only since 1914. The bauxite deposits south of Little Rock, the most important and the first to develop, are still for the most part in the hands of a single Pennsylvania corporation. The potential water resources, second in the South only to those under the control of the Tennessee Valley Authority, still await the moment when they can pass from under the shadow of a single great corporation, organized within the state and taking its name, but probably dependent on outside capital. This corporation—the Arkansas Power and Light Company—built the only two large power dams to be constructed before the recent war. The dams have made power available to many a farm home, but they certainly have done nothing towards flood control. Last spring, as I recall, no less than seven floods took place in the valley of the lower Ouachita. The farmers of that area have no recourse except to sue the company whose dams helped to produce the flood—and such suits always fail.

Here, as elsewhere in America, the thesis still holds that since private enterprise has already accomplished much, nothing more can or should be done unless private enterprise chooses to do it. Perhaps this belief dies harder in Arkansas and in the upper South generally than in any other part of the country, except in the longest settled and least industrial parts of New England. Rugged individualism—which has ignored since the nineties not only the growth of the giant corporation, but also the growth of the giant holding companies—dies hard on the Arkansas frontier, now more a frontier than ever since so many pine forests, useful for pulp, have been cut down in the past ten years and left only wastelands, with the dead tops of pine trees cumbering the ground. Over great areas half the slender trunks are still standing in broken disarray, and forest fires have swept greedily through all. There have been only the feeblest attempts as yet made at planned reforestation, and this for the most part by far-seeing private companies. Arkansas is booming, and the boom will always profit the individual. Someone, perhaps even Jeff Davis, thought differently at first and believed he could make his people aware of what was happening. It could, he seems to have naïvely believed, all be stopped by law. But he was not the law any more than Theodore Bilbo is today.

The mountaineer has nearly reached the fifth decade of the present century on the basis of a life which was primarily designed for a pioneer handicraft economy; and he has not much changed, despite outward mechanization, in his inner characteristics. It is doubtful if he could survive a day if he could not continue being dependent upon the town as a source of supplies and on the mail-order catalogue when the town fails. Here in the Ozarks today, if a man marries early he must abide his luck and call that abiding a virtue, as so many before him have done, or else get out and never return, which has been the solution of all the ambitious and the discontented.

The rural schools, though still understaffed, underpaid, and overworked, have made at least the young people aware that other realms exist and beckon; the battery radio set has done even more; the secondhand automobile to be seen before the doors of the most primitive dwellings has probably done the most of all. I have even heard of a secondhand car which ran up and down the Ozark ridges without brakes and inner tubes for its tires. The tire covers were stuffed with straw.

From 1933 on, much W. P. A. money has been spent, and the mountaineers have not openly objected to taking it. The Agricultural Administration and the Soil Conservation Service have done a great deal through subsidies to change crop practices; the Home Demonstration Agents have set to work to improve the diets of their clients; the flourishing C. C. C. camps once studded the backwoods; yellow school busses full of children now ramble past on roads where ten years ago only wagons and horses could pull through unbridged creeks. Since the war boys from the Ozarks and Ouachitas have gone to remote Europe, or the remoter Pacific; women have acquired a new independence through defense jobs. What the result will be on the mountaineer no one can really say. The old handicrafts, which might ten years ago have been profitably revived, show small signs of reviving. The old squirrel-gun still rests upon two forked sticks nailed to the logs above the fireplace; the flyspecked pictures cut out of old magazines, or the even cheaper chromos, still cover the bare boards of the walls. A bucket and a dipper rest beside the wooden curb of the well; the cheap iron bedstead of forty years ago decks the main room. Shelves of canned fruit alternate with groups of bottles of patent medicines. A battery radio stands on a table, and a secondhand car is in the yard. The radio just now is blaring out news bulletins, following on synthetic cowboy yodelling songs. But somewhere, far and far away, at a remote "forks in the road," an old voice is nasally singing:

"Light down, light down, Lord Banyard," she said;
"And stay all night with me;
And the fairest lady in old Scotland
Will look this night for thee."

"I caint light down, I caint light down,
Nor stay all night with thee;
For the fairest lady in old Scotland
Is waiting this night for me."

Alas, he stooped from his leather-pummell saddle
All for to take a sweet kiss;
She had a knife both keen and sharp;
And she pierced him to his heart.

"Is there a physician in this town?
I pray you bring him to me;
For the fairest lady in old Scotland
Is waiting this night for me."

"There is no physician in this town,
Nor no one close around;
And the fairest lady in old Scotland
Will always weep alone."

Away about the break of day,
She called on her true housemaid:
"Here lies a dead man in my hall,
I pray you take him away."

One tuck him by his lily-white hands,
The other by his feet;
They throwed him in a three-story well,
Just thirty furlongs deep.

"Lie there, lie there, you false-hearted man,
Till the flesh rots off your bones;
And the fairest lady in old Scotland
Will always weep alone."

"Hush up, hush up, my pretty little parrot,
Don't you tell no tales on me;
And I'll have your cage made of yellow-beaten gold,
And hung in yonder tree."

"I caint hush up, I caint hush up,
Nor neither do I want that tree;
For you have killed your own true love,
I'm afeared you may kill me."

"If I had my bow all in my hand,
And an arrow on its string,
I'd let it fly at your golden-yellow breast,
All among the leaves so green."

"If you had your bow all in your hand,
And an arrow on its string,
I'd fly so high above the sky,
That I'd nevermore be seen."

Ever since the day when I heard, for the first time but not the last, this song sung in a leaky-roofed, decaying cabin by an old, blind, and illiterate woman, dressed in flour-sack clothes, whose repertory consisted of nearly a hundred such ballads, I too have regarded the Ozarks as a magic land of unreal possibilities and shadows, where forgotten tragedies and comedies were projected on our present day from an incredible past. That the Ozark characteristics do still persist despite the growth of "rural small industries" and the shift in populations caused by the recent war, may be assumed if we will turn our attention, finally, to remote Izard County in the closing days of 1945.

There, in a region of poor roads, of scattered settlements and frequent limestone caves, lived one Rubert Byler, inhabiting a single-roomed cabin with his old parents, his married sister, Alfie Mae, now separated from her husband, and his second wife, Esther Lee, nineteen years old. Rubert could neither read nor write, nor did he know his own age; he supposed himself to be about twenty-eight, though his mother stated later that he was thirty-four years of age. He could figure out, perhaps, the spots on a pair of dice; and he had learned enough to scrawl his own name on a piece of paper. On December 4, 1945, Sheriff Sarber and his deputy—a man named Tosh—rode northward from Melbourne, the county seat, equipped with a warrant for Rubert. He had succeeded in passing a worthless check some days before in a nearby settlement store. The sheriff and the deputy were both armed—the sheriff carrying a rifle, while the deputy had a revolver. In addition, the sheriff had with him a pair of handcuffs. At sight of the oncoming sheriff's car, the Byler family swarmed out of the cabin and achieved the aim of separating the pair of officers. Somehow, Esther Lee succeeded in snatching away the deputy's revolver; by keeping it pressed to his back she rendered him incapable of giving any assistance. Rubert ran back to the house—but emerged soon after, still unarmed, to confront the sheriff. Sarber, thinking that he knew his mountaineers, tried persuasion rather than force and actually had succeeded in fastening the handcuffs to Rubert's wrists, when, in a sudden show of violence, Rubert wrested the gun from him and wildly shot just as the sheriff, realizing his defeat, was lifting up both his hands. The sheriff fell dead—and the Byler clan scattered into the nearby hills, leaving the deputy to carry the news back to Melbourne.

The next day the Governor appointed Mrs. Sarber, the dead man's widow, as sheriff—and a pursuit of the fleeing Bylers began. That night some unknown neighbors fired the Byler cabin. So the parents, as well as Alfie Mae, willingly came in and surrendered. Not so Rubert and Esther Lee—though it was said later that she was pregnant. All that was seen of the fugitives occurred days later when Sarber's discarded rifle, as well as the handcuffs, were discovered in a cave near by. The couple were then reported as having been seen at the home of an uncle some fifteen miles away looking for food. Officers rode over and warned the uncle that he must persuade Rubert and Esther Lee to surrender at once.

Christmas came and went, and though bloodhounds were brought in, they did not track down the Bylers. In a land of dense thickets and deep caves, not to mention midwinter killing frosts and snows, the trail—if any—soon grew cold. Finally, two full months after the killing, Rubert turned up to surrender at Melbourne, along with his wife. Both were incredibly lean and dirty, and Rubert—a little man, quick and furtive in his movements—displayed a black bushy growth of beard. They had talked to the uncle, and were ready to give up after all—after living on wild persimmons and whatever they could raid from infrequent corn patches for two solid months. At the trial that followed Rubert was quickly condemned to death, but the prosecution of the parents, like that of Alfie Mae, was speedily dropped. Esther Lee—estranged from Rubert, since the family universally had striven to fasten the blame on her at the trial—was soon admitted to bail and has never been brought to court. As for Rubert, though the state supreme court upheld the jury's verdict, he is still, as I write, at the state prison farm. He has now learned to read and scribble a little; and it is generally believed that his sentence will be commuted to the usual twenty-one years imprisonment—the sort of sentence, in fact, that most Arkansas governors still may further shorten by the use of their pardoning power.

The moral to this story—if there is one—may be found by whoever will seek it in the inconceivable remoteness and loneliness of the everlasting Ozark hills. Given another environment, who knows where the mother wit that kept Rubert and his wife alive and away from pursuit for two months might not have led? But Rubert was the prisoner of his environment, as are most of the Ozark people today. They are held captive by the great stillness of the dense-wooded hollows, the thunderstorms and tornadoes, the bad roads, the poor schools, the pitifulness of their own living. Behind the great curtain of ridges running roughly parallel—a curtain of intense indigo blue at sunset—stalks both tragedy and comedy; but these wear a guise but little known to other men.

Twenty

THE SHARECROPPER'S WORLD

The traveller from the East today who drives along the main highway from Memphis to Little Rock will see, for the first sixty-five miles of his course, a good cross section of the sharecropper belt of Eastern Arkansas. Here, from the moment after the Mississippi is crossed, to the quite differently appearing edge of the great rice field which abuts on Brinkley, he passes through a land which was once uniform forest and swamp and which today bears traces of its forests still, in the shape of half-burnt stumps standing in the midst of recently plowed acres. Several of the swamps are yet undrained, and the traveller will not go many miles without a sight of tall, plumed cypresses somewhere on his horizon. There are many shallow and stagnant lakes with cypresses standing in the water close to the shore, such as Blackfish and Shell lakes, which were once possibly the bed of the Saint Francis River; there are plenty of low swampy places where the cypresses stand dense amid willows and cane, and the evergreen smilax runs riot over all. There are shallow drainage ditches running north and south, usually with a low irregular ridge of earth thrown up alongside; and there are rows and rows and endless rows of cotton, varying in appearance from the tender green shoots of late April, to the dark green handsome bushy plants with their pink and white flowers of July, and the brown sun-withered and scorched stalks of late September, covered with the white fluff of the opened bolls. From November to April here, nothing is to be seen but the frost-blackened ghosts of the plant, with a few white strands dangling, or the naked furrows of brown earth, already headed up for future planting. It is then that for some people the cotton fields look most tragically significant, for it is then that the furious winter rains relentlessly wash into the rivers a little more of their fecundity.

Here in Eastern Arkansas at least three fourths of the state's more than a million-bale crop is annually picked; and since the gathering of the lint as well as the hoeing of the plant is still commonly done by hand, here is a whole army of tenant-farmer sharecroppers. According to the 1940 census, the state had a population of 1,949,387. Nearly eighty per cent of this—say, one and a half millions—live by agriculture. It is safe to assume that about half, from seven hundred to seven hundred and fifty thousand, are sharecroppers—that is, they own neither land nor houses and manage to subsist on some portion of the money they obtain by cultivating and gathering the cotton crop for the plantation owners. Most of them are in Eastern Arkansas along the Mississippi or the lower reaches of the Arkansas River, which accounts for the fact that the population of these sections is far denser than in the Ozarks, where the sharecropper system is still practically unknown.

The aspect of one of these great cotton plantations—acreages of three, four, five thousand acres are not uncommon, though the greatest of them all, the giant Delta and Pine, of thirty-eight thousand acres, lies across the river from lower Arkansas in Mississippi—is very different from that of one of the great wheat and corn fields of the middle states of Illinois, Kansas, or Iowa. Where the farm unit of the latter consists of a roomy, comfortable, two-storied farmhouse surrounded by enormous barns, the former conceals the fact that a great many more people live on it, by scattering them. Somewhere along the dusty straight road that leads into the plantation off the highway, there may be located a wide-verandahed plantation home, deeply bowered in trees and often set in a commanding position, atop a low rise of ground. But quite frequently there is no such thing; or, if there is, the owner is away, spending his time amid the luxuries of Memphis, which has been truly called the "absentee landlord's paradise." The road into the plantation seems to lead past scattered groups of small and flimsily built sheds and houses, standing as somber brown, red, green, or poorly whitewashed spots amid the endless furrows. Where the plantation road turns off from the highway, stand the combined plantation store and local filling station, which is often flimsily built and is usually plastered with advertisements of chill-remedy and snuff; but the store usually has a porch in front, where in winter the tenants often loaf about in their overalls, blue jumpers, and high rubber boots. Near by may be seen one or two low, one-story, well-screened, newly-painted, not unattractive frame cottages, usually with trees close by and small flower gardens: these are the homes of the "riding bosses," the overseers. Beyond, facing each other, at uniform distances, in various stages of disrepair, are the scattered cabins of the sharecroppers themselves.

The type varies little. Unplaned lumber and the cheapest grade of roll roofing are invariably used. The only concession to the climate is that the tenant house is set usually several inches off the ground to protect its floor from the torrential rains and the not infrequent floods. Often there is not even a fence in front, and the cotton rows, as they say in the South, "run up to the front and to the back doors." There is never a tree in sight, nor a flower. The interior—one room filled with beds for the entire family to sleep in, and another to eat in, with oil-cloth-covered table and iron, wood-burning cookstove—is papered, if at all, with newsprint or with pictures cut out of cheap magazines. There is, generally, a rough porch in front—sometimes used to store a little extra cotton at the close of some good season, or employed in the summer to sleep on. There is a chopping block and a small stack of wood outside to feed the stove. At the back, usually more decrepit than the rest and oftentimes with nothing in front of it but a brown piece of sacking to ensure some show of decency, stands the open privy. Farther out, a small shed is used to store cotton in during the picking season. Such is the sharecropper's domain, in which he and his family amass an average annual income fairly estimated as being little more per family than two hundred dollars a year. Or so it was stated to be by two independent investigators during the tragic years of the thirties. If it is more now we may thank the Federal government, the present war boom, and God.

Between eight and nine million people, it is estimated, in the entire South, live by sharecropping. Of these, as I have already said, perhaps seven hundred thousand are in Arkansas. No one knows the exact number, and there is no way of telling; for many plantation owners have long since acquired the habit of hiring their hands at the rates paid for day labor, from sixty cents to a dollar and fifty cents a day before the war; and they instantly let them go back on the relief rolls when there is no further need for them. The system, such as it is, probably employs nowadays more white unskilled labor than Negro—the whites outnumbering the Negroes in the rough ratio of 5 to 3, though in some Arkansas counties bordering directly on the Mississippi, the proportion is undoubtedly much higher in favor of the Negroes; and these counties have therefore the highest Negro population in the state. It has been estimated that in the years 1920–1930, the white sharecropper population of the South increased by at least a million persons. And Arkansas, we may be sure, had its share.

The observer from outside of the South, having seen these things or heard something about them, often goes home and concludes in great bewilderment that the South is a hopeless and benighted region, "where every prospect pleases and only man is vile." That a land of such amazing fertility should endure such examples of rural indigence and ignorance seems to him perfectly horrible. What he does not realize is the fact that there is no agreement among the Southerners themselves as to what can be done about the situation. The average plantation owner has directly inherited the sharecropper system from the days of his grandfather after the Civil War. His business is simply to make it work as efficiently as possible. This in itself, be it noted, gives him considerable leeway to display either his meanness or his generosity. The average tenant, unable to do anything else than be a sharecropper, accepts his lot as tenant with resentment or resignation. And if he shows too much of the former, he is quite likely to be run off the plantation.

As a crop, the cotton plant requires a great number of hands to cultivate it, and especially to pick it. Plowing by tractors and disk plows in the last twenty years has, in part, taken the place of the old hand plow drawn by mules, though, as is fitting in this region of conservatism, the old mule-drawn plows probably still have at least equality, if not the upper hand. But chopping-out of weeds has to be done at month intervals from planting time, three times at least, with hand hoes till the plant is large enough to take care of itself. And although cotton-picking machines are imminent, the picking is still done mostly by hand under the dry September sun by stooped figures trailing long bags at their shoulders. It is back-breaking work. There is in it little of the drama and excitement of the northern wheat belt when the travelling threshing-rig is brought to the edge of a great field and the wagons, laden deep with the harvested shocks, are driven up, to be tumbled out with forks to the conveyer belt and there transformed into an endless stream of golden grain falling into the wagons, while another stream of chaff is shot out into the air. The pickers of cotton, like the choppers in summer, move in a spiritless way; and the high-sided cotton wagons, hitched to two mules, wait for the sacks stolidly. At the edge of the "turn-row," where the bags are loaded on, a "checker," usually white, stands with scales to write in a notebook the weight of the bags as they are brought up.

The record "pick" of cotton by an eighteen-year-old youth from southern Missouri, in a field that averaged over a bale to the acre at Blytheville, Arkansas, against 136 contestants from eleven states, in the fall of 1940, amounted to 129 pounds picked in two hours, with all the plants, as they stood, picked clean. But the yield of the runner-up, 117 pounds in the same time, was thought by the judges to have been somewhat more cleanly gathered, with less leaves and other trash in the bags. The cotton was still wet from the result of a rain the night before; this made clean picking of the rows harder to achieve. In other words, cotton-picking remains an art rather than a science. It depends on deftness of fingers, combined with ability to endure a bent-over back for long periods of time. The cotton plant at full maturity is rarely more than three to four feet high; and the blooms and resulting bolls are likely to stand thickest in the lower branches. Two hundred pounds is perhaps a full day's pick for most people; and when one considers that payment for pickers has varied from thirty-three cents hundred pounds to sixty-five and seventy cents for a full day's gathering—one rarely hears of two dollars being paid—one realizes that the thousand dollars won by this eighteen-year-old, who gathered in his big hands 129 pounds in two hours was a bigger fortune than most sharecroppers see in a lifetime. Seven hundred pounds stands as the record day's pick per man on the enormous Delta and Pine plantation.

The sharecropper has, indeed, and frequently, to wrestle with a system which varies so much from plantation to plantation that it is almost never twice alike. In its simple essentials the problem is always the same. The sharecropper is given the rude shelter of a house, a tract of about twenty acres of land, usually tools to work it, and his food during the year; but at the year's end, one half the crop and seed he makes goes back to the landlord for rent; and out of the other half is deducted his expenses for provisions and for everything over and above his housing. This system has innumerable variations. Obviously at bottom it depends on the landlord's sense of fairness as to how the expense account is finally computed; he is an educated man and the sharecropper usually is not. Not all landlords are fair. Then the system varies infinitely from plantation to plantation. Many plantations keep "commissary stores" and demand that the tenant do all his trading with them; others insist on the tenant's buying everything in the open market, and "furnish" only cash, Others, in turn, charge rent for everything: tools, mules, everything except the pitiable shacks; and grant only meager sums to the tenant to buy seed, while they charge him for house repairs, in addition to his other expenses. In fact, the landlords may be classified in two classes: those who try to keep their tenants on the land, and those who do not. There are even some, I have been told, who, spring after spring, raid the always large labor reserve by getting names cut off the relief rolls, in connivance with corrupt relief officers in nearby towns, and who periodically throw these same people back on local relief in the fall.

The system is, at best, a bad system: first, because it creates a permanent class of parasites—the sharecropper who has as much as three hundred dollars to show for his year's labor is indeed a rare specimen and is likely to graduate into the owner class some day—and also because it has increasingly attracted white as opposed to colored labor. The first great migration of colored labor out of the South took place before 1900, when the great depression, accompanied by labor strikes of the mid-nineties, gave way to a new boom in Northern industry that ran from the threshold of the twentieth century up to the panic of 1907. This was the period of "mergers," of giant trusts, and of corporate prosperity. During that time, the Southern Negroes were for the first time urged to go North and to take part in industrial operations. For a time, sharecropper labor was so scarce in Arkansas that Italian and even Mexican imported labor was tried out on many great plantations.

From 1912 on, America boomed again, and wholesale prices of all commodities reached in 1920 a peak comparable only to those of 1814 and 1864. There followed the period of "Coolidge Prosperity" and of the Bull Market Boom of 1927, 1928, and 1929. During this period, particularly after 1918, Negro labor again migrated in droves from the South; and at Harlem as well as in Chicago and in the Oklahoma oil fields, there appeared instances of race friction, sometimes filling the newspaper headlines. In many regions of the South, the poor whites began swarming out of the hills. In Arkansas they had no cotton-mill towns to go to; so they often became sharecroppers. Since to this day the Negro population of Arkansas is only twenty-six per cent of the total, and since of the total of white and Negro population nearly eighty per cent are rural, it follows that probably there are far more white tenants than Negro tenants now in the state. And the white tenant, as any plantation owner will tell you, is less adjusted to the periods of forced labor followed by spells of idleness which the cotton crop entails; he is usually the trouble-maker under the system.

There is much reason to think that the lives of the lowland sharecroppers are far more subject to urban influences than those of the independent land-owning mountaineers. Except for his clothes, his sugar, and his coffee, the mountaineer is far more self-sustaining. Accordingly, it is likely that he visits the town less frequently and buys less out of its shops. As the sharecropper is altogether dependent for his subsistence out of his cotton, he takes part in more money transactions. The leading ambition of the usual sharecropper seems to be to own a second-hand car and to make as many trips away from the plantation and towards the town as possible. Accordingly the towns of the cotton belt: Blytheville, Jonesboro, Marked Tree, Osceola, McCrory, Wynne, Forrest City, Marianna, Brinkley, are likely to be even more crowded on Saturdays than towns of the same size in the mountains; and the crowds on the streets are invariably both white and colored, and a little less friendly in their aspect than the crowds one sees in mountain towns. They drift into mere casual aggregations, and seem almost entirely unaware of the presence of others.

The reason for this is that the sharecropper has no particular function, apart from his labor, in the society that employs him. Mediaeval serfs, though they worked as hard, had plenty of opportunities to display their loyalty to their lords, and took part in a great many local festivals. In most cases the plantation owner—it may be only a company—is someone whom the sharecropper does not even see. His only contact is with the overseer. As he is frequently a transient, moving after the harvest from plantation to plantation, opportunities are few to get closely acquainted with his fellows. Local revivals, so frequent in the mountains, are less common in the lowlands—as plantation churches are rare, these revivals are held in the market towns. The rural schools—such as they are—are being continually filled with transient strangers rather than with neighbors. Accordingly, the sharecropper, unless he has the give-and-take solidarity which is a remarkable feature of the Negro mentality, is likely to become a glum and suspicious individual. Except for his weekly trips to the cotton towns, he learns to do without contacts with the outside world.

During the period between July and September, between the last chopping of the rows and picking, the life of the cropper is one of great monotony. There is little for him to do except to visit his neighbor tenant, attend some revival, go fishing in the cypress swamps. Even the schools are closed. Some travelling show with its assortment of freaks, its gaudily lit ferris wheel, its semi-nude women, its booths where worthless rubbish can be won by successful throwing or shooting, may visit somewhere in the neighborhood—they are usually found touring the roads in the early fall when crop money is more plentiful. But apart from that, the sharecropper has almost literally nothing in the way of employment of his time except to sit on his porch and watch that southern bird, the buzzard, endlessly circling over his furrows through the hot, leaden-looking sky.

Inevitably, as has already happened in the wheat belt and is happening in the corn belt, tractor plows, "steel mules," are taking the place of plowing with mules and by hand. Accordingly, the unit of land that can be controlled by a single pair of hands is growing progressively bigger. Many planters now realize this fact, and they prefer, rather than feed a large number of tenants, to take from the cities hands to chop and pick, paying them at rates current for casual labor a day. After all, this way is cheaper. One cannot blame the planters for displaying human selfishness. But the normal sharecropper who expects to see himself, wife, and family, fed and housed by the system, has increasingly been driven into a corner, and has begun to get the worst of it.

In 1933, at the advent of the Roosevelt administration, matters finally came to a crisis in respect to the sharecropper situation. For some years before—at least since 1930—cotton had been selling around six or seven cents a pound, and not a cent of profit had been possible to the landowner. Plantations began to go under mortgages, or to be sold for taxes; and ruin stared the system in the face.

Finally, in 1933, the New Deal gave out its solution—the celebrated "plow-under" of every third row planted in cotton. When the solution was given out, the planting of the annual crop had already begun; so it was too late for the landowners to do anything. The army of tenants were carried, somehow, over yet another winter; but when the spring of 1934 came, the Agricultural Administration slightly increased its requirements, demanding a forty percent reduction in acreage. There were no reasons why the landlords should keep their tenants any longer, and great numbers were promptly dispossessed. In the momentarily tragic state of American unemployment, there was literally nowhere for any of them to go.

The value of the Southern cotton crop in 1919—a boom year—had been estimated at $3,800,000,000, representing one fourth of the total farm income of the entire United States; and it was grown on about one third of the total farm area. This enormous harvest supported, in the depression year of 1933, in addition to the plantation owners, a tenant population amounting to eight and a half million people. This population was divided into perhaps some five and a half million whites and three million colored people. During the previous decade, the colored population had notably diminished, many going North. In Arkansas a great deal of the most fertile cotton-growing land in the region between the Mississippi and the White River had only recently come under cultivation. It had stood under dense woods and swamps up to around 1913–1915, and in the next decade had gradually been cut over, drained and brought under cultivation. This land was owned almost universally by companies, in some cases by lumber companies, who had simply taken their former logging crews and settled them upon it; or in other cases it was owned by the local banks; and in almost all cases it was controlled by absentee owners who rarely saw their own plantations from year to year. Here, in a population but recently established and about to be dispossessed, was a favorable field for labor organization and agitation.

On July 11, 1934, nineteen sharecroppers on a plantation near Tyronza in Poinsett County, in a region but recently cut over and abounding still in enormous swamps, organized themselves into the Southern Tenant Farmer's Union, and pledged themselves to fight the landlords who had recently dispossessed them, to the utmost of their power. Throughout that summer all through Eastern Arkansas numerous mass meetings were held among the recently dispossessed, still camping at the side of the road. The movement began to spread among the still settled sharecroppers, who began taking pledges to support the Union. At first all these meetings were laughed at by the townspeople, and by the plantation-owner class and their henchmen. But soon the gatherings became more frequent and attracted increasing crowds. They were opened by prayer and accompanied by singing; they were conducted in an atmosphere of religious fervor. A new struggle for humanity and justice was now under way, and the plantation owners were obliged to pay some attention to it. Soon meetings began to be broken up, and local sheriffs began to make arrests among the agitators. The officials of the newly created Union were obliged to move their headquarters to Memphis to be out of the way of the law as interpreted by the Arkansas lawyers in the cotton towns.

At this juncture an able investigator was sent out by the Department of Agriculture in Washington to report on the troubled situation in Arkansas. Her report was filed, but the Department refused to publish it; which led many to believe that the facts it contained were particularly and uncomfortably scandalous. The sharecroppers, on their part, had already issued their own report, made by William R. Amberson, a distinguished physician of Memphis, who estimated the average income of the tenant farmer in Arkansas as standing at around two hundred and twelve dollars a year; a figure later confirmed by yet another observer. Meanwhile the Union went on growing. From the first, it had taken in white and colored members on a basis of complete social equality; and this was particularly galling to the planters and to their "riding bosses." Race riots had once occurred in this same area during the period following the war of 1917–1918; but here was a group absolutely ignoring the rules of race segregation. More and more frequently, agitators for the Union were now arrested, fined, and jailed under old laws which were deliberately revived to suppress the movement.

In the winter of 1934–1935 an able and respected lawyer, C. T. Carpenter, of Marked Tree, whose father had long ago surrendered under Lee at Appomattox, decided to fight cases for the Union without asking for a fee—the Union dues of three dollars a year, though more and more frequently paid by its members, scarcely provided enough to keep its own officers in funds. A meeting at Mr. Carpenter's home town on January 26, 1935, was promptly broken up by county officials amid scenes of great violence. Norman Thomas, contacted through Dr. Amberson, began to take a strong interest in the sharecropper situation and promised to visit Arkansas personally that spring and observe the situation for himself. Notices of meetings held and broken up—of shootings, beatings, threats—began to appear in the metropolitan and even in the Arkansas newspapers. The meetings were now always opened with prayers and the singing of hymns. A religious crusade was on.

In May of that year, at the Southern Baptist Convention held in Memphis, an able speaker drew attention to the fact that many white American families, law-abiding and hard working, were being dispossessed from their homes, without any recourse at law. The papers of America began to evince an even stronger interest in the sharecropper situation. Doctor Amberson invited an eminent English novelist, visiting America, to attend some meetings, now held always under the threat of being broken up by local sheriffs who had been warned in advance by the riding bosses. Norman Thomas visited Arkansas, spoke ably at Little Rock, and departed to spread the news of the tragic situation. In the fall of 1935, an armed mob gathered and surrounded Mr. Carpenter's home; the lawyer went on to his porch unarmed and persuaded them to depart, but not before a shot had crashed through the skylight above his door. In the meantime Senator Bankhead, of Alabama, had introduced a bill into Congress providing for a fund to buy lands and settle the dispossessed on them—a measure that gladdened the hearts of those who had been saying for years that what the South needed was more small farms and more independent landowning farmers.

By January, 1936, at its annual convention, the Southern Tenant Farmer's Union was able to report having no less than 23,000 members. Not all of these, probably, were able to keep paying their dues of three dollars annually, since the budget for the organization three years later reveals only an operating fund of $11,810. A further Congressional investigation was held early in 1936; and Mr. W. L. Blackstone, an extremely intelligent white tenant farmer from the Saint Francis River region, caused a sensation before the committee by pointing out mildly that, so far as Arkansas was concerned, neither the Declaration of Independence nor the Bill of Rights existed any longer. Gifts now began to flow into the coffers of the Union, and proponents of all manner of solutions from coöperative farming to collective farming had their say.

In 1937, following a conference called by the Governor of Arkansas at Hot Springs, a basic form of contract between the planters and the tenants was publicly recommended. Sit-down strikes swept the

United States that year; they were threatened even in the Arkansas cotton fields. Meanwhile, the voiding of the original A.A.A. law by the United States Supreme Court had already thrown the cotton kingdom back into chaos and confusion. President Roosevelt, re-elected for his second term, began his historic fight to reconstruct the Supreme Court that summer. The situation was tense with all the possibilities of mob violence. Senator Joseph T. Robinson, of Arkansas—no particular friend of the sharecropper but deeply loved by the people for his independence and ability—died in Washington, attempting to the last to carry out Roosevelt's plan to break the Supreme Court; and his funeral was a great event at Little Rock and was attended by crowds of people who felt him as having been one of themselves from first to last.

In 1938 at its annual convention, which I attended, at Little Rock, the Southern Tenant Farmers voted finally to affiliate with the C.I.O. This move was frankly opposed by the great body of the delegates assembled in a hall decorated with such mottoes as "God Gave the Land to the People, and the Landlords Took It Away." It meant that they would all have to pay still further dues—which most of them were quite unable to do. But it was demanded by the officers, who were determined to show their power. The Union had steadily grown to over forty thousand members and had spread to Missouri, to Texas, to Mississippi. Many of the white members, disliking the C.I.O. above all things, began dropping out around this time, and the Union became more and more dependent on Negro support. In this year the old race issue was again revived; the landlord of the hall hired for the annual convention refused to let it hold its meetings there after the first day, for no better reason than that whites and blacks sat on the same benches.

In 1939 the officers themselves, at the annual meeting in Memphis, conceded that the C.I.O. affiliation had been a mistake and decided to withdraw from it. Meantime their legal difficulties went on. Two old Negro men and a woman, Dan, Henry, and Beatrice Johnson, all connected with the Union, had boldly distributed handbills calling for a strike of cotton pickers in Mississippi County. For this Beatrice Johnson had been sentenced to four years, and the two men (both over seventy) had been sentenced to two years in the penitentiary for "night riding," under a statute originally intended to apply to the post-Civil War Ku Klux Klan. The case was appealed to the state supreme court, which reduced the sentence to two years in the case of Beatrice, and a year apiece in the case of the two men. So it still stood, to be mentioned in the Southern Tenant Farmer's presidential report for 1940. And as recently as January, 1940, sharecropper indignation meetings were still being held to the tune of over a thousand attendance, along the highway east of Memphis. As late as the fall of that year there was much talk of thousands of tenants being evicted in southern Missouri. Since 1941, however, the South has been faced with a labor shortage; and many of its cotton bolls, for the last five years at least, have not even been picked.

There is still no immediate remedy in prospect for the sharecropper situation. Since 1939, "sharecropper week" has been annually celebrated up north. Though the travelling orgnizers for the tenant farmers finally got a hundred dollars a month for their services (out of this they have to take the expenses of running their cars), the sharecropper movement languished as America began to be drawn into the orbit of the Second World War. The best defender of the cropper system that I know, William Alexander Percy, has said, "Sharecropping is one of the best systems ever devised to give security and a chance for profit to the simple and unskilled," but he immediately qualified that statement by adding, "It has but one drawback—it must be administered by human beings to whom it offers an unusual opportunity to rob without detection or punishment." It has also, as it has worked out in Arkansas, planted people, willy-nilly, at the bidding of vast and mostly absentee companies on acres but recently cut over, started them out as sharecroppers, and then—for no reason whatever—thrown them totally out of employment in a few years. It has tended to make the landlords depend more and more, not on the settled tenant farmer, but on transient day labor. It has driven off the land a considerable section of the population, white and colored, a group by nature least qualified, of all American farm labor, to do anything material for themselves elsewhere. It has also—though this, thank God, is ending—attempted through the connivance of local officers, to suppress free speech and free assembly and to substitute, for the freedoms of man, rule by mob violence.

This is a sufficiently grave indictment. But there is, so far as the Southern States are concerned, always something tragic in the historic facts that have accompanied the growth and development of the great cotton-raising area. After the Connecticut Yankee, Eli Whitney, had given to man a perfect means of separating the lint from the seed in the shape of the cotton gin, cotton became the inevitable crop for the South, so long as Negro slavery could persist. With the fantastically high prices for the staple prevailing in England for twenty years after the Napoleonic Wars, the cotton-growing area was bound to expand; and after 1820 expand it did, the center of it moving westward from the seaboard plain to Alabama, Mississippi, Arkansas, and finally Texas. It has now been freely predicted that even this area will be abandoned in the next twenty years in favor of Texas, Arizona, and Southern California. When slavery could no longer extend its territory and the growth of the kingdom was checked at the source, the South went to war. War again brought high prices, and new fortunes were made, for a time; but the social problem implicit in keeping an enormous army of human dependents in the cotton fields, where most of them are, in fact, unable to find work for more than one hundred and twenty-five to one hundred and fifty days in the year, was utterly evaded. The Spanish-American War of 1898 and the World War of 1914–1918 brought on new cotton booms of greater or less duration, but the essential root difficulty has never been frankly attacked. Now, after the curve of another depression, and amid the boom following another war, there has been much agitation and but little light. The sharecropping economy persists, working always according to the fallible human instincts of those who inherit and wield it, fairly well or badly. Like the old *encomienda* system, devised and practiced by the Spaniards long ago in their overseas possessions, and like the system that prevailed in Poland and Eastern Europe up to 1920–1930, there seems to be no reasonable, nor even practicable alternative, to its existence.

But it would be a mistake to assume that the sharecropper region has not its moments when joy and laughter seem close at hand. Along in September and October, when the big wagons loaded with spoil roll up to the corrugated iron gins, shedding flakes of white cotton to lie at the roadside as they roll along, there is an air of bustle and gaiety on the neighboring highway. The drivers of waiting wagons move back and forth to gossip with each other amid jokes and banter. Even the back-bowed figures dragging their long sacks and picking ceaselessly seem to realize that the crop is at last moving off to the market, and straighten up momentarily in the furrows. There is money for the sharecropper in prospect in those wagons—money to spend foolishly, no doubt, on secondhand cars, trips to the city, new shining veneered furniture and personal luxuries which will make life more pleasant in the stark, ugly cabins. The long gamble with time and the climate has at last won out. Floods, drouth, boll-weevil are all beaten once again. From now on to Christmas, life is no longer a mere matter of fighting weeds and of waiting. The new crop is going off to the gins. Hallelujah!

But the sharecropper belt is even more characteristically itself on some mid-July night, after a day of humid heat, as the chopping of the weeds begins at last to slacken. The monotonous flatness of the land, unstirred by any breeze, seems to breathe out the dense, stored-up heat of the day. One can almost smell the cotton growing. Faint heat-lightening flickers far south above the big cypress swamp, and the straight dirt road, with its sudden sharp turns at right angles around the corners of a featureless field, runs on and on towards oblivion. Here at an intersection there are suddenly seen, silhouetted in the headlights of the car, a gigantic water-oak, and a half-dozen unpainted and rickety cabins. (The average sharecropper shack is worth probably less than a hundred dollars and is not often kept in good repair.) All are unlighted. Near the oak stands a rickety, white-washed, gabled wooden church, lit faintly from within by flickering oil lamps. There drifts out to the road the loud sound of clapping hands, of tapping feet, punctuating the bellowed chorus of a spiritual, followed by dramatic yells and screams:

My Lord, He calls me;
He calls me by the thunder.
The trumpet sounds within my soul,
I ain't got long to stay here.

"Amen, Lord Jesus!" the voices are shouting an answer in fierce antiphonal response. The surface of the intensely black cypress swamp is shrilling with treetoads and frogs in amazing, iterated, persistent chorus. This is still jungleland, despite flame throwers to destroy weeds, tractors, disk cultivators, airplanes to dust the fields in the fight against the boll weevil. Even the threat of the mechanical cotton-picker now on the horizon has not yet changed it. It is haunted, and there is voodoo at its heart. The big thunder-cloud is drifting closer.

It is time to turn the car around and seek again, down some straight-paved and more familiar highway, the comfort of the city. There, to the tune of a jazz band playing in "hot rhythm," or to the tinkle of cool glasses at the Country Club, the sharecropper and his problems may at last be forgotten by most people.

Twenty-one

RICE ENRICHES THE PRAIRIE

In the second week of October, 1940, two travellers proceeding by automobile from Memphis to Little Rock, halted within a few miles of Brinkley—halfway on that route—to observe what was to them an unusual sight. Neither of these travellers, though native to Arkansas and resident for many years in the state, had ever actually seen this sight before. At the edge of one of the great rice fields that begin at about this point, a mechanical threshing-rig was standing, similar in all respects to the rigs used in the Middle West to thresh the wheat harvest. Two white laborers, standing on top of a mule-driven wagon, were feeding into it alternate forkfuls of the harvested rice stalks. A stream of brownish-yellow grain was running out steadily into the bed of another unhitched wagon. Another stream of chaff and straw was steadily blown out into the air. More wagons, waiting to be unloaded, were standing near by; and their drivers, like everyone else in that field, were white. The rice farmer himself, a big-boned, sun-tanned figure of a man in checkered shirt, khaki trousers, with rough straw hat perched well back on his freckled forehead, was sitting on a piebald pony, surveying the scene. To him the two travellers addressed themselves. What they had to ask—as well as his answers—was at last made audible above the steady roar of the thresher.

He had some eighty acres here, all planted in rice of the Early Prolific variety. There were other varieties, especially the Blue Rose, that were popular, but these took longer to grow. This particular field had been planted on the first of May. After about three weeks, water had been put on it, and had been allowed to stand, six inches deep, for seventy-five days. Along in August, the field had been left to dry out, and it had been reaped—by a McCormick harvester, exactly like wheat—only three weeks before the travellers' causal visit. Now the threshing was being done, employing the farmer's own rig—this last was mentioned with a touch of honest pride—and the drooping yellow stalks were producing no less than one hundred bushels to the acre. This compared well with the sixty bushels produced per acre the year before. The farmer was getting sixty-five cents per bushel for his yield. His eighty acres of planting would bring in, accordingly, over five thousand dollars.

The story of the Arkansas rice field, occupying the region comprised, in whole or in part, by Lonoke, Prairie, Arkansas, Monroe counties—and recently spreading north beyond Woodruff County as well as south to the Louisiana border—is the outstanding "success story" of Arkansas agriculture. Most of the Arkansawyers, unless they happen to live within the borders of the field itself, or at the rice-milling towns of Carlisle, Hazen, De Witt, or Stuttgart, seem almost unaware of its existence, except in so far as it provides them every fall with a "sportsman's paradise," where they may find ample opportunity for their favorite sport of wild-duck shooting. The reason, or rather, reasons, for this are two: the Arkansas rice field came late into the picture of state agricultural development; and when it did come, it grew rapidly because of the native energy and scientific farming knowledge possessed by a people who had been grain farmers in Illinois and Iowa before they came to Arkansas—or in other words, it was cultivated largely by "foreigners" and Republicans. For these reasons, the older sections of the state have looked askance at it up to now; and they still know, unfortunately, too little of its life and its ways.

They have no good reason to ignore it. The Grand Prairie, roughly ninety miles north and south and forty miles wide, first observed by Nuttall in 1819 and recognized by generations of travellers since as affording a forest-free route of access from Arkansas Post at its southern tip to the interior of the state, broke the backs and the hearts of its settlers for seventy-five years before one man discovered that rice would grow there; but it now produces the astonishing harvest of a crop which, in 1940, netted 9,741,000 bushels of rice, valued at $6,466,000, and which rose, by 1945, to 14,612,000 bushels, valued at $26,155,000. And all this has happened since 1904, to be exact—in the short space of forty-two years.

Such a result contrasts vividly enough with the conditions prevailing in the past. Arkansas County, in the very heart of the rice district, is nearly the largest county in the state; Prairie County, north of it, is almost equally large. But all this region, though easy of access, attracted but few settlers of any sort until the present century. Let us take, for an example, the case of the Hazen family, after whom the rice-milling town of Hazen now takes it name. Its founder, William Cogswell Hazen, born at Charlottesville, Virginia, in 1806, migrated to Arkansas in the late thirties after spending his young manhood in Tennessee, where he had married and had fathered two sons in 1830 and 1831. He was a practicing physician, a devout Methodist and, in Tennessee, a landowner of substance; in Arkansas he purchased many acres of the Grand Prairie land at the prevailing rate of a dollar and a quarter an acre; and seems to have managed somehow to live on it up to the Civil War. It was then, because of the wild grass that grew upon it, fairly good breeding-ground for cattle. Otherwise nothing was raised.

But when Federal armies swarmed into Eastern Arkansas to run the cattle off and to devour them, Dr. Hazen, with his neighbors, his Negro slaves, and dependents, refugeed into Texas, leaving his two sons behind, both serving the Confederacy. One of them managed to obtain leave from the army for a time and come to Texas, too, shortly after this migration, to see his own mother die—for Dr. Hazen's wife did not long survive the ordeals of the Texas journey undertaken in the summer heat of 1863. In 1865, with the Confederacy utterly gone, Dr. Hazen spent his last thousand dollars—which had been carefully hoarded up in gold—to bring himself and his Negroes back into Arkansas. But all efforts to make his land again productive of anything but an almost worthless hay crop failed; and so Dr. Hazen attempted to begin life anew as a storekeeper at Des Arc. This resulted in bankruptcy; and, since he was now past sixty, the pioneer founder of the Hazens divided his land between his two sons and retired. His sons, finding the land equally unproductive, moved into what is now the town of Hazen, putting up the first house there and slowly selling off all of their lands at low prices. The father died there in 1872; and the elder son, Alexander Richard Hazen, became the first public school teacher in Prairie County and the first rural-route mail carrier out of the town of Hazen, when rural free delivery was established in

1901. It is said that on his first trips as mail carrier he was able to hold all the mail, letters and papers, in one hand. Nevertheless, despite the obvious handicap of grinding poverty throughout his middle manhood, Alexander Richard Hazen managed to hold his own, becoming the most prominent Methodist in the slowly growing small town, marrying the daughter of a neighboring farmer, and leaving behind good and useful children and grandchildren to honor his breed and name.

All this contrasts vividly enough with the German-American wheat farmers from the Danville district of Illinois and the Davenport district of Iowa, who came down to Arkansas in droves between 1905 and 1910 to fill up the empty spaces of Prairie and Arkansas counties and to found the existing towns of Stuttgart and Ulm. During those years and on up to 1920, there took place the largest immigration into Arkansas that had ever been seen since the first great swarmings of 1820–1830 and of 1846–1850; and these newcomers, hundreds of families strong, were all men of substance long before they came. They had been induced to migrate—with money enough in their pockets to buy the rigs and pumping equipment necessary—through clever publicity pamphlets broadcast in Illinois and Iowa by the Rock Island Railroad, which had just recently invaded the great Arkansas prairie region. The coming of the Rock Island and the great migration of the midwestern farmers happened to coincide with a resounding agricultural success, the first cultivation of rice in the state, which came about through the knowledge and persistence of one man.

William H. Fuller, of Carlisle, Lonoke County, had been born, so far as I can ascertain, in Ohio in 1843.* He had come to Arkansas as a young man to engage in what, no doubt, was sufficiently unproductive farming. With this he continued till in 1896 he went for a hunting trip down to Crowley in South Louisiana, in the famed Evangeline country. There he saw rice farming successfully practiced and determined to attempt it in Arkansas for himself. Accordingly, without adequate or reliable pumping equipment, he planted three acres in rice in the spring of 1897. Halfway through the summer his small, inadequate pump broke down, and the crop was practically a total failure. Nevertheless, Fuller had seen enough to convince him that rice cultivation in Arkansas was not altogether impossible.

*A recent article, published in the *Arkansas Historical Quarterly,* Summer, 1946, states that Fuller came from Nebraska.

The next year he boldly moved off to Louisiana, where he remained till 1903—learning by working under the direction of others the correct methods to apply in the matter of rice cultivation. In 1903 he returned to his prairie land near Carlisle. He had now talked and had written to various neighbors about his plans, and it is said that they pooled their resources and succeeded in raising a thousand dollars to enable him to put in a hundred-and-fifty-foot artesian well and to buy a good pump for his field. The thousand dollars invested was offered to Fuller as a bonus, provided he could make good on his claim of being able to produce thirty-five bushels of rice per acre. In the spring of 1904, he planted seventy acres. The yield of 5,225 bushels—nearly seventy-five bushels per acre—amazed everyone. It established Fuller as a true prophet: in a single year, thanks to his tenacity and persistence, rice was seen as the answer to an agricultural problem which had not yet been solved.

It is good to know that this last and greatest of Arkansas's agricultural pioneers did not die until 1922, when, two years before, the rice culture he had started had netted to Arkansas the amazing output of 8,575,000 bushels of grain from 175,000 acres. From that peak—attained mainly because, after the war of 1917–1918, rice, for a time, sold at three dollars a bushel—the production had already fallen off over a million bushels before Fuller died. Yet by 1940 the harvest had again risen to 9,741,000 bushels, selling at prices ranging from sixty-five cents to over a dollar. The yield of 1945 has already been mentioned; in the midsummer of 1946, rice was fetching a dollar and seventy-five cents a bushel.

In the preceding paragraph, the first post-war peak production year of 1920 was mentioned. Up to that time the rice farmer, hauling off his crop to the milling company's plant—established near his own fields from the start—had paid a toll, or bonus, to get his grain milled. Now the growers were faced with a big crop and a falling market. Their solution was typical, but utterly non-Arkansan. They decided to form themselves into a coöperative marketing association, to fight the millers on their own ground and to pay no more tolls. And they succeeded, thanks to backing from the American Farm Bureau, to the support of local banks, and, finally, to a million-dollar loan—it is said, from the War Finance Corporation. Since then, rice farming has been closely cooperative throughout.

Truly, the story of rice farming in Arkansas has been a series of lucky miracles, as compared with the alternate booms and depressions—the lack of any prevailing system—common in the adjacent cotton fields. And still more of a miracle is the story of how closely fitted are the soil and climate to the development of the plant.

The land comprising the Arkansas rice fields is, for the most part, a stiff blue clay, well adapted to holding water. As the Arkansawyers say, it is "hard pan"—that is to say, it does not break easily under the ordinary plow, and is cultivated altogether by multiple disk cultivators. Before cultivation takes place, it has to be diked up, with four to six-inch dikes wandering mazily across it; this job alone is done with ordinary plows; but so tenacious is the soil that the dikes do not have to be renewed except about once every three years. Under the land—in reality an immense flat delta-plain formed long ago between the Arkansas and White rivers—lies the water used on the fields. This is usually found at a depth ranging from seventy-five to eighty feet; but the artesian wells employed generally go down to one hundred and twenty feet, and even lower. The well is drilled at the top of the field, for on this endless plain the land tilts and varies slightly. An electrically operated pump, established in a small wooden shed, jets the water out in a steady stream through an iron pipe jutting up into the air, and it falls into a small earth-reservoir. From this it is conducted through wooden sluice-gates dug in the dikes all over the field. At the end of the flooding period, always estimated as being about seventy-five days long, the field is drained off through wooden gates at the lower edge. Thus the ditches bordering on the highways in the rice-field district have gradually become small, shallow swamps, full of cattails and other aquatic plants, supported by the overflow from the adjoining fields, and much frequented by frogs and by the prevailing redwinged blackbirds of the region.

Almost all of the operations connected with rice growing are carried out by a population overwhelmingly midwestern and white. In 1925, according to an agricultural census, the population of Arkansas County, always the foremost of the rice-producing counties, showed a little over twenty-five percent colored. In Jefferson County to the west, formed out of the rich delta mud of the lower Arkansas, the population in the same year was eighty-two percent Negro; in Phillips County to the east, formed out of the delta mud of the Mississippi, the population was Negro by seventy-six percent. The rice field is also free from the unstable economy of sharecropping. The great plain, empty of anything except small clumps of trees, displays nothing akin to the rows of badly painted, decrepit cabins, the sagging board churches, the well-kept riding-boss houses, the dismal-looking commissary stores. Here are low, one-storied, neat, newly-painted houses, with deep screened porches running all around under overhanging eaves. Near by is usually a large barn for cattle in the midwestern style; close to it is a huge yellow heap of rice straw for the cattle to eat at, for every part of the plant is good for something, and most rice farmers keep excellent small herds. The homes have usually well-tended flower gardens in front; but, since it is so difficult to grow trees on this prairie, they often stand shadeless. Their inhabitants are prosperous and active, despite the terrific heat of the Grand Prairie from June to October; and in Stuttgart, the largest town of the entire rice region, they have been very successfully governed by able Republican mayors throughout recent years. Quite recently the "Flying Farmers of Arkansas" has been organized, mainly among these rice farmers; here, if anywhere, it is possible to sow one's fields, inspect levees, and control irrigation from the air.

Altogether the great rice field is not without its own peculiar charm. It has much the same sense of openness and of breathtaking scale as have the great plains of central Kansas. It is perhaps in early June, when the young rice, about four or five inches high, is first flooded to the depth of an inch that the plain is most beautiful, because of the delicate tender green of the plant and the frequently seen reflections of midsummer clouds caught in some shallow unplanted pool. It is beautiful also in fall, when flooding is altogether over, and the light yellow, heavily drooping, seeded heads hang heavily, ready for the reaper; it is, from spring to fall, the favorite haunt of great flocks of red-winged blackbirds with their swift, darting flight and their delicately sweet song. But the rice country is quite monotonous in aspect, like Kansas again, in late summer, under the heavy rolling thunderclouds of the Delta; and in mid-winter. In winter especially, with the stubble covering the fields with a peculiar tint of ashen grey, and with stray herds of cattle wandering over its empty surface under a sky laden with unshed rain, it has a dreary austerity, unlike anything else in the state, and not soon to be forgotten.

The seed is put into the ground at any time from the first of April to the fifteenth of May. Around the first of May is the usual date; as rice, being essentially a tropical variety of grass, requires warm weather if it is to germinate quickly. After about three weeks' growth, the water is pumped on, and is gradually increased in volume till the plant stands in about six inches of water. Repeated fertilizations of the soil, which have become increasingly necessary in the case of the adjoining cotton belt, are practically unnecessary in the case of the rice field; but there is a common practice of letting a field rest every third year without cultivation. Such fields are sometimes sown in oats or rye in the fall, and are then ready to be reaped when the rice-growing fields are being seeded. The rice farmer usually conducts his operations far more scientifically than the cotton farmer, and the rice fields have as yet shown no signs of exhaustion. The area that the main fields fill is approximately some fifty miles east and west, from five miles east of Brinkley to Bayou Meto beyond Lonoke; and some hundred miles north and south, from the site of Arkansas Post to Augusta in Woodruff County. Approximately, they fill the exact location and dimensions of Nuttall's "Grand Prairie," with a little added over. Here, and in areas beyond which have grown increasingly important, twenty-two and six-tenths percent of the entire United States production of rice is annually harvested, an amount surpassed only by Louisiana and, more recently, by the Texas Gulf lowlands.

The varieties favored by Arkansas farmers are, for ninety percent of the area, Blue Rose or Early Prolific; of these two, Blue Rose is usually planted earlier, as taking longer to ripen. Some sixteen varieties have been tried out at the Branch Experiment Station maintained by the University, between Stuttgart and De Witt, since 1926. No variety, when planted, requires much attention beyond that of keeping the fields under water. Rice does not carry a large population of dependents, like cotton. Prices have recently, in the summer of 1946, as already stated, risen to a dollar and seventy-five cents a bushel. Like the fruit growers of the northern and western parts of the state, the rice farmers have made Arkansas prosperous beyond anyone's earlier dream.

Since the continuance of successful farming in this area depends entirely on the supplies of water still underground, there have been from time to time reports that these supplies were in imminent danger of being exhausted. In the spring of 1934, after three years of steady drought, an investigation was made, and the state geologist reported that a loss of ten and a third inches of underground water had taken place since 1929. This estimate has frequently since then been questioned as being too low; in fact, a recent official report brought out by the U. S. Army Engineers, has stated that, for the past thirty years, the rice area has lost a foot of water every year. Some attempts have been made to remedy the situation by the building of storage reservoirs; and the project of a canal, connecting the Arkansas and the White, across the Grand Prairie, has been publicly discussed. The years since 1936 have been generally wet, and no remedy has as yet been seriously attempted.

The establishment of a great grain-growing area in this region, which harvests its crop usually from the last weeks of September onward, began early to attract many wild ducks which commonly use the Mississippi Valley flyway every fall, on their way from the Canada swamps to the Gulf coast. Since the winter in Arkansas is usually mild up to the New Year at least, thousands of ducks now spend most of the winter season in the lakes and swamps adjoining the rice-field region, where feeding is easy. Thus the town of Stuttgart became not only the rice capital of Arkansas, but also, as it now boasts, the "Sportsmen's Paradise" par excellence of the state. The third week in October Stuttgart celebrates its Rice Carnival; this is followed early in November by another annual festival, which in the fall of 1940 was celebrated for the fourth time: the National Duck-Calling Contest. This is the only local celebration, as far as I know, apart from baseball and football games and horse races at Hot Springs, which is always broadcast in the state. I have never had the pleasure of being in Stuttgart on this occasion, but for some years I have heard over the radio as many as thirty duck-callers give through human lips their versions of the three chief calls of the wild duck: the "flying call," the "feeding call," and the "mating call." There is a wildness in these sounds, especially when heard on a dark November night, with the temperature around freezing and the sky threatening unshed snow. The duck-callers, men who make a living by guiding city-bred hunters to spots in the nearby swamps and bayous which the ducks frequent, and who there call the ducks up to the guns—shooting from a blind, formerly practiced, being now forbidden—must be interesting men to know. The callers, as they have come to me over the radio, have frequently had their efforts interspersed with the loud whistles and whoops of the spectators; it is obvious that Stuttgart knows and admires its skilled duck-callers and is thrilled by a superlative performance. I recall one occasion, indeed, in which it was announced beforehand that, on the afternoon of the contest day, a wild duck had been shot by bow and arrow at the big reservoir south of the rice city. This announcement was received with wild cheers.

It has been stated that there are now annually over seventy million ducks wintering in Arkansas. With summer breeding-grounds in Ontario and Manitoba drained and brought under cultivation in the early thirties, the breed once seemed about to face extinction; but the sportsmen of the United States seem at last, by buying up these grounds, to have restored the wild duck to much of his former glory. It is good that this should be so and that the Arkansas rice field should provide the wild duck with so rich and so perpetual a feeding ground. It is good to think that the Federal government has now established, just east of the rice field along the swamps bordering the White River from Clarendon southward to Saint Charles, the largest game refuge in the entire state, where one may fish but not hunt the year around. The ducks may still go there if they want to escape the hunters. There is reason to think that the fate of the passenger pigeon, still remembered by some of the oldest men in the Ozarks, will not be repeated in the case of the wild duck. By the protection of this species, by the determination to have and to keep "ducks, unlimited," the natives of the state have proved that Arkansas will always be Arkansas. The descendants of Davy Crockett, the "half-horse, half-alligator men," will always seek the swamps adjoining the rice fields at sunrise, the long, brown shotguns held steady in their hands.

Twenty-two

ARKANSAS TAKES A HOLIDAY

Each year, as for some years past, on the night of October 31, the ancient festival of Hallowe'en, Little Rock takes a strange holiday. The festival then celebrated is not a legal one. How it sprang up and developed none can say. The local Chamber of Commerce does not support it. It may at any moment be prohibited by law. Yet it goes on, and it is peculiarly appropriate to Arkansas's capital city. I have seen nothing like it in any other state.

The first time that I ever saw Little Rock's Hallowe'en celebration was on October 31, 1933. At eight that evening I had attended a rather dull meeting of a culture club, at Fourth and Main. When I went to it, the streets were quiet. Previously there had been much scribbling with soap on the windshields of all cars left parked at various curbs, but I had seen the same in much earlier years and had expected it. The windows of business premises standing vacant—a good many, for the depression was still on—were similarly scribbled. Those which were occupied had their plate-glass fronts protected by a coating of glycerine. There was nothing unusual about the size or the appearance of the crowd on the Main Street sidewalks.

When I emerged from the meeting an hour later, all was different. The street on both sides was crowded with a throng afoot. Dressed in a fantastic array of old garments, disguised in papier-mâché masks of every description, the crowd yelled and jostled, blowing horns and whistles, unrolling long curling "ticklers" of paper, hurling thick handfuls of confetti down the backs of all passers-by. At several street corners stood tall, solemn figures in the white robes and peaked hoods of the Ku Klux Klan. Not a policeman, as far as I could see, was in sight. Every streetcar that same along and halted anywhere had its trolley-pole pulled. Automobiles plowed along slowly through the dense mob overflowing both sidewalks. Slapping hands were frequently applied to the rumps of passers-by, women and men alike. The horseplay went on for well over an hour; then I wearied of it and went home to bed.

The next day the newspapers merely mentioned the fact that a leading citizen of the city was angry because the wooden posts supporting his front verandah had been taken down during the night, and had disappeared. Gates and fences were also missing. The soap-scribbles were washed off a day or so later; Little Rock had duly celebrated another Hallowe'en.

The same celebration, with an equal degree of licensed mummery, again took place, despite the war, as late as 1942. Only by 1945 did it show signs of falling off—perhaps because so many other celebrations took place in that year. Since Little Rock was, during the war, a "defense area," named as such by the Federal government, there might have been an attempt made by the military authorities to suppress what apparently was a spontaneous exhibition of rowdy spirit. But the celebration of Hallowe'en in this manner has undoubtedly gone on for a considerable number of years in Little Rock; and whether it can be entirely stopped remains to be seen. It obviously appeals to some innate impulses of the people themselves—perhaps akin to those impulses expressed as long ago as 1820, when the entire town was moved from its site by masked and disguised men at Ashley's bidding. I have never seen anything at all like the Little Rock Hallowe'en anywhere else in the South, or in any other part of the country.

When I was a boy, in the last years of the nineteenth and the early years of the twentieth century, Mardi Gras, though the street parades of the eighties and early nineties had already been given up, was still celebrated by many people's putting on masks and dressing up and going out on the streets. Masked balls were still held on the night of Mardi Gras in Little Rock. At Hallowe'en, on the other hand, various pranks were played, such as soaping windows, stealing gates to fences, overturning iron carriage-stoops, and lighting trash bonfires; but no one then masked or dressed up at night or in the day. Now Mardi Gras exists no longer. Other spontaneous popular celebrations are also going, or gone. The selling and the setting-off of fireworks within the city limits of Little Rock at Christmas or on the Fourth of July have been forbidden by city ordinance. In 1940, Christmas Day in Little Rock was as quiet as any Sunday; only outside the city did the time-honored Southern custom of saluting Christmas Day with firecrackers still go on. Even the traditional eggnog, once ladled from a bowl in every respectable home all through Christmas Day, is now rarely, if ever, seen.

Far simpler and surely less harmful folk festivals have almost completely vanished. The travelling circus, which in the far-off days of my youth appeared in Little Rock at least once every year to create a day of excitement from the setting up of the great gray tents at dawn, the moving of the boarded-up animal cages from the freight yards to the circus grounds, the elaborate street parade, with its elephants and wild animals, which went on from ten o'clock till noon, the two big performances at afternoon and evening, and the final departure of the tired crowd, full of peanuts, popcorn, and pink lemonade around eleven in the evening—all this happens now, if at all, only once in two or three years. The humbler Dog-and-Pony Show, which used to be thought more refined than the circus proper, is today completely extinct. So, as Mr. E. E. Cummings has told us, is Buffalo Bill. In place of all this, there is the travelling "carnival," the "wonder show," which usually tours the cotton belt about the middle of the picking season, in September or October. It is a poor substitute for the circus, this garishly-lit affair, with its giant swings, its ferris wheels, its scenic railways, its tents of freaks, its games of "skill," its undressed girls, and its tiresome barkers.

The Little Rock Hallowe'en, in contrast with these "wonder shows," is not commercial or mechanical; it is spontaneous, human, rough, and rowdy. No one of the many people whom I have asked seems to know just how it arose, or when. As I have already stated, in my boyhood days Mardi Gras brought forth the masking; Hallowe'en brought forth the pranks at night. Now both seem to run together. I have been told that Mardi Gras, during the years in which I lived abroad and became unfamiliar with my native city, led to so many manifestations of hooliganism that sermons were finally preached and editorials written against the celebration of that day. And since Little Rock is in the Bible belt, and since the minority Catholics made no attempt to save what, after all, was their holiday, Mardi Gras was abandoned about 1910. Some years after that, Hallowe'en was taken up seriously, as a chance for popular horseplay and rough fun; and it somehow acquired Mardi Gras's lost characteristics.

But when? I am sorry to have to say that I do not know. I have heard it stated that in the fall of 1917, with America at war and a great number of soldiers from a nearby camp going through the streets, a masked ball was held at a downtown Little Rock hotel on Hallowe'en night. Some of the maskers went out on the streets, walked along the sidewalk for a few blocks; someone flung a few handfuls of confetti, there was much jostling—and then and there Little Rock's Hallowe'en celebration was spontaneously born. The next year crowds in fancy dress, equipped with noise-makers and confetti, appeared as if by magic. Perhaps this was the way the present-day celebration arose. In any case, Little Rock does not easily give up opportunities for such celebrations. This one seems well established, and few can recall the day when it was taken as a needless annoyance by those "respectable elements" which so far have not been able to stop it.

Both the present-day Hallowe'en and the earlier Mardi Gras—not actually celebrated officially in my state till after the Civil War—may owe something to the famed "Callithumpians," which seem to have flourished chiefly during the seventies and the eighties in Little Rock. Nothing whatever has been written about this once-famed organization, so far as I know. From what I have heard concerning it, it consisted of a group of younger society men who, in fancy dress and mounted on horseback, went about the streets from Christmas to new Year's Day and serenaded various people by making outrageous noises on various weird and uncouth instruments outside their homes, until the serenaders were invited to dismount and partake of refreshment within. The whole thing may have been got up as a deliberate parody of the old custom of summer serenading, which went on well past my childhood. On those bygone summer nights, organizations—always of amateurs—went through the streets in wagons, attended by local musicians, to play and sing on the lawns of well-known citizens. Most of the songs chosen were of the sentimental, Stephen Foster variety. To be selected for such a serenade was considered something of an honor. Still later, such serenades were deliberately practiced as a means of raising money. I can recall at least one which visited my father's house in my later boyhood; it had for its object the obtaining of funds for the local firemen. The firemen themselves furnished the playing and singing on this occasion, and they did very well.

Those were the days when—in the spring of 1893 it was—the United States government finally transferred to the city of Little Rock the old Federal arsenal grounds to be used as a public park, and took in its place Fort Logan H. Roots, on top of Big Rock, on the north bank of the river, now a veterans' hospital. When the new park was opened, bicycle races were held in honor of the event; and, as I recall, one of these races took place between two bicycles of the old-fashioned high-wheeled variety. It was not till some years later that the horse-drawn streetcars, introduced in the late eighties, gave way to the newfangled electric trolleys, which seemed so mysterious to me when they first appeared. Except for these, transportation around town was still of the horse-drawn variety. By 1902 there were only three automobiles in Little Rock; and ox-wagons, often mired up to the wagon-bed, were frequently to be seen, plodding into the city, step by step. The age of the horse died hard. Livery stables persisted until after 1914; and there is, or there was in 1941, one old wagon-yard, with its original bunkhouse intact, in the eastern end of the town. The oldest residential streets to this day display many of the familiar stone carriage-stoops, some with names still on them. Hitching-posts, except for a few of the plainest sort, have gone into the limbo of antique shops; but the carriage-stoops, too heavy to take away, remain. The city park on the site of the old arsenal is famous; it has been discovered—since 1942—that no less a personage than Douglas MacArthur was born there while his father, an Army officer, was stationed at the old arsenal. The park now proudly bears his name.

The old town of Little Rock, less than one third of its present size and even smaller when its suburb on the north bank, known to all the old citizens as Argenta, split off and became a separate municipality under its present name of North Little Rock, was, as I recall, a pleasant enough place to live in, provided one did not have much ambition to live somewhere else. The town had perhaps twenty thousand inhabitants, and extended, at the most, twenty streets north and south, and the same number east and west. It was surrounded with woods, little traversed by highways except upon the south and east. To the west, not more than fifteen miles away, lay dense pine forests, in which still might be seen bears and panthers. To get as far west as Hot Springs necessitated a change of trains down to the late eighties. But in Little Rock itself the coming of the Rock Island around the close of the century made people feel that they lived in a metropolis. The town thrived, as did all other Southern towns of the time, largely on its memories of the "Lost Cause." When Jefferson Davis, formerly President of the Confederacy, died at his Mississippi home, practically every house in Little Rock put crepe on its door.

One of the chief festivals of those remote times was Confederate Decoration Day on May 16. The two local militia companies, in which the town took an immense pride, turned out in their spick and span uniforms of gray and blue, with military képis and pompons, and marched afoot to the Confederate Cemetery. They were accompanied by Confederate officers on horseback, in full regalia, and proudly displayed the Confederate flag. At the cemetery, magnolias, rifled from all the town's trees, were solemnly laid on the graves; salutes were fired; there were floods of oratory. As late as the present century, a Confederate general dying in Little Rock was given a full military funeral—a band playing a dead march, muffled drums, the coffin set on a gun carriage, and troops following. The general's favorite horse, saddled and bridled, with the dead man's boots reversed in the stirrups, paced solemnly after the coffin.

In the winter time, when the social season got under way, elaborate cotillions were given at various homes; the annual ball and banquet of the Concordia Club was always a gala occasion; the old Boat House—since burned down and never rebuilt—of the Little Rock Athletic Association, parent of the present-day Country Club, entertained lavishly, though the sport it had been designed to foster—rowing—had never really taken on. In spring, horseback riding around the outskirts, on backwood roads that are now suburban highways, was popular; the German *Turn-Verein,* which had its own building, usually put on a public athletic show; and I have even heard of the risky and daring sport of chasing foxes by moonlight on horseback through the dense thickets of Granite Mountain. Horse-racing went on every spring, too, at the local Little Rock track; the present airport now stands on its site. Baseball arrived in 1895, about the time when West End Park, today the grounds of Little Rock's million-dollar high school, became accessible to the new trolley-cars. And about the same time, or a little later, summer band concerts began to be given in the new City Park and provided another means of outdoor summer entertainment. Glenwood Park, a private entertainment ground up Main Street, had its own active summer theater, as well as numerous entertainments throughout the winter.

This was the period, above all, when local summer resorts flourished. They were usually classified as "watering places," with supposedly marvelous curative powers, and were situated always in the Ozarks, where the nights were admittedly cooler and the scenery more pleasant to the eye. Eureka Springs, one of the first, had been discovered in the late seventies, it is said, by a party of hunters looking for a deer. It rapidly boomed, as its two large hotels, still standing, can testify. It took, at first, a two-day stagecoach journey from Russellville to visit the place; though after Powell Clayton had induced the Frisco Railroad to build a branch line to it, it flourished still more, having sometimes as many as eight thousand visitors. In 1889, the hotel on the summit of Mount Nebo was built; but that spot, though providing a splendid view, never prospered. It began to languish after 1895, when the Eastman Hotel was built at Hot Springs. Some of the more inaccessible and remote "summer resorts," built usually on some commanding site, failed to flourish at all, despite the money spent on them. This was notably the case with the great stone-built ruin of the Hotel Wilhelmina, erected on the summit ridge of Rich Mountain above Mena about 1903. It lasted as a hotel only for two or three years, and then was closed, because—it is said—the guests complained that this particular peak is so often shrouded in low-lying cloudbanks, driven up by violent storms of wind and thunder surging through the plains of southeastern Oklahoma.

Altogether, the late eighties were a good time to be born in—as I was; if they lacked the streamlined efficiency of today, they nevertheless had—until Jeff Davis arrived to upset the apple-cart of the planter politicians—a picturesque dignity, a native aristocracy of manners, that often seem to be lacking in the present day of machinery and mass democracy. Men whose lives were spent in driving horses learned early that life is a matter of personal control and responsibility. The community rested on whatever talent the individuals applied to living. The handling of frequently skittish animals demanded of all those who owned them a less mechanical variety of attention: it made for steadiness and sobriety. Less excitement but more effort were involved in the simplest processes of existence. To travel far entailed—if the trip were made by train—more discomfort, more careful preliminary preparation, a deeper and more stolid endurance of dusty cars and poor hotels. One stayed at home to take greater enjoyment in the not-infrequent visits of touring companies, presenting at the old Capital Theatre such attractions as James O'Neil in "Monte Cristo," Joe Jefferson in "Rip Van Winkle," Colonel Robert G. Ingersoll in his notorious "agnostic" lectures, the world-famous and spectacular "Black Crook," thought to be rather wicked because of its profuse display of girls in tights; and even "Uncle Tom's Cabin," as I recall, which I did not see; or "General and Mrs. Tom Thumb," which I did.

Such were the nineties, now qualified as being "gay" but, in reality marked in the North and the East by violent labor disturbances and huge financial panics. Of these Arkansas heard very little; though perhaps the famed panic of 1893 was responsible for the fact that three years later in Little Rock eggs sold at eight cents a dozen, breakfast bacon was only ten cents a pound, and cotton was seven and a half cents a pound! Off in remote Wyoming and in Montana, the last attempt of the American Indians to find salvation along another road than that taken by the whites had ended in the killing of Sitting Bull and the horrid spectacle of the Wounded Knee Massacre. The Cherokee Strip had been opened in the Indian Territory; and oil, soon after, was struck at Bartlesville, while in the same region many Indians still lived in wigwams and held great annual council meetings. America was changing from the age of steam to the age of the dynamo, and the exact year of the change may be taken as 1898, the year of the Spanish-American War. A year before this, as I recall, on July 4, 1897, the free bridge across the foot of Main Street in Little Rock was at last opened, after many years of agitation and exasperating delays in construction. Up to that time the only way of crossing the stream had been by ferry. There was promised for this eventful occasion the largest and most elaborate display of fireworks ever before seen in the state; and an enormous crowd, shirt-sleeved and perspiring as became a moonless July night, waited long on the river bank back of the old State House to see it. The display was extremely late in starting, because some people, going on a barge down the river, hit a pier of the new bridge in the darkness. The barge was overturned; quite a number of the people were drowned. There was much shouting and confusion and running to and fro, while the expectations of the packed crowd were slowly dampened. It must have been past eleven o'clock when the last rocket expired and the tired people went home—to discuss the drownings rather than the fireworks.

The next year, the year of the Spanish-American War, patriotic meetings were in order; and I recall still vividly how our own home bustled with vast preparations; hundreds of luncheon boxes were filled with fried chicken, biscuits, delicious jellies, and other good Southern things, all prepared for a company of volunteers going off to Cuba. Most of these men sickened and died of the fevers raging around the great army camp at Tampa, as we learned later; so the summer of the Spanish-American War was a holiday for us, but not for them. The nineteenth century, with its spontaneous and naïve reliance on "progress," backed by old folkways, was already on the way out. Edison had invented the electric filament lamp; someone else had invented what was then called "the horseless carriage," and in these facts there lay the seeds of a far-from-noiseless and a long-reaching revolution.

Nowadays our holidays are different. They are for the most part organized affairs—run by some local chamber of commerce, and, since the motor age is upon us, partaking of the nature of massed and organized pilgrimages. Thus, about the first of April, hundreds of motorists travel down annually to the region around Nashville, in the southeastern corner of the state, to see the great orchards of Elberta peaches which grow there, planted in a pine-barren country that began to prosper only after 1890. The flowers of this species of peach tree are of a dark rose color, and not conspicuous; and the trip is not so vividly beautiful as a later one, held at the end of April, to the apple-growing region around Fayetteville and Rogers. Here, as in other festivals, there is the usual crowning of local "queens," which seems to be the inevitable accompaniment to all present-day festivals, the usual street parades with floats containing pretty girls. In the summer there is the White River Festival at Batesville, the Tomato Festival at Monticello, the "homecoming week" at Heber Springs. All of these have their "queens" and "bathing beauties"—the pattern has grown as monotonous and as boring as most of the other products of the motor age—but they draw large picnicking crowds. Only the Baptists notably have succeeded in varying the usual chamber-of-commerce pattern by holding public singing conventions, with quartets—I am sorry to say they are now much influenced by modern stunts on the radio—competing in singing together their favorite hymns, at various places, during the summer months.

Little, however, has been done as yet—and what little there is has been altogether the result of the energy and persistence of some Home Demonstration Agents—to preserve the rapidly vanishing folk music, dancing, and craft skill of the Ozark people. It was only in the spring of 1941 that I finally witnessed in Searcy County one Ozark folk festival, which was fairly complete, and well handled. Such a festival should include dramatization (in this case, the old "Arkansas Traveller" story was acted out again), old ballads, hymn singing (from the "shape note" books), playing by old fiddlers, jig dancing, hog calling, square dancing, and the play party. Folk crafts should also be shown. The difficulty with all such attempts to get the Ozark people to display their vanishing talents is, first of all, that the people themselves are shy and do not much care to show off before strangers; and second, that so much fun has already been made of their supposed coarseness and quaintness, in comic strips and elsewhere, that the mountaineers have even begun to accept much of it themselves. One does not particularly care for folk art when it becomes not a sublimation but a sheer parody; and the uncouth quaintness of the backwoods is a quality easy to parody. A real revival of Ozark folk skills and arts is profoundly necessary, economically as well as morally, today; but the State of Arkansas has still to wait, apparently, till such skills and arts have completely disappeared before anyone can want to bring them back.

There is, however, one folk festival I know of which has the backing of the local chamber of commerce, and which brings visitors from the outside into the town; and this is the Polk County Possum Club banquet, held annually at Mena early in December. This organization celebrated in 1941 its twenty-eighth anniversary, but, after that, all meetings were abandoned till 1945. It is probably the oldest organization in the state to spring directly and spontaneously from local folkways. The folkways in this case are those of the upper Ouachita plateau—and the Polk County Possum Club has lived long enough to foster at least one rival organization of more recent date, and to become an institution.

It was in the fall of 1913 that there took place the historic possum hunt which led to the founding of the Polk County Possum Club. A local judge by the name of Alley challenged the mayor of Mena (the town itself dates back only to 1896, when the first trains on the newly built Kansas City and Southern Railroad ran through it) to a contest. Each man was to go out with his dogs and his hunters—recruited from the neighboring backwoods—one night, and see just how many possums he could bag. The loser was to pay the winner with a banquet. The mayor agreed. It is not recorded which side won, but the banquet was duly held and was so successful that it was repeated about a month later, with the wives of the members present. Thirty-three people attended it on this occasion, and everyone enjoyed the affair so much that it was decided to hold the banquet annually thenceforward. The meat of the possum itself, which tastes like rather greasy pork, served with boiled sweet potatoes, was the chief dish of the evening.

Among the locally recruited hunters on the memorable occasion of the original possum-catching contest was one B. S. Petefish, a denizen of the hills who was equipped with a rich sense of humor and a store of backwoods anecdotes—no doubt one of those "powerful uneducated persons" whose achievements Walt Whitman loved to celebrate. When the group met again, a year after the first banquet, it was decided to set up a permanent club, and it was agreed that they would henceforth meet annually. Mr. Petefish was elected president by acclamation. He retained his office up to 1935.

Mr. Petefish, backwoodsman that he was, no doubt took a great pride in the fact that he had been elected president of a regular organization, meeting annually at the chief town of the district. Any attempt to unseat him from his highly decorative and unpaid office was henceforward resented—and he seems to have clung to his post as tenaciously as the possum itself clings to the branches of a tree. The hunting of this animal, as most Southerners know, does not imply any high degree of skill. It is always undertaken at night, and afoot. The dogs scent the track of the timid animal and pursue him to a tree, which is sometimes climbed, or even cut down. If the tree is a small one, it may be possible to shake the possum down. Mr. Petefish refused to be shaken down; he remained president till the end of his life.

He was, as I gather, stone deaf—and if asked any question, had the habit of covering up his deafness by answering with some anecdote of his boyhood, which had been spent in this remote region of Polk County, in the days when the city of Mena consisted of a single log cabin, and when modern habits were entirely unknown. The chief business of the annual banquets, in the early days of the organization, consisted in "ribbing Petefish," as one of the survivors of the original organization once put it to me. Members would ask him embarrassing questions about what his policy would be if made, say, President of the United States, and would receive replies which had nothing to do with the issue, but which referred to the remote days following the Civil War, when not only possums but bears and panthers and other wild animals were more plentiful and when the inhabitants lived by hunting them.

After Mr. Petefish's death, another backwoods character who had previously attended the annual banquets and who modeled himself on Petefish, was duly elected. This was one English Baker, whose photograph shows him as wearing a deerskin vest and rejoicing in long hair, after the old fashion of the frontier. Mr. Baker, too, had lived mainly by hunting, and he served acceptably as president for two terms, being elected to a third at the annual banquet in 1939, which he was unable to attend. Four days after, he died, and the office then stood vacant till the next meeting.

In 1940 it was again filled, by a character aptly described as "able, stable, and notable," as well as "honest, courageous, and possum-conscious." "Uncle" Rufe Miller, of Cherry Hill, a community some ten miles to eastward, is—for that district—a reasonably successful and independent farmer who can neither read nor write, and who has done not only much hunting in his time but who also has sired and raised up a family of nine fully grown children. He is endowed by nature with a fund of mother wit and a ready tongue: his gift for vivid expression comes out in his own description of his children. As he said on the night of the banquet at which he was elected, "I've got five girls and four boys and haint raised a stark born fool in the lot, and haint raised more'n a right bright one." When I asked him whether he thought he would be elected president, he retorted, "Well, I haint such a fool as to reckon I just caint lose," a remark which reveals much of the true character of the Arkansas backwoodsman.

The proceedings always open with the banquet—though there is an informal gathering of visitors at a hotel some hours earlier. The banquet is held in a large hall, and when I attended in 1940, about five hundred people were present. Possum meat is still served at the feast, but not too conspicuously, the main dish being turkey. The banquet is followed by the initiation of new members. The long trestle-tables are moved back, and a space is cleared before the platform, on which sit the candidates for office, as well as the master of ceremonies, chosen by the local Chamber of Commerce (which obtains a tidy sum annually out of the sale of tickets). At the initiation, women are admitted on the same terms as men—the candidates for membership are taught to give the "possum sign"—right fist clenched with forefinger held bent and upward. They then repeat the "possum oath of allegiance," constructed on a familiar model; and they are submitted to further tests, such as being blindfolded and asked to drink some mysterious fluid known as "possum-juice" from a cup, or are required to stroke and handle a live possum, taken from the half-a-dozen usually seen clinging to branches surrounding the platform. This is then followed by the election. In 1940 no less than three candidates for the presidency presented themselves. These were, in addition to "Uncle" Rufe Miller, who has been already described, Shade Hilton, of Mena, another middle-aged backwoodsman of less genial aspect, and the Reverend W. N. Primer, of remote Acorn, a small community somewhere to northward, who was described as an "independent evangelist" and who presented an aspect recalling, to my mind, the photographs of English Baker. Wearing iron-rimmed spectacles of smoked glass, and with hair that hung in a ragged fringe about this sunburnt neck, he wore, below one blue-trousered thigh, a wooden leg of undoubted home manufacture. Unlike the other two, he was not equipped with a campaign manager (chosen from among the young lawyers of the town) to promise on his behalf repudiation of the national debt, a double set of locks on the Panama Canal, and no third term. He contented himself, instead, with singing and playing to the audience on a guitar. The resultant banging and bawling was truly terrific, though completely unintelligible; and was probably too primitive in its effect, even for Mena, to promote his claims. At all events, he lost, and was forced to content himself with the designation of "secretary at large," while Shade Hilton became vice-president, and "Uncle" Rufe was named President.

The manner of electing the candidates was unique—peculiar to the Possum Club. The electoral committee of five, chosen by the Chamber of Commerce, filed on to the platform, after the candidates had been presented. The audience was asked to vote by shouting and making the "possum sign." At the first ballot, the judges were unable to agree and declared a tie; a second ballot had to be taken. Meanwhile, in the small persimmon trees set in tubs around the platform, a half-a-dozen live possums hung on and looked down, grimly and disdainfully.

A considerable amount of preparation has to be undertaken beforehand each year to make the annual banquet of the club a success. About six dozen live possums have to be found; and these are kept in cages in the various shops along Main Street for a bout a month before the feast takes place. Most of these are then killed and eaten; some half-a-dozen are kept alive to grace the occasion. As fifty possums are, after all, but little to offer to five hundred hungry guests, the possum-meat is served only as a side dish after the main course is eaten. Its general greasiness is not greatly relished by the assembled company in these degenerate days.

The Polk County Possum Club, in short, has become an Arkansas institution—and it has already produced its rival in the shape of the Benton County Possum Club, at which, for several years past, the hill farmers and possum hunters have met—in the open air—to celebrate their exploits and indulge in some good-natured banter, on the model of the Mena organization. In 1940 the Benton County organization held its own public banquet on a ridge east of Rogers on the same night as the affair at Mena, but I do not know what became of it during the recent war. I have also heard that the farmers of Poinsett County in the eastern lowlands are meditating upon yet another such club, to be called the Poinsett County Coon Club. So the old Mena organization, parent of all possum clubs, may well feel proud of its success in having accomplished its object of making those who dwell outside Mena firmly and unalterably possum-conscious!

So concludes the list of Arkansas festivals and state holidays. Others, such as the National Duck-calling and Cotton-picking contests, have already been mentioned. It will be seen that those which are the most characteristic of the state are those which are the most spontaneous; and in almost all, the self-same character of primitive horseplay bulks large. Unlike the English, the people of Arkansas do not take their pleasures sadly. The backwoods humorist here is still an institution. Tellers of humorous and "tall" tales are still in vogue, and certain places are still famous for having sired them. The three favorite contenders for the crown of the late Will Rogers of Oklahoma are today the Van Buren-born Bob Burns and the Piney Ridge-born (originally this place had a different name) Lum and Abner, who found in their own insignificant settlements—not far from the home of the Possum Club and from the spirit of its festival—sufficient of human comedy to make them prosperous for life on the modern radio and screen. The Ozarker does not wish to be taken too seriously. Life for him is so hard and difficult and he is usually so shy and voiceless, that any clown with a fund of amusing expressions, a rich line of talk, is likely to become locally famous. If you can enjoy these local entertainers—always popular though usually unpaid—sufficiently to accept them for what they are, you are of the Ozarks; but if you take them too seriously, you do not belong. To look on the quality of fun too seriously implies criticism of its quality; and the Ozarkers are not grateful for criticism when it comes, as it must, from "furriners," or from the "city slicker" and the "fine-haired."

Twenty-three

THE SWEET HOME PIKE ROLLS ON

On the twenty-fifth of March, 1910, the modern age—which was to rule Arkansas for the next thirty-five years and longer—proclaimed itself unmistakably when four automobiles, containing residents of Pine Bluff, made the run into Little Rock in four hours. The distance, by the present-day motor highway, is exactly forty-three miles; and it could not have been more than a mile or two longer at that time. So these strange vehicles, which in those days frightened all horses, though the animals were still by far numerically the stronger on the streets, had averaged little more than a moderately good horse and buggy and had made the total journey in scarcely over ten miles an hour.

The last five miles of that journey had been made over a road which, so far as I know, was the first hard-surfaced highway in rural Arkansas. This turnpike was constructed on the old Tilford system, a successor to the style devised by that enterprising Scotsman, John L. McAdam. After the ground was rolled, stone blocks of at least eight inches in thickness were laid down, to a width of twenty feet. The heavy steam rollers of those days were used to press the blocks into position. Over the blocks pulverized stone was spread to a depth of three inches, and it was coated over all with gravel and clay. The result was a highway which ran from the Confederate Home (still standing) five miles along the low ridge of Granite Mountain and across the muddy lowlands of Fourche Bayou—where the clay, like red putty, was so tenacious, that it is said it pulled the shoes off the feet of horses passing through—and finally ended in Little Rock.

Had the automobiles passed that way only a year before, they would have been forced to pay a toll in order to enter Little Rock at all. This toll was charged by a private company, for the turnpike had been built as far back as 1885, and the two local contractors who had constructed it had been given a right to charge tolls on all vehicles passing over it for a period of twenty-four years. The list of the tolls is interesting. Footmen were free; horsemen had to pay two and a half cents (probably most horsemen planned to ride both ways and paid their round-trip fare, which made it easier); one-horse carriages or wagons paid five cents; two-horse vehicles, seven and a half cents; four-horse vehicles, ten cents, six-horse vehicles, fifteen cents; cattle, horses, sheep, and hogs in flocks or droves were paid for at the rate of one cent for each animal. Probably a provision for bicycles was added about the nineties; but whether there was ever any toll on automobiles I do not know. They were possibly charged according to the horse-power of their engines; or perhaps they were charged nothing, for the wonder was whether they could run at all along the then-existing mud-tracks.

I have often been out on that road myself in my own early days; and I have a vivid recollection of the Sweet Home Pike, as it was called. The city of Little Rock then ended abruptly even before Twenty-first Street was reached, by Scott or by Rock Street, or by the more recently cut Barber Avenue, whose slight hill was a much-favored spot in our neighborhood for boys to go coasting down on their bicycles. This was the region of the "town branch," which, before my time, frequently flooded Main Street, running unwalled between crumbling banks of red clay, through flourishing cedars and pine woods (useful for Christmas trees), past rickety wooden Negro shacks, an old line of red clay earthworks thrown up by the Federals after the fall of Little Rock during the Civil War, and a newly-built big Negro schoolhouse of brick, still standing; through the redoubtable mosquito-ridden bottom lands of Fourche Bayou, at that time jungle-like in their growth of cypresses and vines. Beyond Twenty-first Street southward, lay nothing but the old Rapley home, a gaunt, burnt-out ruin standing aloof on its clay ridge, and known to be haunted. Going southeast along the highway, one reached the edge of the Confederate Cemetery, with the gloom of its heavy cedars overshadowing files of graves; and beyond that, the road turned south to the Fourche Crossing. The Federal Cemetery, adjoining to the North, had far more graves in it, as well as a monument set up to the Minnesota soldiers who, as we have seen, died here in droves from the fevers brought on by the occupation: but the monument to the Northern men was then ignored by most well-thinking Arkansawyers.

Here, close to the present roundhouse and repair shops of the Rock Island Railroad—not built till 1907—stood the famous tollgate, known to all dwellers of Little Rock in those days as the "Last Chance" gate. The tollgate house, a small, one-story frame affair, was to the left, and the tall roofed, high tollgate swung open by the hands of the gatekeeper, stretched across the roadway. On the opposite side stood "Last Chance" itself: a wooden, false-fronted, whitewashed smithy, usually with a farm wagon or two in front and a leather-aproned blacksmith working hard within shoeing the mules and the horses that had dragged the wagons thus far from Sweet Home, Wrightsville, Woodson, or Pine Bluff. These wagons in the fall were usually laden with a bale or two of cotton, and were frequently seen mired to the hubs with the stiff Arkansas clay. Here was the "last chance" for the farmers of the regions south to get their nags shod at a reasonable country price, or to get a loose iron rim set straight on its felloe.

Beyond lay the cypresses and the rusty iron cantilever bridge, with its rattling planks, which ran across stagnant Fourche Bayou. Here Little Rock displayed its last reminder, or its first, to the passing farm wagons in the shape of vivid advertisements for the "Beehive Store," which then stood on Third and Main and which specialized in cheap workaday shoes and clothing. After these advertisements were passed, nothing remained but the woods, where dogwood and violets and ferns were still obtainable in spring and early summer, and where, in the hot months, lovers went buggy-riding by moonlight. Sixty or seventy carriages full of enraptured couples were not uncommon, then, on a single night.

As I recall, along Granite Mountain itself there was not a single house to be seen till one reached the Confederate Home. The only other structures I remember were two small, red brick affairs constructed long ago for powder magazines, set close to some deserted granite quarries. The woods, though dense, were not composed of big trees. The original forest covering had been completely cut down during the Federal occupation in the Civil War. But here were the clear signs of breastworks and of rifle and gun pits (a few of them there still near the Confederate Home) much overgrown in those days with the dense tangle of trees and underbrush.

It seems strange to think, as one rides along the same road today—now totally denuded of its trees and offering some of the least engaging prospects to be seen in the vicinity of the capital city—that this was once the favored ground for lovers' meetings in times that seem now far distant, though they are well within the memory of many a sixty-year-old citizen of Little Rock. Perhaps, after all, Henry Adams was right with his theory that a new phase, marking the extremes alike of speed and energy and the utmost limit of human thought, was due for the world after 1917. For though the people of Little Rock seem to have changed little in the last fifty years, a great transformation in external affairs has taken place around them. In Little Rock a few oaks still stand that were, possibly, acorns in the days of La Salle; but the human race has not developed in the way the oaks have done. The body of humanity has raced forward to a goal that the mind cannot master or grasp, and we live today at the center of an earthquake that became inevitable when, far off in the eighteenth century, James Watt saw the steam push upward the piston of his first engine. That earthquake may end by destroying Little Rock, along with the Western civilization it fostered; or destruction may be avoided by recovering old spiritual foundations long lost in these days. We have been told that modern man is now obsolete; the question is how far can we avoid, in his downfall, the destruction of ancient and abiding man?

The Sweet Home Pike today is an insignificant five-mile stretch in the network of the state's highways. Today there are five thousand miles of improved state highway in Arkansas, and another four thousand four hundred miles which still remain, though gravelled, akin to the dirt roads of yesterday. The last of the Sweet Home Pike was not completed till 1888 and, as it was being built, it led directly to a discovery which has done more than any other to make the state important in the economy of today.

The road contractor, a conscientious German by the name of Ed Weigel, residing in Little Rock, ran out of gravel for his top surface while busily completing the last mile of this highway close to the Confederate Home. He looked about and discovered near by some crumbly soft gray rock, which he ordered put into the crusher. It produced an excellent road surface and it was used; but Weigel, concluding that he had never seen any stuff like it, decided to take a sackful into Little

Rock and ask the opinion of the state geologist as to its value. Dr. John C. Branner, a friend of Weigel, was then acting in that post; his knowledge of Arkansas's mineral resources far surpassed that of any other man in the state. Accordingly, when the road was finished, and the sackful of rock had been brought in, the geologist, after looking carefully at the gray substance, demanded to know where it came from. Weigel replied, "Never mind where I got it, just tell me what it is." Thereupon Branner informed him that the substance was bauxite, from which the metal aluminum could be extracted. He demanded, again, to know where Weigel had obtained it, assuring him that he would respect this information as confidential and would protect Weigel in his rights of property and discovery. Weigel replied, no doubt with considerable surprise, that it had been found atop Granite Mountain and had been used by him as a road surfacing material; whereupon Branner said, smilingly, "Well, Ed, you can always feel assured that the road you surfaced is now finished with the most valuable road building material ever used on a highway."

Weigel himself did not follow up this free clue or make any attempt to buy up the land bordering on his new tollgate road; but Branner, from that time on, became interested in the mixed formation of sand, clay, and disintegrated syenite that stretches from Granite Mountain back through Saline County towards the town of Benton; and in 1891 he reported to the Governor of Arkansas that in Saline County he had discovered one of the largest deposits of bauxite to be found in the entire United States. This opinion erred, if anything, on the side of conservatism; at this day, nearly ninety-five percent of the bauxite mined in the entire United States comes from the deposits in Pulaski and Saline counties. The Arkansawyers, as is usual with them, were not over-much stirred by Branner's report; and the lands covering these deposits were mostly bought and are now owned by a single Northern corporation, the Aluminum Company of America.

The Sweet Home Pike, paved by the Tilford system, may be said, then, to have led directly to the greatest industry in Arkansas, an industry on which millions of Federal money has now been spent, since aluminum has been so important an adjunct in the manufacture of aeroplanes during the recent war. The old Pike now, like other motor roads in the state (once part of the selfsame toll road system), has long since been merged in the network of the main highways, which in the last twenty years have cost Arkansas over five hundred millions of dollars. A considerable part of this—one hundred and thirty millions in all—was spent around 1926–1927, when the state launched an enormous bond issue designed to make permanent paved roads out of many existing highways. Under the pressure of the largest boom in American history it was felt that such a bond issue would prove a safe investment; and so it was for a time—as the bonds sold readily on the New York market. Three years later, and the payment of interest on the Highway Bond issue had to be suspended. The state could not meet its obligations, and Arkansas had the humiliation of being posted on Wall Street as a defaulting state.

By 1930, when the final stage of the great depression was ushered in with a drought that lasted for two months and a half, without a drop of rain, which beggared cotton and rice and fruit farmers alike and produced on July 29 the highest temperature ever recorded at Little Rock (107.7 degrees) the state was completely bankrupt. In 1932 a candidate for the governorship who promised nothing more than the strictest economy and a slow refunding of the highway debt won over no less than eleven opponents. Out of that dozen, Arkansas chose the one man whose sole philosophy of life was that the miseries of the state and of all the Arkansawyers had been due to their too-eager following of the trends of the machine-age. Thus the natives, faced with the consequences of their own spree of spending, turned to a simple and honest conservative, J. M. Futrell, whose career recalls to a minor degree that of the older Elias Conway, or Elisha Baxter. The refunding program that Futrell then inaugurated remains in force; to this day about a hundred and eighty millions of dollars of accumulated highway indebtedness have to be carried on from one state budget to another. The highways then built are still there—but not much has been added to them over the past ten years, for the reason that the state cannot afford it.

The discovery of vast bauxite deposits—added to the requirements of the motor age—gave to Arkansas the first wave of prosperity it had known since the days of the Civil War. In the decade between 1915 and 1925, the city of Little Rock more than doubled in population. It was open to question, after the great Mississippi Valley flood of 1927 and still more after the depression of 1929, whether the prosperity had not been bought at too high a price. An important oil field centering around El Dorado in the far south of the state began to make its effect felt, from its discovery in 1921 onwards; its yield was sufficient to build many a magnificent mansion and to transform insignificant El Dorado itself into a city of some twenty thousand. To this day one brand of Arkansas-produced motor fuel may be purchased in the state. Apart from new oil-field fortunes, the only magnate's name ever mentioned in the twenties was that of the late Harvey Couch, founder and head of the Arkansas Power and Light Company, already mentioned in a preceding chapter. He had begun his career as a builder of small power lines and dispenser of electricity to farm families along the roads between Malvern, Pine Bluff, and Hot Springs. In the early twenties he constructed two power dams on the Ouachita River, where that stream comes out of its mountains to the south of Hot Springs, taking the steaming water poured out of the springs themselves and merging it in its volume, as it descends to the plain. On an island in Lake Catherine—one of the two reservoirs formed by these dams—Mr. Couch built his own home; and there, throughout the twenties, he surrounded himself with frequent house parties formed mainly of financial wizards of the Coolidge-Hoover epoch. To this day the corporation he founded, through its network of lines and its alliance with the Rural Electric Administration, largely controls the state. But while Couch was being talked about, the activities of Alcoa, as the Aluminum Corporation of America is generally called, were veiled in the silence of anonymity and absentee ownership.

The reason is that, though many tons of bauxite ore were being taken out of the ground by Alcoa from 1918 onwards, not one ounce was being transformed into the metal itself anywhere in Arkansas. Except for a few independent holdings, the entire bauxite region from Benton to Sweet Home, running roughly northeast from Benton to the east face of Granite Mountain and thus covering lower Saline and Pulaski counties at a distance from five to twenty miles south of Little Rock, was under the sole control of this single Pennsylvania corporation; and the corporation found it more profitable to ship all the ore to be processed outside the state. Except for whatever labor was involved in digging with steam shovels and loading the freight cars, Alcoa paid no one in Arkansas. The great open-face cuttings with their brick-red claybanks and gray slagheaps were defacing more and more widely every year this pine and scrub-oak region with its occasional granite outcroppings; but none noted that Arkansas was the loser rather than the gainer by this despoliation. Then, after war broke out in 1941, the changeover in bauxite production figures took an astonishing shape, as witness the following table:

ARKANSAS PRODUCTION OF BAUXITE
*For the Years 1939–1945, Inclusive**

YEAR	QUANTITY (*in short tons*)	VALUE
1939	404,606.72	$ 2,074,954.00
1940	474,076.96	2,501,393.00
1941	911,170.00	4,952,839.00
1942	2,767,315.00	12,029,406.00
1943	7,264,748.00	31,448,573.00
1944	3,018,755.00	13,679,027.00
1945	1,120,469.99	5,002,098.15

*Figures taken from U. S. Bureau of Mines, *Minerals Yearbooks* for 1941, 1942, 1943, and 1944. 1945 figures taken from severance tax records.

What caused this startling leap in production figures was the fact that the Federal government itself had stepped in and had offered to build at least two large processing plants in Arkansas for the precious ore. One of these, the Hurricane Creek Plant, said to be the largest in the United States, arose on the edge of the mining town of Bauxite—a settlement which, incidentally, was quite inadequately served by good highways as late as 1942–1943. This plant functioned under electric power supplied to it from the Hot Springs dams by the Arkansas Power and Light Company. The second plant, known as the Jones Mill Plant, closer to Lake Catherine and Hot Springs as well as to the mineral wonderland of Magnet Cove, had its construction much delayed because the Arkansas Power and Light could not furnish any more electricity—its option on yet another dam site on the Ouachita River having expired a few years before. Bills were now rushed through Congress to give the new plant power brought on wires from over a hundred and fifty miles distance to the northwest, from the Grand River Dam in northeastern Oklahoma, itself only completed by 1940. By the late spring of 1942 the new power line was built; the first invasion of the power company's territory took place through war necessity and government intervention.

Few who have lived through that period can have forgotten it or can have the power to do so even today; for the slow agricultural rhythm of Arkansas, progressing from wet spring to summer drought, from summer drought to smoky fall, from smoky fall to frost and back again via snow and slush to wet spring, seemed definitely to change between 1942–1945. The change had, indeed, been manifest for the state as early as the summer of 1941. Two big army camps—one, near Little Rock, named, as so much else in this area, after the beloved Senator, Joseph Taylor Robinson, who, as Democratic leader, had fallen stricken four years before while striving to drive through a recalcitrant Congress the unpopular purge of the Supreme Court; and the other, near Fort Smith, named after the picturesque prophet of the tank, General Adna Romanza Chaffee—filled the streets of their respective cities with drifts of khaki. In the summer of that year great war manoeuvres were held along the Louisiana border; and immense columns of troops, as in the days of the Mexican War, but this time riding in drab, gasoline-driven trucks, rumbled south along the roads. The next spring saw the coming of a vast artillery proving ground at Hope, the building of a huge incendiary bomb plant outside Pine Bluff, the construction of a picric acid plant close to the old Polish settlement of Marche and the rise of a large shell-case loading plant at Jacksonville. For the first time in its history the city of Little Rock became an overcrowded urban center, surrounded by major industries. Nor did the sudden flood of 1943, doing over two hundred million dollars' worth of damage to the farmlands of the Arkansas valley, blocking most of the highways in the valley itself, and utterly isolating Fort Smith for two weeks, halt for long the prodigious war effort.

The actual amount allotted to Arkansas by the wartime Congresses, as compared with the amount allotted to other Southern States, was small: four hundred and fifteen millions, as opposed to nearly five hundred and forty-five millions for Mississippi and more than a billion for Virginia, Alabama, and Texas, while nearly a billion was spent in Louisiana, Tennessee, and Florida. Yet the contrast with former poverty was so great that it may be said that those critical years of the Second World War made Arkansas, for the first time, conscious of the importance of industry. To all those who would like to see things going on as they had gone in the past, the state had now an answer:

"Build up new industries." That any new industries which can now be built have to rest on a peace time rather than a war time foundation, and have to work in close alliance with the prevailing pursuit of agriculture, may be seen in the fact that all the war time defense plants are today closed down, and no one seems to know as yet what is going to become of them. But the Second World War, none the less, remains a historic landmark in the state, as in many other parts of the South.

Whether the external change really affected the population in any deeper and more psychological way remains to be seen. One important change did take place in the field of politics. For almost the first time in its history Arkansas stepped boldly and vigorously on the stage of international affairs when the mantle of the dead Senator Joe Robinson, of Lonoke, in the cotton- and rice-growing lowlands, descended on the shoulders of a young man from Fayetteville, in the heart of the northwestern Ozark fruit-growing district.

James William Fulbright had been born in Sumner, Missouri, in April, 1905, but had moved with his family to Fayetteville as a boy, where his parents acquired the ownership of a local newspaper. He attended local high schools and moved on to the State University, where he played football and did well in scholarship. Taking his B.A. at Fayetteville in 1928, he became a Rhodes Scholar, acquiring the Oxford M.A. in 1931. Returning to Fayetteville, he married in 1931, taught law at the University, and was, to all appearances, destined for a life as a college professor, when in 1939 he was unexpectedly made president of the University. Two years later and he was promptly ousted by the governor-incumbent in a fit of political irritation. It was the crux of his career.

Urged by one of the Arkansas congressmen, then standing for the Senate, to look for a new field in politics, Fulbright responded with alacrity. He had already, through his personal charm and through the Fayetteville newspaper, still controlled by his mother, built up a considerable following—and he doubtless knew that his expulsion as university president had been but an episode in that undeclared war between highland and lowland, between independent and conservative, which is so persistent in Arkansas. He chose to stand for the lower house of Congress; and in November, 1942, over several opponents, won by a majority of four thousand—the largest in his district for thirty years.

His career as congressman was vivid. He inaugurated it by a speech severely critical of Congresswoman Clare Boothe Luce, who had recently attacked Henry Wallace's internationalism by coining the word "globaloney." He continued by writing, and by getting sponsored, the famous one-paragraph Fulbright Peace Resolution committing a cautious Congress to vague support of the United Nations Organization. In other respects his voting record showed enlightened conservatism. Not being openly in favor of organized labor, and not being directly opposed to the poll tax, he voted for the Federal pay bill, the increased income tax bill, for incentive payments to farmers, more money for soil conservation, funds for crop insurance and for rural electrification, for keeping the Home Owners Loan Corporation in being, and for the O.P.A. With ninety-three others, he voted to abolish the Dies Committee. Two years after his advent to Congress, he was elected to the Senate in a contest in which so much money was spent by all candidates as to lead to a congressional investigation.

Recently he was considered for the presidency of Columbia University, vacated by Nicholas Murray Butler—and has continued his political career by sponsoring and putting through a bill for the international exchange of students and professors between foreign and American universities. This bill, signed by President Truman on August 1, 1946, sets aside three hundred millions of dollars—in part to be raised by the sale of war surplus property—for the following four purposes: (1) to pay the bills of American students in higher education overseas; (2) to permit American professors to lecture in foreign colleges and universities; (3) to assist foreign students working at American nondenominational colleges overseas; and (4) to provide transportation to the United States for foreign students who choose to work at American universities.

This bill may in the end be William Fulbright's final monument as a statesman, for it is hoped that some day it may attract as many as fifty thousand foreign students to this country annually. In other respects, the Arkansas senator's record reveals considerable caution. But, apparently, "Bill" Fulbright, as the Arkansawyers love to call him, has never yet forgotten his Rhodes scholarship or the perspective it brought him.

While this distinguished personal record was being made, Arkansas's new war industries were busily running full blast; and foremost among them stood the two great plants already mentioned, operated by Alcoa and set up by the government at Hurricane Creek and near

Lake Catherine. In June, 1945, with victory in Europe an assured fact, the Hurricane Creek plant was thrown open on a day to visitors, and I was among the throng of thousands who saw it. One recalled later several striking facts: the heat of a thunderous sky with brassy sun aloft, burning through the pine-barrens along the roadway; the vast black aspect of the main plant, with its high chimneys shedding yellowish smoke, behind a twenty-foot mesh fence, and surrounded by vast pinkish drifts and dumps of ore; the neat, white-painted frame canteen and exhibit building alongside, flanked—among standing pines—by rows and rows of newly-built barracks, mostly vacant. The heat in the crowded motion-picture exhibit showing the process of manufacture proved to be too exhausting, and I and my companion soon joined the shirt-sleeved, casual throng, all wearing blue badges as memorials of their visit, in a rapid tour of the building exhibit, showing how what had been an open meadow in 1942 had become transformed into the main plant in less than a year, and also displaying many of the resultant products. From there we went through the high mesh fence into an immense shed, fully forty feet high, with a travelling crane running aloft between its naked iron girders, and with pieces of machinery to be repaired scattered across its floor. This served as the fitting prelude to an equally large main shed, whose corrugated iron walls hold a heat of 120 degrees. From then on, every step was made to the roar and whir of great revolving drums and furnaces: the first huge furnace off to the right, into which we were permitted to peer, displayed a heat of 800 degrees. Further along were the whirring "slurry mixers," where the disintegrated ore was mixed with mud, to be fired again; here escaping steam formed large water puddles on the floor; and here everywhere the peculiar acrid smell of the wet red clay mixed with the smell of metal was very manifest, along with an overpowering sense of superlative power and pressure, very much non-Arkansan in its essence.

From here after a brief inspection of an endless conveyer belt, down which powdered ore ran to be mixed with lime, we passed out again into the open sunlight, to climb to the top of fifty-foot black tanks filled with the brown mud mixture, revolving slowly around between enormous bladed paddles. Then again into a second and third group of corrugated iron sheds, with more "slurry mixers" revolving, and vast cylindrical drums stretching far from one shed to another, all turning together and emitting as they went strangely weird and musical sounds. By this time, I was already growing exhausted with the loud roaring noise, the overwhelming heat, the nervous tension induced by the omnipresent signs of "Danger—High Voltage." So, in the end, I failed to be taken up, by the small, overcrowded elevator, to the top of the four towering, black-rusted, sixty-foot-high storage tanks. The small platform at the summit, thronged as it was, under the four-o'clock fury of the sun, did not promise me that the resultant panorama of machinery might be worth a visit.

Ed Weigel and his fellow-conspirator, Dr. Banner, might perhaps have chuckled from the Elysian fields at my discomfiture as I returned from the scene of activity, for my nasal passages by this time were so clogged by the prevailing fine red dust that it was only by the repeated applications of a handkerchief and by much blowing that they became somewhat clear again. But neither of these men would, I think, have smiled had they discovered, as I did, that the distinct smell of wet clay and metal pervaded all my clothes, which had to be sent to the cleaners a day later.

One might go on from this point along the main highways built since 1926–1927 to pleasanter and even more striking scenes, such as those provided by the seventy-mile-long, beautiful lake behind the great Norfolk Dam in the upper White River country, where the United States Army Engineers, by the close of 1944, completed a concrete barrier that ranks with the six largest dams built in this country, a structure twenty-six hundred feet long and two hundred and forty feet high. This is destined not only to control White River floods, but eventually to provide electric power over a great area of small farms and dense forests. It also provides a marvelous opportunity for fishermen, as I can testify. One might go from there into what yet are but dreams and visions: the further projected dams to be built at Bull Shoals and at Lone Rock, which will effectively harness the White River itself as well as its main tributaries of the North Fork and the Buffalo; or the vast program still more recently worked out by the Army Engineers to make the Arkansas navigable from its mouth to Tulsa, Oklahoma. All these, whether extant or projected, represent the strivings of the New South since the success of the TVA and the coming of another World War; but it is fitting that, for Arkansas at least, we indulge in not too many hopes of the future, but, instead, attempt soberly to evaluate the present. After all, and only too frequently, the history of my state has tended to run backward as much as forward; and what seemed often a fair hope has turned out in the end to be a bitter fruit of disillusion.

In the first place, the Arkansas Power and Light Company has set itself to oppose by every means in its power, including lobbying and propaganda, the idea of constructing further dams for the dual purposes of flood control and electric installations. It has attempted to point out that such dams, because of their excessive cost of construction and maintenance, tend to raise the rates on electric power rather than lower them. Since the corporation controls practically all the power lines within the state, it has succeeded in leasing the power (only one third of what was originally planned) provided by the new Norfolk Dam, to be distributed through the Rural Electrification Administration to its own customers. Whether this new dam will ever be permitted to expand or to sell electricity without the consent of the Arkansas Power and Light Company remains to be seen; at least we can say that the dam controlling the Fourche la Fave at Nimrod, built earlier, had to be put up solely for flood control, and not at all for power purposes. Moreover, and far more symptomatically, the whole question of the state's bauxite production has again fallen into abeyance. Though Arkansas has other important mineral resources—coal, manganese, lead, zinc, and mercury (from cinnabar ores in Howard and in Pike counties, where, incidentally, the only blue-clay diamonds outside of South Africa have been found), yet in bauxite production, Arkansas should stand foremost; and in this field the state has already run into a stalemate. At the end of 1945 Alcoa, wishing to continue its production by extending its three-year leases on the two government built plants, was stopped dead in its tracks by an official order declaring the firm to be a monopoly; and the plants were then offered instead to the Reynolds Mining Company, a considerably smaller competitor. The steam went out from the black boilers, the great furnaces died down, the giant drums ceased to revolve; and, as I write, the question of whether the Reynolds Company can actually operate one plant, while the existing lands and their ores are still in the hands of Alcoa, is very much of an open question.

Truly, one wonders, whether in Arkansas or elsewhere in the South, our Northern critics are right in the stress they lay on racial discriminations between Negroes and whites, and on recent racial outrages. One wonders, rather, whether the racial tensions that do exist do not serve to mask something far more serious and more profound: the fact that the independent-thinking and ambitious Southerner, white or Negro, has come to find his path to a more balanced economy totally blocked by entrenched forces well settled in power. These forces ramify from the local corporations—generally controlled by out-of-state capital—to the local banks and the chambers of commerce; they go into the local newspapers via their advertisements; they rule the ideas of local politicians, and so move upward, on to the houses of Congress and the presidency itself. Any attempt to break them down is immediately ranked as alien, contrary to the American way of life, as just another form of "Bolshevism." Any attempt to make them into more efficient servants of the people is immediately met by streams of skillfully directed counter-propaganda. How little can any individual, however gifted, however ambitious, run counter to the dead weight of Southern economic history!

As in the rest of the South, so in Arkansas: the inert force of ingrained conservatism (not only, by any means, the conservatism implicit in denying to the Negro new measures of social equality, but the greater conservatism implicit in the existence of a poorly educated, misled, unthinking, and economically competitive white majority), stands in the way of any true human progress. Such a progress can come only from within the South, not from without; and it cannot be measured in dollars and cents, but only in better, cleaner, finer ways of living. It is blocked now by private and by public indifference, and by the fact that, behind the smoke screen of talk on the racial issue, the network of established capitalism extends and probably deepens its scope. Only if this difficulty be met and faced, only if it be dealt with day by day to the uttermost of one's powers, through the sacrifice of self-interest and the achievement of complete public and private honesty, can the South as a whole, or Arkansas as a part of the South, make any new advance. Only then can the fine motto of my state, "The People Rule," become an accomplished fact.

ACKNOWLEDGMENTS

The sources from which I have drawn this book vary greatly, from accounts in Spanish, French, and German, to newspaper articles, letters, and personal reminiscences written and unwritten. For the De Soto expedition, I have drawn on the three narratives translated by Buckingham Smith. For Marquette, Joliet, and La Salle I am chiefly indebted to Parkman. Life in Arkansas Post under the French regime, now accessible to scholars through transcripts of official records, seemed to me to have little to do with the main story of Arkansas, and so I omitted it; for the same reason, the brief account given by Schoolcraft of his early trip in the upper White River country was omitted. For the territorial period and the early period of statehood, I am indebted chiefly to Thomas Nuttall's *Travels in Arkansa Territory*, to George W. Featherstonehaugh's *Excursion through the Slave States*, to Friedrich Gerstaecker's work translated under the title, *Wild Sports in the Far West*, and to W. F. Pope's *Early Days in Arkansas*. For the founding of Little Rock, I have depended on Dallas Herndon's *How Little Rock Was Born*, and I have also been permitted, through the courtesy of their present owner, to consult the unpublished and valuable Whittington letters. For the Cherokees and other Indians, I am much indebted to the books of Grant Foreman, especially his *Indian Removal*, a classic account; and have received helpful suggestions from Althea Bass, *Cherokee Messenger*, from Ralph Henry Gabriel's *Elias Boudinot*, and some others, as well as from Cephas Washburn's original journal.

The period from the Mexican War to the Civil War was largely dominated by Albert Pike, of whom no good biography exists, though the work of F. W. Allsopp covers the ground discussed by me from quite a different point of view. I have been familiar with Pike's literary productions from my earliest childhood. As regards Pike's much disputed Civil War record, as well as his negotiations with the Indians, I have found by far the most illuminating account to be that of Annie Heloise Abel (Mrs. George Cockburn Henderson) in her *American In-*

dian as Slaveholder and Secessionist and *American Indian as Participant In the Civil War.*

As to the Civil War itself, I have based my account on a great many published and unpublished sources, so many that I cannot recount them all; and, in addition, I have personally visited the two chief battlefields of Pea Ridge and Prairie Grove, as well as the sites of a good many minor engagements. I have also been indebted, here as elsewhere, to the histories written by David Y. Thomas and his predecessor, Fay Hempstead. The story of Susan Bricelin Fletcher's war experiences I owe to her daughter, Miss Mary P. Fletcher; that of David O. Dodd, I have obtained largely from newspaper accounts; the account written by U. M. Rose of his journey to Richmond appeared in the *Arkansas Gazette* some years ago. My judgment concerning the main actors and events must here remain my own.

For Reconstruction, there is the excellent account, somewhat overcautious, by Staples, *Reconstruction in Arkansas,* as well as John M. Harrell's vivid record of the Brooks-Baxter War. Powell Clayton's book, presenting his side of the case, has also been read and evaluated.

For the development of the Grange, the Agricultural Wheel, and the Populist movement, I am largely indebted to Professors J. H. Atkinson and Granville Davis, of Little Rock Junior College. For Jeff Davis, Governor of Arkansas, I have depended upon the account given by his private secretary, Charles Jacobsen, as well as on newspapers of the period, and on personal recollections. The John G. Fletcher mentioned in the narrative as opposing Davis was my father. For William H. Harvey, I am indebted to his own works—and to a visit to Monte Ne itself.

The accounts of the modes of life practiced by the mountaineers, the sharecroppers, the rice farmers, fall well within my own experience; as does the account of the Arkansas holidays, and of the transformation produced by the Second World War. I have also read many books on the Ozarks, among them works by Wayman Hogue, Charles Morrow Wilson, Charlie May Simon, Don West, and Otto Ernest Rayburn. The ballad quoted in the nineteenth chapter was collected, along with many others, by myself.

John Gould Fletcher

INDEX